1986

WRITERS
ON
WRITING

WRITERS
ON
WRITING

Edited by
Tom Waldrep
University of South Carolina

Random House/New York

First Edition
987654321
Copyright © 1985 by Random House, Inc.

All rights reserved under International and Pan-American
Copyright Conventions. No part of this book may be repro-
duced in any form or by any means, electronic or mechanical, including photocopying, without permission in writing
from the publisher. All inquiries should be addressed to
Random House, Inc., 201 East 50th Street, New York, N.Y.
10022. Published in the United States by Random House,
Inc., and simultaneously in Canada by Random House of
Canada Limited, Toronto.

Library of Congress Cataloging in Publication Data
Main entry under title:

Writers on writing.

   1. English language—Rhetoric. 2. Authorship.
I. Waldrep, Tom.
PE1408.W7715   1985   808'.042   85-1947
ISBN 0-394-34449-9

Manufactured in the United States of America

Dedicated to
Gregory Cowan

FOREWORD

Don Murray has stated that he has apprenticed himself to two trades he can never learn: writing and teaching. I share this apprenticeship and this frustration.

Often colleagues from California to New York (from Elizabeth Cowan, Hans Guth, and Ross Winterowd to Lil Brannon, Cy Knoblauch, and Lynn Troyka) and I have discussed the frustrations of writing and the teaching of writing. Often we have found that both the writing process and the joy in teaching this process are inexplicable. And, even though many of us have attempted to do both for more years than we would like to admit, we are hesitant to share our own processes, finding them personal, internal, complicated. Yet I feel that these various and diverse processes, if we can articulate them, have an extremely practical value for writers and teachers of writing.

I began this project after a class discussion in an introductory graduate course in the Theory and Teaching of Composition in the fall of 1983. Many new, inexperienced graduate instructors (75 percent of the freshman English classes are taught by graduate students at South Carolina) were questioning the pedagogical applications of the theories covered in this course. Many asked, "Do these rhetoricians practice what they preach?" I thought this indeed to be an interesting question. So did many of the rhetoricians/writers/writing professors from California to New York that I asked. Louis Milic responded that my question (how do you write?) "may put a lot of people on the spot, showing divergence between preachment and practice, but so much the better." Ross Winterowd questioned my getting "all those rhetoricians to *act.*"

But many did act, and Lynn Bloom, Joe Comprone, Dick Graves, Harry Brent, Tilly Warnock, and others even said how much fun the essay was to write. Many contributors remarked of the new insight, the new perceptions they gained from such a close scrutiny of their own writing process. And some who could not contribute an essay nevertheless thought the project interesting and timely. Wayne Booth acknowledged

> To do justice to your questionnaire would require more time than I shall be able to squeeze out in the next few months.

vii

Meanwhile, I will say just two things: (1) I do not use any of the standard invention techniques as I write—not consciously as tricks of method. I grapple with my topic and try to think it through, jotting down various half-ideas in my head and then comparing them with each other to find out where they match and where they do not. (2) I revise many, many times, as many times as deadlines allow for. And I always feel that I would have profited from further revision.

Sue Lorch summarized and reiterated the *predominant* feelings of most contributors:

Here at long last is the most difficult essay I've ever written. Self-scrutiny is a challenging occupation. This is about the zillionth draft of this thing, but I am *more* than willing to have at it again if you can use it. If this piece doesn't fit with the others in your collection, I will certainly understand. My hope is that my somewhat oblique approach will contribute variety, spice, or some such, but I'm aware that it may simply be inappropriate. If I have barked entirely up a wrong tree, reject this. It will not affect our personal friendship, which is, after all, the most important thing.

Even though I know only one or two other of the contributors personally, many reflected in their correspondence the same sentiments as Sue Lorch. Their "somewhat oblique approach" was in on time, that is, the "zillionth draft" was mailed in by the deadline date. Since most writing teachers I know are adamant with students about getting essays in "on time," this was reassuring. Yet, interestingly enough, many of those solicited voiced statements similar to students' remarks about writing essays. Many subtly implied more time was needed for yet another revision. Two essayists whose contributions were not in by July 1, 1984, were, like industrious students, very *dutiful* about writing and calling to inform me of their progress or lack thereof, cataloging for me their other commitments and priorities. And three simply were one month or more late with no explanation. Twenty-seven out of the fifty-eight solicited had too many other commitments to participate, which I certainly understood, and only one stated: "I don't think of myself as a 'rhetorician' and I wouldn't be caught dead in that *galère* [my original list of participants]." She further admonished, "Since almost all rhetoricians write very badly, I can't see any advantage in having accounts of how they go about producing the dreary stuff that passes for theory these days."

The essays, not at all "dreary stuff," are in alphabetical order with the exception of Elizabeth Cowan Neeld's. I felt that since this collection is dedicated to the memory of my good friend Greg Cowan, and since Greg's life and his writing still affect many of us, including Elizabeth, the exposé of her writing process should, in fact, be first. She and Greg were collaborators, coauthors, lovers, partners-in-life. Professionally I owe much to both of them, and many of the contributors in this collection are indebted to Greg for his innumerable contributions to our profession.

CONTENTS

xi

Essentially we're both sponges absorbing information, events, and personalities around us. It's in this initial and informal brainstorming conversation that we hear ourselves and each other talking. Somehow this process gives us a focus on ideas that might otherwise escape our attention; thus, this interchange becomes a primary advantage of team-writing.

I must confess that rarely do I consciously follow the advice I give my students about the composing process. I wander through the woods, occasionally intersecting one of the sacred pathways of invention or arrangement, but never following it for very long. Asphalt roads have their place . . . when you're traveling straight and by clear design, but I like to wander when I write, create my own roads.

It was really the student newspaper . . . that developed me into a writer: 2 A.M. at the printers, a ten-inch hole on page one, Mr. Barta yelling that he would go home in an hour whether we were finished or not, someone on the phone calling in the facts, and me writing those ten inches, nearly as fast as I could type—ah, the virtues of formulaic writing.

I loved writing essays, then. . . . You could, in the midst of composing an essay, actually forget, at least for the moment, the look of your handwriting. And once the idea was finished you could go back and polish, satisfying Sister Rita Anne's mania for writing on the lines and correct spelling, and appealing simultaneously to your parents' uneducated fascination with two or three pages of words strung together in a relatively sensible form.

art, to speak to friends, or even to conduct pedestrian business as long as a telephone is handy.

ing. I think about the introduction, what examples to use, how to develop the main idea, what kind of conclusion to use. I write, revise, rewrite, agonize, despair, give up, only to start over again, and all this before I ever begin to put words on paper.

We are culturally averse to a shared understanding [of the composing process] because we value doing it differently; we sincerely hope that we are weird. No wonder then that as Emig and Flower and Hayes have concluded, individual accounts of the composing process are idiosyncratic, more concerned with feelings about writing than with the act itself.

All writing . . . has the feature that it is difficult, lonely work, and satisfying mainly when finished. I face writing with enthusiasm when I am rolling the topic around in my mind and I enjoy the attendant research, but I genuinely dread the moment when I have to put pen to paper—or, for that matter, put fingers on the keyboard in front of the green screen.

Writing is easy; it's *not* writing that's hard. The writing comes in a bolt, one moment there is nothing and the next there are a thousand words or more, an always unexpected burst of language that is frightening in the power and complexity of its connections, in the sudden clarity where there was confusion a moment before. It's easy to receive a bolt of lightning when it strikes; what's hard is to create conditions that cause lightning to strike —morning after morning—and then wait for the bolt to hit.

Writing is acting. It is choosing, shaping, arranging, rearranging, shifting, adding, deleting, discovering. To

write is to perform, to reveal, to show. The performance may sometimes be perfunctory, but it is a show,
nevertheless. A writer can "do" a paper in the same
sense that she can do a dance, do a magic show, do a
rope trick.

extends beyond the limits of a flat sheet of paper and involves seeing connections between my past experience, the writing task at hand, and the impact of some writing on an audience, known or imagined. A Write Idea centers on *having a sense of the possibility of managing and completing a piece of writing.*

Realistically, I guess I am always trying to "become" a writer; I think a writer "becomes." That person "becomes," I am becoming, as a result of my experiences: my observations, my perceptions, my training, both formal education and at-home rearing.

To write at all under [certain] circumstances, you have to accept that the best way you can is good enough, though it will never be good enough, not even for yourself. What a business this writing is! What cartwheels it has us turning!

How did I take the plunge? How am I still learning to write? How do I help students begin writing and join the community of writers? How am I learning to overcome the excuses of time, busywork, head-tripping, and hems of [poets'] garments to avoid writing? Most important, I believe, I am learning to write, not alone, but with others.

A great deal of my writing time is spent building a storehouse of writing material. I squirrel away passages of writing, anything from a short sentence to a long character sketch. Not generated by particular projects, these writings are, rather, "savings" put aside for the future.

WRITERS
ON
WRITING

ENGAGING WITH THE ENCOUNTER: HOW I WRITE

Elizabeth Cowan Neeld

Is this encounter... strong enough for me to be willing to engage completely with the process of writing? How I answer a question like this, I've learned over time, is the single biggest clue to how successful my writing will be. ... If I'm not willing to engage with the encounter—really interlock *with it,* pledge *myself to it —then there is no point in beginning. And I don't.*

Dear Tom,

The best way I know to answer your question, "How do you write?" is to catch myself in the act. That isn't easy. Because there seems to be some inherent contradiction between *writing* (which is a private act, even though aimed for a public audience) and *talking about that writing* (which requires an observer who is always awake and noticing, and a commentator who is always analyzing and taking stock).

Each role—being the writer and being the observer/commentator —naturally stands to influence the other. So we will never know how "pure" my answer to your question is. (This would probably be so even if all I did were *comment* on how I write—how could we be sure I was remembering and describing "the truth"?) What I do know, however, is that I will not cheat. I will stay honest by including the work I do in every stage of the writing process. As much as possible, I will distinguish between myself as the *writer* and myself as the *observer/commentator talking about the writing.*

I think it was Robert Graves who wrote a book called *The Reader over My Shoulder.* I invite you and the readers of this book into that relationship with me as I write.

THE SETTING

I've just come in from our deck where I've been sitting, watching the sailboats turn on their sides in the rough winds of the San Francisco Bay. Doing nothing with my mind. Being peaceful and alone. The morning has been hectic; my schedule, impossible. I have deliberately set up this still time to bracket the writing I am about to do.

I come inside, go to my computer, put the disks in, and set up the screen. I'm now ready to begin to write.

THE ENCOUNTER

The first thing I do is reflect on "the encounter" that led me to sit down to write. (I define an encounter as anything that "shows up" and gets my attention enough to make me deliberate whether or not to engage with it.) The encounter for this essay was an external one—your request ("Will you do a chapter for this book?") and my response to that request ("Yes, I will."). However, for the writing I will do with you and the readers of this book looking over my shoulder, the encounter comes from an internal motivation: my intention to write a book about my father's life. My first step toward this book is to write a short synopsis of the book, which I can show to an agent.

I now spend two or three minutes examining this self-generated encounter that led to the writing I'm about to do. I've discovered over the years that there is a lot of valuable "information" in the nature or the essence of the encounter—sometimes the mood of the piece or the location of the writing in an appropriate universe of discourse, perhaps even the direction in which the writing is going to go. I'm now looking, as I begin to write the first words, for those shadowings, those hints, that might inform the work I am about to do.

Next I stop to ask myself a very important question: Is this encounter (my desire to write a book about my father's life) strong enough for me to be willing to engage completely with the process of writing? How I answer a question like this, I've learned over time, is the single biggest clue to how successful my writing will be.

I have tried writing when I wasn't engaged with the encounter. The result was not satisfying—most often, the writing turned out to be little more than "ransom-note writing." This is my word for writing that has no inherent power, that has only the power of a gun behind it— writing that is like a big black word cut out of this magazine, a small red word cut out of that one, all spelling out something like, "If you don't put $25 million dollars in the trash can at the corner of Pike and Celantro, you'll never see your dog alive again." Ransom-note writing happens all the time. It's surface schemata—in Norrie Fry's words, automatic fluency, turning on the tap and letting a lot of bumble emerge. I've done it myself. But enough's enough. If I am not willing to engage with the encounter—really *interlock* with it, *pledge* myself to it—then there is no point in beginning. And I don't.

EPISODE

Since I *am* willing to engage with the encounter of writing a synopsis of a book on my father's life, I'm ready to do what comes next: begin "the writing episode." (*Episode,* in its usual sense, of course, refers to any event complete in itself but forming a part of a larger whole. In its Greek derivation, however, *episode* means "following upon the entrance to the road or the way; to go, whence?"). I think of a piece of writing always as being an *episode* in my life, in both senses of the word: as something with a beginning/middle/end that is a complete segment in my ongoing work and as something that "follows upon the entrance to the road or the way." This way of thinking provides a very powerful context for holding all the twists and turns the writing might take as I find out what it is I want to say.

This context of writing as episode also allows me the freedom *not to know* when I begin to write. And for this book synopsis, that's a good thing; because I have never written anything connected with my father's life. I have no notes. No drafts. Not even any doodlings. Everything, therefore, will appear unpracticed when I "enter the road or the way; to go, whence?"

THE CREATING STAGE

This is the stage where I write the first words that will ultimately lead to a completed synopsis of a book on my father's life. During this creating stage, I will experiment with possibilities. Although I begin with no strong ideas on the subject, I do have a commitment to be in action—to put words on the page so that I can see what I think. The heuristic with which I always begin is *looping.*

Looping

LOOP NO. 1

A book on my father's life? Today in *W* magazine I read a quote by the president of the New York Botanical Gardens, in which he said that until you had gardened you didn't know what it was to be in touch with the universe. And I thought of my father, Tommie Harper. A farmer turned fundamentalist preacher. Who thinks a title for a book about his life should be *From the Plow to the Pulpit.* What is in this? Where is the line that leads to the line that leads to the line—to quote Bill Stafford's poem about the authentic? What is the connection between a hard life as a farmer in the red-clay hills of Georgia, in the Gone-with-the-Wind country that never was anything close to a movie for anybody's life, and a life as a fundamentalist preacher who could pray a life-threatening blood clot away (to the complete amazement of every specialist in the hospital!) and who could preach you right into alignment with the rules of the church, no matter how resistant you thought you wanted to be? Is there a connection between a life as the community hellion—who always carried a pistol and got called to handle every incident that occurred, the guy who went to the old tent in the cow pasture to cut the ropes so that the revival services could not go on—and the man who ended up in the mourner's bench hearing in the background the refrains of "He's the lily of the valley, the bright and morning star"?

This is the farmer who preached the very next day, to the mules as he plowed the field. Who gathered the community together by the third day after that evening in the altar and preached his first public sermon, after preaching to the railings on the front porch. Who went to Bible school, paying for his tuition with chickens in a crate—and, when that exchange was used up, took care of the furnace for his keep. Did somebody *really* come to his family's house a fateful winter Sunday when he was twelve and put a hand on Tommie's head, saying to Miss Willie, his mother, "This boy will be your preacher man"? What evidence then or for years and years to come does anybody have that this mean and threatening man would be God's voice in the mountains of east Tennessee?

Center of Gravity of Loop No. 1
The center of gravity in this loop seems to be: intrigue with the direction this man's life took.

LOOP NO. 2

Emerson once said that the line of a ship on the water looks zigzag, zigzag, but that when you see it from enough distance away it straightens itself out to the average tendency. How far away will I have to get to see the line of Tommie's life straighten itself out so that I can follow its movement as it became what it was? Am I interested in this book's showing the relationship between his boyhood escapades, meannesses, hard times, and hurts, and his powerful life as a preacher who spoke the words he heard from on high? No, it's not some kind of Ericsonian psychological study I want to do—not that that wouldn't be interesting, but I don't have the knowledge to do it. All I could do in that arena is some kind of amateur guessing that this incident in his life turned him this way and that incident turned him that—I'm not interested in that. What am I interested in? I'm interested in the power of a man. I'm interested in how a man stays true to his authentic self his whole life long. I'm interested in what is the source of an uneducated man's power to "move mountains," to guide people to change their lives. And I'm not even in my Daddy's church! So it won't be some support for the doctrine that he preached, for the way he says the world works. What is there, though, underneath? What is the power that makes the man? What is there to say in the early 1980s about a 76-year-old man who speaks words when he is in the pulpit, words that move . . . ?

Center of Gravity of Loop No. 2
The center of gravity in this loop seems to be: the question of how to interpret my father's life.

LOOP NO. 3

Perhaps in the incidents lie the key. The time his grandfather whipped him with the basket strips, holding his neck to the ground with his foot. The many hunts in the woods alone, solace to the young boy's soul. The lynching he didn't do and got the credit for anyway—which enormously increased his stature as "the man to leave alone." The move to Michigan during the Depression to make money to send back home. Marrying the quiet young Rachel that October day, giving the preacher a possum for his pay. Riding on the bus to those early revivals, where the offering for the entire three weeks was $3.35. Staying in a room strung with tobacco, with a young baby, fighting mosquitoes all night long. What's in these incidents? The movement of a life. Reminds me of Heidegger's admonition to follow the movement of the showing. But what do you tell an agent about the book? How do you make definitive enough a book that won't be what it is until it's written? Maybe there's encouragement in the fact that agents are known for seeing the possibilities in embryonic ideas. So forge ahead. Remember what Whitman said in *Leaves of Grass:* "You understand enough . . . Why don't you let it out then?"

Center of Gravity of Loop No. 3
The center of gravity in this loop seems to be: the decision to proceed on the synopsis, even though I don't know yet what the drift of the book is going to be.

So there's the first creating stage. Ten minutes per loop; total of thirty minutes. After I entered upon the road or the way in this writing episode, how did those loops move me along?

One thing I notice is how much my enthusiasm for writing the book was kindled as I wrote the loops. I *want* to write this book. I am excited about writing this book. This surprises me. I also realized, while writing the loops, that I won't know what my father's life "means" until I write a draft of the book. That is enticing to me—I'll find out what the book wants to be! Lurking somewhere in the shadows, too, as I wrote those loops, were thoughts about the unpredictable power/force that my father seems to live in. What's to come?

I think I'll do one more heuristic in the creating stage. This time, *chaining:* a question, then an answer coming directly out of that question; then a question coming directly out of that answer. In a line. Where to begin? (One way to locate a starting place is to ask myself what I want to know more about. I'm interested in that reference to Bill Stafford's poem—"the line" playing around in all this. And in the zigzag line of the ship that showed up in the Emerson quote. Maybe that's a place to begin the chain.)

Chaining

Q. What do you remember about Bill Stafford's poem?
A. That it talks about authenticity as the line that connects to the line that connects to the line.
Q. Is the line straight?
A. No. That's what makes it authentic. This part leads to that part and that part leads to the next, and on and on.
Q. Then you don't have to make a decision about some part of a thing because it doesn't seem to be going in a straight line, or because you don't see the connection?
A. No, and I think that's what's intriguing—that the connection isn't seen. You don't know where each part is leading. And somehow, in all of it, there's a form.
Q. Do you really think that?
A. I don't know. Maybe there are lives that aren't lived authentically because the line doesn't lead to the line but just turns in upon itself to rotate around in a senseless orbit with nowhere to go?
Q. What about your father's life? He would never have thoughts like this—Bill's poem wouldn't mean anything to him. In fact, wouldn't he be embarrassed at talk such as this?
A. Yep. I think that's part of the intrigue for me.
Q. Hey, I just thought of something—is a big thing in this book the question of what determines the direction for a naive, unlearned man's life? For all our lives?
A. A live spark in there! What if what is so about life is something that

can't be spoken in a creed, caught in rules, made part of doctrine? What if the irony of it all is the unexplainable, the unexpected?

Q. That's surprising to you, isn't it? You were not thinking of that question at all.

A. You're right. I don't even know what I "believe" about all that. I just know there is something in the power of the words my father spoke, believed, and read. Wonder how much you really have to know?

That chain took a totally unexpected turn. At this point I'm not able to pin down the questions that have turned up. Later—we shall see.

EARLY SHAPING STAGE

Next comes the discovery draft of the synopsis.

Discovery Draft

Working Title:
From the Plow to the Pulpit

This book, set in rural North Georgia (*Gone with the Wind* country), is an account of the origins of a fundamentalist preacher who started boyhood as a hunter and a farmer, became a community hellion, and ended up behind the pulpit.

The first third of the book will cover the inauspicious beginnings of this preacher man—the poor farming life, incidents from childhood (shooting the first gun, making rabbit stew, whippings, preparing the chewing tobacco, deaths of two babies, siblings in the family) and will have as its focal point the unexplained appearance of a mysterious preacher man who put his hand on Tommie's head and said, "This boy will be the preacher in the family."

The second third of the book will cover Tommie's mean years— rough riding a horse, brandishing a pistol everywhere he went. Privy to lynchings. Threatening and never threatened. Called to handle every fracas. Yet falling in love with a girl ten years his junior, angelic in her quietness; the awkward years of courtship while the man waited for the child to grow old enough to marry. The reformation that came with the love for Rachel. The early years of marriage—farming, cutting and selling wood, buying sausage once a week and canning it in jars to last the next seven days, making undershorts from flour sacks and pinning them for want of buttons to fasten them with.

The last third of the book will be from the point of Tommie's conversion on. Beginning with the trip to the tent to cut the ropes (reformation hadn't gone that far—this traveling tent revival was too much a threat to the stable community) and ending up, unexplainedly, in the altar bench. Then the early startings—brush arbor meetings, stories of "shouting powders," sleeping in tobacco-hung rooms infested with hundreds of mosquitoes, being quartered at a house where they ate only oatmeal as their food three times a day, stories of someone blaspheming and then being struck by lightning while hanging up the clothes, the miracle of stopping the blood when the doctors could think of nothing else to do. A man who still alternates his praying with catching the fish that he finds on his line.

The value to the reader can include (a) interest in a way of life that is fast disappearing from the American scene, (b) the drama of radical, inexplicable changes in a man's life, (c) wonderment about what sets and unfolds a human being's life, and (d) the depiction of a man's integrity and perseverance and dedication to what he stood for: a man's stand.

What does this discovery draft show? That I am still thinking. I cannot yet, in Heidegger's terms, "follow the movement of the showing." What the book is all about hasn't shown up yet. The writing, therefore, continues to be—at this early shaping stage—finding out what I think.

Time out now to go to a movie—to see Marcello Mastroiani fall in love in a Brazilian film set in the cacao groves in 1925! I am going to put this project on the windowsill to cool—like a row of pies. For expediency's sake, I wish the first discovery draft had been "the one." But it wasn't. But it *was* an opportunity to see what I hadn't thought about in relation to the book I am planning to write. This draft showed up the areas in which I need to continue to think. If I had not written the discovery draft, I wouldn't have known what was missing. So I am very satisfied with the way the piece is developing. Now for my break.

- - - - - - - - - - - - - - - - - - - -

Well, Tom, it's now several days later. Only three days to go until the essay is due to be mailed to you. The short timeline, although uncomfortable, is valuable. I use my commitment to a timeline to manage myself through the stages of writing. And I *do* have to manage myself—there's no magic in my getting a piece of writing done. I probably have as much reluctance as anybody else. Sometimes this reluctance is little more than laziness; at other times, it is more like a fear of having nothing to say. However, I've learned over the years that I can count on myself to keep a commitment to a timeline, so I unashamedly use having to produce on a timeline to manage myself so I get the writing done.

Writing that last sentence reminded me of a second ally that helps me manage myself to write: my fascination and proven experience with the *process* of writing itself. I treasure the surprises that crop up in a discovery draft. I am often in awe of the connections that emerge during a creating stage. I watch in wonder the development of a thought. Like a scientist in a laboratory, I wait to see what the outcome of my dialogue with the words on the page will be.

And I always know that every piece of writing will "turn out." It may not be my best work ever; it may even turn out not to be something that anyone else ever sees. (And it may also turn out to be the most satisfying thing I have ever written, and something that other people respond to favorably as well.) I accept every piece of writing as it finally turns out, whether I've had time to work it through every possible opportunity or whether I've gotten it to a level where, as the French poet Valéry says, no writing is ever complete—it just has to be abandoned. The important thing is that my reliance on the writing process has proven that I can finish every piece of writing and that something useful—no matter how I might come to value it critically—always shows up.*

Late Shaping

I'm now ready to do a second draft. One more draft only—that's all I have time for. Then, using whatever I have—in this case the loops, the chain, the two discovery drafts—I'll make something that will satisfy me as a final copy. I'll edit that final copy, put it into immaculate manuscript form, and that will be it for this writing episode!

Second Discovery Draft

Working Title:
From the Plow to the Pulpit

The story of one man's life. And not a famous man at that. Why would you tell it?

First, there is the sheer adventure—the "and then what happened next?" A boy born in the red-clay hills of North Georgia into a family so poor that they got oranges and bananas only one time a year, but a family whose prized possessions included a small, elegant pistol with a butt of solid engraved gold ("Your great-granddaddy carried this pistol in the Civil War," I was told from the time I was a child). A family who, on occasion, still dug for the legendary silver hidden by the soldier's wife when Sherman marched through Georgia. But a family that throughout my father's life chopped cotton, plowed potatoes, shoed horses, and cut wood in order to get by.

---

*If I can't find any other value for what I have written, I fall back on what Annie Dillard calls her "crackpot notion" about "why write?"—a notion she modeled on Buckminster Fuller's theories about entropy in the universe (Second Law of Thermodynamics). Annie's notion holds that writing—because it makes a whole of fragments and brings order to what was formerly chaos—may serve the purpose of keeping the universe (with its tendency to natural entropy) from falling apart! It's a saving thought on a bad day when what you've done seems to be only a disappointing piece of work!

What is the "stuff" of a boy's everyday life growing up in the early 1900s in such hard times? What's there in those first ten years to hint of the direction a man's life is going to go? The solitary hunts in the woods, which combined bringing a rabbit home for making stew and being alone far back in the trees. The days at the plow when he thought he would die before Blanche came with the water jar across the field. The challenge of making twists of tobacco, using the weight of the corncrib to pack it down. Being so shy that he ran home from the fieldhands' table on the farm where he'd been hired out—because he turned a glass of buttermilk over while looking at a red-haired girl.

What was there to hint at what was to come? And did a stranger *really* turn up at the family table one Sunday and, upon leaving, put his hand on this young boy's head, and say, "Miss Willie, this boy will be your preacher-son. You watch and see."?

Then there were the hell-raising years. The community rogue, the man everybody sent for when something mean needed to be done. The man who got credit for lynchings, even though he wasn't in miles of the place—credit, however, that could only enhance his reputation as the man to be feared. Riding his horse, pistol always on his side, this man terrorized anyone who dared to get in his path.

This was the same man, however, who chose Rachel as his bride— deep, quiet, calm Rachel, for whom he "reformed" most of his meanness and with whom he began to build a struggling farmer's life. The meanness wasn't all gone, though. There was the night he slipped away to cut the ropes on the revival tent that represented intrusion to the community. But instead of cutting the ropes on the tent, he found himself in the mourner's bench with the sounds of "He's the lily of the valley, the bright and morning star" ringing in his ears. This was the man, then, who the next morning began to preach to the mules as he plowed. And by the third morning had a public sermon prepared, which he had perfected by preaching to the railings on the front porch. Within weeks he was in Bible school, having paid his and Rachel's tuition with the chickens they brought in crates from the farm.

Then began the years of brush arbors, sleeping in people's homes while he, Rachel, and the baby were on the revival trail, sometimes in tobacco-strung rooms so full of mosquitoes that you heard motors in your ears all night long, sometimes eating only oatmeal three times a day, but always in touch with the purpose for it all—service to God. A man who knew about healing and about people who blasphemed and then were killed by lightning hanging washing on the line. The man who, long after retirement, still maintains a first-hand acquaintance with what he knows—"Excuse me a minute, God; I've got some fish on this line. I'll be back after I get them caught."

A man whose life has no explanation. A man who just is who he is. So authentic that there's nothing else to say. The story of one man's life.

LATE SHAPING STAGE

This is the part I don't like. Revising for the final draft. I know the importance—and *especially* the opportunity—of revising; and I always *do* revise. But I still don't like it. Nevertheless, here goes.

This final draft I want to be no longer than two pages, single-spaced. I will use this length as a constraint, to discipline my work. I also will revise with a closer ear to my audience—in this case, an agent who might take on this book. I will pay special attention to taking out maudlin comments or emotional theatrics. Let's see how it turns out.

Final Draft

Working Title:
From the Plow to the Pulpit

This book will depict the unexpected and even unexplainable turns in the life of a fundamentalist preacher in the South.

His beginning was inauspicious for what he was to become. But the element of the unexpected was present even then. He was born into a family so poor that they had an orange and a banana only once a year, but a family whose prized possessions included a small, elegant pistol with a butt of solid engraved gold. ("Your great-granddaddy carried this pistol in the Civil War," I told from the time I was a child.) A family that told with pride the story of the soldier's wife's courage in hiding the family silver the day Sherman marched through Georgia, while they, with equal pride, chopped cotton, plowed sweet potatoes, shoed horses, and cut wood just to get by.

What was there to hint in these early years of the direction the man's life was destined to take?

The solitary hunts, which combined bringing a rabbit home to make stew and being wondrously alone deep in the woods. The days at the plow when you thought you would die before Blanche came across the field with the water jar. The challenge of making homemade whiskey in the homemade still, and of packing a twist of tobacco using a corncrib's weight. Being so shy that you ran away from the fieldhands' table on the farm where you'd been hired out—because you turned over a glass of buttermilk while looking at a red-haired girl.

And did a stranger *really* turn up at the family table one dark Sunday in late December and, upon starting to leave, put his hand on the young boy's head and say, "Miss Willie, this boy will be your preacher son."?

The prophecy could not have been more wrong in the next ten years. Mean times for the boy becoming a man. Riding a horse and brandishing a pistol everywhere he went. Privy to lynchings, called to handle every community fracas, a threat to anyone who dared to cross his path. The same man, however, who fell in love with sweet, young Rachel, ten years younger, angelic in her quietness, still and deep. Spending long awkward years waiting for her to grow old enough to be his bride, reforming to make a home for him and his wife.

The early years of marriage—farming, cutting and selling wood, buying sausage for 5 cents a pound once a week and canning it all in jars to last the next seven days. Making undershorts from flour sacks and pinning them because no buttons were to be had.

The reformation hadn't gone far enough, however, to keep him from going to cut the ropes on the revival tent (a threat and an intrusion into the community's stable way of life). And the unexpected wasn't all in the past. Stalking up to the tent side, open knife in his hand, the man, inexplicably, found himself next in the mourner's bench, the strains of "He's the lily of the valley, the bright and morning star" ringing in his ears.

This was the man who, the next day, preached his first sermon to the mules as he plowed. Who in three days had his first public sermon prepared, after practicing his delivery to the railings on the front porch. Within weeks he was in Bible school, third-grade education and all, having paid his and Rachel's tuition with chickens brought with them from the farm.

Then the early startings—brush arbor meetings lit with lanterns hung in the trees; stories of "shouting powders"; he, Rachel, and the baby on the revival trail. Sleeping in tobacco-strung rooms swarming with mosquitoes that could bite you as many as two hundred times in one night; staying with a family who served only oatmeal to the guests three times a day. The stories of the inexplicable—someone blasphemes and is killed by lightning the next day, hanging wash out on the line; the miracle of stopping blood when nothing the doctors could do had worked. A man whose ministry took him to forty states and whose power never diminished. Who, in his retirement, alternates praying with catching the fish that he finds on his line. ("God, you wait. I'll be right back as soon as I see what's on this line.")

This book will capture a way of life that has virtually disappeared from the American scene. It will also be the story of a man's life that does not lend itself to easy explanations, the story of a man whose existence illustrates the unpredictable, mysterious flow of life. The book will rotate around the wonderment of what sets and unfolds a human being's life. Finally, it will reveal the power of a simple man's integrity, perseverance, and courage to live the unexplainable life.

THE COMPLETION STAGE

So, Tom, that is the final draft. I will edit what's here and then send it off.

Edited Draft

Title:
From the Plow to the Pulpit

This book will depict the unexpected, even unexplainable turns in the life of a fundamentalist preacher in the South.

In light of what he would later become, his beginning was inauspicious. But the element of the unexpected was present even then. He was born into a family so poor that only once a year did they get to have an orange and a banana; yet among their prized possessions was a small, elegant pistol with a butt of solid engraved gold. From the time I was a child I was told, "Your great-granddaddy carried this pistol in the Civil War." Proudly, this family told the story of how the soldier's wife courageously hid the family silver the day that Sherman marched through Georgia—while they, with equal pride, chopped cotton, plowed sweet potatoes, shoed horses, and cut wood just to get by.

In these early years, what was there to hint of the direction this man's life was destined to take?

There were the solitary hunts, offering twin blessings: a rabbit to take home for stewing and the wonder of being alone deep in the woods. There were the days at the plow, when he thought he would die before Blanche came across the field with that water jar. There was the challenge of making homemade whiskey in the homemade still, of packing a twist of tobacco using a corncrib for weight. There was the shyness in these pre-hellion days—so much shyness that he ran away from the fieldhands' table on the farm where he had been hired out, just because he had turned over a glass of buttermilk (while looking at a red-haired girl).

And there was this oft-told story: A stranger who turned up at the family table one dark Sunday in late December, started to leave, then turned back to put his hand on the young boy's head and say, "Miss Willie, this boy will be your preacher son."

For the next ten years, no one could possibly have believed such a prophecy. The boy-becoming-man turned mean: rode a horse and brandished a pistol everywhere he went. Was privy to lynchings, was called to handle every community fracas—a threat to anyone who dared cross his path. Yet this same young man fell in love with sweet Rachel—ten years younger; angelic in her quietness; still, and deep. Long, awkward years the young man spent waiting for her to grow old enough to be his bride, reforming in order to make a home for himself and his wife.

These early years of marriage, they farmed, cut and sold wood, bought sausage for 5 cents a pound and canned it all in jars to last the next seven days, made undershorts from flour sacks and pinned them because no buttons were to be had.

His reformation, however, didn't prevent him from heading for the visiting revival tent (which he saw as a threat and an intrusion into the community's stable way of life) with a knife to cut the tent ropes. He stalked up to the tent side, open knife in hand. Instead of cutting the ropes, however, he unexplainably found himself in the mourner's bench, the strains of "He's the lily of the valley, the bright and morning star" ringing in his ears.

The next day he preached his first sermon—to the mules, as he plowed. In three days he had prepared his first public sermon (practicing his delivery to the front-porch railings). Within weeks he was in Bible school, third-grade education and all; the tuition, his and Rachel's, he paid for with chickens from the farm.

Then came the early startings-up: Brush-arbor meetings lit with lanterns hung in the trees. Stories of "shouting powders." He, Rachel, and the baby on the revival trail, sleeping in tobacco-strung rooms swarming with mosquitoes that could bite you as many as two hundred times in a single night; staying with a family who served only oatmeal to their guests, three times a day. Stories of the inexplicable: Someone blasphemed, and the next day was killed by lightning while hanging out the wash on the line; doctors gave up on a patient, and this young preacher performed a miracle—stopped the blood.

His ministry took him to forty states, and his power never diminished. Now, in his retirement, he alternates words of the preacher with words of the fisherman—"God, you wait; I'll be right back as soon as I see what's on this line."

This book will capture a way of life that has virtually disappeared from the American scene. It will depict the story of a man's life that cannot be explained away, the story of a man whose very existence illustrates the unpredictable, mysterious flow of life. The book will rotate around the wonderment of what it is that sets and unfolds a human being's life. Finally, it will reveal the power of a simple man's integrity, perseverance, and courage to live the unexplainable life.

FINAL OBSERVATIONS

In these, my final observations, Tom, I see that even in the last draft prior to final editing—even at that late stage—something surprised me. Until that draft, I didn't see the possibility of using *unexplainability* and *unexpectedness* as the mythos for the book. I suspect that I will make this narrative theme indirect and unobvious—yet I also suspect that in itself it will gather and organize much of what I have to say.

I also see that, as with most things I write, I will satisfice with this synopsis rather than write out all the possibilities that I might perfect and explore. "Satisfice" is one of those concepts that when you learn it you wonder why you never knew it before. Satisfice means getting a piece of work to an acceptable level, then working on it only as much as you have time and/or inclination. At the point where you have no more time and/or inclination, you call the piece complete. You satisfice.

So, now that I have edited this final version, I call the writing complete, I satisfice.

Doing the synopsis has been a valuable experience. I have much deeper insights into what this book will be. I have an expectant, quiet passion to do the work. I was informed by the writing process. I see possibilities to be explored, am thinking of areas I intend to research (e.g., pre-Depression days in North Georgia; the fifty years between the Civil War and my father's birth).

As you can see, Tom, as I wrote that synopsis I made discoveries that can begin to help me make meaning out of a subject that has greatly affected my life. It's because of what I come to see, what I come to know when I write, that I set a time to put words on paper every day. There is no doubt that writing takes committed work. It calls for grappling with pieces that don't fit together until they do. Writing calls for trust, for receptivity, for the willingness to "fail." Writing, done authentically, keeps one "living in the question" often much longer than it is comfortable to be there.

But the rewards are rich. Writers engaging in the writing process discover what an encounter "means." They are surprised by what turns up to be said. They hone their thinking and sharpen their skills. Writers engaging in the writing process *act.*

Writers make. We create. We form.

Like the ancient Chinese poet, writers knock upon silence for the answering music.

So that, Tom, is how I write.

Love,

Elizabeth

Books for Everybody to Read

A Glass Face in the Rain, William Stafford. New York: Harper Colophon, 1983.

Becoming a Writer, Dorothea Brande (foreword by John Gardner). Los Angeles: J. P. Tarcher, 1934, 1981.

The Breaking of the Vessel, Harold Bloom. Chicago: University of Chicago Press, 1982.

The Creative Imagination: Enlightenment to Romanticism, James Engell. Cambridge, Mass.: Harvard University Press, 1981.

Living by Fiction, Annie Dillard. New York: Harper & Row, 1981.

On Becoming a Novelist, John Gardner. New York: Harper & Row, 1983.

One Writer's Beginning, Eudora Welty. Cambridge, Mass.: Harvard University Press, 1984.

Stories That Could Be True, William Stafford. New York: Harper Colophon, 1977.

The Mind's Best Work, David Perkins. Harvard University Press, 1982.

The Timeless Way of Building, Christopher Alexander. New York: Oxford University Press, 1979.

David Bartholomae (Ph.D. 1975, Rutgers) is associate professor of English and director of composition at the University of Pittsburgh. He served on the board of directors of the National Council of Writing Program Administrators and on the executive committee of the Conference on College Composition and Communication. He is currently a member of the college section of the National Council of Teachers of English and codirector of the Western Pennsylvania Writing Project. He was a Fulbright lecturer in American literature in 1982–1983. He has published articles on composition theory and composition teaching, and won the 1980 Braddock Award for his essay "The Study of Error."

AGAINST THE GRAIN

David Bartholomae
University of Pittsburgh

As I think about how I write, I know that my work will always begin with other people. I work with other people's words, even as I do my own work; other writers make my work possible, even as I begin to shape projects of my own. I don't put much stock in what I hear about invention and originality. I think it is a myth teachers foist on students in order to make teaching easier or less risky.

Do we choose a tradition or does it choose us, and why is it necessary that a choosing take place, or a being chosen? What happens if one tries to write, or to teach, or to think, or even to read without the sense of a tradition?

Why nothing at all happens, just nothing. You cannot write or teach or think or even read without imitation, and what you imitate is what another person has done, that person's writing or teaching or thinking or reading. Your relation to what informs that person is tradition, for tradition is influence that extends past one generation, a carrying-over of influence. Tradition, the Latin traditio, *is etymologically a handing-over or a giving-over, a delivery, a giving-up and so even a surrender or a betrayal.*

—*Harold Bloom*, A Map of Misreading

I

How I write is against the grain. I think this has always been the case, although now that I've been doing it for several years—doing it to the point, now, where I think of myself as a professional writer—the terms and conditions of interference have changed. There are things that get in the way of my writing and things that I put in the path of my writing that are different now than they were when I was younger, but the essential resistance—both mine and writing's—remains.

19

Writing gets in my way and makes my life difficult, difficult enough that I sometimes wonder why I went into this business in the first place. There is work that comes easier to me. Writing gets in my way, but when I write, I almost always put up barriers—barriers to show my sense of duty—to stand (like parentheses) in the way of writing. I feel, as a matter of principle, that writing should not go smoothly and that when it does, unless I'm writing a memo (but even there I try to plant buried jokes or unofficial countervoices), when it does go smoothly, it's not doing the work of a professional or showing proper respect for what Thoreau referred to as the "extra-vagrance" of things.

I think of writing primarily as a matter of resistance. At the same time, however, I will quickly admit that I have developed habits and changed habits to make writing more efficient. I've learned to revise, I've learned to use a word processor, I've learned to develop a schedule and to find a place that can make regular writing possible. Writing still, often, makes me unhappy, makes me sick, makes me do things—like smoke, for instance—that disgust me. I have my habits and quirks and behaviors, like other writers, and I've learned that thinking about them has helped me to put them to use, and I've learned that talking about them can help me speak with greater authority to my students. I can remember, in fact, the day when, as a graduate student, I was talking to my freshman composition class about topic sentences and came to the troubling realization that while I knew what they were I did not know if there were any in anything that I wrote. What I did know was that I never thought about topic sentences while I was writing, and I vowed that I would try never again to say words to a class that made no sense to me as a writer.

What are my habits and quirks? I revise a lot and, as a consequence, I push my students to do the same. I spend a lot of time letting a paper bounce around in my head before I start writing. I begin my papers always with *things,* never with ideas or theses. I begin, that is, with a folder full of examples, or two books on my desk that I want to work into an essay, or a paragraph that I cut from an earlier essay of my own, or some long quotations that puzzle me and that I want to talk about and figure out (like the Bloom passage above).[1] I like green pens, I never outline, I work with two yellow pads (one to write on; one for making plans, storing sentences, and taking notes). I've learned to do all these things and they are a part of who I am and what I do as I write, but they strike me as unimportant when weighed on the scales of the Western tradition.

I'm not just being snide here. I feel a sense of historic moment when I write—not that I'm making history, but that I am intruding

[1] Harold Bloom, *A Map of Misreading* (New York: Oxford University Press, 1975), pp. 31–32.

upon or taking my turn in a conversation others have begun before me. I feel a sense of the priority of others. Some of them, I think, are great writers, some of them are my colleagues and contemporaries, some of them are my teachers, some of them are strangers or students. I feel a sense of historic moment when I write that I'll confess I never felt at marches and rallies and that I never feel at university committee meetings or other public occasions.

What interests me most, then, and what I think about when I think about the composing process is another kind of drama altogether. There is another form of struggle, resistance, and achievement that I experience more profoundly when I write, and I will call it, drawing a phrase from Harold Bloom, the "dialectics of influence."

Bloom, in the passage at the top of this essay, says that "nothing happens" without imitation and, therefore, tradition. I take this very literally. For me, nothing happens, or could happen, until I imagine myself within a discourse—a kind of textual conversation/confrontation with people whose work matters to me and whose work, then, makes my own possible. But I experience another kind of personal confrontation as well, one with a figure—or sometimes figures—not immediately addressing the subject or argument of the paper I'm working on (a person not likely to appear in the footnotes, for example). This is the most powerful influence and it is the influence of another writer, a person represented by a verbal, textual presence—a set of terms, a sound and a rhythm, a sensibility—that I cannot push out of my mind or erase from my own writing. When I write I find I am appropriating authority from others while trying to assert my own. This is the dialectic that I feel when I write and that shapes what I do when I put words on a page.

When I talk about the pressure of another writer's work on my own, I am talking about a particular person—not Writer in the abstract, but someone I know or someone that I am reading. There have been several who have functioned this way for me, but two most powerfully. These were not my composition teachers—actually I never took a composition course—but my writing teachers nevertheless, people whose writing would not leave me alone but stood, and stands still, as a challenge, an echo, a model, a burden. If I think of my own experience as a writer, the most powerful terms I can use to discuss the composing process are not prewriting, writing, and revision, but tradition and imitation and interference and resistance.

II

When I was an undergraduate, my career as an English major was more distinguished by my enthusiasm and my love of abstraction and glossy generalization than by my skill as a writer. I hated to write, partly because it was such an uncomfortable thing to do but also because I think I believed that it wasn't important—not as important as my ideas and my energy and my enthusiasm—and with the lingering sense that writing gave the lie to my expertise as a student of literature and language.

I figured that I could attend to writing later and learn to take my ideas and report them more efficiently or elegantly. I was playing football at the time (not as successfully as I was doing English) and learning that what distinguished the really good player was not that he was bigger or stronger or had more skills than I had, but that he understood the game and movement and fitness in ways that I did not. I learned early on that I was not yet in the league with those players and I learned what it would take for me to get there. I don't know that I learned the same lessons about writing. Roger Sale says that the first real lesson he learned about his writing came when he was out of graduate school and in his first teaching job. He was carrying on, he says, about something when a colleague asked, "Why do you talk in that boring way?" It was said in a way and at a time in his life when it could make sense. For Sale, the message was, "Quite simply, I did not know what I meant most of the time I spoke or wrote." And, he says, after that writing got harder and harder.[2]

Maybe these lessons are impossible for undergraduates. I could learn what made a serious football player but not what made a serious student of English. No one asked me why I talked and wrote the way I did, and I was comfortable believing that my performance on the page didn't matter, was essentially irrelevant to the work I was undertaking. When I think of what it was like to write then, how I did it, I think of my nine-year-old son, who has so many things he wants to do on a Saturday afternoon, and such strong feelings about it all, that he sits and morosely stares at the wall, or flits from comic book to TV set to the refrigerator. My teachers characteristically said that my papers were full of interesting ideas but poorly written—turgid, difficult, disorganized. I received mostly As and became determined to make a career out of English because one of my teachers, David Osborne, insisted not that I write well but that I at least know something. He taught the Victorian period and made us learn names and dates and read documents that were neither novels nor poems.

I don't think I really learned to write until graduate school, and there learning came through two deeply—I think I would say pro-

[2]Roger Sale, *On Writing* (New York: Random House, 1970), pp. 52–55.

foundly—felt experiences. My dissertation adviser rejected my dissertation because it was poorly written, and I came into contact with the first strong teacher of my academic life, Richard Poirier.

The dissertation story is an easier one to tell. I wrote the whole thing, about 350 pages or so, while I was away for a year in England, and when I gave it to my adviser he wouldn't read past page 100, saying that it was all just too poorly done. I think I knew that writers reworked or revised what they were writing—in fact, I think I told my students that this was true—but I had never done it, and so, for the first time in my career, I began to revise. I knew how writers acted, but I did not act and, as far as revision is concerned, had never acted like a writer. It all seems so matter-of-fact in the telling, but I still remember it with all the force and resonance of those experiences where we first learn the deep, troubling significance of something we thought we had known all along. I reworked the whole dissertation, and the final draft bore little resemblance to the first manuscript I sent from England. It was better than the first draft, and I learned a lot about my subject (Thomas Hardy) from doing the work.

When I went back to the first draft, after returning to this country and after a year of teaching, I saw two problems. The manuscript was sometimes incomplete, sometimes overdone, and often disorganized. And so I learned to add, subtract, and rearrange—the kind of revision that comes when you can step back, look again, and rework a piece you have begun. I find this kind of work to be fundamentally different from the kind of work that is involved in putting words on the page for the first time. I am, frankly, grateful to be able to do this kind of revision, since it allows me a certain grace or forgiveness when I pound out a draft. I don't think that it is hard to learn to do this, and I don't think it is difficult to teach.

The other problem I saw with the first draft was harder to solve. It remains for me one of the problems central to my writing. I was less troubled by the disorganization in the first draft than I was by its glibness. The writing seemed to me a sign of someone who knew how to do a dissertation (or do English or do school) but who would never be taken seriously by teachers or readers who paid attention. The problem here was not so much what I had to say about Thomas Hardy but what I did with what I had to say and how, in fact, I went about saying it. It's hard to learn how to deal with this—with the pressure of language to be pat, complete, official, single-minded; with the pressure of language against complexity, uncertainty, idiosyncracy, multiple-mindedness—and it's very hard to teach students to work against fluency, the "natural" flow of language as it comes to a writer who has a grasp of a subject.

I still feel a combination of bitterness and gratitude when I sit down to rework a paper. I find adding, subtracting, and reorganizing to be comfortably routine—not easy, that is, but manageable and predictable. I do this at least until I get to the parts where I am confused or clearly wrong, and then I try to see if I can save what I've said by making it reasonable or convincing. What I still find hard is pushing against my own language, resisting its smooth finish or apparent direction, trying often to complicate rather than simplify, or to disturb rather than quiet the rhythm of my sentences. The work I do here—resisting, interfering—goes on also when I am writing for the first time.

In practice, however, revision for me has never been a line-by-line matter. My revisions still bear little resemblance to my first drafts. I will, for example, begin pushing at the first sentence and find myself writing ten pages, following a line of thought that was repressed in the first writing. This business of stopping and reworking a passage until it grows and grows and takes over the paper occurs also when I am working on a first draft. In fact, I often work with two or three yellow pads at a time, each containing a level or a layer of the piece I am writing.

I often think of writing as multilayered, although not in the sense that there is a center, like the center of an onion, that can be revealed or discovered once the layers are peeled away or sloughed off. I think, rather, that I revise to add a layer, often discordant, over a layer that will also remain—so that there is a kind of antiphony. One layer speaks the words that are authorized. It speaks departmentally, professionally, carrying out the work that is charged by the institution. The other layers speak the words of my teachers, of the books I read; and they speak of my need to locate myself in all of this as a person who has read, and who can do respectable work, but who has the need to assert his own presence as well.

I revise to figure out better what I can say and to say it in such a way that it seems eloquent, in an Emersonian sense—so that it seems to assert the presence of someone who speaks as more than the representative of an institution or a brand of research or a discipline. I try very hard to interfere with the conventional force of writing, with the pressure toward set conclusions, set connections, set turns of phrase. The lesson I learned when I revised my dissertation radically changed the way I write. When I write I dump and revise, and then I continue to revise until I feel finished or until I can no longer ignore a deadline. What I learned first as a behavior (working on a paper for a second or third or fourth time), I've come to think of as a matter of belief or principle (working against the "natural"—that is, the conventional—flow of words on the page).

III

I find I cannot talk about how I write without talking about matters of belief and principle. I did not invent the principles that guide my writing. I suppose I could say that I inherited them. There is certainly a long Western tradition of writers, writing styles, and theories of writing, which is set against the belief that writing should be clear, brief, and sincere, or against the belief that good writing is efficient writing, or against the belief that writers shape and express their own meanings. I have learned to be able to make allusions to ancient and modern texts to borrow authority for my beliefs. At the level of belief, however, or at the level of deeply felt experience, the tradition exists for me through my contact with strong teachers, the teachers who influenced my writing.

I use the word "strong" to echo the way Bloom uses the word when he refers to strong poets or strong poetry and to the anxiety of influence. I think if we are lucky we come up against strong teachers, teachers whose presence, whose sensibility, whose manner of speaking and writing define almost completely our own historical moment, the context within which we might think, speak, read, or write. Bloom, in the passage I've put at the head of this essay, says, "You cannot write or teach or think or even read without imitation, and what you imitate is what another person has done, that person's writing or teaching or thinking or reading." This is no simple matter, however, since the young poet/student (like Shelley) faced with the older poet/teacher (like Milton) struggles to assert his own presence or priority in the very poetry that the older poet made possible. Or, as Bloom says, "A poet . . . is not so much a man speaking to men as a man rebelling against being spoken to by a dead man (the precursor) outrageously more alive than himself."

The force of this argument for me is the way Bloom argues that tradition exists functionally for us through the presence of a single person, a person who cannot be ignored, whose speech we cannot help but imitate and whose presence becomes both an inspiration and a burden. Through this encounter we place ourselves in and thereby invent a cultural, intellectual history. My own experience tells me that I have learned more, or perhaps learned more deeply, through these encounters than through a regular exposure to books and ideas and classes and so forth. The most dramatic educational experience I had was my contact with Richard Poirier in my first year of graduate school. The first three years of my graduate career were driven by a desire to be able to do what he did—to be able to read and speak and write like him. I would, for example, copy out difficult or impressive sentences he had written in order to get the feel of them. I can feel them now in many sentences I write. It is a mixed feeling. I state it simply, but it was not simple at all. I tried for a whole semester to write a paper using the word "language" as he used it in talking about how language "worked" in "Upon Appleton House." It took me a whole semester to use the word in a sentence that actually made sense to me. I felt that I had gained access to a profession by exercises such as these. At the time it did not feel like surrender. It was inspiring to feel that I could use his language and mimic, as I could, his way of reading and writing.

I remember very well how shocked I was when one of my other professors, after admiring a paper I had written, commented, "Don't you ever get tired of that Poirier routine?" It was not then, nor could it ever be for me now, simply a "routine," largely because what Poirier taught and how he taught and how he wrote were and remain central to my own beliefs and my professional identity. I felt ashamed, however, and began in my dissertation to try to write myself free from his influence, to find a project and a way of talking that I could claim for my own. This was a difficult and unsettling thing to try and do. I felt that I had found a place for myself, a way of thinking and talking that located me in the world of professionals, and now I had to push against it. This is not a battle that a writer wins, but for me it marked the next dramatic stage of my education.

As I think of the key experiences in my intellectual life, they all follow a similar pattern. My academic life has been marked by people, not by ideas or theories alone or in the abstract, and my development as a writer has been marked by my attempts to take on and then struggle free from the presence of others. The experiences, obviously, have not all been so intense; and not all, particularly the most recent, have been through teachers I actually see and talk to. I have recently been reading and rereading two essays by Emerson, for example, and I can't seem to get them out of my head.

The other equally key moment for me was meeting and working with Bill Coles. I knew about composition and work in composition before I met him, but I never really entered the field until I met him, felt the force of his presence as a teacher, and read his prose. I could never have imagined his eloquence or his wisdom on my own. I can leave it at that. He gave me a place to begin as a teacher and student of composition. There is nothing that I have written that I could have written without that starting point. As my teacher, I believe, he made eloquence and wisdom possible and defined for me how and why I would work in the field. In what Bloom calls the "dialectics of influence," this has been a matter of working with him and a matter of working against him, a matter, in its way, of interference and resistance, of giving over and giving up, of surrender and betrayal. This is how I think a writer learns, by learning to write within and against the powerful writing that precedes him, that haunts him, and that threatens to engulf him.

IV

I have learned one more important lesson about writing. It is the last important lesson I think I have learned, so perhaps it marks a later stage of development. When I was thirty-two, I wrote on my own for the first time in my life.

Now I have been arguing that no writer ever writes on his own but always in the presence of others. Learning to write means learning this and learning to handle it. So I don't mean that I wrote something fresh and original, or that I wrote something I made up completely all by myself. What I mean is that I wrote something without having to. Actually, even this has to be qualified, since I was still untenured, but as I felt it and as I think back on it, I wrote an essay, actually two of them, both fairly long, just because I had to write them. I know that teachers talk about self-sponsored writing and expressive writing, but these terms never made much sense to me, except perhaps as metaphors.

There are, I think, things that writers are compelled to write about—subjects or themes that try as they might they cannot evade. I know this is true of my own writing. These themes may be said to "express" something basic to the makeup of a writer. The point I want to make, however, is that the presence of such themes doesn't naturally or necessarily give a person the motive or the ability to write about them. What does, or what did for me, was the moment in my career when I had a project—when I found myself in the midst of work that had gone on long enough, that had, in a sense, developed its own force of tradition so that the next step became visible, necessary, and inevitable. Because of what I had done, and the coherence of what I had done, there was a next step rather than a "starting all over again." For years I had felt that every paper I wrote meant that I had to figure things out for the first time. I am not sure what happened—whether I learned to see or insist on the coherence, or whether I had built up a critical mass of work to make the next step possible. I do know that I suddenly felt that there was work that I had to do. Bits and pieces of things that I would read, for example, would jump forward as if magnetized because of the way they could serve the project I was working on. I have heard people say that artists have a special vision, that they don't see the world the way the rest of us do. This never made much sense to me until I thought of it in my own terms. If artists have something, it is a project, a body of work that is ongoing, that defines their professional lives, and that makes them notice things that seem invisible or unimportant to others.

There is, perhaps, a point at which a writer has written so many sentences, read so many books, had so many arguments about a subject, that his work, and the progression of his work become inevitable. It's not so much the preoccupation with a theme that counts as the storehouse of words, the available sentences, the anticipated arguments, the general sense of having a place and a role in a discourse. In my mid-thirties, in the middle of my first job, I had the feeling I had in graduate school and early in my career—the feeling that I had found a place for myself. Now I worry a lot about this routine I've established, about the problems of self-parody, and about the debts I owe to others.

V

As I think about how I write, I know that my work will always begin with other people. I work with other people's words, even as I do my own work; other writers make my work possible, even as I begin to shape projects of my own. I don't put much stock in what I hear about invention and originality. I think it is a myth teachers foist on students in order to make teaching easier or less risky.

I think of Whitman as a strong and risky teacher. For me, he represents the paradox of teaching and learning:

> I am the teacher of athletes,
> He that by me spreads a wider breast than my own proves
>   the width of my own,
> He most honors my style who learns under it to destroy the
>   teacher.

He knows, however, that teachers don't die so easily, "I teach straying from me, yet who can stray from me?" And he concludes this section of "Song of Myself" with these lines:

> My face rubs to the hunter's face when he lies down
>   alone in his blanket,
> The driver thinking of me does not mind the jolt of his
>   wagon,
> The young mother and the old mother comprehend me,

The girl and the wife rest the needle a moment and
    forget where they are,
They and all would resume what I have told them.

As for my teachers, I resume what they have told me when I move
to speak in turn. But never willingly and only sometimes with a most
difficult grace.

Lynn Z. Bloom is professor of English at Virginia Commonwealth University. She earned a B.A. (Phi Beta Kappa), M.A., and Ph.D. from the University of Michigan, and has taught and directed writing programs at Butler University, the University of New Mexico, and the College of William and Mary.

Bloom is the author of Fact and Artifact: Writing Nonfiction *(1985);* Strategic Writing *(1983);* American Autobiography, 1945–1980: A Bibliography, *with M. Brisco and B. Tobias (1982);* Forbidden Diary: A Record of Wartime Internment, 1941–45 *(1980), and numerous other books and articles on writing, biography, and autobiography.*

She has received many awards and grants, including grants from the National Endowment for the Humanities, and has served on the editorial boards of several composition-related publications. She lives in Williamsburg, Virginia, with her husband, who is a professor of social work, and two college student sons.

HOW I WRITE

Lynn Z. Bloom
Virginia Commonwealth University

As I write, as I edit, I continually ask two nagging questions, "What do you mean?" *and "How do you* know?" *Ultimately, as I write and continue to rewrite, I have to be able to answer these questions about every phrase, every sentence, even every choice of word and punctuation mark.*

I wake to sleep, and take my waking slow.
I feel my fate in what I cannot fear.
I learn by going where I have to go.
                                        —*Theodore Roethke**

For years I have misremembered the opening line of Roethke's "The Awakening" as "I wake to dream," for waking to dream is for me the essence of how I write. I take that waking "slow" in the sense that for most writers, as for most teachers of writing (or anything else), the creation of any piece of writing takes all my life. I can give it no more; I would give it no less.

Even though I begin with an idea that intrigues, excites, pleases me, I can't predict at the outset a great deal of what I'm going to say; I indeed "learn by going where I have to go." In some ways this epitomization of my writing process is a variant of E. M. Forster's comment on his own manner of writing, "How do I know what I think until I see what I say?" However, for me learning by "going where I have to go" implies, in addition to developing the content, learning throughout the process of writing how I am going to handle the structure, organization, and style of given paragraphs, sentences, of this particular whole essay.

Most of my writing is nonfiction—articles for professional conferences, journals, and compilations such as *Writers on Writing;* entire books for general readers, scholars, and students; and book reviews for newspapers as well as for academic readers. All of it is meant for publication; much of it is commissioned. Thus I write each piece, short or long, with a specific or generically identifiable audience in mind—literary or composition scholars specializing in the subjects of my re-

*Excerpt from "The Waking" from *The Collected Poems of Theodore Roethke.* Copyright 1953 by Theodore Roethke. Reprinted by permission of Doubleday & Company, Inc.

search; college and high school teachers of writing; college students of designated levels of ability and involvement with the subject, from freshmen to graduate students. Unlike the audience Gertrude Stein had in mind when she said, "I write for myself and strangers," for me even the strangers are friends, people I know generically, if not specifically. These include my colleagues throughout the academic nation; my own students (composites of the students I've taught for the past twenty-five years at universities, private and public, in the North, South, East, Midwest, and West—reinforced by the tastes and abilities of my own college student children and their friends); my neighbors in Cleveland and St. Louis and Indianapolis and Williamsburg; people I meet at parties (political and otherwise), the supermarket, the League of Women Voters, the library, and the swimming pool.

From the time I first learned to read, smitten with the joys of Dr. Seuss, I wanted to write. I thought at the age of six that to delight readers with words was the most wonderful thing in the world. Forty years later, I still think so, having adopted Joan Didion's view stated so compellingly in "Why I Write": "In many ways writing is the act of saying I, of imposing oneself upon other people, of saying listen to me, see it my way, change your mind." Given my audience and the subjects on which I write—rhetoric and composition, biography and autobiography, twentieth-century American writers—it is inevitable that I want also to teach. I want to show my readers what I've discovered, to convince them that my understanding, my view of the subject, my way of doing it—whatever it may be—is the best. And the most enjoyable. Indeed, Sir Philip Sidney's contention that the aims of imaginative literature are to teach and delight, and that a well-written tale will hold "children from play, and old men from the chimney corner," applies to nonfiction, as well.

I write for myself and my friends in the same language in which I'd talk to them if we were discussing the subject in person—friendly, knowledgeable, I hope, but not condescending, though with less slang and fewer personal references than an oral conversation would contain. (Indeed, although I'm pleased to have the chance that *Writers on Writing* provides to analyze my own writing process, I have for so long kept autobiographical details out of my writing that I am uncomfortable here at putting them in—a paradox in light of my critical specialty.) I try to maintain an authoritative, up-beat persona who talks in real language that real readers use and understand.

I know that this persona and my dislike of stuffy, jargony language were fostered by two years of working closely with Benjamin Spock, M.D. (yes, *the* Dr. Spock), as I wrote my first book after graduate school, *Doctor Spock: Biography of a Conservative Radical* (Indianapolis: Bobbs-Merrill, 1972). Having written a dissertation on biographical method, I wanted to try practicing what I was preaching, and chose Dr. Spock because he was an interesting major figure accessible when I was at home rearing small children. Writing this biography knocked the dissertationese clean out of my style. Spock writes the way he talks, and since I included many quotations from interviews and from his writings, my own style had to be compatible with Spock's or the disparity would have been too disjunctive for readers. Spock himself is a conscious stylist, as the forty-year popularity of *Baby and Child Care* attests. He writes with absolute clarity, no ambiguity (especially when a child's health and safety depend on it), careful but nontechnical explanations of terms, friendliness. Spock is the Strunk and White of baby book authors, so I had a good teacher. A careful analysis of Spock's style taught me to simplify overly technical language, to define specialized terms in nonspecialized language, to break up long sentences and paragraphs to rest the ear and the eye. Spock composed aloud, and from him I learned to listen to the words, the music, the sounds of silence.

A writer is always writing. I write when I swim, I write when I cook (favorite daily activities); I write when I dream, asleep or awake, especially during an hour of semiwakefulness I've come to cherish early every morning after five or six hours of sound sleep. James Thurber has described well the process of incessant writing:

> I never quite know when I'm not writing. Sometimes my wife comes up to me at a party and says, "Dammit, Thurber, stop writing." She usually catches me in the middle of a paragraph. Or my daughter will look up from the dinner table and ask, "Is he sick?" "No," my wife says. "He's writing something."[1]

Sometimes my mental writing consists of random speculations, searching for a golden needle in a haystack that is mostly straw. At other times it means looking at a more familiar subject from a deliberately unusual perspective, or series of perspectives, to see anew—because I don't want to see—or say—the same old thing. Often, one idea will lead to another—my home garden variety of Linda Flower's "issue tree" and branching.[2]

When I get a good idea, one that seems right, or so obvious that I wonder why no one ever thought of it before, I recognize it immediately. Aha! It took me five years and one minute—the latter six hundred pages into the final rewrite—and a catalytic suggestion from a friend to discover the right title for my most recent book.[3] I take casual, fragmentary notes on this thinking, usually jotting down key words and phrases, and names of books and authors to consult. If ideas don't come, I read. When the material is relevant I continue to take sketchy notes, or to

[1]James Thurber in *Writers at Work: The Paris Review Interviews* (New York: Viking, 1957), p. 96.
[2]See "Build an Issue Tree," *Problem-Solving Strategies for Writing* (New York: Harcourt Brace Jovanovich, 1981), pp. 87–100.
[3]*Fact and Artifact: Writing Nonfiction* (San Diego: Harcourt Brace Jovanovich, 1985).

dog-ear pages. When the material is irrelevant—the daily papers or a novel when I'm wrestling with a critical issue in autobiography—the reading is merely a diversionary activity, a facade for the thinking about the *real* issue that I'm working on beneath the surface. If good ideas still don't come, or if I find it hard to concentrate creatively, I stop and turn to something entirely different, maybe even a less demanding kind of writing. I know the hard part will continue to simmer on a mental back burner until it's pliable enough to work with.

If I'm writing an article or a chapter of a book, I spend as long as I need to (usually, anywhere from two to three days to as many weeks or longer, if necessary) blitz reading key texts—professional journal articles and books central to the subject at hand, to get a focused overview of the research or literature that's accumulated since the last time I studied the subject. As I read I again take fragmentary notes, consisting of key words, phrases, and page numbers—nothing formal, nothing fancy. As long as the books are indexed, I can find what I want; otherwise, I use the notes. As I read and the topic begins to take shape I find that I'm focusing, narrowing the topic and sorting out ideas—some self-generated, some stimulated by my reading—into relevant topics and rejects. The latter are either irrelevant, unoriginal, badly done, too complicated for the length and level of the paper, or simply uninteresting to me.

I group the usable ideas into topical categories, and arrange these categories to fit whatever organizational plan emerges as my thinking develops. Although this is fluid and may change as I write, I am careful to give the greatest emphasis and the most prominent space to the Very Important Ideas, and to keep the lesser thoughts subordinate in the overall pattern and in development.

From time to time I stop and simply sit and think; it looks as if I'm not doing anything. Or I take a brief nap, or drink tea and read the newspaper, or exercise, or cook, or do (horrors!) housework. And let the ideas cook awhile. Sometimes I discuss my ideas with my husband, a social psychologist who's been not only my best friend but my best—and most unsparing—critic for nearly thirty years. During this casual-seeming time of intense gestation I try to keep out distractions, especially those that involve concentrated thought and effort in other areas of life. Indeed, to the extent that I can, I try to compartmentalize categories of major effort; teaching and paper grading get done on teaching days; writing gets done on writing days; social activities and errands get pushed into gaps between these larger blocks of time. (This method of composition during extended blocks of time differs consider-ably from the way I used to write when my children were little. I could never say to them, "Don't bother me; I'm writing about Dr. Spock." Without the leisure for a warmup period, I learned to concentrate instantly and to write in whatever batches of time were available, even as short as a half-hour, with the children playing in the same room.)

I block out my writing commitments week by week, month by month, and year by year. I use an abstract and perhaps impossible goal —to write an article a month and a book a year—to keep myself writing steadily; although I don't necessarily accomplish this, I get more done by setting such goals than I would with less demanding goals in mind. To reinforce my informal commitments to myself, I make formal commitments by agreeing to submit work according to schedules determined by editors, organizers of sessions at professional meetings, and others. The closer I am to a deadline, the more concentratedly I work; indeed, I use the imminence of a deadline to ensure efficiency. Yet this form of writing roulette produces uncomfortable tension (and an occasional late manuscript) if unanticipated distractions or calamities occur. My husband, who writes as much as I do, and I reward ourselves with trips to celebrate the completion of major projects; visions of the Alps, Yeats country, Carcassonne, and Cordoba keep me hard at work to accommodate the deadlines that, puritanically, I must meet before I can have my just dessert.

I write at home and on airplanes—both places with limited access and unlimited vistas. Home is best. Woods, wildlife, and a garden with a view (never mind the weeds) outside; a woodstove within. Everything I need (except a Xerox machine) is, literally, at hand—reference books, journals, my personal library, annotated and highlighted; volumes lugged home from the university library; copies of mind-jogging articles, published and unpublished; a vintage collection of student papers; correspondence files with editors' instructions and readers' critiques; ever-increasing piles of successive drafts of my current manuscript. Comfortable chairs (my office furniture, like my office, is designed to fit a cubist's imagination, not this all too human frame). Comfortable dress, ranging from an elegant and cheering quilted robe to bare feet, in season. Good lights, sufficient for the major surgery I continually perform. And especially, my electric typewriter and my personal computer.

Until two years ago, I always composed prose on the typewriter (and poetry in longhand on yellow lined tablets). Because I write as I think, and think as I write, the faster I can get the thoughts down the easier the writing is. Hence the switch to personal computer. The computer also allows unlimited revisions as I write and rewrite. Sometimes I edit each sentence several times before I go on to the next; after I have enough text to work with I move sentences and paragraphs around to see (which one can do literally with a computer) which way looks best. The boundaries of the computer's screen have made me aware of the great extent to which I rely on the text I've just written as a guide to what is yet to come, and the enormous amount of rescanning I do in the process. As a nervous computer novice—and a realist (VEPCO often reminds us small-town folk of its power by turning it off at unsettling intervals)—I print out the text every ten pages or so to have a working draft in hard copy; that makes the rescanning easier, too. What a pleasure to have a clean copy to mess up instead of having to cut and paste a scribbled-over typed text already too cluttered to work on without retyping.

As I write, as I edit, I continually ask two nagging questions, "What do you *mean?*" and "How do you *know?*" Ultimately, as I write and continue to rewrite, I have to be able to answer these questions about every phrase, every sentence, even every choice of word and punctuation mark. If I can't justify something, out it goes. As Marianne Moore observed, "A writer is unfair to himself when he is unable to be hard on himself." I have to be my own toughest critic in order to meet my friends—other tough critics—out there in the audience.

After a slow start in the morning, my energy, ability to concentrate, and creativity build throughout the day and evening, with time out for meals, an occasional nap, and an invigorating evening swim. On a good writing day I begin low-level tasks around ten in the morning—editing the hard copy of the previous day's manuscript, feeding the changes into the computer, often rewriting more as I do so. Later, in the afternoon and throughout the evening, I work on the harder tasks—new writing—until I can't stay awake any longer, usually between midnight and 1 A.M. Before I stop, I jot down fragmentary thoughts to keep the hot topics from cooling overnight. During the school year, I try to arrange three good writing days a week. During vacations, I schedule five to six such days at a stretch, this strenuous mental workout punctuated by the necessary (for me) antidote of a day of intense physical activity, with no writing at all.

After a first working draft is roughed in, I fill in the gaps, looking up supplementary information, checking quotations, finding references. When I get a draft that's good enough to show someone—usually after two complete rewrites, though the tough spots may have been written a dozen times or more—I impose it on my husband and try to feign indifference while he reads. That never works. I want him to like what I write, to like it well enough so I won't have to change anything, to leap up with admiration as he finishes and shout "Hats off!"—as M. Grand, Camus's wretched aspiring writer in *The Plague,* imagined all masterpieces should be received. That seldom happens. When it does, I'm so happy we celebrate with wine and chocolate.

Most often, he thinks some parts are fine (he's learned over the years to start tactfully) and that other parts need work. We discuss the problem spots, and ways to solve the problems, in considerable detail —sometimes, alas, generating more heat than light if I'm too close to the draft to see it any way other than as I've written it. If so, there's no choice but to put it aside and come back to it at intervals, which, depending on the deadline, may extend anywhere from a few hours to several years. I try not to spend more effort on the rewriting than the importance of the piece warrants. I might work over the problem parts of an ephemeral book review twice, at most, but I will rewrite major articles or book chapters as many times as I need to to get them right. I usually write long the first time, and then arbitrarily cut the manuscript by a third to tighten it up without loss of meaning.

When I get a respectable penultimate draft (better than everyday pottery but not the bone china), I try it out on a knowledgeable typical reader, whether a scholar, student, or general reader. (I like to think that my teenage children became good writers as well as critical readers from being impressed into editorial service on occasion.) And sometimes, on still another. That's about as many external points of view as I can cope with before sending the work out to be reacted to by editors and their readers. Over the years I have developed a sufficient sense of the integrity of my own ideas and style so that I don't feel obliged to accommodate all readers' remarks; if a camel is a horse invented by a committee, a knockoff TV sitcom must be the literary equivalent and, no thanks. Though it took more courage than I thought I had at the moment, I once rescued the manuscript of a book over which I'd labored for four years from an editor who plastered over all my witty remarks with dull, Latinate verbiage. The new editor restored both the wit and my equilibrium.

Once a manuscript is off to the editor, I'm mentally done with that work and am on to the next. So when I get editorial queries or suggestions (read "commands") for revision, or galleys to correct, I have to emerge from the "deep well of unconscious cerebration" (wherein Coleridge's creativity resided, according to John Livingston Lowes) and refocus on what is now to me an old and distant work, no matter how much I like it. I can see it then with the critic's cold eye, and edit it again with rigor. I seldom read my published works. I already know them by heart—and by the time they appear, I'm so deeply involved with the new paramour that when someone congratulates me on my most recent book my instinctive reaction is, focusing always on the work-in-progress, "But it's not done yet."

Do I finish everything I start? Every prose writing for which there's a contract or a commitment. Although a dozen years ago I spent a year learning to write poetry and more or less completed a poem a day, my concentration on prose interferes with finishing more recent poetry. I have scraps of poetry, mostly single ideas or images to explore, stuck in drawers all over the house, in my purse, amongst the unpaid bills. In my mental recipe file simmers the Great American Super Succulent Cookbook. And in my head and heart is a world of short stories and novels that extends from Kilimanjaro to Yoknapatawpha. Someday . . . But in the meantime,

I wake to [dream], and take my waking slow.
. . . .
I learn by going where I have to go.

Hal Blythe and Charlie Sweet are professors in the Department of English at Eastern Kentucky University. Their articles have appeared in such publications as College English, College Composition and Communication, Writer's Digest, Poe Studies, *and* Studies in Browning and His Circle. *They have written stories for such diverse magazines as* Ellery Queen's Mystery Magazine, Home Life, *and* Woman's World, *and they have created scripts for both educational and commercial television. Currently they are working on a novel.*

COLLABORWRITING

Hal Blythe and Charlie Sweet
Eastern Kentucky University

Essentially we're both sponges absorbing information, events, and personalities around us. It's in this initial and informal brainstorming conversation that we hear ourselves and each other talking. Somehow this process gives us a focus on ideas that might otherwise escape our attention; thus, this interchange becomes a primary advantage of team-writing.

Two heads are better than one might be a cliché, but in our case the old saw still cuts it. As partners in crime—well actually, writing about crime—we have found that what we call collaborwriting pays (though not enough).

Since the Longfellowian April of '75, we have turned out as a team everything from a critical piece on the motivations of Browning's Ferrara to a monthly column in *Byline* to the lead novella in this month's *Mike Shayne Mystery Magazine.* For almost ten years we have collaborated on over 250 published works, and all of them are products of a single methodology on whose cornerstone is inscribed WRITING DEMANDS DISCIPLINE.

Perhaps the best way to illustrate why Hal and Charlie (a/k/a Hal Charles, Brett Halliday, Charlene Herrald) can write is to take you through an ordinary writing day. Since our primary profession is teaching and we both have families, we have a limited amount of time to devote to writing. Fortunately, writing is a full-time occupation we have learned to practice part-time.

Our teaching schedules, we make certain, are set up so as to allow us a compatible block of time during the day. Our synergy level peaking early, we arrange to be free from classes every day between 10:30 and 1:00. Perhaps this very brevity forces us to use our time efficiently. We write only on weekdays, but in our ten years of collaboration neither of us has ever missed a day because of illness or other commitments. We write forty-eight weeks a year, allowing two weeks at the end of each semester to recharge our individual batteries. This discipline has caused us at various times to write in homes, hospitals, and airports.

Normally, though, we write at one specific place. When we were just getting started, we received a very useful piece of advice from a Hollywood writer who was visiting campus. Jack Sowards, who wrote *Star Trek II* among other things, told us that instead of setting aside a room at his house, he got up every morning and drove to a rented office in downtown L.A. Separated from the usual associations and demands of home life, he found the typewriter and books put him in the right frame of mind for writing—the separate office reinforced his professional commitment. For us, getting away from the constant interruptions at our office by colleagues, students, and book salesmen is a similar necessity. Unfortunately, we can't afford to rent a downtown office. Our compromise? For a mere 70 cents a day we can get two cups of coffee and a booth at the local McDonald's. After all, Scott and Ernie labored in the smoke-filled haze of Paris bistros, so why not work under the glow of the Golden Arches? Furthermore, Papa couldn't get a Big Mac. After six years of sitting in the same booth five days a week amidst the cheerful muzak and Happy Meals, in fact, we were honored. While he couldn't present us with the Pulitzer Prize, the owner dedicated our booth by placing over it a plaque and our portrait ("Hey, Sundance, who are those guys?").

Each writing session is structured. While we absorb that first jolt of caffeine, we talk over anything interesting we've run across in the media or personal experience. "Where do you guys get all your ideas?" we're always being asked at writers' conferences. Essentially we're both sponges absorbing information, events, and personalities around us. It's in this initial and informal brainstorming conversation that we hear ourselves and each other talking. Somehow this process gives us a focus on ideas that might otherwise escape our attention; thus, this interchange becomes a primary advantage of team-writing. Then, too, we subscribe to what we call the three burner theory. Besides the primary piece we're bringing to a boil on any given day, we like to have a second starting to bubble, and a third we've just put on the stove. Usually we jot down what we discuss and try to rough out vaguely what we might do with it. One day we might come up with a query letter for *Writer's Digest* while another time we might mention a key idea to help bring a bubbling plot to a boil.

Stage two is the read-through of what we wrote the previous session. Hal's reading the material aloud helps us correct any problems in form or content. Misspellings, overused sentence patterns, unnatural-sounding dialogue—all are exorcised at this point in our daily ritual. Further, this reading shifts us into the flow of the piece. It is here that we leave the booth in a Kentucky McDonald's and enter the mean streets of Miami or the wine cellar of Montresor.

Stage three is the actual writing. Charlie plays scribe because Hal writes as though he has a medical degree. Here as in everything else the collaboration is total. Our idols Manny Lee and Fred Dannay (Ellery Queen) divided up the chores so that one wrote the plot outline, the other filled in the story, and on Fridays they met to revise. We, on the other hand, write every word facing each other across the paper-filled Formica.

During this stage we usually work from a rudimentary outline constructed in an earlier session. It's a free exchange of ideas. Hal might say, "What if . . .?" and Charlie will pick up the cue and supply some details. If we reach the point in the wood at which the roads diverge and Hal wants to travel one while Charlie the other, we talk out the situation until we both take the same path. The more we write together, the less we encounter divergences and the more we seem to be able to finish each other's sentences. We usually work out scenes by dramatizing the parts. A scene really comes alive when Hal playing Mike Shayne interrogates Charlie the Gat. Once, in fact, we got so wrapped up in the role-playing that a McDonald's employee who overheard but didn't know us, asked almost hopefully, "Are you guys . . . detectives?" Three cheers for credibility! We try to end each writing session at an exciting juncture, making the starting point of the next day's writing easier.

Stage four is the only time we work alone. Every night Hal does any necessary research for the next day and handles our correspondence. Meanwhile, Charlie plays with our newest investment, transferring the day's material onto a floppy disk and running off a copy for the next day's proofreading. Changing over from the old Smith-Corona to the Apple IIe in the last year has improved both the quality and the quantity of our writing. We're more open to revision since the magic of word processing makes the chore easier than in the old days, when even a minor change meant a totally retyped manuscript. Our word count—and yes, we do consider that part of the discipline—has more than doubled. When Charlie types, he also provides an extra reading.

The next day we repeat the cycle. When the project is ready to be taken off the burner and presented for consumption, we do a final read-through, checking for any errors in logic or mechanics. The finished product, then, has usually been through at least five readings in part or in whole.

Establishing a routine and following it religiously has the same value we believe for the writer as it does for the athlete. The whole process, like a Boston Celtic guard dribbling behind his back, has become second nature for us, something we rarely consider. It's only when we get the inevitable writers'-conference question, "Why do you guys write together?" that we stop to analyze. Actually, there's more than one reason we continue our collaboration.

How many writers have complained that writing is a lonely, agonizing time? For us, it's not. It's a period when we can socialize, when we can exchange and fictionalize our views on everything from departmental gossip to nuclear terrorism. One of us is a big-city, Southern Baptist good-ole-boy, while the other is a small-town Connecticut Yankee. Part of the fun of our cross-pollination is reconciling our two varied viewpoints on many issues.

All writers need reinforcement and support. Consider Gustave Flaubert, who wrote his first work in a vacuum. When he showed what he thought was the finished product to a circle of friends, he was devastated by their criticism. Our support is constant, and so too is our criticism. If Charlie suggests what he considers an innocent line of dialogue, Hal, seeing it in a different light, might point out its lack of logic. We've long since passed the point of individual egotism and thin-skinnedness. Even now, rereading this paragraph, we can't remember if Hal said this or Charlie said that; *we* said it all. Some of our colleagues have commented, in fact, that our greatest fictional creation is Hal Charles.

Maybe our collaborwriting isn't so much two heads but, as psychological studies are showing, an instance of being able to integrate Charlie's right brain and Hal's left brain. We're not saying that we're a pair of half-wits, but that we have complementary personalities. Let us illustrate with the genesis of a Mike Shayne story published in the August 1984 issue of *Mike Shayne Mystery Magazine.*

The bulk of our fiction originates from an isolated idea Charlie has —in this case he had three. In our brainstorming portion he threw out a trio of plot seeds that intrigued him:

1. What if Santiago and Manolin had been trolling the Gulfstream circa 1984 and had found not the big fish, but a floating bale of marijuana?
2. A newspaper article that described a teenager paying for a new Mercedes by pulling $40,000 out of his lunchbox.
3. A couple who kept their marriage from becoming stale by pretending she was a prostitute and he was a regular.

Hal, being the Mr. Spock of our enterprise, ran the ideas through his mystery filter and suggested combining all three. Logical, Charlie said, but how? For Hal, the figure in Charlie's carpet was a crime ring, a drug-smuggling Fagin who employed street kids as runners and whose operation was threatened by a blackmailing streetwalker who had stumbled into his illegal activities. Fine, said Charlie, how do we get Mike Shayne in? Oh, he needs a client. Who? Suppose the prostitute shows up dead and one of her clients retains Miami's number-one P.I.

Why hire Shayne? Suppose the john cared? Why would he? And so it goes.

In essence, what we do is eventually apply the usual pattern of a hardboiled mystery to set up our episodes. By continually asking a kid's favorite question, "Why?" we evolve a rough outline of the plot that we feel free to add to or subtract from as we write. And scholarship/criticism begins the same way. For instance, after teaching Browning, Hal once expressed a dissatisfaction with the traditional explanation of Ferrara's motivation. Off the top of his head, Charlie wondered if the Duke might have been impotent. "Why," Hal asked, picking up on the chance remark, "did you say that?" Charlie didn't know. A close examination of the text offered tenuous support. Hal noticed an image cluster, and then we did some research. With two of us, that takes half the time. Bits and pieces were culled from previous scholarship, an outline was constructed around the usual pattern for a critical paper, and the writing process began. The end product appeared in *Studies in Browning and His Circle.*

Another advantage to collaborating is that we rarely encounter the traditional nemeses of writers. One of the reasons we haven't missed a day of writing in so long is a sense of obligation. On a particular day Charlie may feel like anything but a trip to Ronald's Room, but he knows Hal is depending on his being there, so he shows up. Writer's block? Never! One of us always has a fresh idea or a new slant on an old one. False starts? Hardly! Because we talk out virtually everything step by step beforehand, we usually have a pretty good idea of our destination as well as a map of how to get there before we start the actual work. Burnout? Impossible! With our constant exchanges, frustrations are always brought into the open and never allowed to fester. And with the three burners operating, if we get tired of one project, we can always switch to another.

In our new math, then, $1 + 1 > 2$. And now that we've finished revising this piece, you'll have to excuse us. It's time for a Big Mac.

Harry Brent is associate professor of English and director of writing programs at Baruch College of the City University of New York. In addition, he has taught at Rutgers University, the universities of Wisconsin and Nevada, and Jilin University in the People's Republic of China. For four years, he served as chair of the college section of the National Council of Teachers of English and as a member of the NCTE executive committee.

Brent has published and lectured widely on a variety of topics relating to the teaching of English. Among his most recent publications are Rhetorical Considerations, *with William Lutz, (4th ed., 1984), and, also with Lutz,* The Perennial Reader *(1984). Scheduled to appear this year is his* Writing in the World.

EPISTEMOLOGICAL PRESUMPTIONS IN THE WRITING PROCESS: THE IMPORTANCE OF CONTENT TO WRITING

Harry Brent

I must confess that rarely do I consciously follow the advice I give my students about the composing process. I wander through the woods, occasionally intersecting one of the sacred pathways of invention or arrangement, but never following it for very long. Asphalt roads have their place . . . when you're traveling straight and by clear design, but I like to wander when I write, create my own roads.

NO, VIRGINIA

If I understand my assignment correctly, I am supposed to answer for my own hypocrisy. Everybody knows that rhetoricians and teachers of writing do not follow the advice they give their students. My task in this article is to explain this contradiction, at least in terms of my own experience, and to plead *mea culpa*.

Do rhetoricians really take their own advice, do they really go through all those stages of free writing, pre-writing, drafting, revising, editing, and so on? The question has vague associations with the one

45

that Virginia asked about Santa Claus. We all know that the reply she hoped for was the one she got. In this case things are not so neat. No, Virginia, I do not engage in "brainstorming."

I must confess that rarely do I consciously follow the advice I give my students about the composing process. I wander through the woods, occasionally intersecting one of the sacred pathways of invention or arrangement, but never following it for very long. Asphalt roads have their place, especially when you're traveling straight and by clear design, but I like to wander when I write, to create my own roads. I usually manage to make it through the wilderness, but I couldn't tell you how. Like the boy in Faulkner's "Bear," I left my compass on a tree.

The last time I taught Faulkner was at Jilin University in China, up in Manchuria where there is lots of wilderness. I learned that the Chinese like clearly defined paths. This is, after all, the era of the "Four Modernizations." The lectures I gave in composition theory were studded with phrases like "the five roads to invention," "the eight important transitions," "the six ways of revising." My students were teachers and graduate students. Their English was excellent and they had read much. There was interesting content in their lives, derived from actual experience—in the recent "Cultural Revolution" and from what they had read. They wanted information on rhetorical form, on how to organize and present their ideas clearly and effectively. They liked asphalt roads.

While I was in China, I was mildly disturbed at the reluctance of my students to ask questions. They seemed to take down my words as gospel truth, as if there really were "six" ways of revising. Nobody ever asked whether there was a seventh. This reticence, I learned, is a Chinese custom based upon recognition of the teacher's authority and a reluctance of students to be seen as arrogant in questioning that authority. Their silence made me guilty, for I fully expected questions that would reveal my own lack of reliance on the formulas I gave them.

In retrospect my guilt has vanished, largely because I think that my Chinese students had backgrounds and interests that would tend to make their writing interesting no matter how it was organized. The material they got from me was ancillary—a set of options for organization and development. Unlike most American college students whose experiences, at least as reported in their essays, tend toward the trivial, my Chinese students had much to say. The problems I had with their writing were very much like the problems I have with my own: getting out the deadwood (theirs tended, paradoxically, to be very flowery deadwood) and giving interesting material some observable sense of organization. At the end of the course, my students' essays were quite organized and often very predictable, but, unlike the essays I read from students in this country, they were rarely dull.

My experience in China taught me that organized systems of rhetoric *by themselves* do not produce good writing. The primary element in good writing is not form but content. With advanced writing students who have interesting experience to draw upon, whether directly from their lives or vicariously from reading, rhetoric lends options for organization, for surprise in presentation, and for fluidity of style. With other students, and these are mostly freshmen, the story is otherwise.

Freshmen are different. They usually have not read very much, and their experiences, though often meaningful to them, tend to be the common stuff of adolescence. Dreadfully boring are their judgments, at least from an adult perspective, and repetitive in the extreme are the papers I get. I teach them how to organize, but in my heart I see little point in applying principles of adequate development to the topics of dead cats, college registration difficulties, or their last book read—that thing by William Golding with the kid whose glasses symbolize civilization. Or, now that 1984 has passed, *Nineteen Eighty-Four*, although usually the Monarch Notes version thereof.

I can assign these students readings in the hope of thereby enriching their experience and giving them something to write about, but even when I do this, their essays are predictable and most often based upon some quick judgment or visceral reaction. I am not likely, for example, to get reactions based on *other* readings. If I have freshmen read an essay by Sartre, they are not likely to read independently an essay by Camus or Freud as part of the process of formulating their own response.

This difference between our own backgrounds and those of our freshman students is why the advice about writing I give in class differs from my own writing practices. At the risk of sounding arrogant, I must say that my world is richer than theirs and that thus my way of dealing with the content of that world is necessarily different. I don't "brainstorm"; I read. And I place much more emphasis on revision—wandering and rewandering in my essays—than on invention.

Frustration with the intellectual poverty of our students is, I think, one impetus for the recent focus on invention as a major component of writing. As teachers, we are readers (in addition to being correctors), and when confronted with student essays we thus naturally yearn for interesting subject matter. The problem, as I will go on to explore in this essay, is that we have failed to place the demands on our students regarding subject matter that we place upon ourselves.

I don't think that there is very much difference in the way that we and our students write. The major difference is that we have more to talk about than they do. I remember that during my first or second year of teaching I was watching a TV interview program on the intellectual maturity of college students. The panelists were all well-known, respected educators. I can't remember anyone in particular, but they were all Barzun-van Doren types. In reaction to a line of argument much like the one I'm now pursuing, one of the panelists made the statement: "Wait a minute, a seventeen-year-old kid has had a lot of experience. He's got a lot to write about." I was rooting for the person who said this, and I felt gratified that he validated my own prostudent prejudices. But, as with most of those comments that stay with you for twenty years, there was something naggingly wrong about this one. Two decades later, I disagree. Tens of thousands of freshman themes have convinced me otherwise.

We and our freshman students have very different writing problems. Thus it is appropriate that we *not* use the devices we tell them to use. My most difficult problem is getting what I have to say into the best form. The most important problem with student writing is not form but content. As far as the process of writing goes, we and our students tend to do roughly the same things. To illustrate, before continuing my discussion about the importance of content, let me remark on how I am writing this essay.

HOW I AM WRITING THIS ESSAY

Right now I am sitting in my office at my word processor. In the room next door, the faculty lounge, there is a party going on. I do not like getting sloshed in the middle of the day—especially when I have a karate lesson this evening—so I'm pretending that I have lots of hard work to do. My colleagues are having a good time and thus are not likely to disturb me.

The main problem I'm experiencing right now is that I do not particularly want to write at this moment. However, the deadline for this piece is seven weeks away. That sounds a long time off, but I've got one major book to finish up and another to get started on in those same seven weeks. Doing this essay has been increasingly on my mind for about two weeks now. Like my need to lose weight, I've been thinking about it at least three or four times a day. The only way to get it out of the way is to get it out of the way. Besides, Tom Waldrep has gently nudged me with a follow-up letter.

Let me try a little stream of consciousness: Interruption. A phone call from a book salesman—wants to have lunch next week—nice guy —I've got to keep on my diet—he had trouble today with a chemistry manual—wonder why one of my teacher's manuals was published a month late—how come two of my publishing friends didn't show up at my wedding—maybe I should check out the party—no I should concentrate more on this.

Enough stream of consciousness, and enough writing for today. The process isn't much different, at this stage at least, from what my students tell me they go through. As I move through this essay I'll comment from time to time on how I'm writing it. In the last section I'll briefly review the process in its entirety.

TRUTH AND EXPERIENCE

It is about a quarter after eight on a Thursday morning, and I am at home in front of my word processor, with a cup of coffee. My aim this morning is to continue this essay by focusing on the relationship between writing and experience. My first thought is that in effective writing, experience is rendered with a felt sense of honesty. This thought leads me to a consideration of the nature of "honesty." To explore and develop this consideration, I focus on my experience of the last hour.

My fiancée and I got up about forty-five minutes ago. She is off to work. I began the day by making the coffee and finding the stale French bread from last night—good in the morning with raspberry jam.

The McNeil-Lehrer report is rebroadcast in the mornings in New York. I turned it on for a few minutes this morning. It ended with a tribute to George McGovern, who had just dropped out of the Democratic presidential nomination race.

In the bathroom, I picked up an old copy of *Harper's,* the one with the article by Simone de Beauvoir about Sartre's death. I had been reading this article off and on in the bathroom for about a month. This morning I came to the part where Sartre dies. After the funeral scene, there is an appendix containing an interview with Sartre by de Beauvoir in 1974. The subject is death and God. De Beauvoir asks Sartre what he thinks about death. He responds in part about his writing:

> . . . I wrote which has been the essence of my life. I've succeeded in what I longed for from the age of seven or eight. I have written what I wanted to write, books that have had an influence and that have been read. So when I die I shall not die as many people do, saying "Oh, if I had my life again I should live it in another way. I have failed; I have made a mess of it."

As I read Sartre's commentary on writing, I listened to McGovern talking about honesty in his campaign. His remarks gave me the impetus to write as I am now about honesty in writing. McGovern discussed how, because he did not make winning his prime object, he felt free as a presidential candidate to say what he really wanted. McGovern and Sartre seemed to connect. For an instant or two I had one of those experiences in which one not only understands, but feels, the essential truth of some insight. To be able to say or to write exactly what you want, to speak directly and sincerely, is a central thing in one's life. The fact that few people really get a chance to be absolutely honest in their writing, especially publicly and consistently, is one of the central contradictions of the writer's art. Honesty motivates us to write, yet when we revise we temper our honesty.

The honesty I'm talking about is not the moral kind. Nor is it the rhetorical honesty Aristotle discusses in terms of what he calls "ethical stance." The honesty I mean has to do with our impulses to tell the truth when we write and the process we go through in smothering those impulses little by little, especially as we revise, so that the real content about which we are writing gets covered up. In the piece I am now writing and which I am now revising again and again at various "nows," which you are "now" reading, I am tempted at this very moment to return to the first paragraphs and "cover up" some material.

In this sense, all writing is as Derrida says, "under erasure." Underneath what you are "now" reading there are at least five or six layers of draft. Each one of these was produced by mental processes in which one shade of an idea covered or erased another. And as you, my reader, read this you highlight and erase as well.

In revision we erase for style, for continuity, but also to cover up, to subvert honesty. What is there to cover up, for example, in this essay? Well, some things about my personal and intellectual life. If this were a "normal" essay, not one where I have the job of discussing *how* I write, I would probably delete the description of the morning rituals. I would certainly never let the inference be drawn that I read Sartre only in the bathroom. And I would be especially careful to cover up the fact that I came upon the quote by Sartre almost by chance, or that my decision to write about honesty originated in a chance turn of the TV dial, that making this decision and finding the material from Sartre was not the result of an organized plan of research.

I suppose that if this were a "normal" essay, I would indirectly try to convey to the reader the impression that what I am writing proceeds from an orderly and logical plan, that in line with what we tell our students, I have done my "pre-writing." But, in truth, I hardly ever write anything according to an orderly and logical plan. Nor, as I told Virginia, do I ever engage in those warmup exercises we call "free writing" or "brainstorming."

THE PRIMACY OF NARRATIVE

Unless my writing assignment is extremely narrow and technical, such as the self-study report I wrote last year on the composition program I direct, I tend to write the first draft of anything I do partially as a personal narrative.

There is a catch to this. I would not want colleagues reading this article to suggest that their students write their first drafts as personal narratives. The reason again sounds arrogant. It has to do with my earlier comments on writing and subject matter: Our students don't live the same kinds of intellectual lives that people reading this article are likely to live. A narrative of a freshman student's typical day is not, except for class assignments, likely to be filled with the kind of reading and intellectual exploration we go through every day.

There are exceptions to this rule, but as a generalization I think it holds. If you doubt, ask your students to list the books and magazines, other than those for class, that are in places other than shelves in their rooms. Then do the same for yourself.[1] You are

---

[1]The reading material (short titles) next to my side of the bed on this particular day includes the following: *The London Times* (one copy); *Newsweek* (two copies); *The Village Voice* (one copy); Eric Partridge, *Origins: A Short Etymological Dictionary of Modern English;* Freud, *Moses and Monotheism;* Jules Verne, *Journey to the Center of the Earth;* Sybil Taylor, *Ireland's Pubs; Penthouse* (five copies); *Playboy* (three copies); Henri Focillon, *The Art of the West,* Vol. I, *Romanesque;* James Joyce, *Ulysses; Hachette World Guides: Israel;* William Katz, *North Star Crusade* (an adventure novel); *The All Color Book of Science Facts;* Lin Yutang, *Imperial Chinese Art;* Robert Elegant, *Manchu* (a novel); Israel Shenker, *In the Footsteps of Johnson and Boswell;* James Joyce, *Finnegan's Wake;* Evans and Pollock, *Ireland for Beginners;* Felicia Rosshandler, *Passing Through Havana* (a novel); *The British Isles: A Symphony in Colour;* M. F. Hearn, *Romanesque Sculpture;* Mandanjeet Singh, *Himalayan Art;* W.E.B. Griffin, *The Brotherhood of War II* (an adventure novel); R.P. Kapleau, *The Three Pillars of Zen; The Book of Bests;* R. P. Long, *Castle Hotels of Europe;* Joseph Campbell, *The Masks of God: Creative Mythology;* Hilda Hookham, *A Short History of China;* Colin Platt, *Medieval England;* Norman Simpson, *Europe: Country Inns and Back Roads;* Stanley Bonner, *Education in Ancient Rome; Adult Erotica Catalogue; Gourmet* (three copies); A. M. Schenker, *Fifteen Modern Polish Short Stories; Touring Guide to Britain,* Vols. I and II; the 1984 CCCC Program; *Harper's* (two copies); *English-Polish/Polish-English Dictionary;* Judith Huxley's *Table for Eight* (a cookbook); Barbara Tuchman, *Stilwell and the American Experience in China; Cosmopolitan* (one copy); *Cheri* (one copy); W. Rahula, *What the Buddha Taught;* Clogan, ed. *Medivalia et Humanistica,* New Series, No. 8; *The Secular Spirit: Life and Art at the End of the Middle Ages; Where* (one copy); *Brown Alumni Monthly* (one copy); *Islands* (one copy); *New Look* (one copy); *Vogue* (one copy). Now not all of this was placed by the bed by me. My dear wife (who a few paragraphs ago was my fiancée—several revisions in this essay and in my life since then) must bear some of the responsibility, notably for the Polish dictionary, *Vogue,* and much of the art material, as I bear some of the responsibility for the books

likely to find the piles of books and magazines next to your bed richer in interesting material than what you'd find in your students' rooms. Thus a narrative of your daily experience is likely to include much reaction to and speculation about what you read. Narratives that move from conversations with Socrates to observations about the politics of Angola tend to be more interesting than those that report the trivia of campus life. Of course, students have no monopoly on trivia. There is much trivia in my own life, but, at least vicariously, there is also much else.

In a certain sense, this exercise is unfair. For one thing, students have less time for "extra" intellectual reading than we do. For another, they typically have less money with which to buy books and magazines. Nonetheless, I think the point holds. Ask your students to list honestly the kinds of reading material they have lying around in their rooms in the summer when their reading time is not taken up by class assignments. Ask them if they ever read anything out of class. How many own library cards?

Students, for the most part, lead different lives than we do. Thus, for example, to ask them to write an argumentative essay arising from a narrative context is a very different thing for them than it is for someone with greater breadth of experience, especially vicarious experience derived from reading. With some marked exceptions, student essays focus on mundane daily experiences. Anyone who has graded batches of student themes knows well what I'm talking about. While all of us have experiences just as mundane, at least we tend, as a matter of course, to connect them with what we read. Thus even a simple narrative assignment is likely to focus on complex subject matter.

---

on her side (with the solid exception of the business administration titles). On her side may be found: Porter, *Competitive Strategy;* Edward Hoagland, *African Calliope: A Journey Through the Sudan; National Geographic* (three copies); Charlotte Brontë, *Shirley;* R. W. Southern, *The Making of the Middle Ages;* Melvin Konner, *The Tangled Wing: Biological Constraints on the Human Spirit;* The Catalogue of Rutgers University-Newark; W. B. Yeats, *Memoirs;* Lehmann, *The Dow Jones-Irwin Guide to Using the Wall Street Journal; College and Research Libraries News* (one copy); Morris Berman, *The Reenchantment of the World;* Edgar Snow, *The Lost Revolution; Business Week* (eight copies); *Penthouse* (one copy); *The Wilson Library Bulletin* (one copy); Colin Mc Evedy, *The Penguin Atlas of Medieval History;* Doris Stenton, *English Society in the Early Middle Ages;* Conrad Arensberg, *The Irish Countryman; W Polsce Po Polsku/An Elementary Polish Course for English Speakers;* A. Schenker, *Beginning Polish,* Vol. I; Darst, *The Handbook of Bond and Money Markets;* The Faculty Handbook of Rutgers University; Daniels, *Business Information Sources;* O'Reilly, *Country Inns: Castles and Historic Hotels of Ireland; The Holiday Guide to Israel;* Wright, *On a Clear Day You Can See General Motors;* Aristotle, *The Politics;* Said, *Orientalism; Ireland: Where to Go What to Do;* Angier, *The Master Backwoodsman;* de Meun and de Lorris, *The Romance of the Rose.*

WRITING AND SUBJECT MATTER

One cannot discount the importance of subject matter to writing. No matter how well-formed an essay might be, if the subject matter is simple, linear, or based on adolescent experience, the resulting essay is likely to sound trivial to the mature reader. To help students build a sense of maturity in their writing requires some basic rethinking of current approaches to the pedagogy of writing courses, perhaps a shift of the pendulum once again toward the importance of content in student essays and the usefulness of reading as a prelude to writing.

I am not advocating a rubber-band return to the days of imitation as a central strategy for student writing. Asking students to read and imitate a few pieces of well-written prose may help make their writing more orderly, but it will do little to make their writing richer. What I am advocating is a bit more honesty with students about the importance of subject matter in writing, and about the necessity to get that subject matter from books. I am not suggesting necessarily that we have students write *about* specific pieces of reading material, but that they make reading an ongoing part of their lives and that they bring the fruit of their reading to their writing.

There is a certain pointless sentimentalism in a lot of composition teaching. We give students assignments asking them to compare their hometown with the college community, to chart the process of registration, to describe an interesting person they've met, or to argue for or against raising the drinking age. We pretend to be interested in the results, but in truth we would rather read a chunk of a good book than fifty such student essays. Then we lie to the students by telling them how "interesting" their writing is. Many of my own comments on poorly written student essays begin, "While this essay is interesting, ..." Usually there is little of interest in student essays apart from an occasional bizarre true-life incident.

There currently is a film, *Before the First Word,* that points up this problem. This film has nothing at all to do with actual writing (sequels are planned in which this focus is promised). It has to do with content, with the gathering of information as a prelude to writing. The reason why many of my colleagues claim that this is "the best movie about writing I've ever seen," has, in my opinion, more to do with the people and places in the film than with the film's relevance to the writing process.

In this movie, two students from a New York college go with note-pads in hand to interview the old-time residents of a street in the middle of New York City's chic district of Soho. The inhabitants are largely elderly first- and second-generation Portuguese and Italian people, fearful of displacement by young urban professionals. The students in the movie do no actual writing. They interview these people.

My reaction to *Before the First Word* is mixed. I applaud its indirect statement about the importance of subject matter to interesting writing. What I don't care much for is the sentimental quality of that subject matter.

For viewers of the movie the hook is the students. How can we help but feel sympathetic toward two fine-looking, energetic young people as they encounter crusty old-timers? Our reactions are entirely predictable as we watch through student eyes the unfolding of the conflict between affluent newcomers to the neighborhood and people with roots, the salt of the earth. We like seeing these students enriched by their contact with this world. There is nothing negative about human enrichment—except that the kind portrayed here tends toward the trivial and lacks real complexity. The conflict between the old immigrant residents and the young professional newcomers is predictable journalism.

I doubt that many of us would want to watch a movie of the same two students reading Sartre. I don't mean a movie in the Andy Warhol sense where we would simply *watch* people read, but one where we might read along with them and observe their thoughts and associations, perhaps follow the notes they might make in the margins or on a pad.[2] Such a movie would be too "serious." It would lack the sentimental appeal of the students in the streets of the old neighborhood.

Before the First Word is a positive step in the teaching of writing insofar as it establishes the importance of content to the writing process. The problem with the film is the kind of content. The juxtaposition of the experience of the old neighborhood residents and the idealism of the young kids is too close to the sentimental perspectives of adolescence, the kinds of perspectives our students should be trying to grow out of in order to develop as critical and interesting writers.

It will be interesting to see whether sequels to *Before the First Word* emphasize the importance to writing of background reading and critical analysis, or whether the students end up writing nice journalistic essays about the poor old folks in Soho and their all-too-predictable conflict with the inevitability of change and displacement. It will also be interesting to see whether those sequels tell the fairy tale that the path to becoming a good writer is as quick as a trip around town with a pad and pencil, or whether they tell the truth: that it takes a long time

[2]I am not suggesting here a movie in which the students would tell us what they think as they are reading. This form of protocol analysis has little value for analyzing thinking, as the act of reflecting on a thought necessarily interrupts and changes the thought itself.

to learn to write well and that good writing requires a great deal of reading and the honing of one's critical faculties.

QUICK RESULTS

The great difference between our writing and that of our students is a difference in experience, especially with regard to reading. It is important that we recognize this difference and use it in our teaching. How to use it? Do we lock our students in windowless rooms with great books? Do we expect them to become well-read overnight?

There is an aphorism in Japanese that goes something like this: "Don't have high expectations, don't look for quick results, concentrate on the task at hand." I learned this saying from my karate instructor whose point was that learning the martial arts takes a lifetime. The Japanese karate experts say that to learn to stand correctly takes three years, to learn to form a fist correctly three more years, and to learn to throw one correct punch still three years more. Nine years for one technique!

In our composition courses we look for quick results: a week on narration, two weeks on comparison, maybe three on argumentation. By the end of one or two fourteen-week courses students are supposed to have evolved into good writers. I feel bad for many of the students who get As and Bs in such courses. They walk away with false confidence, born of having met our very limited expectations. Their experience is not unlike that of someone who takes a six-month course in karate or judo and gets a black belt, a distinction that is rightly earned only after years of intensive effort. My point is not that we should give students lower grades, but that they should be made to understand the limited contexts of those grades. The strategies for invention and arrangement we teach in freshman courses are all shortcuts dictated by the limitations of time. The real learning of writing involves processes well outside the reductionism of our pre-writing exercises and strategies for modal development. These are devices to be used temporarily and discarded as the student develops through life as a writer. As students develop they will have to face the same questions: "Who is my audience?" "How can I make this sound interesting?" They will just learn to answer those questions in different ways.

In karate, there is a story about the belt system that illustrates this point. The lowest-level belt is white, the highest black (of which there are over a dozen levels, the highest of which have never been attained). In between the white and black belts there are various colors depending on the system one follows. The story goes that in old times in Japan there was only one color belt, white. As one progressed in study, the belt naturally got dirty, became brown, and finally black. Someone with a black belt had studied long and hard. But as he studied more the belt wore down, became threadbare and finally white again.

Writing, like karate, is something one works at one's whole life, an art in which one always faces the same problems, and in which there is always a higher degree of mastery to be attained. In this sense we have an important bond with our students. However, we know more about writing than they do. We know that mastering a list of pre-writing techniques and strategies for arrangement does not make one a good writer. To teach our students a few white-belt tricks, give them a good grade, and leave them with the impression that they have mastered an art is seriously to mislead them. The point of the story about the belts is not so simple. When the belt turns white again, the wearer does not forget all he knows. He does not go back to the beginning and start over. He sees that there is more to see. That is the most important lesson for our students—that there is always more to see, that the techniques of freshman composition are not the end of the road.

STORMS IN THE BRAIN?

Has the recent emphasis on writing as a process detracted from a serious focus on the importance of content in writing? I think it has, but I say so not to condemn process-oriented pedagogy, much of which I practice. The extent to which I apply this pedagogy to my own writing is another matter.

How did I write the first section of this article? Did I do free writing? Did I draw a diagram with spokes off a wheel? The kinds of things I tell my students to do. No I didn't do any of this, I never do when I write. I usually just sit down in front of the word processor and write. I revise a lot, but the first draft of anything I do is never preceded by what generally goes under the rubric of "pre-writing" activity.

There is one thing I especially did not do when preparing to write this article: "brainstorming." To my great displeasure I find myself using this word occasionally. I have even used it in class, though I doubt that it produced many neural hurricanes. I suppose that what I mainly don't like about "brainstorming" is the term itself. There is nothing inherently retrograde in terms of one's intellectual development in making lists of items as a prelude to writing. There is a little bit of retrogression, however, in using the word "brainstorm" in a serious discussion with one's peers. Whenever I hear the word, I involuntarily start humming "Little Sheila," a rock tune from the fifties. It has a line, "Her brain drives me insane."

But even if "brainstorming" were called by another name, let's say "mindchurning," I still wouldn't do it as part of my own writing process. I have too much churning, too many storms, up there already. To whip up any more would send me to the psychiatrist, who would likely advise that I calm the cranial seas. Again, at the risk of seeming arrogant, let me advance the notion that brainstorming works for students because many of them do not typically experience much cerebral agitation as part of their daily routine. For one thing, they don't read much. Thus an artificial mechanism has to be introduced to stir up the neural brew.

Stirring up the same old neurons is not going to make any new stew, and certainly not any cervelle mousse. It goes without saying that a college curriculum that continually stirred up students' minds would find "brainstorming" superfluous or even excessive. If the world had taken the advice of my favorite scholar of the Middle Ages, Siger of Brabant, there would now be no need for "brainstorming." It was he who said, "Question everything." Students today don't question anything—hence the necessity of "brainstorming," "mindchurning," or whatever. Back in the sixties students asked too many questions, so "brainstorming" was not widely talked about as part of the writing process. Teachers had some difficulty coping with all those antiauthoritarian ideas. In the eighties, by contrast, there is much relief over the stereotypical student—supportive of the status quo and willing to do anything in order to become a six-figure executive. These are the people for whom "brainstorming" has blossomed as a theory. Some sort of force, Aeolian or other, is required to blast them away from the contemplation of money. While I still have much criticism for the aimlessness in the pedagogy of the sixties, at least "brainstorming" was not necessary then. There were problems in the writing classrooms of the sixties, chief among them the teaching of organization. But there was no dearth of interesting conversation. I secretly long for the sixties and often wish I could trade a class of proto-managers for six hippies who read. Oh wonderful era when students came to class with prestormed brains!

PRE-WRITING VS. PRE-THINKING VS. PRE-BEING, ETC.

The whole notion of pre-writing is a strange one. As a buzzword in rhetoric circles, it has held on for a remarkably long time. I suppose that it belongs in the category of *inventio* in classical rhetoric, although the activities usually subsumed under its heading, except for finding a topic, clearly are part of arrangement, *dispositio*. The question that readily presents itself with regard to pre-writing is whether a focus in its direction has consequences for the end product of writing, the completed essay. Is actual writing better or worse for this focus? My own notion is that the orientation toward process and toward the activities leading up to writing are necessary for our beginning students, partly because those students do not come to writing assignments prepared with material to write about. Past the freshman level, however, such techniques rapidly lose their importance. As writers mature, they perform their "pre-writing" chores intuitively as part of daily life. There is no need to churn the mind artificially.

This difference in the application of writing process theory has not been widely appreciated and has led to a false division in emphasis between "process" and "product." The distinctions in approaches associated with these terms tend to correspond with age differences—younger writing teachers waving the banner of "process" and older ones insisting on the consideration of "product." In certain institutions the conflict between these groups has become intense, the "process" people acting like evangelists, the "product" people taking as their watchword, "No pasaran!"

I have a colleague in the "product" camp (I refuse identification with either side) whose response to the notion of "pre-writing" is *reductio ad absurdum*. He does a mock shudder with his hands raised above his head and his eyeballs bulging every time I use the word "pre-writing." His notion, like mine when I'm not teaching a composition course, is that real "pre-writing" involves all of one's experience up to the point of writing; that perhaps "pre-writing" continues on and through the processes of writing and revising; that if "pre-writing" is allowed as a legitimate term in conversation, it must necessarily refer to a state in which we all share prior to, and even during, the act of writing. Every person, then, is continually in a state of "pre-writing." A corollary to this position is that if there is "pre-writing," there must also be "pre-thinking" and "pre-being." One gets in a terrible logical jam when using the term "pre-writing."

I continually remind my friend that "pre-writing" accurately refers not to a state of being but to a series of techniques. He usually responds that he sees no need for these techniques in his own writing. I must agree, since I don't use them either in mine. Here is where I come into conflict with my "process" friends, many of whom insist that "pre-writing" is a necessary, or even biologically innate, part of the writing process. As you can see, this debate can get out of hand and well away from issues close to the teaching of writing.

Modern pre-writing is really pre-invention. Those who link pre-writing to classical rhetoric reinterpret invention. It was always assumed in the classical tradition that one had some *thing* to write about,

thus the focus in invention not on discovery of *subject,* but on appropriate mode of development, ethical stance, etc. Today's attitudes about
"pre-writing" assume a writer who does not deal with sophisticated and
interesting ideas in daily life. Thus the point of pre-writing exercises is
often to get the student to transform mundane, boring (and usually
sentimentally viewed) experience into the stuff of interesting writing.
The students in the movie mentioned above, *Before the First Word,* go
through an experience typical of strategies for "pre-writing."

The subject matter I use in my own writing does not come as the
result of any "pre-writing" activity. It comes from my daily life, which,
I am fortunate to report, is rich with interesting things, such as the
books around my bed. Pre-writing and brainstorming have no place in
my writing process. My focus is on revision. Whether focusing on revision is process-oriented or product-oriented you can decide.

REVISION

Every piece of writing I do demands revision, if just to break the im-
possibly long and prolix paragraphs I tend to construct, or to vary
sentence structure here and there, or, simply so that people won't think
I'm uneducated, to fix some usage "errors" such as the sentence fragments for which I would lower a student's grade but which I find
perfectly acceptable in my own writing.

My larger purpose in revision is twofold: to clarify my ideas and to
illustrate them. In early drafts, I tend to write around my subject instead of approaching it directly. I tend to forget my own advice to my
students about audience, that readers need signposts, that in addition
to explaining and developing an idea, you have to name the idea itself.

As a practical matter I leave out examples when I write. To stop
for an hour to look up a quotation would break the flow, so I don't do
it. I add the examples later, often having to modify my text when the
examples are not exactly as I had remembered them and don't quite
illustrate my point.

Transitions are a particularly vexing problem in revision, especially
now that I have a word processor and can insert material with ease
wherever I want. One of my most common problems is discovering that
the insertion of a paragraph has broken my general line of development. To get around this I either modify the paragraph in terms of
content to make it fit with those around it, or I take the longer route
of reviewing the whole line of development and changing my cues to
the reader both before and after the new paragraph so as to make
reference to the new material.

It goes without saying that I revise for grammar, usage, spelling, etc., though sometimes leaving glaring errors, especially in spelling. I was born with an optic pit and just don't see them.

A RETROSPECTIVE: HOW THIS ESSAY WAS WRITTEN

This essay was written over a period of about ten weeks. The total time spent on writing it was probably about thirty hours, twenty of the thirty in revision—and I'm obviously still writing.

I began this essay on two separate occasions, following two lines of development. In retrospect I wish I had not done this, as it necessitated synthesizing not only different kinds of material but differing rhetorical approaches. In this respect the essay has the structure of a sandwich. The part in the middle concerning theory was inserted into another essay about my personal writing habits. Getting the parts to fit coherently required over five revisions. Trying to strike a consistent tone was particularly difficult.

Why did I follow this difficult procedure? Simply because when I started the second time I forgot that I had already begun. I do not always do this, nor would I recommend this method to you. It is especially difficult to coax a central idea out of your material when following this method. I hope that you will recognize that my main point here has to do with the primacy of content in writing. I did not start out by looking for a central idea or formulating a thesis. "Coax" is perhaps a good word for what I did to my material to work toward a central generalization.

I began writing this essay both times on Kaypro II computers using Perfect Writer software. One Kaypro is in my office at home. I have three others at work. For the past year I have consistently composed on them. Prior to acquiring computers, I composed in manuscript about half the time, on a typewriter the other half. Only rarely do I compose in manuscript any more. I never compose on a typewriter. The computer doesn't make the writing itself any easier, but it saves enormous amounts of time. I could have produced this same essay with pads, pencils, pens, and a typewriter, but it would have taken me three or four times as long.

One disadvantage of the computer is that you have to be careful when using it or you can lose your material. When I attempted to join my two original files, both entitled "Waldrep.mss," together, I forgot to change the name of one of them, a necessary procedure to place them on the same disk. When I wrote File 1 onto the disk already inhabited by File 2, the second file was erased. Fortunately I had a backup copy of an earlier version of File 2, but I did lose the results of about five hours' work. It was one of those things I realized just as I was doing it —a microsecond too late.

I tend to see my approach to writing as like a potter's approach to making something out of clay. I begin with the material, and then try to coax it into various forms. If one form does not seem to be taking shape correctly, I may try a different form. Or I may add new material and let the project take another direction. Never do I start out to "develop an idea." I always build *material* into an idea, thus the primacy of content. I like to wander and let the point of the journey emerge.

Perhaps still best known for "Rhetoric 2001," which won the Freshman English News *Prize in 1974, Richard M. Coe has taught in Canada, China, and the United States. He presently teaches rhetorical theory, composition, and drama at Simon Fraser University. His* Form and Substance, *an innovative textbook, is now distributed by Scott, Foresman. He is presently doing empirical research in discourse analysis and contrastive rhetoric, hopes to move on soon to some more theoretical work, and says he has an idea for an excitingly new kind of handbook.*

FORMING SUBSTANCE

Richard M. Coe
Simon Fraser University

It was really the student newspaper . . . that developed me into a writer: 2 A.M. at the printers, a ten-inch hole on page one, Mr. Barta yelling that he would go home in an hour whether we were finished or not, someone on the phone calling in the facts, and me writing those ten inches, nearly as fast as I could type—ah, the virtues of formulaic writing.

Dear Tom,

How do I write?

Ah, who but you would think to ask?

I do many kinds of writing—and that matters because my rhetorical strategy (and hence my process) varies considerably with purpose, audience, and occasion.

I write about rhetoric, discourse analysis (including the analysis of literary and literary critical discourse), and composition (theory, practice, and pedagogy) for a variety of audiences—scholars, teachers, and (occasionally) the public. I also do some journalism (under a *nom de plume*) as a stringer for a foreign newspaper. Then there are proposals, reports, letters, and memos: course proposals, grant proposals, video treatments, research reviews, business letters, bureaucratic memos, consumer complaint letters, letters to authors whose work I have admired, letters of recommendation, letters to friends, and so on. These, of course, vary significantly from one type to another. In the past, I also wrote some fiction, poetry, and popular science.

Most important is the type of writing that *we*, not I, do. Some of this is collaborative, some genuinely collective—a type of writing that I find very exciting and fertile, productive of higher quality products (and a solution to the loneliness of individualistic writing).[1]

[1]I have long been amazed that, despite the clear importance of collaborative and collective writing in modern societies, virtually all composition pedagogy embodies the as-

The first time I wrote for publication I produced little narratives —mood pieces—for the junior high school yearbook. My father, largely by example, encouraged my writing: an old Underwood typewriter is as much a part of my image of him as his pipe. Before revising school compositions, I used to bring the drafts to him for criticism.

Later, at university—after concluding (perhaps unfairly) that the Psychology Department would help me understand only rats and the Philosophy Department only abstract mathematical logic, I slid into an English major. Within the English major at the City College of New York (later part of CUNY), there was a stream that emphasized writing and literature, rather than academic literary criticism. Largely because this stream allowed a completely free choice of literature courses, I chose it. Thus I took lots of comparative literature (instead of the standard English major selection of Chaucer, Shakespeare, Milton, and one course from each of the past five centuries) and a number of courses in journalistic, critical, and expository writing.

But it was really the student newspaper, which I eventually edited, that developed me into a writer: 2 A.M. at the printers, a ten-inch hole on page one, Mr. Barta yelling that he would go home in an hour whether we were finished or not, someone on the phone calling in the facts, and me writing those ten inches, nearly as fast as I could type— ah, the virtues of formulaic writing.

The writing courses did lead me to look at texts from a writer's point of view. And the comparative literature reinforced my tendency to pay attention to forms and contexts. This point of view and these tendencies served me well a bit later when, like so many other graduate students in English, I was given two textbooks, two days' training, a syllabus, and fifty freshman composition students. I was certainly not properly prepared to teach English 101; but unlike teaching assistants schooled exclusively in New Critical approaches to English/American literature, I at least approached the problem of freshman composition from an angle that gave me a reasonable chance of discovering a passable solution.

The peripatetic nature of my life has left me pretty flexible about where and when I write. Medium is much more important: I want my writing instrument to come as close as possible to keeping up with my thoughts. Consequently, I have since junior high school composed on

sumption that all writing is individual. (See my "Writing in Groups," *Working Teacher*, 2:4 [1979].) Surely, most pieces of public writing (in which category I would include documents produced within corporate and governmental bureaucracies) have in some significant sense been written by more than one person. We have virtually no studies of —or even speculations about—group writing. (I was, therefore, happy to hear that Lisa Ede and Andrea Lunsford recently received a Shaughnessy grant to do some such research.)

a typewriter, falling back on pen only with great resistance and when it was clear no typewriter would soon be available. Now I find myself going through the same pattern on a new level: I use a typewriter only when it is clear that a word processor will not soon be available. I suppose my ideal writing instrument—at least for producing first drafts —will be a word-processing computer that takes dictation. Invent soon please the technology to make that cheaply available. (In fact, one way —the easiest way I know—of producing drafts is taping a talk or lecture and then transcribing it.)

However expository the task, my ultimate motive for writing is almost always rhetorical: Each piece of writing is an attempt, or part of an attempt, to improve the world by changing ideas and/or attitudes —perhaps even by moving someone to action. Augustine's notion of writing to teach, to convince, and to move suits me well (better some-how than Cicero's original version). Because of this motive, I often find my thesis statement in the middle of a piece: If I am presenting an idea my readers will initially disagree with, some preparation—reframing— is necessary before the overt presentation.

Perhaps I want to convince composition researchers that certain crucial questions cannot be answered by empiricist research tech-niques. Perhaps I want people living in the United States to realize that Canada exists, that Canadians are culturally distinct from Americans. Perhaps I want some high school teachers to begin using a process approach to composition in some way more meaningful than attaching a few pre-writing exercises to the old curriculum. Perhaps I want my department chair to assign me more courses in rhetorical theory and discourse analysis. Perhaps I want North American working people to realize that U.S. support for repressive regimes in third world countries means repression of labor unions, which means lower wages in those countries, which means that corporations are motivated to move their manufacturing operations to those countries, which means higher unemployment and lower wages for people working in North America. Perhaps I want parents to understand why grammar drills are not an answer to the literacy "crisis." Perhaps I want the corporation that sold me a greenhouse window to renegotiate the price because what I re-ceived was not quite what we had contracted. Perhaps I want to write a poem that evokes contradiction as a classical haiku does.

The hierarchy of constraints within which I create is implicit in these rhetorical contexts. Often the subject matter with which I deal is of such complexity that it cannot be reduced to a simple statement: In this sense, the nature of the subject creates certain constraints. Purpose, audience, and occasion—what I call the rhetorical context to avoid repeating the tripartite formula—obviously constrain. Occasion in-troduces both constraints of the particular situation and also constraints of the genre: Certain journal editors prefer articles in the 12–1,500 word range; a business letter rarely can run over 400 words and still get read closely; a leaflet usually must be much shorter than that. Moreover, the business letter must usually begin by stating why the letter is being written and end by stating what I want. Such constraints, by narrowing the possibilities, speed my process (as well as creating problems when they seem to contradict the complexity of my subject and purpose).

I am happy to report—now that you make me look—that I actually use all the invention techniques I recommended in my textbook: talk-then-write, free writing, brainstorming, meditation, keeping a journal, research (including interviewing and experimenting as well as library research), contradictions (i.e., negative thinking), heuristics, and formal patterns.[2] (Brainstorming I use mostly when writing collectively.)

I often use a pattern defined by the genre, as in a business letter or news reporting. I use the journalists' five Ws to produce the lead of a news story and the assumption that editors cut from the bottom as a guide for ordering the rest. I can write a letter of recommendation fairly quickly because I have a formula (which demands that I decide first what is the main point I want readers to retain; once I have settled on that and made a jotted list of secondary points, the formula virtually writes the letter).

Though I emphasize free writing in my teaching because it offsets certain typical problems of student writing, I use it myself only when stuck. (Though I am presently experimenting—in part as a type of free writing, in part to save my eyes—with turning off the screen on the word processor while inserting the preliminaries that will become the first draft.)

When I was writing *Form and Substance,* I got seriously stuck (for about a month) at the preface (i.e., at the last part of the writing). Finally I said to myself, "Okay, schmuck, do what you always tell your students to do"—I yell at myself a lot when I'm trying to do anything well (be it writing or skiing); since I essentially love myself quite well, this creates no problems. The problem with the preface was an incredible contradiction of subject matters: I wanted to explain my understanding of humanism (with appropriate reference to Classical and Renaissance precedents) and of a humanistic approach to writing; I wanted to explain how the book was organized and the different ways in which instructors could use it; I wanted to justify the inclusion of certain material explanations that went beyond the immediate "practical"

---

[2]Invention by "negative thinking" or contradiction is a technique I started teaching after reading dialectical writers, e.g., Kenneth Burke and L. S. Vygotski, who (consciously or unconsciously) apparently use this kind of invention. Cf., *Form and Substance*, pp. 51–61. Any dialectical theory of form, moreover, clearly must treat form not only as *dispositio*, but also as generative.

needs of the students; and I wanted to acknowledge—to honor—a rather large number of people who had shaped the thinking that produced the book. How to explain humanism and humanistic pedagogy in 500 words? How to make that fit with practical explanations of exercises and epitaphs? How to transit from one to the other and thence to ac-knowledge-ments? The constraints were overwhelming: they seemed to rule out *all* possible solutions. A long free-writing exercise produced five typewritten pages—and three days later I had a preface.

Do I revise? What a question. The quality of my sentences, insofar as it exists, is the product of revision. Drafting, I focus on getting ideas down. Sentence structure is just too much to consider. The result is that my sentences are a mess, usually a complex mess. If my published sentences are good, it is because they have been revised extensively, usually to simplify and clarify them. I also do a great deal of cut and paste (blessed be the word processor), usually to find a structure that will be easier or more persuasive for my audience, sometimes for logic. My technique for doing this is what I have dubbed "outline later."[3] I also do some "nutshelling," but usually only after I've completed a draft.

Often I do some revision (whatever comes easily) while drafting, but the bulk of it comes later, usually several days or weeks later. Revisions are innumerable. The major ones are additions including both long substantive additions and many qualifiers of overstated ideas, but it would probably be accurate to say that I do one to four major revisions, depending upon the importance of the piece.

I must immediately insert a disclaimer: my generalizations must be taken as generalizations.[4] My writing process varies so much from one type of writing task to another. The more formulaic a piece (e.g., a news report, a business letter, or a letter of recommendation), the more contracted the process: I search for an angle that will focus the material, write one draft from jottings, and do one revision (perhaps while typing the neat copy). The more a piece involves the *creation of meaning,* the more time spent generating, focusing, and organizing, the more drafts, the more revision. The more a piece involves persuasion, also the more revision—but reenvisioning suasive effectiveness involves a different level and type of revision than does reenvisioning subject matter.

Although I certainly have false starts, I rarely throw out anything when I am doing "serious" writing (i.e., writing that involves the creation of meaning). That is, I may throw something out of a particular

[3]*Journal of Advanced Composition,* 1:2 (1980). See also, *Form and Substance,* pp. 91–95.
[4]We ordinarily do not take generalizations as generalizations—i.e., as *generally* (but not always or entirely) true—which is why so many people object to "generalizations." This indicates something significant about the intellectual structures of our culture (and also about North American anti-intellectualism).

piece, but I usually find I can use it elsewhere, perhaps several years later. For example, in 1973, I wrote the first hundred pages of a popular science book on human nature;[5] I never did finish that book, but many of the ecological examples got used elsewhere, often as analogies to convey notions of interrelatedness, freedom of development within definable constraints, etc. See, for instance, my explanation of the principle of selection in writing by analogy to wolves culling caribou herds.[6] Similarly, a piece written at the behest of *Modern Drama*—I still suspect the editor thought I was Richard *N.* Coe (and decided not to publish the piece when he discovered I wasn't)—about the use of paradox in Pinter's *Homecoming*—became the basis of "The Rhetoric of Paradox."[7]

So beware: If you don't publish this, pieces of it will probably find their way into print in some less worthy context.

[5]I was motivated by the popularity of Robert Ardrey, Desmond Morris, Konrad Lorenz, et al.—and by the unpopularity of various academics who so conclusively refuted their most dramatic assertions—surely, I thought, a good rhetorician could use Ardrey's form to convey the scientifically correct information.

[6]*Form and Substance,* p. 75.

[7]Later published in *A Symposium in Rhetoric,* 1975. The Pinter piece ended up in the *Educational Theatre Journal* (1975), apparently accepted on its own merits.

Joseph J. Comprone is director of graduate studies at the University of Louisville, where he works closely with students in Louisville's Ph.D. program in rhetoric and composition. He has previously directed writing programs at the universities of Minnesota, Cincinnati, and Louisville.

Comprone has published two composition textbooks and is at work on a third, has published thirty articles in professional composition journals, and has delivered papers since 1970 to the Modern Language Association, the National Council of Teachers of English, and other national and regional conferences.

COMPOSITION, INTELLECTUAL LIFE, AND THE PROCESS OF WRITING AS PUBLIC KNOWING

Joseph J. Comprone
University of Louisville

I loved writing essays, then. . . . You could, in the midst of composing an essay, actually forget, at least for the moment, the look of your handwriting. And once the idea was finished you could go back and polish, satisfying Sister Rita Anne's mania for writing on the lines and correct spelling, and appealing simultaneously to your parents' uneducated fascination with two or three pages of words strung together in a relatively sensible form.

MY BACKGROUND AS WRITER

Early Schooldays

I attended parochial schools in the Philadelphia area from the first through the eleventh grades. My elementary school years at Our Lady of Perpetual Help school were filled with overcrowded classrooms, populated with the daughters and sons of poor but not destitute Irish, Italian, German, and Polish second- and third-generation American families whose mothers were always, everlastingly home and whose fathers seemed to be forever coaching Knights of Columbus, Catholic Youth Organization, Babe Ruth, and Little League baseball, basketball, and football teams. I remember, it seems, endless weekends spent collecting meager donations in sterile suburban 1950s shopping centers—the enclosed mall had yet to appear in the Philadelphia area—displaced city kids foraging the suburban fringes for the funds to buy tee-shirts and caps for a softball team, the plastic helmets and humpbacked shoulder pads of a Pop Warner league midget (never "pee-wee") football team. My earliest reading experiences were reading and rereading one-paragraph articles in the local newspaper describing the Prospect Park Termites victory over the Folsom Falcons in midget-league football. I played for the Falcons.

Sometimes there were as many as eighty kids in my elementary classroom, all wearing the prescribed white shirt and tie if male, the dark-blue skirt and white blouse, if female. Most of us were terribly clean, scrubbed around the ears and cheeks, and our clothes were as worn from frequent washing as they were from contact with macadam playgrounds. We were not allowed to talk in class. We hung our coats and set our galoshes in pine-paneled cloakrooms, always in orderly fashion, one child after another leaving his or her seat to walk the black and white-tiled floor, enter the cloakroom, quietly hang the coat on a brass hook, and return with measured steps. The desks, set in ordered rows across the room, were short and fat, with inkwells set in the middle of the front, and with a gradually sloping pine top that could be lifted when books needed to be placed in the desk or when you needed protection from the missiles (erasers, spitballs) thrown by students in the desks in front of you. Sister Rita Anne, I remember, compiled each student's "neatness" grade for the term by averaging together daily evaluations of these desks. If books were properly arranged, papers in orderly stacks, and ink stains at a minimum, you received a little red, silver, green, or blue star. A certain number of stars by the end of term, and you had an A in neatness to offset a C in sentence diagramming.

We wrote a lot in these crowded classrooms. Sometimes we wrote to display our penmanship, Palmer-method slants and ovals embellishing our sheets of scarce white lined paper. (We had to write our names in small print at the top, left-hand corner of the page, never taking up too much space, so as to leave enough room for several exercises. We used less paper that way.) Sometimes we wrote to fulfill assignments, summarizing our reading in a history or religion text or in response to questions in a worn and recycled catechism. Sometimes we wrote one or two sentence proverbs or maxims, often with religious content. Even our arithmetic papers were punctuated with brief sentences, such as "This is addition" or "The Multiplication Tables are next." (Sister Rita Anne always demanded *complete* sentences.)

We copied whole poems and short stories, word for word; these copies were checked first for accuracy, second for neatness, and third for quality of handwriting. All the poems we copied were in the Christina Rosetti mold, expressing high sentiments and idealized versions of the life of labor, femininity, the religious life, agrarian life—but never the realities of industrial life in Delaware County, where oil refineries, shipyards, and General Electric and Westinghouse factories dwarfed the row houses and walk-ups that filled our neighborhoods.

Amidst all these mechanical exercises were interspersed, never too frequently, those occasions on which we were allowed to write essays. I loved writing essays, then. They seemed so wonderfully free of the drudgery of copying, imitating, correcting, writing over, summarizing, and paraphrasing. You could, in the midst of composing an essay, actually forget, at least for the moment, the look of your handwriting. And once the idea was finished you could go back and polish, satisfying Sister Rita Anne's mania for writing on the lines and correct spelling, and appealing simultaneously to your parents' uneducated fascination with two or three pages of words strung together in a relatively sensible form. Essays were an infrequent and much-loved ego trip. We stopped, at least for a moment, the cycle of using writing to say what someone else had said, to perfect our use of prescribed written forms, and used writing to develop our own thoughts.

Most of the writing I did in my grade and high school years continued in these two patterns. Most often my writing served the purpose of learning and relearning the written forms and ideas of the writers of textbooks, stories, and poems. It also very obviously served the purpose of assuring my teachers and parents that I was indeed learning the prescribed forms of American English; that, postimmigrant children of the industrial revolution that I and my classmates were, we were becoming, through our education, the kind of productive and potentially employable and middle-class citizens that our parents envisioned us becoming. Language, of course, was important to that social transition; writing, moreover, was the best and most precise way of checking to see that those social-linguistic skills had been learned. I remember Sister Agnes Marie, our seventh-grade teacher, telling the girls in my class that their good handwriting and correct spelling and punctuation would most assuredly result in future bank teller and secretarial jobs.

The nuns who read the bulk of this practice writing seldom looked for ideas. They simply *looked at* the papers and exercises. Sister Rita Anne had trained her eyes to spot a misplaced *i* or *e* in a second or two's glance at a paper. Handwriting slanted in an improper direction took even less time to note and mark off. Even the summaries and paraphrases were evaluated by what nowadays we call primary trait methods: Ideas from sources were marked by key words and phrases, which then became the teacher's cues to low or high grades as they read student exercises. All eighty of my classmates and I were immersed in writing as product, in writing as a craft and form through which the results of reading or exercises were reported.

Despite this overwhelming emphasis on writing as craft, however, we never completely ignored the creative. It was as if we earned creativity by submitting to the disciplines of craft. Every so often, usually on a Friday afternoon when the week's work was done to our teacher's satisfaction, we cultivated the essay form. The essay gradually became, for me at least, a symbol of what the discipline of writing could accomplish. It could enable one to discover and shape one's own thoughts and communicate them to others. It became an instrument of the superego, along with athletics, the most possible way of gaining some kind of recognition from authorities in an overcrowded and not terribly verbal everyday world.

Later Schooldays

My early schooling continued in this pattern through high school. I was exposed by priests and brothers to Latin and classical rhetoric. The exercises in copying, imitating, and paraphrasing were not then called rhetoric, but my later studies enabled me to see them for what they were: somewhat watered-down *progymnasmata* in an overcrowded and less-than-genteel urban high school where the exercises were often used to reinforce order rather than because they were ideal teaching methods. I continued to write essays, whenever allowed, as an escape from the formal exercises of writing. My elementary school habits continued, even when I wrote essays: I would carefully check each phrase as it appeared on my white lined page, dutifully conserving space, marking through mistakes with two straight horizontal lines, checking spelling and punctuation as I progressed across the page, belaboredly comparing what I had just said with what I wanted to say, often sounding phrases aloud in an attempt, first, to have them right and, second, to have them say what I thought I wanted to say.

Rewriting was often impossible because of strict deadlines; I, as a result, rewrote as I wrote. When, very occasionally, I did actually rewrite by starting again, the whole methodical process was repeated, line by line, until the paper was rewritten.

There was a curious factor involved in this seemingly painful process of development. What now seems to me to have been pure drudgery and pain was not so painful at the time. Certainly I did not contrive writing experiences as moments of relaxation. But, as I think back, I realize that the slow process of poring over the words I had produced on a page, crafting phrases, searching for the right word, correcting to standard English—only marginally concerned with what I was saying—resulted in two distinct advantages for me as a developing writer.

First, and most obvious, for all its Freudian implications, this mechanical approach to producing words on a page developed in me a generally satisfying feel and respect for the craft of writing. I was continually aware, during my exaggeratedly methodical writing process, that I was producing an artifact that would be *seen* by others, by those in my community who held the keys to social advancement. I sometimes hated them intensely for holding those keys, but I wanted the doors open in any case, and those essays became my primary academic means of turning those keys. Key turning aside, however, my respect for writing as product and craft gradually became a motivation of its own. Later, in college, I remember understanding my own labors with writing better after I had read Yeats's "Sailing to Byzantium," where the Grecian goldsmiths hammered out tributes to kings. There were no kings to whom I might dedicate my artifacts, but my respect for the craft itself had been reinforced and clarified.

A second advantage evolved from these years of exercise and belabored composing. I think that I created, during these early years, a foundation for composing when in later years what I had to say was as important as or more important than how I said it. By the time, in college and graduate school, that I was asked to write creatively on topics or subjects that I had studied, I had so mastered the habit of doing several things at once while I wrote that the burden of writing essays was lessened. The current debates in composition theory between those such as Elbow who advocate free writing first and editing later and those such as Flower and Hayes who contend that fluent writers compose recursively, moving back and forth from the writer's to the reader's perspective, seem to me oversimplified. Writing is craft; it is the production of an artifact that will be seen and then read. As artifact, writing must literally be shaped, formed, reworked, and polished, before, during, and after actual composition. But writing is also the transcribing of a conceptual act; it must be true, as well, to the thinking that informs it. It must be the record of an idea developing, first in the mind of the writer and then in the mind of a reader. Of course, these two perspectives on writing—as craft or as mind-thinking—are *both* important to good writing. My early years as a writer emphasized craft over expression of thought; my later years in formal education began to foreground thought and background craft. But most important to me was the fact that neither ever left the other alone.

Entering the "Profession"

There came a time in my life as a writer when this balance of craft and expression needed to be subsumed by a larger purpose, when my sense of audience needed more definition than my earlier sense of what the experts and authorities, the "adults" of the academic world, could supply. This time occurred for me toward the end of graduate school, when I began working in the field of composition under Walker Gibson's tutelage. Gibson's influence was primarily intellectual: He became for me the symbol of someone who used writing as a means of ordering what he firmly believed was the essential chaos of experience. Gibson valued writing as craft and as expression of thought, but he saw its true purpose most clearly in the act of composition. Intellectual life, the examined life, the conscious life—however Plato or Virginia Woolf might have expressed it—was, for Walker Gibson, centered around and on the act of writing. The more we learned about a subject or the world in general, Gibson suggested to me, the more we were threatened with confusion, the Tower of Babel, the clash of contending facts and philosophies. To live a responsible intellectual life, one had to write, because writing was the individual intellectual's primary means of giving coherent and individual expression to the potential chaos of experience that intellect and learning created.

I oversimplify what in actuality was a complex epistemological perspective in Gibson's teaching. Even my oversimplification makes the point: Writing became, for me, a moral responsibility at this time. It was no longer simply something I did to gain the recognition of authority; it was a means to an individual and social end, a way of ensuring that my perspective on experience could be, first, defined and, second, communicated to other thinking people. On however modest a level, I felt I was joining a community of people who wrote because they thought; who, ultimately, thought because they wrote. I thank Bill Gibson for that.

Gibson's influence combined at that time with a more mundane professional influence: I spent 1968–1969 as assistant director of composition at the University of Massachusetts in Amherst. I talked with young composition teachers, attended a few composition conferences, and worked with Gibson in constructing composition program materials, selecting textbooks, and advising on grievances. It was not exciting work, but put alongside the more ideal development of a sense of the intellectual purpose behind composition, this practical experience provided me with an immediate audience to which I could direct my ideals. Composition teachers were beleaguered and ignored; writing, what for me had recently become *the* central activity of an intellectual life, was the tolerated but often despised skill in the college curriculum. Teachers hated to teach it; students hated to do it; yet all superficially proclaimed its importance. I had, in other words, discovered a community that needed to know what I had to say about writing and teaching writing. On one side of my ideal audience were all those beleaguered teachers who needed and wanted to know what made writing work and how to teach what made it work. On the other side of that ideal audience were the rest of the English teaching profession, despising the need to teach writing but lamenting the poor writing of their students. The composition teachers were eager to learn but sceptical of ideas that did not mesh with their experiences with writing; the English teachers had to be persuaded that the writing process was complex and difficult to teach, but their ignorance of those complexities made them a more captive audience once they had been persuaded of the importance of composition.

I have spent the rest of my writing career addressing this dual audience. As composition has itself come of age as an academic discipline, both the audience and I have changed. We know more now about the complexities of language and composing. There are more of the converted, and those English teachers who despise teaching writing are usually crafty enough these days to keep their feelings to themselves. But the essential difficulty of and purpose behind writing for this dual audience is still there. We have a moral responsibility to explain how writing can help the thinking person organize, express, and communicate the results of their struggles to make sense of their experience and learning. To think without writing is to learn without shape or form; learning without shape or form often produces the isolation and despair that have beset modern intellectuals. Certainly a phenomenon that threatens professional intellectuals can debilitate the student.

MY WRITING PROCESS NOW

This has been a long preamble to an essay that purports to explain how I write now. But I believe this preamble will explain why I do what I do when I write. Before I proceed to describe what I do, let me briefly summarize how my past experience as a writer has influenced my present writing behavior.

Specific Perspectives

All working writers, I imagine, have quirks. Mine have evolved in a relatively clear pattern from the two aspects of writing I have been discussing: the sense of writing as craft, developed during my early schooling, and the sense of writing as personal expression and individual control, developed during my later experiences with the essay form. My sense of craft continues to make me compulsive about the mechanics of putting words on a page. I have to be able to spread out, with drafts and books and materials related to the writing task arranged around the yellow lined pad on which I write. Dark-colored ball-point pens are a necessity. I am productive in two- or three-hour spurts, here and there, usually in the morning, sometimes twice a day; and I write articles in seven- to ten-day periods. I *never* type first drafts because I am a poor typist and the keys seem to get in the way of the flow of ideas. Also, because my short- and long-term memory seem to get out of touch when I use a typewriter, and writing becomes a completely mechanical, technical activity. My handwriting is a curious mixture of printing and cursive. I think this comes about because the printing keeps me from moving too fast, the cursive from moving too slow. The result, I think, is a pace and rhythm of putting words on the page that suits my accustomed mental-physical writing pattern. I want time to look back and rewrite, to reread key paragraphs that remind me of the gist of what I have said so far and prod me toward the next stage of my plan. And I do edit while I reread, often substituting more apt words or phrases, often checking spelling and repunctuating in minor ways. But, as a writer, I do not want these regressive activities to result in my losing my train of thought or momentum. Anxiety sets in at both ends, for me. Too slow, and I become anxious about the empty space at the bottom of the page; too fast, and I become anxious about the form and sound of what I have already written. The trick of actual composing for me is to strike the right balance, to keep patterns of retrospection and progression going simultaneously, so that one reinforces rather than blocks the other.

These physical obsessions and scribal-psychological activities develop from all those years of copying, paraphrasing, imitating, correcting, conserving paper, perfecting cursive style, practicing spelling—endless hours doing the kinds of things that control the physical activity of writing while they also contribute to the production of consumable writing products, to our sense of writing as artifact. These activities, taken together, become my strategies for bringing mental activity to a point on a page. They become the minor disciplines that keep the act of writing connected to both the writer's mind and the reader's sense of convention. They are the stuff of composition; they control the rhythm of thought as it becomes written language. Without them, I would become scribally neurotic, constantly looking back to check what I had said, simultaneously worrying about what I yet had not said. I would be, in such a state, a working model of what experts in cybernetics call an "overdetermined" communications system.

The Bigger Picture

Where, then, does the personal element, the expressive aim, enter into this process? Where does the idea of composition as the center of intellectual life, as the organizing ground for the shaping of experience, as the individual thinker's attempt to give shape to his or her reality come into play? For me, this overall sense of purpose hovers at the back of my mind, at the fringes of every act of composing. It is the audience and the aim of everything I do as a writer. When I write well, it is what gives my writing a point, a "center of gravity," to use Peter Elbow's words. Each article, each chapter in a book may have its own self-contained thesis, but it is this general sense of the moral necessity and central function that writing has for me that I want, in everything I write, to communicate to others, whether fellow composition teachers, English teachers in general, or the general public. Without this sense of central purpose, despite all my obsessive attention to craft, my writing would sound and feel hollow were I to detach it from a desire to say it all in every piece of writing that I produce.

Of course, as a writer, one must balance this desire, this psychological need to say it all with a more realistic, ideally ironic, sense of the limits of writing. When I describe this delicate balance, I use writers such as Richard Selzer and Loren Eiseley to help illustrate my meaning. Both are writers who write because they are certain kinds of thinkers —Eiseley a biologist and natural scientist with a holistic perspective on the world and man's place in it, Selzer a surgeon with a clear yet almost mystical sense of the importance and nature of his occupation. These are premier essayists, I believe, not because they are excellent craftsmen, which they are, but because they have a mission and their craft is simply and magically a way of transforming that mission into a clear and complex perspective on experience for their readers. Selzer's doctoring is no longer simply a profession for him; it is a way of life, a way of seeing experience whole; his writing both helps him see life whole through his profession and helps him get that whole image of life across to a reader.

The Whole Picture

I shall return at this point to my actual experience as a writer. I have already described in specific terms how my sense of writing as craft influences my writing behavior. How does this concurrently held broader grasp of my intentions in writing influence my composing process?

My first answer to this question depends upon a definition of the kinds of occasions on which I write. At this midpoint in my professional career, about two-thirds of what I write is generated by my own reading, teaching, and professional activity. As I read, teach, and attend conferences and other professional activities, I gradually develop a sense of what I want to contribute to the community of teachers and scholars. Usually this general sense derives originally from an article that I have read, a paper that I have heard, or a hallway or coffee-room conversation. Then, more talk and reading, often with some related teaching experience interspersed, helps me clarify what I think I have to say to other teachers and scholars. At the same time, I begin to refine my sense of audience, moving from broad audiences such as teachers of writing to more restricted audiences such as "teachers of writing who want to use literature in their courses" or to "teachers of writing who are interested in speaking-writing relationships." But this refining of audience is not as simple as I have made it seem. At the same time that I refine and restrict audience I find myself holding tenaciously onto my intention of addressing a large and far more pluralistic audience, those people who know that writing is the center of a thinking life, those people who grasp the significance of writing in a relativistic world, the Walker Gibsons of my past. Without this dual sense of audience, I feel that my writing would be too pat, too simple, too sure of itself, too comfortable with its own clarities. But without the more restricted sense of audience there would be no clarities, no comfort, no confidence at all. Again, I express the need for balance.

The other third of my writing is commissioned by editors of professional journals or by commercial publishers, or takes place in such professional contexts as academic committee reports, program descriptions, memoranda, and letters. It is due at preset deadlines. It, too, is related to my ongoing intellectual-academic life, but it is always half out of synch and half in synch with my intellectual life. In this remaining third of my writing life, nothing is ever just right; there is never a perfect match between assigned writing chore and the latest of my ideas about composition. This other third of my writing may include a chapter from a textbook that I have been writing over a two-year period, on a preset, chapter-every-other-month schedule. Or it may include a paper to be delivered, again by prearrangement, to a university audience on a subject I wrote about years before but on which I have done little recent research. The difficulty with this kind of writing is that it never connects as directly and easily as I would like with the intellectual side of my writing life. I have to discipline myself to reread, to go back over already-written and already-read articles and books in order to discover relationships with my current thinking, to strike a spark that will provide new heat and energy for an old idea.

This tension between what I have thought and written in past periods of my career and what I am currently thinking as it is manifested in these two kinds of writing projects is, I believe, a central, generating force in my writing life. Without the friction between what I have read and written before and my current writing, my composing would probably be more fluent—words would flow across the page with few interruptions, qualifications, or elaborations. Ideas drawn from my teaching, professional and general reading, discussions with fellow teachers and writers, would generate a great deal of prose. This uninterrupted flow would feel good, at least for a while, but there would soon come a time when these piles of words would worry me. And left alone they would, after awhile, make me neurotic because I would begin to imagine them heard or read by other writers and teachers, people whom I respect in the field or discipline and whom I know would have a difficult time with this unedited draft. Only when my composing is interrupted, first, by echoes and reverberations of former ideas and writings, second, by the questioning assertions of others who are thinking about the same topics, am I really sure that what I write will do some justice to the subject's complexities. These ongoing interruptions do make the writing of sentences and paragraphs more difficult, but they also make me feel far more confident than my uninterrupted writing does that what I write will not embarrass me later, in front of that more general audience of intellectuals who never read a piece simply for what it says about a given topic but always for a specific message that also says something about human experience.

Overall, then, both kinds of writing tasks result in a similar composing process. That process—never too fast, never too slow—allows for the interference of other topics, other ideas, responses from other writers and readers, and it allows my writing to continue to exist as the record of an idea developing, at the "cutting edge" of my current thinking. In fact, I have come to think, only lately, that the writing process is no more or less than my attempt to control the interrelationships of past and present in my mental life.

Writing an Essay

I need to illustrate all this with at least one specific discussion of a recent composing experience. For two or three years now I have been interested in the work of Walter Ong on literacy, particularly oral and written relationships within the general history of literacy. So far I have read and reread five of his major publications, delivered four or five papers at universities and academic conferences on the relevance of his work to the teaching of composition, begun to assemble and read a variety of commentaries on Ong's work, and composed two article-length pieces. I have also begun to pull past and present reading on literacy together with my work on Ong's ideas.

Several patterns of composing activity emerge from this experience with Ong's work. First, I am aware that oral composing, through conversation and dialogue and more formal presentations, makes up at least half of my composing life. I believe these oral activities fulfill the function of connecting my ongoing thought processes with my evolving sense of audience. They give me a chance to try out my ideas on real people in informal and formal settings. It is also important to note here that what others actually say to me in these oral contexts is often not nearly as important as what I think in reaction to what they say. My thoughts, in other words, continue to develop along their own subjective lines, but they are fed and influenced as much by the nonverbal, verbal, and written responses of others, and by the sound of my own voice externalizing my thoughts, as they are by my reading, self-reflection, and writing. Through oral activity and response, the circle of my composing broadens, but without my losing a sense of the relationship between my own intellectual processes and my projections of that inner life into the area of personal experience. What I have to say to others about Ong's interpretation of the shift from oral to written culture in seventh- to fourth-century B.C. Greece, and their responses to my words, become my means of keeping a continual thought and composing process going.

The other half of my composing experience on this project was about evenly divided between ongoing, systematic research and writing. Once I have gotten beyond the initial stage of deciding upon and at least generally defining a new intellectual direction—as I did with my work on Ong after about a year or two of teaching rhetoric courses in which I included his work and informally talked about his interpretation of the history of literacy with other teachers —I reverted to my earlier school habits and began to set down in my mind a systematic and general plan of reading and research. I took two kinds of notes as I read. The first I call "chapter and article summary notes." In these I summarized the chapter's or article's significance in relation to my research topic. An article from *College English,* for example, on literacy and composition I would summarize only in ways that would immediately relate to my evolving hypothesis concerning Ong's work and its relevance to composition. I continued to write—drafts of papers for conferences, various kinds of expressive statements on the topic—as I progressed through this research process. All this took time, of course, and it combined with my planning and teaching of classes in rhetoric and literature to create an ongoing process of composing, one that operated sometimes through talk, sometimes through formal presentations and teaching, sometimes through writing. But most important to me as writer was the sense of connected inner speech—sometimes monologue, sometimes dialogue with an imagined interlocutor—that this process created in me.

It was, I believe, this ongoing inner speech that distinguished my thoughts about Ong's work (which were taking shape on paper). It is precisely this convergence of all the communication arts around a developing thought that distinguishes the knowledge we gain by writing from the knowledge, far more loosely conceived, that we gain through most other cognitive processes.

The trick in controlling this complex process is to balance in new and ever more complex ways writing as craft and writing as intellectual process. When this balance is successfully struck, writing an essay begins, develops, and closes around an interactive combination of talking, thinking, reading, writing, and crafting. Actual writing—of papers, articles, chapters in a still hypothetical book—simply interrupts this process to bring the writer-thinker, always essentially a narcissist, back to a renewed and better-formed sense of self in relation to a subject. These writings bring others into the writer's intellectual process.

Before I close, I should say something about the final stages of this complex process. Seeing writing as intellectual process and as craft helps me to explain a central composing paradox. In the broader, intellectual sense of a developing topic or problem, there is no definite closure in the writing process. I fear I shall never write the perfect draft, on Ong's sense of the history of literacy, on any complex topic. There will always be need for revision, for re-seeing from new perspectives, for turning an idea around to know it anew, for hearing and including someone else's original perspective, for fine tuning of one kind or another. In this sense, writing is always an open-ended process. Every sentence I write, extracted from a full, intellectual context, is a paltry thing, a "tattered coat upon a stick."

But there are points within this overall process where I must close an idea, complete a rhetorical situation with a particular text. These are important times for me in several ways. First, these points of closure relieve my writer's neuroses. I understand better my writing as craft, manifested in my need to address a particular audience on a particular occasion with a particular text. During these moments of actual composition, if I can manage a balanced perspective on what I am doing, overall process and particular textual composition come together and I both discover new perspectives on my subject and craft an essay that, although it *could* be revised, will withstand the pressures of other minds.

Second, at these points of actual composition, if I have stayed with an idea carefully and long enough, I am ready for others' responses to my writing, to the way I have tried to match thinking and written language. It is at this point that I am prepared to hear the editor's criticisms of style and usage, the fellow Ong scholar's comment on a particular misreading or misinterpretation of one of Ong's ideas, or a colleague's more general remark on the irrelevance of Ong's work to his or her primary concerns. I am prepared at this point, in other words, to bring the private process of composition into the community of people who are committed to the intellectual life.

Third, and finally, "going to paper," as one of my colleagues puts it, serves an important psychological function. It is purgative. It makes me feel that I have actually done something. It gives me a draft to read, to feel in my hands. But, above all, it gives me the opportunity to see my thinking and to imagine it as others might see it. I feel at this kind of moment, if it is successful, a clear sense of my own thinking and the support of an intellectual community. Writing, at these moments, becomes for me one of the very few occasions when my inner life and my sense of community come together in a single process of knowing.

This essay makes no claims to have presented a systematic procedure that I follow as I write. Instead, it stakes its claims on the synthesis of knowing and communicating that occurs in any good piece of writing. But its claims have further implications, I think. They establish, at least in my mind, a potentially central place for writing in a university curriculum. The act of writing, for me, has gradually become the center of gravity of all that I do. It helps me pull together my reading, which, in recent years, has drawn increasingly on disciplines other than English. It helps me gain distance and control over my own thinking processes. And it helps me find and communicate with people who, I hope, need and want to hear what I have to say. And, finally, it is the satisfaction gained from having my thinking organized and communicated that pushes me to recall and reuse those years of summarizing, training memory, paraphrasing, translating, practicing spelling and vocabulary, that otherwise I would have been pleased to forget. Writing as craft and intellectual process are mutually reinforcing, or they are nothing. They are the central skills, the unifying skills, the synthesizing skills, and the controlling skills of all we think and do.

Edward P. J. Corbett, who holds an M.A. degree from the University of Chicago and a Ph.D. from Loyola University, is currently professor of English and director of the advanced composition course at Ohio State University. He has served as director of freshman English not only at Ohio State but also at Creighton University in Omaha, Nebraska. Professional offices he has held include president of both the Ohio and the Nebraska councils of Teachers of English, executive secretary of the Rhetoric Society of America, and editor of the journal College Composition and Communication.

Among his many publications are Classical Rhetoric for the Modern Student *(2nd ed., 1971);* The Little English Handbook *(4th ed., 1984);* The Little Rhetoric and Handbook *(2nd ed., 1982);* The Rhetoric of Blair, Campbell, and Whately, *edited with James L. Golden (1968, 1980);* The Writing Teacher's Sourcebook, *edited with Gary Tate (1981); and* The Rhetoric and Poetics of Aristotle, *Modern Library college edition (1984). Recently a festschrift was published in his honor:* Essays on Classical Rhetoric and Modern Discourse, *edited by Robert Connors, Lisa Ede, and Andrea Lunsford (1984).*

THE RITES OF WRITING

Edward P. J. Corbett
Ohio State University

One does learn by doing. Sometimes what one learns by doing is trivial or ineffectual or downright wrongheaded. But if one continues to reap bad or inferior fruit from doing and is shrewd enough to recognize the imperfections of the harvest, one will usually and eventually change or modify the doing.

In a front-page article in the *New York Times Book Review* for May 20, 1984, Hortense Calisher talked about the curious reluctance of American writers to talk about their personal lives or about their writing. As evidence of this reticence, she pointed to the scarcity of autobiographical writing by the major American writers of the mid-twentieth century—Faulkner, Hemingway, Cather, Dreiser, Fitzgerald, Cheever. And indeed, in comparison with European writers of this and the previous century (think, for instance, of all those garrulous English Romantic poets), American writers have been remarkably reticent about their private lives and their writing processes. With his *Notebooks,* in which he talked about the "germs" and the evolution of many of his stories, Henry James was a rarity among American writers. (But then James always did seem to be more European than American, and he sealed that affinity by becoming a British citizen before his death in 1916.)

The world will little note nor long remember what the American writer Edward P. J. Corbett said or wrote (who he?). In fact, if I had not been asked to contribute to this volume, I probably would never have had the opportunity to talk about my writing habits and processes. And after reading Hortense Calisher's article, I asked myself whether I too shared the typical American writer's reluctance to talk about the dynamics of the writing process. My answer to my own query, after some deliberation, was that I was *not* indisposed to talk about my writing. I was, on the contrary, quite eager to talk about it.

Why was I different from those American writers of fiction and nonfiction who have established their place in the literary histories of the United States? My readiness to talk about my writing processes was due, partly and maybe mainly, to my longtime profession as a teacher of writing. Fresh out of graduate school, with no formal training whatever for teaching writing, I was assigned, in my first year as a university instructor, to teach four sections of freshman composition. I was handed a syllabus and a clutch of textbooks and was shoved in the direction of the classroom. *Panic* is the mildest word I can think of to describe my emotional state in those early weeks of my teaching career. I was desperate for guidance about what to do in the classroom. Looking back now, I can see that I did many foolish things in those composition classes, and I have many times wished that I could recall the students who were in those muddled classes and apologize to them for wasting so much of their valuable time.

But one of the smart things I did, in my desperation, was to ask myself what *I* did when I was assigned to do a piece of writing. By becoming introspective, I was trying to recover the dynamics of my own writing processes. Fortunately, by that time, I had done a great deal of writing—probably more than most people of that age. I had written not only the usual quota of themes and reports and term papers for my classes in high school and in college but an unusual amount of self-initiated writing—mainly short stories. The ambition that seized me very early in life was to become a creative writer—more specifically a fiction writer. I have a whole suitcase full of short-story manuscripts and rejection slips from magazine editors. Because I hadn't been successful in selling any of my stories to the mass-circulation magazines during my undergraduate years in college, I thought that maybe I could prepare myself for a career as a fiction writer by becoming a journalist, as writers such as Ernest Hemingway, Sherwood Anderson, William Faulkner, and Katherine Ann Porter had done.

So when I was with the U.S. Marines in North China, helping to repatriate the Japanese after World War II and waiting to be discharged from the service so that I could attend graduate school on the GI Bill, I wrote to the University of Chicago asking them for information about their school of journalism. They wrote back to me, saying that they did not have a school of journalism but that if I wanted to attend a journalism school in the Midwest, they advised that I enroll at one of the noted journalism schools, such as the one at Northwestern in Evanston or at Marquette University in Milwaukee or at the University of Missouri in Columbia. But they strongly recommended that I take an advanced degree in some subject-matter field and then pick up some journalism courses.

To make a long story short, I elected to take a master's degree in English at the University of Chicago, and having to earn some money to support the family that I had just started, I accepted a job, right after graduation, as a teacher of English at a Midwestern university. And that's where I left off a few paragraphs back—a bewildered first-year teacher, desperate for guidance in helping the hundred or so students in my four sections of freshman composition to cope with the themes I assigned them to write once a week. As I said, I was smart enough to recognize that one of the fruitful things I could do was to introduce them to some of the techniques and strategies that I used when I wrote.

One does learn by doing. Sometimes what one learns by doing is trivial or ineffectual or downright wrongheaded. But if one continues to reap bad or inferior fruit from doing and is shrewd enough to recognize the imperfections of the harvest, one will usually and eventually change or modify the doing. I am sure I learned some valuable lessons about particularity and concreteness from my experience in writing short stories. And I probably also gained a measure of facility in putting words on paper. But after I got caught up in the academic world, I gradually abandoned the writing of fiction and, out of sheer professional necessity, concentrated on the writing of academic discourse. For that kind of discourse, I had to learn a different set of conventions, strategies, and styles. I suppose I learned those new sets from a combination of observation, imitation, and practice. I know that I never had a course in how to write academic discourse.

It is hard for me now to recall what I learned in school that helped me in my writing. I was fortunate in having exceptional teachers in the late elementary grades and throughout my high-school years. My English teachers were particularly good. The teacher I had in the seventh and eighth grades made me a whiz at diagramming sentences. And in my first year of teaching, I set the students in my composition classes to diagramming sentences. I wonder now what I hoped to accomplish or what I expected my students to learn from that exercise.

My resorting to that futile exercise indicates how desperate I was then for something sensible and effectual to do in those writing classes. From my perspective today, I can say that I did not permanently harm any of my students by requiring them to diagram sentences but I did not do them much good either. How much more fruitful it would have been if instead of asking them to diagram sentences that someone else had composed, I had required them to compose sentences of their own on the model of those sample sentences. Still, those exercises in diagramming could not have been a total loss for my students. Down through the years, I have found that my ability to diagram sentences has been immensely helpful to me when I had to untangle the syntax of a garbled sentence I had written or to recast a sentence that struck me as being awkwardly phrased.

But what else from my early schooling helped me as a writer and as a teacher of writing? The English teachers I had in high school regularly exposed me to first-rate literature—mainly British literature of the eighteenth and nineteenth centuries. As I recall, those teachers were exemplars primarily of the emotive school of criticism. They would read a passage of literature to us and then exclaim ecstatically about it: "A gem! A perfect gem!" It was not always clear to me that the passage which had elicited that exclamation was indeed a gem, but who was I to challenge the taste of my revered teacher?

The ultimate effect of all this exclamatory response to literature was that I and most of my classmates developed a real passion for literature. In our relatively leisurely summer vacations, we regularly visited the neighborhood public libraries and came away with an armful of enticing books, which we read under a shady tree in the backyard or in a swing on the front porch in those rare hours during the daytime when we were not playing baseball in the empty lot across the street. It is impossible to calculate, I suppose, just how much all this reading of "great literature" did for me as a writer or as a teacher of writing, but I am sure it did something. Not every omnivorous reader becomes a good writer, of course, but there are no good writers who are not also insatiable readers.

One of those teachers of literature engaged us in a practice that I know has helped me to improve as a writer. This teacher set short passages from literary texts for us to copy verbatim and turn in every day at the beginning of class. At first, I regarded this assignment as so much "busy work," but after a while I got caught up in the excitement of the discoveries I was making of felicitous choices of diction and phrasing. Subsequently, either consciously or unconsciously, I began to incorporate into my own writing some of the words and the structures that I had encountered in my copying of passages written by accomplished writers. And I was delighted by the extensions and refinements of verbal powers that I was noting in my own prose.

After five or six weeks of designating the passages we had to copy each day, the teacher encouraged us to copy passages from writers we admired. For some reason, I was enamored at the time of the prose of Thomas Babington Macaulay, the noted Victorian essayist and historian, and having been turned loose by the teacher to choose passages of prose that I admired, I copied tens of thousands of words from Macaulay's essays. That concentration proved to be both a mistake and a benefit. I did pick up many of the distinctive virtues of Macaulay's prose style: the specificity and concretness of his diction, the clarity and variety of his sentence structure, the pace and the drama of his narrative style—and some of those features still mark my prose style today. But it is always a mistake in this regimen of copying to stay with one author too long. You are likely to begin sounding like that author, and that eventuality is a consummation devoutly to be avoided. You want to develop your own voice and your own style. It is better to flit from one author to another than to stay with one author for an extended period. From that kind of ranging, you are likely to pick up a variety of verbal niceties from a variety of authors—but still retain your own voice.

In any case, no finger exercises that I have ever engaged in or that I have engaged my students in have yielded such immediate and demonstrable benefits as this verbatim copying of prose passages. I have seen some of my students display incredible improvements in their prose style after only three or four weeks of this straight copying. Those students who genuinely wanted to improve their writing made the greatest leaps forward, but even students who indulged only half-heartedly in the copying manifested a measurable improvement. Try it. You may like it.

I suspect, however, that what had the greatest effect on me as a writer and as a teacher of writing was my exposure during the four years of high school to the study of Latin and Greek. There is no doubt in my mind that this fortunate and somewhat fortuitous encounter with the Latin and Greek classics turned my life around and made me, for better or for worse, what I am today. I wish I could specify what the benefits of this experience were, but I can talk only in general terms about those benefits—about a reinforced reverence for quality no matter how old it is, about a sharpened sense of the potentialities of words, about a growing awareness of the similarities and differences in the dynamics of a family of languages. I wish too that I could recall what we did in those classes as we struggled to learn the grammar of those languages and to translate those highly inflected languages into the basically word-order language that is English, because if I could recall those approaches, techniques, and exercises, I might have some practical advice to pass on to my readers about what they could do in coping with a foreign language that could prove to be useful to them in learning how to write. I am not even sure that studying Latin and Greek— or any foreign language, for that matter—is an indispensable requisite for becoming a competent writer. I just know, in a vague but firm way, that the study of Latin and Greek proved to be the crucial catalyst for me. If nothing else, it disposed me toward the intellectual life in general and toward the humanities in particular. It may be significant that historically almost all of the enshrined British and American writers through the nineteenth century had been exposed at least to Latin and in many cases to Greek also.

One definable contribution that the study of the Latin and Greek classics made to my development as a writer and as a teacher of writing is that it introduced me to the formal discipline of rhetoric. Actually,

I did not discover rhetoric through my study of Latin and Greek in high school. I came to rhetoric indirectly, many years later, through a serendipitous discovery of Hugh Blair's *Lectures on Rhetoric and Belles Lettres* (1783) during my first year of teaching. Reading the fascinating lectures that this Scottish rhetorician had delivered for almost a quarter of a century at the University of Edinburgh led me back to the origins of the formal study of rhetoric in the schools of fifth-century Athens. I started out with the rhetorical works of Aristotle, Plato, and Isocrates and went on to the works of the great Latin rhetoricians, Cicero and Quintilian. Eventually I discovered that Hugh Blair, along with his compatriot George Campbell, came at the end of the long reign of rhetoric in the curriculum of the English schools, a reign that began when rhetoric was a part of the trivium in the medieval schools and that flourished in the Tudor grammar schools and universities during the English Renaissance of the sixteenth century.

In their book *Rhetorical Traditions and the Teaching of Writing* (Upper Montclair, N.J.: Boynton/Cook, 1984), Cyril H. Knoblauch and Lil Brannon have questioned the relevance and the value of classical rhetoric for the modern composition classroom, and they present a strong case for their claim that the rhetoric which developed out of the scientific, empirical system initiated by such seminal philosophers as René Descartes and John Locke is much more pertinent to the modern classroom than is classical rhetoric. Nevertheless, I know that my study of classical rhetoric proved to be pertinent and useful to me as a teacher of writing. Before I discovered rhetoric, I thrashed about futilely in the composition classroom because I did not know what I was doing. With my discovery of rhetoric, I learned what the act of communication was all about, and I gained some valuable insights into the process of writing. Consequently, my activities in the writing class began to be purposeful and, in a measure, efficacious.

I cannot adequately convey how excited I was when I made the rather commonplace discovery that the act of communication involved someone saying something to someone else for some purpose. It is remarkable how much of a change that epiphany effected in me as a teacher of writing—and also as a writer. I came to realize that writing was more than just the sequence of sentences that I scribbled on a blank sheet of paper. It was a complex of elements that had to be brought into some kind of harmony. Instead of being concerned only about those words I scribbled on a sheet of paper, I had to be concerned about the image of myself that I projected to my readers and about the disposition of those readers that I was addressing. Moreover, the *something* that I was trying to convey to my readers had to coincide with, had to be true to, the "reality" out there that I was talking about. As a result, I had to make that *something* a finely tuned complex of those three modes of appeal that Aristotle dealt with in his *Rhetoric:* the ethical appeal, the emotional appeal, and the logical appeal.

The ethical appeal mainly concerned me, the *someone* in the communication act, because it concentrated on creating a trustworthy image of the writer that would be projected to the readers. The emotional appeal was mainly concerned with the readers, the *someone else* in the communication act, for it dealt primarily with putting the readers in the appropriate mood or disposition to receive the message. The logical appeal was mainly concerned with the text being composed, the *something* in the communication act, for it focused on making the what-was-said true or plausible or responsible—in short, on making the what-was-said as consonant with the reality-out-there as the circumstances permitted. In speaking of the relationship of each of the modes of appeal to the particular element in the communication act, I have said "mainly concerned," because I did not want to create the impression that each of the appeals is confined to just one element in the triad. Just as the speaker/writer, the listener/reader, and the text (the *something*) constantly interact with one another, so each of the three modes of appeal frequently deal with one of the elements other than the principal element I assigned it to above. For example, if the text says something that is illogical or untrue or irresponsible, the image that the speaker or writer wants to project to the audience will in some measure be tarnished.

The principal contribution that the formal art of rhetoric made to my development as a writer and as a teacher of writing is epitomized in the previous paragraph. I did not get all of those insights from classical rhetoric alone. My know-how was considerably enhanced by the extensions and refinements of those insights that rhetoricians of the eighteenth, nineteenth, and twentieth centuries have provided—and also by the commonsense observations that I myself began to make once I had been enlightened. But it is still amazing to me how much of a difference the discovery of ancient rhetoric made in my development as a writer and a teacher. I was "born again."

I have been speaking about those experiences in my own schooling that influenced me as a writer and a teacher. It is time now for me to speak somewhat particularly about my writing habits. The rhetoric texts, ancient and modern, give us prudential advice about how to compose a piece of discourse. I myself have written some rhetoric texts that are used in the schools. In my own writing, do I always do what the rhetoric texts tell us to do? Do I have my own "secrets," my own "gimmicks," which I do not share with other writers even in my textbooks on writing?

The aspiring writer should be suspicious of any rhetoric text that presents a single, lockstep way of composing a piece of discourse. There are no absolute do's and don'ts about the writing process. What works well for one writer may not work at all for the next writer. I learned that cardinal truth very dramatically a few years ago when I circulated a questionnaire among my graduate students that asked them about their writing habits.

One of the startling revelations of that questionnaire was that more than 90 percent of that group of students wrote the first draft of any piece of writing in longhand—curiously enough, on a yellow legal tablet. Since I always wrote every draft on the typewriter, I was stunned to learn that other writers did not compose on the typewriter too. I am practically inarticulate with a pen in hand. But think how damaging my advice to my students would be if I told them that they must, or they should, write the first draft of their papers on the typewriter.

Another shock came from the graduate students' response to a question about how they went about writing the sequence of sentences in a piece of prose that would later be read by somebody. I asked them whether they wrote off the sentences in a "white heat" and then went back and made corrections and changes, or whether they had to get each sentence "just right" before they could go on to the next sentence. Again to my surprise, the overwhelming majority of that group of students—two-thirds of them—said that they had to be satisfied with the phrasing of each sentence before they went on to write the next sentence. For years, I had followed the advice of most modern rhetoric texts that one should write the first draft straight ahead, not pausing to correct spelling or grammar or punctuation but just getting one's thoughts laid out on a piece of paper. And before I circulated that questionnaire, I would have bet that most people who did a fair amount of writing wrote in that manner. A little later on, I am going to reveal how my writing habit in this respect has changed now that I am doing most of my composing on a word processor.

I also asked my students whether they did any kind of outlining before they began writing their papers. I myself have never drawn up a formal outline before writing—that is, a topic or sentence outline in which all the coordinate elements are phrased in parallel form. Sometimes I had been required by my teacher to submit a formal outline along with the final draft of a paper, but I drew up that formal outline *after* I had finished writing the paper. Most of my students confessed that they too never drew up a formal outline, unless they were required to do so. But like me, all of them did some kind of organizing before they began to write. Maybe it was just a list of points that they wanted to cover; maybe it was a sequence of rectangles into which they scribbled a suggestive word or phrase or sentence. For me, the hardest part of organizing a discourse is finding a suitable starting point. Once I can settle on that starting point, I know what the subsequent parts must be and the order in which those parts must be arranged. For that reason, I cannot go on in a piece of writing until I write my introductory paragraph(s). Some rhetoric texts advise the writer to plunge right into the body of the paper and then, after the body of the paper has been written and maybe the conclusion too, to come back and write the introduction. For some reason, that technique has never worked for me. Teachers must introduce students to a variety of techniques for organizing their papers, and encourage them to try out the various techniques in order to discover the method that works best for them.

From this questionnaire and from many years of conferring in private sessions with my students, I found that the greatest variety in writing habits appeared in students' techniques of invention—that is, in methods of discovering something to say in a piece of discourse. If there is any area of the writing process where teachers must be sure to introduce their students to a variety of strategies, it is the area of invention or, to use the Greek term for the process, heuristics. In my *Classical Rhetoric for the Modern Student,* I introduce writers to only one method of invention, the *topics,* because that is the heuristic system that the Greek and Roman rhetoricians devised to help the speaker or writer find something to say. (In my *Little Rhetoric and Handbook,* however, I introduce writers to a wide range of heuristic systems.) In my *Classical Rhetoric,* I reduce the common topics to a list of five general topics subdivided into subsidiary topics. Because this is not the place to elaborate on the system of the topics, I will give only the five general headings here: (1) Definition; (2) Comparison; (3) Relationship; (4) Circumstance; (5) Testimony.

Because I made such a big thing out of the topics in my book, I have frequently been asked whether I myself ever used the topics to find material for something I had to write. My answer to that query is, "No, I have not consciously resorted to the topics." By the time I learned about the topics—quite late in my graduate-school work—I had already developed my own system of invention. When I look back on any piece of writing I have done, I can see that, in a sense, the topics have yielded material for various parts of the discourse. Here I am engaged in defining a term or a concept; there I am engaged in demonstrating a cause-and-effect relationship; in this part of the paper I am comparing two things. So often have I found that kind of evidence in something I have written that I am convinced that the classical topics reflect the characteristic ways in which the human mind operates when it is trying to discover what it knows about a subject or what could be said about a subject. But I have not been very successful in consciously using the topics to find something to say. Nevertheless the topics have proven to be very productive for some of my student writers.

Never having been taught any formal system of invention, I had to develop my own system. Now when I have to deal with some subject that I cannot write about off the top of my head, I do a lot of meditating and reading—sometimes for several days, sometimes for several weeks. I take copious notes, especially when I am reading. Most of the time, I am not just paraphrasing what I am reading; I am copying passages verbatim. I do a lot of verbatim copying, not only because I might later have occasion to quote those passages in my paper but simply because writing out the words helps me to understand and to fix in my memory what I am reading. I steep myself in the subject I am going to write about and always gather more material than I can use. Then I just let all that material stew in my subconscious for a while. I may jot down some key points that I want to discuss in my paper and may even try to put those points in some kind of order. But as I said earlier, I cannot really get going in my writing until I have written an introduction that satisfies me. Getting that introduction just right helps me overcome my inertia and points me in the direction that the piece of writing must go.

But one of the most profound observations that I have made about my own writing process in recent years is that writing the first draft is still part of the invention process for me. The mere act of verbalizing what I have discovered in my pre-writing stage suggests additional things I could say and even suggests the final organization of the paper I am writing. It may be pedagogically convenient to break the writing process into the three stages of pre-writing, writing, and revising, but that kind of compartmentalizing of the process is not very realistic. Invention goes on in all three stages, even in the stage of revision. A number of recently published rhetoric texts have recognized that fact.

I think it is too early for me to make any final pronouncements about what changes the use of a word processor has effected in my writing habits. I have been composing on a word processor for over a year now, and I am ecstatic about this wondrous machine. I can say definitively, even now, that the word processor has increased my productivity at least three times. And I can also say that I now do much more revising than I ever did before. Previously, I would write off the first draft without pausing to make any corrections, alterations, or additions in my prose. After typing that first draft, I went back over it and made lots of changes—not just changes in wording and punctuation but substantive changes as well. Then I moved directly to typing up the final draft. I usually made some additional changes as I was typing that final draft. But that was the extent of my revising.

With the word processor, however, it is so easy to erase or insert words, so easy to transpose sentences and paragraphs, so easy to add new passages—all without the prospect of having to retype the page or the whole paper—that I am constantly revising the paper. I hinted earlier that the word processor had made one change in my writing habits. Whereas I used to write the first draft straightforward, without pausing to make corrections or changes, I now tend to do what I discovered most of my graduate students did: I am inclined to get each sentence "just right" before moving on. I write a sentence or a paragraph, and then I stop to reread it. If I am not satisfied with the sentence or paragraph, I am now likely to fix it up right then and there. But it is so easy to make changes on the word processor that I do not find that the constant "fixing up" delays the overall composition process very much.

As I said, it is too early for me to declare definitively what permanent changes the word processor will make in my writing habits. And it may also be too early for any of us to say what significant changes the word processor will make in the writing habits of students in general. I suspect that it will benefit the already competent writer more than the inexperienced writer, because the latter does not yet have enough lexical and syntactical resources to be able to take advantage of this marvelous facility.

In any case, the word processor has helped me put together this exposition of my writing processes. And I, having written this exposition, have learned something about myself that I only vaguely knew before. This experience has proven once again what is perhaps the paramount truth about writing: Writing is not only a means of communication but also a means of discovery.

Robert Gorrell is emeritus academic vice president and professor at the University of Nevada-Reno; having also taught at Deep Springs College, Indiana University, Helsinki, Hawaii, and California at Los Angeles. He is past chairman of the Conference on College Composition and Communication and of the college section of the National Council of Teachers of English, and past director of the NCTE Commission on Composition. He was NCTE distinguished lecturer in 1971.

Gorrell's publications include Modern English Handbook, English as Language, *and* Writing Modern Language, *all with Charlton Laird;* Writing and Language, *with Mable Brown; other textbooks; and a variety of articles on rhetoric, language, and the teaching of writing.*

OF PRACTICE AND PREACHING

Robert Gorrell

The translation of analysis to theory to precept is hazardous. Francis Christensen examines 4,000 sentences and discovers that 75 percent begin with the subject. What advice, if any, does his information justify—that we should begin sentences with the subject 75 percent of the time, or usually, or that we should vary the pattern 25 percent of the time?

I remember, some years ago, receiving from a national committee an elaborate questionnaire, intended, its preamble explained, to find out from some two hundred professional writers how they went about writing and therefore how writing gets done. I'm not very patient with questionnaires, but I suppose this one flattered me by including me in some pretty fast company. I tried to answer it, and I got through the biographical data with no trouble, and through the questions about whether I use a pencil or ball-point or typewriter and whether I smoke or chew my fingernails as part of the composing process.

And then I remember something like "Where do you get your ideas?" I had one line for the reply. I gave up fairly easily. I did salve my conscience a little by writing a letter, presumably about my writing —actually about why I couldn't answer most of the questions, at least not in one line.

In a way, I'm still facing the same difficulties. But the problem posed here is more confined, and more interesting. Whether rhetoricians practice what they preach is a valid and relevant question.

Furthermore, I think that any writer's subjective observations about writing are more important than our scientific time dares consider them. George Campbell, two hundred years ago, advocated a kind of sophisticated intuition:

> The earliest assistance and direction that can be obtained in the rhetorical art, by which men operate on the minds of others, arises from the consciousness a man has of what operates on his own mind.

99

I think that most of the comments I have made about rhetoric—at least those that have any claim to originality—have grown from my experiences in writing and reading. And with more age I have become less cautious.

To begin, I should point out the obvious, that different people—even rhetoricians—write differently and that I write differently on different projects. In general, I write more slowly than some. I've done a lot of collaborative writing, especially with Charlton Laird, and I find that other writers work at a different pace from me. When we work together, he turns out copy twice as fast as I do, but revising his takes twice as long as revising mine. His method offers freshness and liveliness, but also sometimes a lack of clarity; mine offers clarity but sometimes stodginess. Larry may blot too little, I too much. We both compose on a typewriter, probably because of early newspaper experience. A friend whose writing I watched, the late Walter Van Tilburg Clark, wrote a tiny script with an orange Parker fountain pen that had belonged to his father, and often did half a dozen versions of a chapter before he was satisfied.

I write or have written several different sorts of things, as I suppose all of us do: textbooks, allegedly scholarly articles, a weekly newspaper column about usage, reams of committee reports and recommendations, political speeches and press releases for my wife, some fiction—unpublished—poems—mostly unpublished—and quite a lot of material about rhetoric, about how to write.

For each of these the immediate motivation is somewhat different. The weekly column becomes a matter of routine; the political speeches met a present practical need; some articles resulted from invitations with deadlines that seemed remote enough to be safe; poetry and fiction in some ways answered a challenge; textbooks, at least partly, were inspired by the crass need to pay the light bill. To a degree, with all writing and less impressively than with Milton, fame is the spur. But with all of these, including the textbooks, the necessary motivation for me is confidence that I have something to say. This requires a certain amount of immodesty, but some immodesty is essential to any creativity. And I am convinced that you can't write successfully just to imitate or fill a formula or make money. A desire to do something better or at least differently is the necessary motivation for any kind of successful writing.

There are also, of course, habits and mechanical procedures common to all the writing I do. I have used a typewriter almost as long as I can remember; my father ran a weekly newspaper, and we had an old Underwood at home that ultimately became mine. I learned shorthand in high school and still take some shorthand notes—partly because they're more legible than my longhand. Except for attempts at poetry, which I scribble, I compose on a typewriter, although I keep a pencil and pad beside me to make notes about ideas I want to use later and am likely to forget. I have recently shifted to what I reluctantly call a word processor. (Writing should not be called "processing"; I think of processed cheese as bogus.) For me this seems to work out as only a somewhat more efficient typewriter, one with which I can ultimately turn out clean copy.

I try to write regularly, but I am less conscientious about this than I used to be. The time of day doesn't matter. I used to work late at night, especially with a deadline threatening, but these days I get sleepy. I still have to discipline myself to get writing done. It's easy to rationalize that fixing a leaky faucet is more demanding than dealing with a stubborn paragraph. Writing is work for me, but I can't help doing it. For forty years I never wrote without a pipe in my mouth. I quit smoking five years ago, and I detect no ill effects. I have always had some sort of spot I could call a study—for many years a tiny room in the basement protected by black widow spiders, and I associate writing with such a spot, with books around. I seemed to get less done during periods when I was on leave and writing on a kitchen table on a portable typewriter. But these are superficial considerations. You can write on the kitchen table or on your lap if you need to.

The important question here, and the most interesting, is what use I make of various rhetorical principles. I propose to consider a few of these and to try to determine how I use them, or whether I do. But first I need to make three observations about my attitudes toward rhetoric.

First, I want to cite a reminder that there are different sorts of rhetoric, not all applicable here. In a 1977 article speculating about a "generative" rhetoric, I tried to distinguish "five faces" of rhetoric, five common meanings of the word *rhetoric:* an academic discipline, a theory of discourse, a description or grammar of discourse, a body of precepts, or whatever all these deal with—the writing or speech itself.

I am concerned here with the fourth of these, with rhetoric as it is practical, as a body of principles for generating discourse, as advice about composing. These principles, if they are sound, grow from rhetorical theory that must square in some way with rhetoric as a grammar of discourse, with what actually happens. The translation of analysis to theory to precept is hazardous. Francis Christensen examines 4,000 sentences and discovers that 75 percent begin with the subject. What advice, if any, does his information justify—that we should begin sentences with the subject 75 percent of the time, or usually, or that we should vary the pattern 25 percent of the time? I need to remember that pursuit of rhetorical precepts led to the kind of stultifying prescription and proscription that for generations made rhetoric a way to petrify students and ossify prose.

Second, I want to urge that a rhetorical principle or description is not invalid or useless just because I or someone else doesn't use it. In particular, some principles or procedures seem to me valuable for teaching, as finger exercises, even though they may not be useful for more experienced writers. For example, I have written about patterns of continuity in prose, describing what goes on in the linear movement of discourse as a series of commitments and responses. I have assigned exercises to students in which they produce a sentence and then experiment with different sorts of responses to the commitment that sentence makes. The exercise seldom produces distinguished prose, but I think it helps students understand a general principle that discourse should track, that one thing should follow another logically. I don't consciously think of alternative responses to commitments when I am writing, but I think that work with this part of a descriptive rhetoric, or perhaps rhetorical theory, can help students. Another kind of exercise with a long history has blossomed into prominence with a new title, "sentence combining." It has pedagogical usefulness, as does the ancient practice in imitation.

Third, I am thinking primarily of rhetorical principles that apply generally. I am not concerned here to distinguish the different forms of discourse or different strategies a mode may require. I do rely in various ways on the following general principles.

PRE-WRITING

In our textbooks these days we still talk about pre-writing, writing, and revising or editing, and I think there is some virtue in thinking about these procedures independently. Recent criticism of texts, based on the alleged discovery that these are not separate, sequential activities, seems to me largely thrusting at a straw man. Anyone who has written realizes that these procedures are recursive, that the minute you think about something to write you start revising your thoughts, that with every sentence you write you're involved in pre-writing for what is to follow.

I do usually indulge in something that might be called pre-writing, in the sense that it occurs before I put anything on paper. This may go on for ten years or for a day. It may take the form of stewing at four in the morning about why I don't get started on an article I've promised to do. It may involve trying to think of an approach, a theme if you will, for that article. What have I got to say that hasn't been said ten times? I may think of a possible sentence that seems to me clever at the time, or a possible good line for a poem if I only had the rest of the poem to go with it. I sometimes enjoy reading less than I should because I tend as I read to think of things I want to write, because I disagree with some comment or get an idea for something similar to what I'm reading or some expansion of its ideas. I suppose I think more about things to write while I'm reading than at any other time.

Sometimes ideas keep turning up vaguely over a long period and finally jell into something usable—or sometimes, for various reasons, never quite jell. I have, for example, a large stack of cards from some research on relations between broadside ballads and Jacobean drama. For more than twenty years I have rationalized not getting that project finished into an article. Or I keep from time to time going over in my mind ideas about the importance of considering tone in interpreting metaphysical poetry. I think of examples and ways of getting started, but I haven't started.

A good deal of my daydreaming concerns writing I should do or want to do or writing I am actually working on. I think of possible approaches or things I've forgotten or why what I'm doing won't work. Sometimes I speculate about the audience and how it will react, especially if I am preparing something for a specialized group. Much of this I forget—as I should.

Sometimes I take notes from mental rambling of this sort, and occasionally the notes are useful. I have never kept a journal or notebook, but I've always planned to start.

All this is pre-writing of a sort—reading, speculating, agonizing. It gets somewhat more orderly when I decide I'm going to start a specific project. Before I started writing this comment on my writing, for example, I thought occasionally for three or four weeks about what I might do. From my random thoughts three notions survived. I remembered that I had been asked years ago to talk about something like how I learned to write. I found notes in the file and was reminded of a questionnaire I had received about that time. It seemed to me a possible idea for an introduction. As I am writing now it is the introduction, although it may not remain. I also speculated about whether there was any way to keep this from being merely a combination of aimless reminiscing and ego gratification, and decided to focus on the ways in which I made use of certain specific rhetorical precepts. And that suggested a rough pattern of organization—aspects of practical rhetoric as main topics.

In other words, I did at least some of the things the textbooks tell us to do in getting ready to write—thought about a main idea, thought broadly about organization, even did some minor research. I did not ask myself questions involving particle, wave, and field, although I suppose I might have, but I did develop a basis for pertinent questions about what kind of rhetorical advice I customarily heed. I think that I usually do something of this sort.

ORGANIZATION

I did not make an outline for this discussion, but I did jot down topics I wanted to remember. For a full-length textbook, I find an outline essential; and it has to be constantly revised in order to avoid repetition and also to get everything in. For most writing, especially of shorter pieces, a formal outline seems to me mostly a waste of effort. This is true partly because the organization frequently emerges, or at least changes, as the writing progresses.

I am, however, generally much concerned about organization, uncomfortable until I can see some kind of pattern developing. I sometimes even try to develop a gimmick, more or less arbitrary, as an organizing device. For example, I remember a few years ago writing a paper on progress in the teaching of writing over the past thirty years, and I held it together partly with Hamlet's taunt to Polonius that he might get younger "if like a crab you could go backward." This expressed a generalization about the subject on which I could focus; I used the quotation as title and introduction and referred to it from time to time to provide transitions. I am probably more partial to this device than I should be, since it may be artificial and may influence thought more than it should.

TRANSITIONS

I think that I have more trouble contriving ways to clarify the organization than in any other part of the writing process. To produce transitional sentences and paragraphs that are both clear and graceful I find difficult, but I try. And I sometimes remember the kind of advice I give —to repeat part of an idea from a previous paragraph in introducing a new one, to keep the reader constantly aware of where he is and where he is going, and so on.

DEVELOPMENT

For development or invention the most useful precept I know is to work for specification, and I do find myself following this advice. That is, most of my thinking as I write attempts to find examples, illustrations, specific instances to support whatever generalizations I'm wanting to establish. Some material of this sort has occurred to me during whatever preliminary thinking I have done, and for any kind of research project material is presumably already in notes. But for most writing I find myself filling in as I write—relying on logical development or memory much of the time, but often stopping to look at notes or check a book. I don't systematically ask myself questions according to a pattern of heuristics or explore Aristotle's *topoi,* although I think it might sometimes be helpful if I did.

PARAGRAPHS

I tend to compose in paragraphs, to be conscious of their form. I am, of course, aware of various studies showing that the prescriptions of Alexander Bain and all his successors do not consistently reflect what happens in good prose. I do not suggest that good writing requires composing paragraphs. But I am more comfortable thinking of paragraphs as more than punctuation—as units of prose, partly, I suppose, because at some stage I was taught they should be, but mainly because I admire prose that develops in paragraphs.

I have in textbooks attempted to describe the movement of prose as a series of topic-comment units. These units may be independent or may be combined in a few ways, usually in some kind of hierarchical relationship. I try to organize the units in paragraphs, depending on how they can be logically fitted together. I even like to try to work with a topic sentence of some sort; and when I can manage, I like the notion of a concluding sentence. I'm especially pleased on the occasions when I can end a paragraph with a sentence that provides a succinct summary, is not repetitious, and seems to me clever. I think of the ironic turns that end a lot of Samuel Butler's paragraphs.

I do not want to suggest that paragraphing is the most important procedure in writing, even that it is essential. But I find it useful, especially in revision, to look at paragraph patterns in order to check on other aspects of the writing. I don't check systematically. Francis Christensen used to say that he thought about levels of coordination and subordination in his paragraphs as he wrote. I think he probably did, because in his rhetorical analyses of prose he had described paragraphs in those terms. And I can't avoid thinking of prose in the terms in which I have described it—as sequences of commitments and responses and topic-comment units. These relationships are in the back of my mind as I write and revise, although I am not consciously testing them. Considering them, at least casually, may reveal inadequacies in development, for instance, or a break in the continuity of the ideas.

In revision I sometimes move indentations—that is I break up the topic-comment units differently, usually more frequently. I don't always turn out paragraphs that fit a pattern, and that doesn't bother me.

REVISION AND EDITING

I revise a good deal while I am writing a first draft—redo sentences often several times, go back and insert something I have forgotten, move things around. I'm uncomfortable about leaving matters I know are wrong for later revision. I tend to stop progress to check a fact or fill in a quotation. I sometimes even take time to retype a paragraph I've messed into illegibility to be sure I'm satisfied with it. The word processor cuts the time on some of this revision; but I have not yet learned to do final editing on a screen. I'm not comfortable until I have a printed copy to work with, and I almost always find additional changes to make.

Because I do so much agonizing over a first draft, I write relatively slowly, but I also find that I need less time for later reworking. My usual procedure is to let the first draft sit for at least a couple of days and then go over it thoroughly word by word. Then I check on that revision with another run-through, and then I'm usually ready for a final copy. There are exceptions to this procedure. For one thing, I sometimes keep tinkering with the first draft for several days as I get new ideas. I may think of a better example or illustration or a new way of clarifying something I've had difficulty explaining, and I may tear up the manuscript fairly extensively. Furthermore, something like a full-length textbook, especially one written in collaboration, may require much more extensive revision. Laird and I have redone some sections of an edition of *Modern English Handbook* a dozen times. On the other hand, a newspaper column may have to get into print in a hurry.

Both in revising as I write and in later reworking and editing, I more or less consciously follow a few procedures that depend on rhetorical precepts, especially concerning sentences and diction.

With sentences, I automatically consider continuity from one sentence to the next, the logic of the predication, unintentional repetition of words or sounds, rhythm. Occasionally I read a passage aloud. When I am hit with a sentence that somehow jars, I rely on a couple of specific approaches to revision. I check on the subject, try other possible subjects. This, of course, leads to trying other basic sentence patterns. I find this useful because it pushes me toward recasting the whole sentence rather than tinkering with what is usually the wrong pattern. I look for sentences that might best be broken up. I'm suspicious of my semicolons.

I usually in revision spot a few words that seem not quite right. I can spend a good deal of time fussing about them, especially if I am sure that exactly the right word exists if I could only think of it. I sometimes even try a thesaurus, occasionally with success.

I also in revision work consciously to tighten, to cut repetition or unnecessary words. I try to stay especially alert to a few specific characteristics of my first drafts—a tendency to overqualify, for example. I keep a sharp eye out for the word *some,* for *I think* and *it seems,* for *a kind of.* I watch for an excess of transition words, since I tend to pile up sentences beginning with *but* and *and,* partly, I suppose, to reassure me on the first draft that I know where I'm going. Whenever something strikes me as not quite right, I consider first the possibility of cutting it.

As I look back over this, I suspect that I have exaggerated the orderliness of my habits. Not everything I have mentioned occurs every time I write. I am certainly less occupied with procedures when I write than I may have suggested here. I don't sit down and say to myself, "Now I am going to do pre-writing" or "Now I will consider the subjects of my sentences." On the other hand, I am a little surprised, as I try to describe what I do, at how often what I do seems consistent with the rhetorical principles I consider most important. This may be, of course, only my way of defining what I consider important. But I find in it some reassurance that sometimes, at least, I either practice what I preach or preach what I practice.

Richard L. Graves is professor of English education at Auburn University. He teaches courses in rhetoric composition and in the summer serves as director of the Sun Belt Writing Project. Much of his time and interest is devoted to assisting Alabama teachers develop programs in composition.

A native of Texas with a Ph.D. from Florida State, Graves has published articles in various NCTE journals and most recently has edited Rhetoric and Composition: A Sourcebook for Teachers and Writers *(1980). His major interests center around the composing process and the continuing growth of adult learners.*

A DANCE TO THE MUSIC OF THE MIND

Richard L. Graves
Auburn University

Writing is a distinctive human act: it defines the human condition, wrenches order from chaos, turns darkness into light, and gives life and meaning to what was once ordinary and dead.

The metaphor which best describes my composing routine is that of dancing. When everything is just right—the ideas are clicking, the words are coming—then writing is like dancing. Mind and pen move in concert, mind leading and pen following, but both together, graceful, sure, fluid, and true. When my ear catches the music, I am lost in a reverie of thought. Someone passes my office but I don't notice. Time slips away. On the telephone I lie. "I have an appointment" is the excuse I give so I can be alone with my work. I am conscious only of the words going down on the page. I lip read each one. Inhale. Exhale. Scratch out. Move forward, searching for the right word, the right turn of expression. I try to hold on to some elusive thought slipping in and out of my mind.

At the outset there is an outline, a pattern, a routine of steps to follow. But so often the dance itself takes over and creates its own choreography. It moves spontaneously to some distant music. Listening, enchanted, I am caught up in the music.

Then, later, the spell is broken. I go back and reread, decipher the scratchy notes, searching for the essence of the idea, listening again for some hint of the music that lies buried there. This is the revision stage. This is like watching a videotape of your own mind. Now I'm the director, critical, demanding, and arrogant, but always just below the gruff exterior is a haunting memory of the music. I am at my desk. At the left is a scratchy page from yesterday, or perhaps just an hour ago.

109

Now I am writing in neat cursive script, copying word for word, still lip reading, going slowly, meticulously examining words, rejecting some, choosing others, carefully crafting the whole thing. Most of all, I try to make the language match the subtle rhythm of the music. "When I have finished, will the reader hear what I have heard? Do my words really do it justice?"

This process then repeats itself, sometimes up to four times, before I send a sheaf of yellow pages down to those beautiful people who neatly type everything. I've just realized that I don't "send," but invariably hand-carry every important piece of writing to them even though there is no chance that anything could be lost. Subconsciously, symbolically, carrying the sheaf to the typist is like carrying a gift to the altar. In those yellow pages is the distilled essence of my life. What is there, for better or worse, is the best part of me. I have come to understand what Quintilian means in saying that "It is writing that provides that holy of holies where the wealth of oratory is stored." The act of writing is a holy act. It distills the essence of our thought, the essence of our being. Writing is a distinctive human act: it defines the human condition, wrenches order from chaos, turns darkness into light, and gives life and meaning to what was once ordinary and dead.

I normally write every morning (except weekends) from about eight o'clock until ten. When confronted with a deadline, however, I sometimes work in the afternoon or early evening. If I spend more than two or at most three hours in concentrated effort, my writing tends to lose its edge. I like to let it simmer, to see how it looks on the page, and test it against my original thought. I write with a Pilot pen on a yellow 8½ × 11 tablet. I fill up a page, which is always scratchy and messy, then neatly copy, editing as I go along. When I have finished the neat copying, I carefully number the pages at the top and put a circle around the numbers. This will remind me later that a particular page is not a rough original but edited copy. Days turn into weeks, and the collection of numbered pages grows. Finally, when I have finished, I go back and reread the whole and start the editing process all over again. When the manuscript is in good shape I take it to the typist. The typed copy is returned to me, and the editing process starts again. Usually there will be three or four typed editions of a paper before I send it to an editor. The process of writing a fifteen- to twenty-page manuscript normally takes some three or four months. My students know I'm an easy mark when they ask for more time to finish their work. I need time too, and understand.

These are the exteriors of writing, the fetish part. These are the small, personal idiosyncrasies that become more or less habitual and make the inner process more comfortable. If for some reason I were deprived of these externals, I don't think it would appreciably alter my work, for writing is first of all an internal act. Writing originates in an idea, a small seed, and the externals are there just to protect and nourish the seed. Like the flower in the crannied wall, writing sometimes has to grow out of a hostile environment. I wonder. If my environment were more hostile, would that force me to improve the quality of my work, to pay closer attention to my thought? It is strange that we continually seek to make ourselves more comfortable, but sometimes discomfort prods us into action. Sometimes pain creates a starker beauty, finds a deeper truth.

Recently I have started keeping a process journal, an informal record of my thoughts and writing activity. What triggered this is an idea that came to me and still continues to haunt me. The idea is that we teachers of composition should teach writing as a spiritual act. That is, we should encourage our students to write about subjects that are of supreme significance to them. Originally I thought that the idea could be developed into an essay for a professional journal, but more recently I have begun to see it as a book-length manuscript. The rough notes give a clear picture of the embryonic pre-writing stage of a manuscript. Most important, they bring back to my conscious mind ideas that over the weeks may have been lost. Reviewing the process journal is like seeing in bright sunlight a picture that was originally painted in darkness.

I tend to work on several projects simultaneously. My process journal was devoted exclusively to the idea of writing as a spiritual activity, yet at the same time I was working on the manuscript you are now reading. Looking back, I see that this is a way of life with me. Several things will be going on at once, each in a different stage of completion. Thus in a way my mind is like an assembly line, one idea just beginning to find shape while another is being finished in final form.

There is yet another aspect of my writing which is important, the influence of my students. We don't dare tell our students that they are the teachers and we the learners, yet there is so much truth here. Over the years my students have profoundly influenced my writing. The reason for this is that I think of my classroom as a kind of laboratory; I like to try things and experiment. I like to engage the minds of my students, much the way Clayton Lewis describes in the Spring 1984 issue of *Freshman English News.* When something I believe in doesn't work, I go back to my office and ask why. Consequently my syllabus is always flexible; it is never more important than the students' growth as writers.

Some classes always stand out. Last spring I taught an off-campus graduate seminar on the composing process. We were all experienced teachers and all interested in becoming better teachers of writing. Each Tuesday evening we met for four hours, which normally would seem an eternity, but the time seemed to fly by—at least for me it did. It was indeed an animated and stimulating group. I included various activities in the seminar—reading current composition theorists, panel discussions, individual reports—but the overall success, I think, can be attributed to two activities. Each evening we devoted time for individual writing, and we read our work aloud in small groups. As the quarter progressed, I sensed a growing bond among the members of the group. Through reading our own writing and listening to the writing of fellow teachers, we came to appreciate one another more fully. Our writing permitted us to know one another in ways that would not be possible in the typical lecture setting. The growing bond was symbolized in the time we allotted for a snack. During the first meeting there was no food, but we asked if two people would volunteer to bring a snack for each of the following sessions. As the quarter progressed the snacks became more and more elaborate. It was as though the care put into preparing the evening meal symbolized the growing bond among members of the group.

I learned much from the seminar. I was reminded of the awesome power of writing. The pen is indeed mightier than the sword—than the computer too! The experience brought into focus the importance of human relations in the teaching process. The people I came to know that spring are so much more than just social security numbers on mass-produced printouts. Now some mornings when I walk down the hall and inadvertently eavesdrop on a colleague lecturing some fifty sleepy sophomores, I smile, inwardly, and remember the seminar last spring. I think about engagement of the mind. About dialogue. About listening, intently. About asking and probing, gently. But most of all I think about writing. I think about what education really is, or could be. I go back to my office and ask myself about the meaning of learning and growing, and how it (not "they") happens.

During that spring quarter I also taught a 101 section of freshman composition. Some readers will already have caught the ominous note here: 101 in the spring quarter. This is the class for those who failed 101 in the fall, for transfer students, for high-school students entering college early or late, for students with registration problems. In short, 101 in the spring quarter is often a collection of misfits, failures, and dropouts trying to drop back in. There were twenty-six in my class that quarter; some of them admittedly were good students, but most had severe writing problems. It turned out to be one of the most satisfying teaching experiences I have ever known.

The class began as one would expect. On the surface there was sullen hostility and cool detachment, which was really a mask for the depression, humiliation, and impotence of mind and spirit which we English teachers sometimes unconsciously promote. Certainly these students exhibited problems with the conventions of written English, but in so many cases their real problem was a human problem: a profound lack of confidence in themselves as writers.

The methods I used in the class were quite ordinary. First of all we spent time writing in every class session. From time to time we read our work orally, and sometimes put it on overhead projection. We read selected essays, usually "selected" by me for their broad general interest. I believe the key to the eventual success of the class derived from the students' freedom in choosing their subject matter for writing, their constant immersion in the writing and revision process, and the encouragement and positive reinforcement they received for their work.

Not that the class was totally successful. There were two Fs, one because of excessive absences, the other because of a consistent pattern of error that showed little change over the quarter. Nevertheless it was gratifying that nine students who at the outset demonstrated severe problems in syntax, usage, and mechanics made remarkable gains during the quarter. The more they wrote, the more their hostility melted away. They began to trust their instincts as writers and to lose their paralyzing fear of making an error. They began to focus on *their* message. In short these young, reluctant writers discovered the joy and power of writing. They reminded me of someone who had been crippled from birth and now had learned to walk for the first time. I cheered their halting steps. I encouraged them. They grew stronger, and I could see their growth.

The class confirmed for me what a magnificent thing believing in yourself really is. Writing needs the magic of belief in order to reach out and achieve all that is within the realm of human possibility. It needs a warm and caring environment. What about basic skills, style, and all the other conventions of English? When there is a lot of writing, rewriting, and group reading, then errors tend to fall by the wayside. When there is little writing and a lot of teacher talk about errors, then errors tend to multiply. That's just one lesson I learned from a 101 class during the spring quarter.

But the quarter is short, and I ask myself, "Who will their next teacher be? Will their next teacher build on this foundation? Or will it be someone who is too quick to criticize and punish, someone who is anxious to display his or her own erudition but unconcerned about students' growth as writers?" I have hopes, but I fear there is too little communication among us teachers, and too much emphasis on the traditional paradigm.

In conclusion I would like to mention some of the larger aspects of life that influence my writing indirectly. These often go unnoticed but are nevertheless important. For example, maintaining good health, cultivating friendships and good human relations, and finding time for solitude and reflection all contribute to the writing process. All these are parts of a larger pattern, a rhythm of living. All fit together, each part important in its own way yet contributing to the welfare of the whole. I am one of those who believe that regular exercise and a good diet are necessary for keeping a keen mental edge. Consequently, I try to allow some time each day for vigorous physical activity, and I try to keep plenty of fruit, vegetables, cheese, and white wine in the pantry. Good human relations are also important. A lively party, a family camping trip, or just being with friends all contribute indirectly in their own way to the quality of time spent in writing.

So many forces influence our work, it is difficult to sort them all out. We can point to some specifics, but there are so many unspoken influences, some of which may be more important than we consciously realize. However, there is one idea with which I feel certain all the contributors to this volume would agree: "Writing itself is a great teacher."

Hans P. Guth is professor of English at San Jose State University in California, where he was chosen Outstanding Professor in 1972. He received his Ph.D. from the University of Michigan at Ann Arbor, where he also did his first teaching.

*Guth has published numerous articles on rhetoric and composition, including "The Politics of Rhetoric" (*College Composition and Communication, *1972) and "Composition Then and Now" (*Rhetoric Quarterly, *1980). His articles on Spenser, Kafka, and other literary subjects have appeared in* Proceedings of the Modern Language Association *and other journals. His best-known composition text is* Words and Ideas *(5th ed., 1980); more recent books include* New English Handbook *(2nd ed., 1985) and, with Renée Hausman,* Essay: Reading with the Writer's Eye *(1984). As the author and editor of high-school texts, Guth helped pioneer productive sentence work and modern approaches to composition at the high-school level.*

In June 1984, Guth codirected with Gabriele Rico the first annual Young Rhetoricians Conference at San Jose, which was devoted to the current upgrading of composition as an academic subject and brought together young-in-spirit rhetoricians for a lively festival of the art of rhetoric.

HOW I WRITE: FIVE WAYS OF LOOKING AT THE BLACKBIRD

Hans P. Guth

San Jose State University

What makes inductive writing self-activating is that we have a built-in human need to order our perceptions, to make sense of the flow of experience, to find our way in the world. To use John Dewey's terms, just as there is a "hunger of the eyes" for color and texture and shape, so there is built into our minds a search for order and a quest for certainty.

How do I write? The "how" part of this question is easier to answer than the underlying more provocative "why": How do we as writers do what we do—and why? What compulsions activate our typewriters? What disks program our word processors? What tunnels limit our vision? Equally provocative (or perhaps only more sobering) is the implied "so what" part of the question: Assuming that we can rationalize what we do, of what use is such an understanding to other writers?

To shed light on the provocative "why" and the sobering "so what" under the puzzling behavioristic surface, let me take up in turn five ways of looking at the process of writing—five paradoxical dimensions of my own practice as a writer that may (or may not) have parallels in the experience of other writers. Certainly, by the time we read the third or fourth story or book by an author such as Doris Lessing or Charles Dickens, we begin to develop a sense of the same writer at work: We begin to recognize the particular window through which the author makes us look at the world as well as the kinds of phenomena most likely to catch our eye there; we begin to recognize the grievances to which the author returns or the mental adversaries with whom he or she does battle; we begin to recognize the rhetorical strategies and forensic flourishes in which she or he delights; we begin to recognize a characteristic stance toward the reader—confidant, disciple, fellow victim, or coconspirator.

As we subject our own more humble writing efforts to similar scrutiny, we may well discover a similar range of essential motives and procedures, of underlying purposes and instrumental modes. Above all, we are likely to be struck by the common denominator that our writing (when it is any good) shares with that of the great compulsives: True writing is *self-activating:* Whatever its external occasions and incentives, it is in large degree self-motivating, generating its own energy and its own punishments and rewards. In fact, the most basic task of any teacher of writing is to push this essential ON button—to make the student writer discover the intrinsic, built-in rewards that make the equally built-in disappointments and perplexities worthwhile.

GENESIS: THE RITUAL OF WRITING

Back to the how. Looking in the mirror to limn this self-portrait of the practicing writer, I see a member in good standing of the Gutenberg Brigade, one of the print people, surrounded by the paraphernalia of his trade—pen in hand at a cluttered desk, hemmed in by stacks of manila folders sticking out from their too small pigeonholes built into crowded shelves, facing piles of proofs, drafts, clippings, offprints, and miscellaneous stuff (which I MUST CLEAN UP!). My behavior in this familiar setting is of a kind that no doubt the graphs and electrodes of some ingenious Masters and Johnson of the writing process could ferret out, although it might strike them as a strange, erratic, fumbling ritual indeed. It is, however, a kind of ritual and, as such, has method in it. Perhaps we do in fact start to think of ourselves as writers when our at one time intermittent, ad hoc writing efforts become a familiar ritual, and often a compulsive one (and when other claims on our time, no matter how meritorious or unavoidable, begin to be felt as impositions or intrusions). I write; therefore, I am!

Actually, in keeping with the nonlinear, nonsequential nature of the process I am about to describe, a vital part of the ritual does not take place at a desk at all; it is done standing up, without using the hands. While taking a shower, or while pretending to listen politely to a colleague's conversation, I am mentally sketching a paragraph or roughing out a chapter, fitting together incipient ideas and bits of prose like a plumber assembling lengths of pipe, or like a cabinetmaker tentatively fitting together the pieces of wood that will eventually become a beautifully interlocking, smoothly fitting specimen of the cabinetmaker's art.

This is a stage of half-formed ideas, of thoughts in ferment, but also of hitting on a (to me) felicitous metaphor or on a (to me) clever or inspiring line. This is the stage of free association, of the creative momentum —it is often the happiest stage and has in it some of the feeling of dawn, when we sense with Thoreau that indeed the morning wind forever blows and the poem of creation continues uninterrupted.

Gradually, this first stage gives way to a second, a stage of anxiety —there is a strong urge to get something down on paper lest, like Coleridge's vision of the Khan's pleasure dome, it fade when the euphoria wears off. This rough-draft stage is the scribbling stage, when I fill soon-to-be-crumpled-up pages with notes and reminders to myself, with some key ideas and key phrases spaced out on a still half-empty page to be soon crowded by details and salient examples while, like some humble Michelangelo of the writing process, I apply paint to flesh out or realign what was at first only a very rough design. There is much crossing out and rephrasing going on at this stage, with a whole paragraph or passage eventually transferred to an intermediate cleaner page—or left in limbo for a time while I am busy on some other part of the scaffolding, attending to some crucial later (or earlier) part of the argument. (My friends who rely on the INSTANT-REWRITE buttons and the verbal garbage disposals of their word processors watch this whole inefficient second stage with knowing winks.)

The rough-draft stage soon begins to shade over into a third stage of impatience, of pushing toward completion—I begin to type (as I am typing this article before the rough draft is finished and while I am still thinking). The thesis, the outline, and the vital connections have emerged in their quasi-final shape. I will fill in the still very fragmentary final section (in this article, on audience) with some crucial ideas that I jotted down at lunch. I am still hunting for a quotation or two and an excerpt from a student paper that I know I have somewhere in my notes. I will make strategic revisions while I type, and some crucial oversights or weak links will come to me as I drive or feed the cat. It is now just a matter of pounding away at the typewriter—and voila! it is written. It is ready to go forward to be greeted by the quibbles of editors, the plaudits of the faithful, the measured praise of the judicious, the carping of the bilious, and the strictures of a James C. Sledd.

INDUCTION: THE RHETORIC OF DISCOVERY

Having painted this self-portrait of a writer—drawing on notes and files, establishing tentative connections among disjointed materials, always seeming to work on several levels of the scaffolding at once—I am ready to ask the question that my high-school biology teacher used to ask:

What does all this tell us? It tells us first of all what most of us already know: Writing is not an orderly deductive process. Textbooks that used to describe it as such always seemed to me to withhold from the student writer vital information, like recipes failing to tell us to wait for the dough to rise when baking our own bread. Handbooks that asked students to write a theme by following a beautiful outline always seemed to me to skirt the vital question: Whence the beautiful outline? Instructors who asked students to start with a thesis and then proceed to fill it in with "vivid" examples always made me want to shout: "No, no! You've got it backwards!" A theme in progress, like a book in the making, is a struggling *toward* a thesis; it is a body of material *in search of* an outline.

No doubt my aversion to premature abstraction, my suspicion of ready-made patterns, resulted from a personal spiritual history: When I started teaching freshman composition, the aim of the young ambitious academic liberal was (forgetting for the moment about the comma splice) to promote the great urban renewal of the mind—to clear the minds of our students of the small-town Republicanism of their Midwestern parents in order to provide the *tabula rasa* on which bold, fresh thoughts and new insights could then be sketched. We were the spiritual heirs of the writers whom the intellectual and moral bankruptcy of two world wars had left with an abiding contempt for glib talk, for resounding abstractions, for self-righteous announcements. (George Orwell: "Official war propaganda, with its disgusting hypocrisy and self-righteousness, tends to make thinking people sympathize with the enemy.") We taught that "A poem should not mean / But be"; with Archibald MacLeish in "Memorial Rain," we tuned out the felicitous words of the French ambassador eulogizing the grateful dead to listen, with the bones in the sand, for the rain. We taught short stories by Ernest Hemingway, with characters in them who had acquired a deep-seated suspicion of all beautiful and edifying claptrap—determined to hold on to a few simple realities, without "all this talking."

Ours was the ideology of anti-ideologists, the party line of independents; our middle name was Irony; years later, we still wince at the big beautiful words (excellence, love) that roll trippingly off the tongue and cost nothing. Years later, we still watch in sardonic silence people making a big show of instituting school prayer for students who do not have a prayer; we watch with grim satirical eyes some of our less advanced fellow citizens inveighing against the theory of evolution.

In the intellectual climate of my own beginnings as a writer, the only honest way to write seemed to be to write *inductively*—to build a piece of writing from the ground up. In graduate school, I wrote seminar papers fiercely adhering to the *docta ignorantia* model, brushing aside the derivative cant of critics, moving into Restoration comedy, for instance, to ask: "What have we got here? What do these people do? What do they say?" With luck, the graduate professor reading the paper with the patience of Job would be rewarded with a carefully traced pattern of action and interaction, of witty protagonist and ironic foil, that took shape the way the lineaments of a human face emerge under the restorator's hands from under the grime and incrustations of centuries on a Greek bronze statue newly fished from the bottom of the sea.

I wrote my first composition text the way I had graduate papers. Such books then were full of unctuous, self-approving, condescending professorial talk (students were forever being "careless" in their writing); they were full of half-truths that for decades one New England schoolmaster had copied from another; they bored me to tears not only with their wooden, unreadable prose but with the irrelevance of the opaque formulas they offered my students in order to improve their writing ("The subject complement is the predicate nominative that modifies the subject of the verb"; "Use the inflectional -*s* ending for the third person singular of the indicative mood of the present tense of the finite verb"). The only remedy seemed to be to proceed inductively (forget "what the market wants"). Since a textbook in a writing course should be about writing (then a revolutionary idea), the thing to do seemed to be to look at actual examples of student writing, at actual student themes, to ask: "What have we got here? When it works, how does it work? When it fails, how does it fail?" ("We publish," said the rejection slip from Norton, for a book that went on to sell a million copies, "only material of the highest quality." It was then the fashion to print student papers only as horrible examples, bleeding red ink all over the page.) I remember the faces of several of the students whose writing I printed (and pondered) in the book—one of the true compensations of teaching composition, to me, has always been that the students who come to us first as mere anonymous numbers in a computer printout gradually, through what they write for us, become human beings in whose successes and failures we share and who cheer us with their native intelligence and mother wit.

The book talked about the voyage of discovery, the charting of unknown continents, that is honest writing. Writing is the art of making up one's mind, it said. Start close to what you know, it said—close to authentic observation, close to what you have lived through or witnessed at first hand. Mobilize your resources. Use your eyes and ears. Write inductively. This does not mean that you will not often (in fact, most of the time) start a paper with a strong thesis or a paragraph with a topic sentence. It does mean that such a key assertion will be an *earned* generalization, an *informed* opinion.

What makes inductive writing self-activating is that we have a built-in human need to order our perceptions, to make sense of the flow of experience, to find our way in the world. To use John Dewey's terms, just as there is a "hunger of the eyes" for color and texture and shape, so there is built into our minds a search for order and a quest for certainty. People who know something about how to teach children to read and write talk about "storying"—about the primordial, archetypal human need to fit events into a meaningful pattern. Here is the crux of writing, and of the teaching of writing: The successful writer has developed a sense of how a meaningful pattern emerges from honest but at first miscellaneous observation. The successful writer knows how to work out a structure that unifies and informs a rich body of authentic material. This is where the true satisfaction and excitement of writing come in, as order emerges from confusion.

We sense the satisfaction that results from the honest search and the excitement of discovery in the occasional truly first-rate, truly illuminating piece of literary criticism: Adrienne Rich, in "Jane Eyre: The Temptations of a Motherless Woman" (reprinted in *On Lies, Secrets, and Silence*), takes us along in search of Charlotte Brontë's version of "what it meant to be born a woman"; she retraces with us the spiritual pilgrimage of her heroine—"a person determined to live, and determined to choose her life with dignity, integrity, and pride." We see the pattern of Jane Eyre's life take shape—from her early encounter with callousness and economic dependence, through "the central temptation" of "romantic love and surrender," to her discovery of women "in real and supportive relationship to each other," to her refusal to be used by a man (St. John) for his own however noble cause. We share in the critic's sense of fitness and satisfactory completion when at the end of her essay we see Jane Eyre joining in marriage with Rochester "in economic independence and by her free choice" and "without sacrificing a grain of her Jane Eyre-ity"—thus illustrating Charlotte Brontë's ideal of a true "erotic and intellectual sympathy," of human relations "without painful shame or damping humiliation."

What does my admiration for the honest search and my deeply ingrained affinity for inductive procedures mean for the teaching of writing? Like everyone else today (so much for trying to be different), I stress the students' gathering and shaping of materials. I stress preliminary exploration, the *working up* of material for the students' themes, so that the thesis of a paper will not be half-baked or opinionated or only half-believed but instead an assertion that resulted from honest observation and fresh thought. I try to break through the cliché barrier by sending students out into the city with a pad and pencil, so that they will come back and tell me what they saw:

An old lady groveling at a rummage sale
Antiseptic hours painted on a banker's door
Giant clocks

Alternate one-way streets
And people . . .
Beggars waiting for eternity in the park
Pickets for hire
Thrift shops and teenagers . . .

Increasingly, I run through sets of exploratory questions or construct sample outlines for a paper as a group activity in class, so that my students can experience as a group the shaping and pulling together that is at the heart of composition. I teach modes and patterns not as rigid formulas created on the eighth day but as possible organizing strategies, to be adapted and implemented by my students for purposes of their own.

No doubt, in much written-to-order writing, we cut the cloth to the customer's specifications. Nevertheless, within the constraints of an assignment, the writer's true challenge and reward are to make a pattern take shape that does justice to the subject and to the task at hand. The first piece of writing I was ever paid for was a translation and adaptation of a British detective novel that I prepared for serialization in a German newspaper. I vividly remember the euphoria (aided no doubt by innumerable cups of tea) that accompanied the cutting and rearranging and shaping I did to turn what had been a good story for a British audience into a good story for the German reader. Our students, through a series of gradually more challenging assignments, have to develop their competence and confidence in doing some shaping and rearranging and pulling together of their own. That is what a good composition course is all about.

DIALECTIC: THE RHETORIC OF DIALOGUE

However, . . . On the other hand, . . . Admittedly, . . . It is only fitting that a look at the dialectic dimension of writing should start with a large *However*. The balance in our teaching of composition may be tilting from the deductive models of the past to the inductive models of the present; however, we should not forget the limitations of induction as a model of how we think and write. Skeptics will be quick to remind us of the creative hypothesis, the unacknowledged agenda, the intuitively seized configuration (or gestalt), or the hidden premises that shape much of what goes on in our minds. There is of course no real *tabula rasa*. We do not really, like "Adam and maiden" in Dylan Thomas's poem, walk with the spellbound horses onto the pristine fields of praise; instead, we walk onto fields already crossed by well-trodden cowpaths and littered with other people's milk cartons and McDonald's wrappers. More often than not our *docta ignorantia*, our "learned ignorance," is not a real starting at the beginning but a studied, deliberate ignoring of the scholasticism of others in order to clear space for doctrines of our own.

Much thinking takes place in the give-and-take of dialogue; rather than generalizing cautiously and judiciously, we *react,* find fault, provide alternatives, or shore up our defenses. Looking back from this different, and more dialectic, perspective at my history as a writer, I realize how much of my writing has always been triggered by the assertions of others. Much of it has been *counter*statement, *counter*-argument. I write about Kafka, for instance, to protect him from critics reading into his anxious prose religious or psychoanalytic certainties alien to the spirit of his earnestly argumentative characters forever trying not to lose their bearings in a universe that at any turn in the road threatens to turn absurd. "I must with improvised ingenuity somehow fit all this together in my head," says his country doctor, who speaks also for K. of *The Castle,* forever earnestly searching for the rational clues to the workings of an irrational world.

For me as a young student of language, my culture heroes (and the true leaders of our leaderless and fragmented profession) were the language scholars and linguists and lexicographers doing battle against traditional ways of teaching (?) mastery of our language. They were people such as Jespersen, Fries, Marckwardt, Perrin, Pooley, Bryant, Roberts, and Gorrell, who pitted their erudition, their love of learning, and their love of language, against the traditional pedantries. Their weapon was by definition the counterargument, the strategic counterexample. (The verb *steal* "expresses action," but so surely does the noun *theft,* not to mention the word *action* itself.) There was a grim satisfaction in quoting the truly great on the more whimsical of the "rules" invented by school grammarians: "Give me that man / *That* is not passion's slave" (Hamlet); "My father and my uncle and *myself* / Did give him that same royalty he wears" (Hotspur in *Henry IV,* Part One). Re the traditional rule banning the possessive case for inanimate nouns: "This is my *play's* last scene, here heavens appoint / My *pilgrimage's* last mile . . . My *span's* last inch, my *minute's* latest point . . ."

Four inanimate possessives in six lines of a poem by John Donne. Pow! Touché! This is not to say that the challenger is always right. Rather, the promise of dialectic is this: From the clash of thesis and antithesis, some fuller, more balanced, or at least less desperately dense and parochial view will emerge. (I spent a large part of my doctoral dissertation arguing against what I considered excessive inductive leaps in the early writings of Kenneth Burke, only to find myself at the end converted to many of his basic views on the private agendas that motivate writing.)

Our teaching of both language and literature turns stale when it is not dialectic enough. My literary heroes and heroines have often been the characters who *talk back:* Antigone talking back to the imperious demands of the state; Hotspur playing the glorious rebel to the ingrate, politic Bolingbroke; Milton's Satan defying the Almighty "in dubious battle on the plains of Heaven"; Thoreau teaching disobedience to the rule of the jingoistic majority. The great confrontations create the drama (both literal and figurative) of literature; Shakespeare's drama provides the ideal school for apprentice critics because it forces them to weigh the rival claims of the lovers and Mercutio, of Richard II and Bolingbroke, of Caesar and Brutus.

The students in our composition classes need to experience the charge of adrenalin that results from the confrontation of opposites; they need to experience the urgency and excitement that a writer feels when prodded into action to say: "I have listened to this long enough —now my turn!" A composition class begins to succeed when students forget that the topic is merely an assignment and tell us (or each other): "On this *I* have something to say!" For several years, when prodded by teachers to demonstrate what I mean by true writing (as against phony writing), I have read a passage from a paper written in one of my classes by a vaguely Oriental-looking student who wrote as follows on the topic "Is Prejudice on the Decline?":

> I, personally, am very sensitive to verbal reactions. There is always the question, "What are you?" The mere fact of being questioned makes me stiffen with resentment at the ignorance of those who felt that they had to ask. There have been times when I have been completely at a loss for words on how to reply. I could answer, "American," "Japanese," and "Japanese-American," but somehow I feel unnatural and placed in an awkward situation. I do not consider myself totally American, because of obvious visible differences, nor do I think of myself as Japanese, since I was not brought up with the strict traditions and culture. Being thought of as a member of a minority makes me slightly uncomfortable, and responding to that question has made me sometimes regret my existence.

The reason we know that this is true writing is that it catches us off guard. We forget for a moment our conventional role as grader, corrector, or editor of student writing. Instead, we have for a moment become a reader, responding to real writing.

The minority student rebelling against ethnic labels, the Mormon student setting out to correct misconceptions about Mormons—these students have discovered one of the powerful basic motives that makes much true writing self-activating: the need to set the record straight, the need to talk back to the stereotype, the need to get a hearing for the unfashionable view, the need to assert that the prevailing version is not the only one. We are all "revisionists"; we are all in the business of revising and adapting inherited think schemes to make them fit our own experience and our own needs.

Once our students begin to feel that their version will be heard, we can hope to move on to the stage where they in turn will give a fair hearing to the versions of others. They will begin to see that writing is a transaction between writer and reader, not a manipulation. They may be ready to write papers weighing the pro and con, to write the "Yes, but" paper, to wrestle with the complications and stubborn contradictions of a genuine issue. They may begin to share our admiration for writers whose genuine soul-searching makes their prose shine with a kind of fierce integrity.

MIMESIS: THE RHETORIC OF IMITATION

One more "However, . . ." I have in these earnest chartings of what motivates and guides writing left blank a large other side of the moon. As is our wont as rhetoricians, I have neglected much that is not equally earnest or at least only indirectly so. Actually, like some of the fellow rhetoricians I know best, I have a large frivolous streak imperfectly suppressed. How much of my writing over the years has been parody, occasional verse, hoaxes, *jeux d'esprit!* Why do I burden my files with collections of Creole proverbs ("He who knows how to talk can buy on credit"); with desk-top graffiti ("To the memory of those who died waiting for this class to end"); with famous last words of the illustrious about to expire (Oscar Wilde: "Either this wallpaper goes, or I do"); with imaginary titles for the world's shortest books *(The Humor of Rhetoricians);* with imaginary titles for composition texts that would simultaneously please both the avant-garde and the rear guard *(The Ivy and the Grass, The Whole Error Catalog, The Compleat Radical, Aristotle Now)?*

Parody is the tribute talent pays to genius, Samuel Johnson said (or should have said); and it is often a loving tribute, such as Cornelia Otis Skinner's "For Whom the Gong Sounds," an early entry in a sheer endless line of Hemingway parodies and Ernest-Hemingway-Look-Alike-Contests:

> "This is the Ingles of the street car. He of the boardwalk to come soon."
> "I obscenity in the unprintable of the milk of all street cars." The woman was stirring the steaming mess with the horns of a Mura bull. She stared at Robert Jordan, then smiled. "Obscenity, obscenity, obscenity," she said not unkindly.

My own efforts at parody have ranged from Hamlet on the merits of early retirement ("Whether 'tis nobler in the mind / To take the golden handshake and depart") through the Legend of the Red-Pencil

Knight in Spenserian stanzas to Popeian couplets on the best of all academic worlds:

> Far as the sprawling college plant extends
> The scale of academic rank ascends,
> Where all must full or not coherent be
> And all that rises, rise with due degree. . . .
> What is, is right. Whoever would begrudge it
> Is out of step and sins against the budget.

Parody—playful imitation—and other kinds of word play are of course less frivolous than they might seem to our more terminally earnest colleagues. They are what play is to the child—an exploring of possibilities, a delightful discovering and acting out of new patterns and new powers. Playful language use is powerfully self-activated and self-motivated by our native curiosity and our delight in experimenting with new styles. We know a student is well on the way toward becoming a writer when we read her imitation of Wallace Stevens's "Disillusionment of Ten O'Clock," in which the houses are haunted by white nightgowns—none "green, / Or purple with green rings, / Or green with yellow rings":

Disenchantment at the Dance

> The dance is crowded
> With blue denim.
> There are no dresses
> Of shiny, red satin
> Or shimmering silk.
> No bright feathered hats
> No rhinestone buttons.
> People aren't dancing
> The foxtrot or cha cha.
> Only, once in a while,
> A few underclassmen
> In T-shirts and jeans
> Clap their hands
> Shuffle their feet.
> —Anne Louise Bader in the *English Journal* (May 1980)*

"Art, Nature's ape," said Edward Taylor. Individual artists, in turn, have often gone through an apprentice stage of aping—of discovering and trying out—the styles of other artists. The experimental, playful use of other people's style is similarly a most useful phase of the training of the apprentice writer. It promotes such essential qualities as fluency, a sense of pattern, and a sensitivity to style; it extends the writer's range of possibility. A fuller sense and a fuller command of our linguistic and stylistic resources come partly from reading but also in large measure from trying on styles and strategies for size. By promoting such experimenting (and not by writing *awk* in the margin) do we help the novice overcome the handicaps that beset the inexperienced writer: the tin ear, the wooden prose, the labored transition, the plodding progression, the somniferous monotone.

Classroom work that however diffidently activates the built-in motives and intrinsic rewards involved here is likely to surprise the instructor who is geared to the "find-the-error-in-this-sentence" approach. Some of the most readable writing we are likely to get from an average class is the kind of work with sentence imitation that helps develop the students' sense of pattern, of sentence rhythm, while at the same time allowing them to bring their own intelligence and imagination into play. If we give them a model pattern such as Alexander Pope's "To err is human; to forgive, divine," they will write:

> To whine is childish; to ask is adult.
> To hear is easy; to understand, difficult.
> To prepare is success; to wait, failure.

If we give them an aphorism such as George Bernard Shaw's "Economy is the art of making the most of life," they will write:

> Cooking is the art of making the most of food.
> Procrastination is the art of avoiding today's mistakes by putting
>   them off until tomorrow.

If we give them a sentence with somewhat of a rhetorical flourish (actually simple inversion) such as "Stronger than the mighty sea is almighty God," they will write:

> More precious than a rare gem is a moment alone.
> Heavier than a ton of bricks is a depressed heart.
> More disgusting than sludge is a two-week-old banana.

American education tends to lurch like a drunken sailor from heady intervals of liberated creativity to long dreary spells of "Back-(lash) to Basics." In the literal-minded times when the premium is on gray, drab prose and the twenty-seven rules for the comma, we must not betray our love of language, our commitment to the life of the imagination. We must more often than is our custom express our solidarity with fellow professionals like Martha Mills, who had her students in an Oklahoma middle school write the "Alphabet Challenge," in which each word in turn takes up and begins with the next letter of the alphabet:

The ABC of Questions

Are butterflies carnivorous? Do eagles fly? Goats have infants? Jackals kill lions? Maybe not. Or perhaps questions require solicitude, tenacity, ubiquitousness, vigilance, why? Extraordinary! Yes! Zany!

An Alphabet Challenge

Are birds, cats, dogs endangered? False! Generally, humans ignore jeopardized kinds like mongooses, nightingales, ocelots. People, queerly, rarely see those unusual vertebrates—wonderful extraordinary yellow zebras. (Collected by the Oklahoma Council of Teachers of English, 1976; reprinted by permission)

The best expository prose is alive with the natural rhythms of our language; it testifies to the schooled eye of the author for the apt metaphor and the striking concrete detail. It testifies to a command of and pleasure in language that come in large part from exposure and emulation.

AUDIENCE: TO (AND ABOUT) THE READER

One more look at the blackbird: Looking back over what I have written about writing, I realize that I may seem to have slighted the writer's audience. Like most people, I certainly do not think of my writing as putting messages in bottles that occasionally wash up on the right beach. Perhaps, on the contrary, I take a sense of audience too much for granted. As a situation comedy on television plays to the accompaniment of the laugh track, so my writing proceeds to the accompaniment of the pleased smiles, the puzzled frowns, and predictable objections of the imaginary reader. I backtrack to fill in necessary explanations and shed additional light on the subject; I worry about missing links; I go out of my way to meet legitimate objections; I weigh the strength of forceful assertion as against due caution; I tone down (somewhat) a certain natural tendency toward exuberance and talking with my hands.

An essential part of our task as writing teachers is to help students develop their own sense of audience by *providing* an audience. We act

130 · Hans P. Guth

out for them, in our oral and written comments, the smiles and frowns, the enthusiasm and the recalcitrance, the sensitivity to nuance and the obtuseness of the imaginary reader. Our students need to develop their sense of the help, the incentives, and the rewards the reader needs to respond to their message. Like all true teaching, developing this sense of audience for our students requires a careful balance of positive reinforcement and validation (the well-placed "well done," "well said," "touché!" and "I agree") with judicious criticism and pointed advice.

In spite of the importance of the implied or imaginary audience in all purposeful writing, it seems to me that awareness of audience can easily be mistaught or overtaught. Much modern communication theory places the sender and the receiver too rigidly at opposite ends of the message. Much public relations and advertising works on the assumption that we are here and the audience out there, to be worked upon, conditioned, manipulated, researched, cozened, exploited, presold, suckered, and snowed. Personally, I am always suspicious of the (often very successful) kind of contemporary author who, while seeming to jump through the hoops for the reader, is actually always too deliberately at the controls of the machinery that takes the delighted and bamboozled and terrified audience on the rollercoaster ride toward "the right stuff."

This "I-do-unto-thee" perspective on the audience creates a polarity that we do not sense in much truly first-rate writing. Instead, we find there a sense of solidarity that ideally unites writer and reader in a common enterprise. The writer, no matter how aggressive, bitter, or wrongheaded at times, basically respects the reader. The reader, in turn, in Virginia Woolf's phrase, becomes the writer's "fellow worker and accomplice."

Some of the true classics in our rhetoricians' repertory of first-rate prose convey this sense of community between the writer and the imaginary ideal reader, sharing standards of rationality, sensitivity, or humanity. Although Jonathan Swift often seems to look at human imperfection with savage contempt, he writes for readers whom he assumes capable of sharing his indignation or his outrage. When Marian Evans earnestly preaches to her readers in the programmatic sections of her novels, her basic stance is that of a writer merely bringing out the best in us, appealing to shared human values. The secret of some of the great masters of the modern essay, from George Orwell and E. B. White to Marya Mannes and Adrienne Rich, is that in reading them we find ourselves more intelligent, more sensitive, more honest, or more caring than we are when we are not at our best.

For our students, the discovery of an audience can be a disaster or a revelation. ("Rubbish!" exclaimed my oldest son's stereotypical English teacher after listening to this student's earnest explication of a poem.) It is a tremendously self-motivating and self-activating experience *to be heard,* to get a respectful hearing. Our student writers must have the revelation of discovering that someone actually cared to read, and to take in, their story of false arrest, or of the empty house after the parents' divorce, or of the barrier of silence between father and son. A writer's confidence begins and grows with discovering the power to hold the reader's attention. With growing confidence, our students (like we before them) can hope to discover the more advanced satisfaction that comes from actually making a *difference,* making a dent.

Power in writing means the ability to move the audience one step beyond what it would normally be ready to accept. There is great personal satisfaction in feeling that we have, in whatever small way, made the audience over in our own image.

A FINAL WORD

As teachers of writing, we need to balance our large doses of "do-as-I-say" with adequate helpings of "do-as-I-do." When watching fellow rhetoricians teach, I am cheered by their references to their own experiences and practices as writers; I relish whatever anecdotal lore they can muster about what other writers faced and tried. We need to help our students translate the rules and guidelines of our textbooks into the procedures of the practicing writer. The best advice remains sterile unless our students make it their own through practice, exposure, and emulation. For the benefit of impatient administrators, we talk about writing skills as if they could be isolated and cost-effectively taught. All the time, we know that we are actually dealing with intellectual and linguistic resources that are built up over the years, and about intermeshing habits of observation, structuring, and strategic thinking ahead that we teach by example as much as by fiat or exhortation.

One crucial contribution we can make even in the minimal one-shot composition class is to help our student writers discover the motivations that will make their future progress at least in part self-teaching and self-motivating. These basic built-in motives include the need to make sense of the world—to fit our data or observations into a coherent story; the need to assert ourselves, to talk back to whatever party line or popular prejudice prevails at the moment; the discovery of the delight that comes from using language well; and finally the need for validation, the need to be recognized and to be heard. When we cannot bring these (or some of these) motives into play, the teaching of composition is all uphill, drudgery for student and teacher alike. When we *can* bring these motives into play, we help students progress toward the self-definition, self-assertion, and self-realization that, notwithstanding the lip service these concepts are often paid, are at the core of a liberal education.

C. H. Knoblauch is associate professor of English and director of writing at the State University of New York at Albany, having also taught at Brown University, Columbia University, and New York University. He has published numerous essays on rhetoric, composition theory, and eighteenth-century literature; a textbook on the teaching of writing, The Process of Writing: Discovery and Control *(2nd ed., 1982); and a new book with Lil Brannon,* Rhetorical Traditions and the Teaching of Writing *(1984). He has recently completed a study of eighteenth-century rhetorical theory.*

In addition, Knoblauch has lectured widely to public audiences and presented papers at meetings of the Modern Language Association, the National Council of Teachers of English, the Conference on College Composition and Communication, the American Society for Eighteenth-Century Studies, and other professional organizations, and has served as a consultant to numerous schools and businesses both on the teaching of writing and on writing in the corporate and professional world.

HOW I WRITE: AN IMPROBABLE FICTION

C. H. Knoblauch
State University of New York at Albany

The pen is not a natural extension of my hand in the same sense that my TV remote control is. I don't write to discover myself, to fend off depression, to record my life, to amuse myself or others, to complain to newspapers or department stores, to pass the time, to create art, to speak to friends, or even to conduct pedestrian business as long as a telephone is handy.

It's an immodest venture, but I've been invited after all, so I'm going to tell a story about my writing. I'll be the hero, naturally, and what I say will always have suitably heroic overtones. Unseen villains will be lurking here and there to lend a necessary element of antagonism to the plot, but they will be apparent to the careful reader only in my subtle insistence that what I do is normal and right, while what other people do is peculiar, neurotic, or unproductive. Everything I say will be fictitious, of course, since autobiography cannot be anything else. But I'll try not to lie outright, except as is necessary to satisfy the requirements of logic, organization, and artistic effect—always strictly in the service of portraying my heroic writer-self while assuring my reader that the activity of writing is orderly, rule-governed, and researchable to the last nose scratch and significant pause. To sustain the veneer of plausibility, I plan to create an absolutely unimpeachable narrator, an earnest, even at times solemn, explorer of the mind's mysteries, embodying the detached rigor, the cool efficiency, of the true Researcher. He will weave, I vow, so seductive a tale that a veritable Model of Composing will emerge with hardly a whisper about the secret recalcitrance of the data comprising it. The reader who believes this earnest truth-teller will find satisfying affirmation of a dominant myth of our age—the Myth of Objectivity. My elegant fiction will have been mistaken, as such fictions often are these days, for a reassuring glimpse of the very Nature of Things. The reader who rejects the overwhelming empirical necessity of my model, poor soul, can only be condemned, before the god of the Normative, to unfashionable raving about her presumed distinctiveness.

Where to begin? With a need to write, I suppose, for the why surely has some bearing on the how. In my case, it's a mixture of fear, since I must write to earn a living, and egotism, since seeing one's pronouncements in print can be quite exhilarating. Both of these motives are carefully masked, of course, as a sense of professional responsibility. I'm neither a "born writer" nor a particularly good one. The pen is not a natural extension of my hand in the same sense that my TV remote control is. I don't write to discover myself, to fend off depression, to record my life, to amuse myself or others, to complain to newspapers or department stores, to pass the time, to create art, to speak to friends, or even to conduct pedestrian business as long as a telephone is handy. As the day labor of a professional academic, my writing is essentially a blue-collar task in which the pen (or typewriter or word processor) is the equivalent of a street repairer's jackhammer or a welder's torch— the distinctive instrument of my trade, nothing to get poetic about and nothing to pine for when the clock has been punched, dinner is on the table, and a ballgame is about to start. I write books and articles about rhetoric, writing, and the teaching of writing. I write to understand the composing process, to communicate whatever I've learned, and to offer opinions about what it all means for teaching and, at a stretch, for the quality of human life. The writing is obligatory in my line of work: It's the way academics talk to each other. I write when I'm asked (that's mainly egotism), when I must (that's fear), initially to get tenure, now to get raises and new infusions of praise, to vindicate myself in the face of hostile reviews, and when I feel so inclined (which is seldom except under the influence of fear or ego).

This is not to say that I dislike writing or find it drudgery. I only dislike it and find it drudgery *sometimes.* Often, I quite enjoy writing once I get started at it—enjoy the process of coming to clarity out of confusion. I enjoy the prospect of telling people what I think (at least as long as I believe they will agree with me and fall down in admiration at my feet). But it also frequently gives me both a headache and a backache, just as the jackhammer does, I imagine, when a worker has spent all day vibrating over it. Worse, writing causes endless anxiety about that most dreaded of academic catastrophes—the saying of something indefensibly dumb in print, where it cannot be denied, disowned, or restated as though it had never happened. I'm constantly confronted with the hazards of my trade, obtuse editors who never see the truth as fully as I do, readers who believe that what I've said is either something they already know and therefore trivial or else something that fails to accord with their own opinions and therefore wrong-headed. I must live through my own humiliating, fortunately infrequent (?), but always unavoidably public lapses into genuine stupidity. Consequently, writing is never, for me, the pure joy some people insist it can be. At its best, it is, for me, somewhat like chess, an intriguing intellectual game, distinguished by endlessly evolving patterns of attack and defense, exploratory moves, advances and retreats, errors of judgment, and occasional master strokes. It's an adventure in making coherence out of chaos. It encourages (and sometimes rewards) intellectual discipline, concentration, imaginative risk, and sheer, plodding perseverance. When everything comes together, I'm elated: I've won the game. When it doesn't, or when some myopic editor or reader says it doesn't, I lose and, after a suitable period of mourning, begin again. As in chess, success is never guaranteed but it is eternally possible.

Let's start with the outside: my work habits, so natural and efficient that they should constitute a national standard. I can write at almost any time between 8 A.M. and 2 A.M., optimally between 10 A.M. and midnight, on any day of the week, at any time of the year, both before and after the vernal equinox, although extremely unpleasant Albany Februarys are especially productive periods. I don't depend on visitations from the Muse because she doesn't pay my salary. I've grown accustomed to the feeling that I'd rather be doing something else, just as the welder has, so it doesn't usually get in the way. There are times, to be sure, when I quickly realize that I might as well be doing something else, when the admirably righteous discipline of sitting at my desk is offset by the irretrievably mediocre results of the effort. During these times I avail myself of one of academe's few privileges, the one that justifies its low pay: I declare myself on holiday. Ordinarily, however, I can write when I must—not every day, I hasten to add, but as often as sustaining the illusion of respectable professional effort requires. Some people insist that they do write every day, but I choose to believe that they are either lying or, if telling the truth, inefficient and potentially obsessive. I make no effort to write regularly, and would feel quite sorry for myself if I had to. When I do come to the task, I prefer being at home to being anywhere else, prefer long stretches of uninterrupted time, prefer working at a large, uncluttered desk or table, and prefer cheap ball-points to pencils, typewriters to ball-points, and very expensive word processors to typewriters. I've spent much of my career functioning in unpreferred conditions.

I like to write for long periods of time—eight, ten, even twelve or more hours at a sitting. The first couple of hours are rarely as productive as the later ones, a warming up period where more is eventually thrown away than retained. My concentration seems to improve as the hours go by, to the point finally of blocking out everything else, to the point of requiring an hour or more of decompression time before sleep. I prefer noise while I work, music, even the television—I don't pay much attention to it but miss it when it's absent. Silence is distracting. Once at work, I don't procrastinate much, don't raid the refrigerator, don't chew pencils, don't break for *Days of Our Lives,* don't call up friends, don't read the mail. In fact, I will think of little else but what I'm working on even when I'm briefly away from it, and I will react gracelessly to unanticipated interruptions. I do, of course, sometimes procrastinate prior to writing, for as long as I dare. Knowing that I can produce articles in a few days' time enables me to wait until precisely those few days are left before getting to work. The determining factors are my interest in a piece and my sense of its degree of difficulty. Fascination or panic will drive me early to the task, while insouciance or intellectual hubris will frequently encourage a test of my crisis responses. However, I hate missing deadlines and seldom do, not out of moral conviction but only because of a doubtless neurotic regard for punctuality somehow related to my sense of the order of the world.

I'm a plodder, a nitpicker, a schoolmarm, a malcontent. I'm tyrannized by my own rituals, hence a normal writer in every respect. Prior to getting a word processor (dark days they were!), my habit was to draft in ink on legal-size paper about one and a quarter pages of single-spaced text at a time, stopping at that point regardless of where I was in a paragraph. If the page and a quarter was so full of additions and deletions that it was barely readable, I would handwrite a second version, continuing to revise in the process. Once it was reasonably clean, I would type the draft, still revising constantly, then return to handwriting on legal paper. The moment I became aware of new deficiencies in the typed portion of a manuscript, I would turn to eliminating them before going on. Even if the inadequacies required substantial revision throughout the manuscript, I would feel obliged to complete everything before continuing. Now, with a word processor, I can nitpick far more efficiently, albeit with no greater devotion to the task. I still chisel sentences, revising constantly, and still repair earlier statements before making new ones, but without the tedious shifting from pen to typewriter or the time-consuming paper shuffling that I had learned to endure while my habits were being formed. I now regard the typewriter as a medieval instrument, only slightly more effective than stylus and stone tablet, a sadly deficient moment along the technological time line of human development.

Now, the inside of my composing—the truest test of the story-teller's mischievous art. Most of my writing concerns the same general ideas: the nature of composing, the history of Western thinking about discourse, the relationship between that thinking, over the ages, and the teaching of writing. Therefore, despite all the textbook exhortations to first "find a subject," I always have one close at hand and don't need to look. I'd hazard the guess that most blue-collar writers don't "find" subjects; rather, ideas for writing are implicit in their situations. My business is rhetorical theory; someone else's might be lingerie or money or furniture repair; one's business is one's subject. My way of learning about rhetoric is to talk about it, read about it, and eventually write about it. All three activities are mixed together, continually energizing each other. An article or book will begin as a response to talk or reading or some earlier text that I've written. The stimulus may be curiosity, a desire to find out something I know little about: I might wish to determine, for instance, exactly what Adam Smith contributed to rhetorical theory, and will therefore read Smith, read what others have written about him or his era, and write something myself to create a knowledge of Smith that is truly my own, a personal connection to whatever I've found out from others. Or the stimulus might be puzzlement, a desire to clarify something that I don't understand—let's say, the way a writer's sense of genre conditions choices about what to say or how to say it. Sometimes the stimulus is combative, a wish to represent my understanding of something as it disagrees with someone else's: I might read somewhere that the paragraph is an essential unit of discourse and then write a counter-statement expressing my own views. Sometimes the stimulus is pedagogical, a desire to tell others something I'm quite sure of myself and think they will profit from—let's say a suggestion to teachers that writing can have heuristic value in their classrooms. Finally, I might write in response to people who have written about what I've written—such is the nature of academic conversation. In any case, I'm always writing about the same broad subjects, though with different aims and focuses at different times. I never seem to be able to say exactly, once and for all, everything I think I mean. So, I keep blurting out parts of it in the hope, eventually, of getting it right.

My audience is nearly always some blend of the professional scholar and the teacher—a construct in my own head created out of personal judgments that a typical reader of my work will be very much like myself and will know as much as I do about my subject but not as much as I know about the particular things I wish to say. The only catch is that the scholar part of my imaginary reader often wants me to behave one way while the teacher part wants me to behave another. Hence, my writing is a constant effort at mediating between the two. My scholar wants theory, research, historical reflectiveness, and footnotes, an authoritative but unostentatious display of erudition. My teacher wants examples and practical advice, some sense of what theory and research mean for the real world. The scholar tends toward thoroughness, the teacher toward general essentials. My scholar wants careful, modulated writing, thought-provoking but emotionally neutral, while my teacher wants prose that is lively, entertaining, and committed. Sometimes my sense of an editor-reader helps to adjust this mix, whenever I know the preferences and hobby-horses of a given journal regarding style or tone or mode of argument or type of information. Other times, the subject I'm working on—somewhat more theoretical or somewhat more practical (I don't think I'd care to write on something altogether one or the other)—provides a clue. In any case, this sense-of-a-reader is quite palpable at the start of my writing, helping me to gauge the effect of different choices I might make about what to say or how to say it. That doesn't mean, of course, that I always guess correctly; it only means that I have a reason to try, a motive for making choices.

My writing depends significantly on dialectic: that is, I am far more likely to be argumentative than neutrally descriptive or dialogical in my habits of expression. My customary strategy is to look for opposition, contrast, difference, counterpoint, disjunction, as the way of clarifying, both for myself and others, whatever I mean to say. As a result, my writing tends to be aggressive rather than benign, challenging rather than reassuring (the author as Don Quixote). It provokes, I've come to discover, a stronger kind of disagreement than less pugnacious prose will do. The dialectic helps me to penetrate issues that puzzle me: Are Aristotle and Kenneth Burke saying the same things about discourse? What does "organization" really consist of? What is the meaning of "symbolic action" and how does it work? Is writing teachable, and if so, exactly what about it is teachable? Are people right who say that students need to learn grammar first and the five-paragraph theme later? I find I can grope toward personal answers to such questions more successfully through posing arguments, making distinction after distinction, than through reviewing the literature and counting up opinions on all sides (the author as Librarian, a villain to my hero). My way of thinking about the issues in my field is to place perspectives and statements in opposition to see what kinds of sparks are thrown off: Classical rhetoric versus modern rhetoric, formalist versus epistemic views of discourse, teacher-centered versus student-centered classrooms. The disadvantage in this habitual practice is a tendency (my detractors tell me—but what do they know?) to create straw arguments, or to oversimplify, or even to distort in the effort to locate dissonance. The advantage, when I'm successful (which is nearly always!) is, I fancy, a more sharply delineated position, with more precise discriminations, than I could have achieved in the absence of counterpoint. I walk the tightrope strung across overassertiveness and intellectual distortion (the author as Death-defying Circus Performer), more often falling off in other people's eyes perhaps than in my own.

Once writing, the most significant unit of composition for me is the clause. I am not an Elbovian, evacuating pages of material at a time from hidden fountains of creativity. I do not write whole, unpalatable sloppy first drafts, then return to the beginning to make them progressively less unpalatable. I require perfection as I go, one sentence at a time. Do I know where I'm going? Well, I do and I don't. I know in a general way that I want to cover certain issues and say certain things, though I will always end up covering other issues as well and saying things that I hadn't expected to say. Given my dialectical habit, I usually have some sense of the oppositions I will try to establish. But I never write outlines or other full-scale plans regardless of the size of the projected work. I don't seem to know actual lines of argument in advance, discovering them rather along the way, usually by assessing what I've already said to see what it may necessitate or make possible. Nor do I see a work in advance as composed of sections —introduction, body, conclusion, and the like—except for monograph-size writing, when I will try to anticipate chapter divisions. I sometimes end up with introductions and other such ancient rhetorical boxes by accident, but I never set out to create them. I just jump in with a first sentence, not exactly composed at random but at least written with the belief that, among so many equally possible choices, this one is as good as another (and I'll probably change it later anyway). Then I go to the next sentence, which seems to arise out of implications in the one before it, implicit suggestions about other things to say. A third sentence arises out of the context of the two before it, and so on. I seem able to keep in mind the larger concerns of the writing while focusing most of my attention on the particular sentence at hand. Consequently, I will fuss over that sentence until it communicates exactly what I want, unconcerned that I might forget some other idea not yet formulated. I will often pose structural challenges within individual sentences as a device for thinking more rigorously—for instance, beginning with a subordinate clause, unsure what it will finally add to my meaning, just to keep the sentence open to richer expression as long as possible. I will revise a sentence endlessly as long as I sense that it isn't yet what I mean. Or I will go back to it, having been working on others, the moment that I find it unacceptable. Paragraphs evolve through gradual, painstaking accretion of utterly perfect sentences, linked together by means of the entailments that I perceive as I fashion the system of statements.

To keep the system evolving coherently, I reread what I've written over and over and over and over and over, every sentence once completed, every two sentences to be certain of their connection, every paragraph in its connection with every other, back and forth, obsessively. At the start of each day's writing, I read everything I've done so far (in the case of an article) or at least everything in the chapter I'm working on (in the case of a monograph). I'll make corrections as I go, not beginning new material until the old satisfies me once again. No one page is really finished in my own mind until the whole work is finished. The rereading gives me a fresh view of individual statements in an ever-expanding context: I can check for intellectual consistency, embed clues that anticipate later insights, sharpen the coherence and directedness of the evolving argument, locate words, phrases, sentences that might tend to mislead a reader about the meaning of the whole. As important, through the perpetual rereading I can discover new things to say by assessing the implications of what I've already said and following their lead. The interesting point here seems to be that I'm *discovering* system/order/coherence as I go rather than planning it in advance (the author as Tristram Shandy). It emerges gradually from the process of making consecutive statements: I only half-see it at the moment of composing and come to learn more about it through endless rereading. As I catch new glimpses of it, I add more statements to shore it up (or to change it if I don't like where it's leading me). I'm helping a reader, of course, through this process of making a perceived order as visible as I can. But what really matters is that I'm becoming clearer myself about what that order is going to consist of by tinkering with it until it "reads" properly to me.

An interesting puzzle comes to mind. How do I know that something I've said is not yet exactly what I mean even though, in a certain sense, I don't yet know what I wish to mean—and can't know until I've found satisfying language? Sometimes, the source of discomfort is easy enough to locate—I perceive that the meaning of the statement (word, phrase, clause) fails to correspond appropriately to my impression of the meaning of the context to which it contributes. Or I may think of different words with which to compare it, noting how it suffers in the comparison. The problem might be, at other times, aesthetic, a feeling that the language is clumsy or wrongly pitched or uneconomical or rough-hewn. In that case, the perception of inadequacy doesn't depend on an awareness of something unsaid that "feels" preferable but only on a realization that the words there on the page don't function properly, create a wrong effect somehow, and require change, though not necessarily a particular change. But what I have in mind is that curious feeling that the meaning of a statement is just off the mark—acceptable in its context, doing no damage to the system to which it contributes, aesthetically adequate, but wrong, insufficient, unsubtle, naive, simplistic. What is the standard by which such an estimate is made? I can tell that something else or more needs to be said, but what causes me to know that? Sometimes, I suppose, the statement simply fails to measure up to the implications it is designed to make explicit—in that case, the subtlety of the whole reveals the inadequacy of an offending part. Sometimes, too, a statement will introduce ideas, issues, or directions of inquiry that are not sufficiently pertinent to the purposes I'm trying to achieve. But sometimes, I just "know" that the language in front of me doesn't adequately convey some meaning I'm quite sure exists even though I haven't yet expressed it. Perhaps the knowledge comes from having read, spoken, or written some other formulation of the idea, vaguely recollecting it as richer then than now. Perhaps it comes from lived (rather than verbalized) experiences of something I'm trying to describe (as here where I try to explain my composing by recollecting occasions when I've engaged in it): my "understanding" of the experience itself seems fuller somehow than the statements I make about it. Anyway, this is puzzling to me and will require more writing somewhere else.

My paragraphs tend to be quite long, typically a manuscript page in length. I like to imagine that I have worked out an entire "segment" of an argument within a paragraph, though I'm not sure what I mean by a "segment"—it's something more aesthetic than logical, a perception of wholeness or sufficiency, of balance and rhythm and completion. Everything I have to say here about my paragraphs I'll try to say in one of them. Since my paragraphs are of roughly uniform length, the size has little to do with how much information I have on a given issue, or how complicated it is, or how inspired I am to make statements about it. I have no sense of necessity motivating the production of paragraphs except the urge, born simply of habit, to make all of them the same length, a manuscript page. Indeed, the crisis point in my writing, the point where I must struggle hardest to conceptualize, is the moment when I have only half a manuscript page (though potentially a "natural" paragraph break) and must find something appropriately pithy to fill up the other half. A pint-sized paragraph constitutes, for me, intellectual defeat, a concession of inadequacy, like not managing to do ten chin-ups every time. I suppose, then, that the visual space of the paragraph serves a function similar to the incomplete syntactic pattern in a sentence: it's a formal challenge to think more fully or carefully, to qualify or extend or specify, to work a little harder. Sometimes, abundant intellectual riches will force me to halt a paragraph at its customary size with more material still to be integrated, in which case I'll begin another. Too long a paragraph is also a defeat, suggesting my inability to synthesize and focus in an economical way. But luxury is not nearly as commonplace a condition as poverty, the perception of a vacuum waiting to be filled.

Just as I know I've said enough in a paragraph when it gets to be about a manuscript page in size, so I know I've said enough in an essay or book when it has reached the page limit an editor or publisher has stipulated or is willing to accept. As near as I can tell, there is no necessary termination to writing, although there are devices that signal a decision to terminate on a particular occasion. It's impossible to run out of information, ideas, relevant issues and problems, connections, themes, arguments, insights, meanings, or language. Only time, space, and energy can be exhausted, not writing. The trick is to fashion the system of assertions in a way that makes it appear to be necessarily of the length it has achieved, neither shorter nor longer than it should have been. Sometimes, I find that I've miscalculated the relationship between available space and the strategy selected for treating some subject, but that doesn't mean, on the one hand, that I've run out of things to say or, on the other, that I have too much to say for the space available. It only means I've miscalculated the relationship. So, if I haven't yet said enough, I go back inside the argument to extend and clarify, perhaps to raise an issue or two I had earlier decided not to introduce, perhaps to add more evidence, perhaps to make the line of reasoning more explicit. The "bare bones" of the argument, I then rationalize, have been "fleshed out" and made truly substantial. If I've said too much, I hack and slash at the text until it shrinks to acceptable size. The hacked off part is henceforward designated as "fat" while what remains is "meat." In either case, creating the rhetorical illusions of completeness and sufficiency is what matters: Arguments don't find acceptable sizes; rather, judgments about space define the character of arguments. I usually imagine that I haven't said enough; my editors usually insist I've said too much. Meanwhile, readers who approve of what I say will rarely fault my text for leaving things out or padding, while readers who don't agree will almost always do so.

Which reminds me: I don't like to hear from readers while composing. When a manuscript is, in my best judgment, finished, responses are very helpful, though I will defend my choices vigorously and make changes only when someone I trust has argued me into them or someone I don't trust insists on them as the price of publication. But while some writers enjoy response from readers all along the way, I find such intervention extremely distracting. I feel entirely confident that I know what I'm doing or at least will eventually figure out what to do. If I'm lost, I must find my own way out; if stalled, must restart my own engines; if stuck, must free myself. Advice at such a point only represents someone else's solution to a very personal, and sooner or later personally soluble, problem. If, by contrast, I'm proceeding happily along my own track, response only diverts attention to other, perhaps equally useful but not equally personal avenues of inquiry. I will always defend the value of writing centers in schools but would neither work in one nor seek aid from one. I think there must be writing-center personalities in the world: They enjoy each other's company during the often lonely process of composing; they find reassurance in the advice and support of those who are sensitive to the difficulties of their task. More power to them. But for me there is a time to listen and a time to write: The two are mutually energizing but also, as activities, mutually exclusive. I can barely organize what *I* think is in my head without trying simultaneously to organize other people's impressions of what's in my head, or worse, their preferences about what ought to be there. This is not to say that I can't hear readers when they make sensible recommendations or pose disturbing counterarguments. Timing is the key: I have to be ready to listen. As long as I realize myself that a manuscript isn't ready, I look inward rather than outward to assess the deficiencies. But at that point when I can no longer sense inadequacy, instead of assuming (foolishly) that there must be none left, I look to trustworthy readers to continue the revision process now that I no longer have the ability to sustain it alone. That is, when the timing is right, I'll treat another reader's response in the same way as I treat my own: as a stimulus for changing the text.

The tale is nearly told (notice my strategy for signaling the close of a text; I could just as easily have said: "Now, on another matter of crucial importance . . ."). However, (ah, the reader thinks, we're tapering toward the conclusion but not quite there) I should just add that my writing seems to have changed over time even though my habits have remained essentially the same, which leads me to conclude that one never stops learning to write. I note, for instance, since my dissertation days a gradual shortening of sentence length, a preference for fewer subordinate clauses in particular. Some might say it signifies maturation, the discovery that one's intellectual sophistication depends on the quality of thought more than on the complexity of syntax. Others might imagine that the change is a shrewd tactic, born of the realization that readers are much happier when they know that decoding sentences will not require a break for lunch. My own deep faith in empirical science, however, leads me—reluctantly—to suspect that the degeneration of my T-unit size is inescapable evidence of the onset of senility, or at best second childhood. Another change I've noticed is the loss of professional voice—that neutral, neutered, pompous, omniscient, oracular, cold-blooded, professorial sound that makes academic discourse so . . . monumental. The cause may be cranky individualism, another symptom of age, together with recent experiences of collaborating with another writer whose Dixie dialect makes me forget what professors, who often tend linguistically to be Yankees, sound like. Sometimes I remember again, but permanent amnesia wouldn't distress me and probably should be wished for. I'm also developing, of late, a very convenient new tolerance of my own imperfection, with little consequence that I can see for the actual degree of imperfection in my writing. I take less time to produce the same quantity of prose, possibly just because I've mastered the genre of Journal Article, possibly because my powers of concentration are degenerating along with my formerly robust T-units. Finally, the word processor is having certain effects I had not anticipated. It allows me to be more experimental, more "creative," even playful, realizing that whole chunks of text can be moved, rearranged, or zapped with godlike ease. Writing has assumed some of the attractiveness of *Pacman,* and lost some of its similarity to the labor of galley slaves. In time I could come to like it more as a sport than as an occupation.

Behold, then, the Composer Extraordinary. There are deeper questions, of course, to which I have no answers. I don't know where the words come from, or the structures into which they so religiously form themselves. Still less do I know where the ideas come from, at least the freshest ones, the ones I'm proudest of. I don't know how or what (or even if) I'm thinking in that fraction of a second before a word or string of words appears on the page in front of me. I don't know how I call up appropriate strategies from a range far broader than my conscious understanding has ever revealed to me. I don't know how I solve intellectual or technical problems. I've tried composing aloud, which is like playing the violin and simultaneously explaining finger movements along the strings, but it hasn't helped me to answer such questions. I could take a stab at answers but fear that my readers' broad tolerance of fiction might not stretch as far as fairy tale. I, the Researcher, am not without integrity! So, instead, I'll rest content with the modest tale I've told here, never letting on for a moment that I've fudged a little from time to time, uttered just the tiniest of fibs, to make things come out right. And so as not to end on a down note, I'll do even a bit more. Ever hopeful of results from relentless positivistic inquiry, let me offer solemn assurance that, once I've had a chance to compile more clause-length statistics, count more nose scratches, chronicle more invention heuristics, identify more plans, measure more significant pauses, and generate more flowcharts of The Composing Process, I may just nail down the answer to those messy questions right to the last decimal point and pass them along all neatly ordered in tables and graphs. Then I can lay to rest for all time the business of how people write and get on to what really interests me—the electromagnetic basis of creativity. That story, I promise you, will be a hoot.

Janice M. Lauer directs the graduate program in rhetoric and composition at Purdue University. She is author of Four Worlds of Writing *(2nd ed., 1984) as well as numerous articles published in the leading composition journals and in such collections as* Classical Rhetoric and Modern Discourse *and* Eight Approaches to Teaching Composition. *Lauer gives talks and workshops at many institutions throughout the country and has for nine years directed the annual rhetoric seminar* Current Theories of Teaching Composition.

REASONS
FOR WRITING
Janice M. Lauer
Purdue University

My composing processes have yielded various results: answers whose cogency holds up over the years, insights that solve immediate problems but which are qualified by new work, and answers that turn out to be superficial or wrong. Even when my composing ends up in my file, I value it because it serves a heuristic function, leading to other writing, to new pedagogy, to graduate courses, or to dialogue with colleagues.

What usually compels me to write? As I reflect on this question, I think of William Carlos Williams's image, "rolling up." My writing rolls up. The motion starts with a nudge from either within or without. I become aware of some theory in the field that doesn't completely satisfy me, that seems to explain inadequately some aspect of writing. Back in the sixties, I was troubled by a lack of understanding of how writers reach judgments, a broad concern that led to many minor puzzlements. More recently I have been disturbed by several trends: misunderstandings about the nature of an art, conflicts about the appropriate modes of inquiry for composition studies, confusion over the sources and levels of knowledge in our field, and negative assessments of the rhetorical tradition. These intellectual enigmas have propelled me into writing.

External pressures have also motivated me to write. As a teacher of composition and a mentor of graduate assistants' teaching, I continually puzzle over ways to help students write to reach new understanding rather than merely to fulfill assignments, over how to help them interact with readers and develop arts of investigation. These concerns motivate me to begin composing. The seeds of some of my essays I can trace to dialogues at conventions and at the summer rhetoric seminars, to battles with readings, and to pressures at the university. I mention these catalysts because I consider them one of the most important parts of my writing process—its initiation, the cognitive dissonances that cast me out of my complacency, out of routine into composing.

From these dissatisfactions, I try to tease out questions to clarify the direction of my investigation. Some questions I have posed include the following:

1. What kinds of changing situations (academic, pedagogical, or professional) do composition instructors find themselves in today?
2. What new kinds of *topoi* can guide students to examine subjects more imaginatively, analytically, accurately?
3. In what senses can composition studies be considered a discipline? What is a discipline?
4. What is the nature of each of the modes of inquiry in composition studies? Are these modes complementary or competitive? Should one be privileged? What is the relationship between descriptive and experimental research?
5. How has the concept of art changed in the rhetorical tradition?

I have investigated each of these questions, using thinking and written planning: I recall and jot down what I already know that bears on my question, and I draw connections between my subject and other ideas. This planning occurs over weeks and months in which I devote several concentrated sessions to written plans. As new ideas occur—in the shower, while driving, during reading—I add these to my lists. I find that this kind of planning, freer than free writing, helps me investigate my questions more fruitfully than mental planning alone or endless drafting. During this time, I try to identify the distinctive features of what I'm pondering, for example, inquiry processes in composition studies, the nature of heuristic procedures, the essence of descriptive and experimental research, the genesis of writing as inquiry. These acts of naming are tough, entailing analysis and often leading to further reading and dialogue.

I also probe the dynamic side of my subjects, tracing their changes and processes, for example, the interactions between writers and readers, the processes of composing and inquiry, the changing conceptions of art in rhetorical history, the evolving worlds of composition instruction, and the history of issues in invention. Because I seldom take this dynamic perspective on my own, I am often surprised at what it reveals about my subjects.

My exploring also includes creating connections. These links come to mind at odd times: while cooking or waiting in line, upon waking up, or when working at my desk. Many of these connections never surface in finished texts but act to stimulate further investigation. A few connections find their way to publication. Here are some examples:

- classical invention/ heuristic procedures
- the field of composition/ a phoenix arising from ashes
- knowledge in composition/ social knowledge
- composition studies/ a discipline
- writing/ creative problem solving
- contexts for composition/ worlds
- rhetorician/ mastercraftsman
- composition studies/ true comedy/ dappledness

Where does this planning take me? Sometimes to answers. If answers come during planning, I note them down but allow myself more time to continue to explore. In some cases, my early answer satisfies me; in other cases, I find a better resolution. To clarify and test emerging insights, I put them in the form of hypotheses. In the light of articulation, sometimes their "brilliance" doesn't hold up: I see that I have been asking the wrong question or that I need more pondering.

When I have a tentative answer, I begin drafting, guided by my hypothesis and a rough mental plan of organization that forecasts large sections of my initial draft. For a longer piece, I jot down an organizational plan. Usually my working hypothesis suggests an organization. For example, "Composition: Dappled Discipline" called for sections explaining the features of a discipline possessed by composition studies. "Issues in Rhetorical Invention" entailed a historical organization. "Modes of Inquiry in Composition Studies" prompted a comparative design. These large organization schemes realize themselves through multiple drafts, which clarify, substantiate, and occasionally change the guiding insight that was seminal in their production. For example, when planning for my essay "Issues in Rhetorical Invention," I at first hypothesized that one view of contemporary invention reflected an Aristotelian position while the other mirrored a Ramian view. But as I worked through several drafts of the essay, giving talks along the way and reading additional secondary scholarship, I revised my judgment to conclude that both contemporary views had their historical roots in conflicting interpretations of classical texts. The same shift occurred during the drafting of my more recent article on theoretical and empirical inquiry. My planning suggested that these two modes were different but complementary. As I worked through drafts, however, I came to see that the modes are essentially similar with only superficial differences, that they operate on a continuum of probability.

Drafting is not the only act that prompts changes. Reading, discussion, feedback from colleagues, and talks contribute to a reasonably finished piece of writing. My intended readers also influence the shape of my finished texts. Many of my articles begin as talks. As I revise them for publication, I make changes to offer the background and substantiation that various kinds of readers require. For journals at the growing edge of the field, I do not explain the significance of the subject because they know the important problems in the field; nor do I bring them up to date on the scholarship or provide extensive background information. I refer to the relevant scholarship, but I do not explain it. However, this tailoring for journals, as I have discussed elsewhere, is tricky because of the developing nature of composition studies. Sometimes when I send an article to a journal that I consider to be at the growing edge, the editor requests background for readers innocent of current scholarship. In these cases, I either revise or send the article elsewhere. Such adaptation remains a continual challenge.

When I review the writing I have done, I realize that writing has served me essentially as a means of inquiry, as a way of tackling questions important to me as a teacher, researcher, and member of a profession. My composing processes have yielded various results: answers whose cogency holds up over the years, insights that solve immediate problems but which are qualified by new work, and answers that turn out to be superficial or wrong. Even when my composing ends up in my file, I value it because it serves a heuristic function, leading to other writing, to new pedagogy, to graduate courses, or to dialogue with colleagues. Painful and exhilarating as I have found the processes of writing to be, they enable me to reach new understandings and, at times I hope, to contribute to the growing body of knowledge in composition studies.

Richard Lloyd-Jones has taught writing at the University of Iowa since 1952. In 1956 he took over the programs in technical and expository writing, by 1959 he directed all of the advanced composition programs, and in 1976 became department chair and director of the School of Letters at Iowa.

He has chaired the Conference on College Composition and Communication as well as the teaching of writing division of the Modern Language Association. He has been a director of the Association of Departments of English, and in 1984 became president-elect of the National Council of Teachers of English.

Lloyd-Jones has published poems, essays, professional articles, and reviews. With Richard Braddock he wrote Research in Written Composition, *and he was later codesigner of the Primary Trait System for mass scoring of student writing. He also has written reams of reports and memoranda.*

PLAYING FOR MORTAL STAKES

Richard Lloyd-Jones
University of Iowa

The real pleasure of writing is . . . somewhere in the wild. . . . The words lead you on, and sometimes they fade away, and you are lost in a strange place with only your adrenalin to keep you searching.

How I compose depends on what and why. In a general way I suppose writing requires certain acts more or less in sequence; otherwise, how would theorists make plausible talk about a writing process or how would teachers and editors provide rules and examples? For all of that assurance of regularity I have a sense of starting over each time I write seriously—it's a new path in a strange wood. Oh, I know some wood-craft, of course, and I don't drop into the middle by parachute.

Not all woods are new to me, either. The letters that come to the office today are much like the ones of yesterday and require much the same answer. Some of the responses are really recitations of old texts, individualized only as a computer individualizes. At best that's a park with asphalt paths, but there is a need for parks. Even computer in-dividualizing creates the illusion of community, and mowed lawns are better than deserts.

The real pleasure of writing is found somewhere else, somewhere in the wild. It's harder, riskier, sometimes a bit exotic. The words lead you on, and sometimes they fade away, and you are lost in a strange place with only your adrenalin to keep you searching.

When I was young, I aspired to poetry. I still do, but I'm not so hardy, and so I often settle into prose of a sort. When I wrote poems, I stumbled onto lines, or words, or tendrils of tunes. That was why I liked John Donne; I suspected him of finding a line or two, a puzzle of images, and then getting a bit bored after he had charted where the images would lead him.

Once I saw an image, I'd ask what it wanted. If a drop of rain on

153

the hot pavement smelled just so, what did it mean? Did the scorched earth scorch the rain? What would it mean, scorched rain, if it were to mean anything?

Those schooled in the matter-of-fact know that rain cannot be scorched, so the idea has its meaning in a dislocated world of the will, in perceptions of absurdity; but one of the logic of such radical re-arrangements comes the creative vision. Given the truth of the initial absurd assumption, I'd follow step by step until meaning emerged.

Perhaps the image of scorching really comes from the searing heat of the pavement on a bare foot, a misery so profound that the body can pay attention only to its survival. The rain, when it comes, brings relief, but even more it brings an awareness of the pain which before one had to deny. Or perhaps the scorching means that the life in water is killed when it turns to steam on the pavement and the acrid odor is truly the smell of death. I don't know. I used the image once or twice, and then discarded it unexplored. I am still struck by the pungent fact now and then, but the language has never seemed to resolve itself into a poem.

Still, one way of generating language is to accept the promise of an image or a tune or a rhyme and then follow where it leads. Committed to iambs, one must make more iambs. Take a rhyme scheme or a verse form and more rules are set. Even choosing to start a sentence with the verb commits a writer not only to the sentence but to a role in relation to an audience. What situations permit sentences to begin with verbs? One must know one's system of rules, though, and the system isn't much fun unless there are lots of rules; it's got to be hard enough to challenge the will, so the better you get, the more rules you decree. Each decision about how the language is to be used reduces the options for the next step, and the next, and eventually a finished text emerges. I often read with surprise what I have made.

Still, I imagine that a similar procedure governs the composition of most personal letters—the letters home, for example. The main function of most such letters is to keep open the lines of love, to say that although nothing is really to be said, everything is sayable. The information that fills up the sentences is of no account. Some theorists might call this expressive writing; in its most intimate form the letter says, "Here I am, down to that last veil or two, so look at my mind and self." One assumes the reader cares. Otherwise life would be grim.

In less intimate situations, still expressive, personal letters and essays show the companionable person letting the mind apparently create what it will, now and again arguing a case or reporting information, usually of no consequence, but mostly self-centered and dependently social. In order to say, "Look, Ma, no hands," the bicycle rider/child has to depend much upon the opinion of Ma. And although Ma may be very strong, she depends upon that dependency. And that's what one kind of composition is about. When the personal essay develops literary pretensions, the premise is that the illusion of exploration is powerful in leading the reader to some idea and profoundly social in gaining acceptance for it.

When I write personal letters, even personal letters with some segment of business, I'm usually producing lazy art. I don't have the courage or strength to write poetry or a real essay, so I let the mind drift, and sometimes a rather nice fragment or two will emerge, asking to be made into something substantial. Some people write journals to find fruitful fragments. I like having an explicit audience to show off for, hence the letter, but some journal writers think of an alter ego, or God, or posterity, although some claim just to write. I doubt it. My audience may at times be very hazy, an occasional shadow in the fog, but I don't think I write without some sense of reader, and I doubt that others do. Perhaps language is so much a shared machine that no one can be wholly without an audience even if the reader is but some externalized piece of one's self.

Frankness requires me to say that to some degree I compose this way in all but the most mundane and repetitive situations. I tidy up a lot in revision, and the revision goes on in my mind long before the ink hits paper. In fact, I talk through most writing, usually several times. But even so the first text on paper explores itself as it goes along. I usually know my conclusion and my general points for getting to it with a particular audience, but the exact phrasing, and hence the precise meaning, comes only when the relatively vague plans of my mind's disjointed private speech are turned into the hems and haws of conversation and then are given a temporary firmness in a written text. Once built it is usually remodeled.

Well, I've brought up the mundane twice, so I should accept the rules of recursive foreshadowing and deal with how I manage worldly prose. Anyway, the mundane represents a pole on the axis of creation and convention, and I've exhausted the energy of the metaphor which suggests that writing is exploration.

Much of the writing I live by is highly conventional. I have in recent years chaired a large academic department in a large research university. Much of the role is that of a functionary. For example, the morning mail requires answers to inquiries I've answered before for other people I know only as askers of questions. The relationship is practiced, the phrases in the answer are set. So also are the thank-you notes to contributors, or the explanations to requests for funds, or the acknowledgments of applications or recommendations. The business of any office goes on with ritualized grunts, not less sincere for being highly stylized. It is bureaucracy, and I am a bureaucrat doing my job. I try to do it in the morning, both to get it out of the way and to start the mental juices flowing, as one does mental jogging. Hardly anything gets revised, except incrementally over a period of months; sometimes all of the material is dictated, and often a standard form is merely modified slightly.

Even as a bureaucrat I sometimes have to compose official documents not so clearly set in routine. In sheer volume most work in a large organization is simply the quiet meshing of gears, but sometimes real decisions must be made and a different kind of game must be played out in words carefully fitted to the need. The audience is more complexly defined in its role by the particularities of the decision to be made, and the ideas require more than routine naming. Real explanations must be devised. A funding agency with its implicit jury of peers is different from a financial vice president or the director of building maintenance or the academic dean. Whatever the people may be like, their roles set up expectations, and I must figure out what they are.

I also must discover my competence. I may be an expert on the research project I want funded, but I may know little about indirect costs or the fire alarm system I want installed, and I know both relevant and irrelevant information about a colleague I want promoted (and though I've known and liked the person for some years, I don't really know much). I had better be clear about the competence I claim and disclaim if I am to be perceived as a reliable reporter.

And I must know the competence of the reader beyond the role. I may not be able to find out much about the anonymous jury in a government agency, but I can discover that the vice president is a lawyer, not an accountant, and the building super is an electrical engineer by training, and the academic dean is a positivist with a yen for charts.

One may find in this some of Aristotle's advice about persuasion. I have to know the materials and territory well enough to be reasonable, to seem reasonable in my competence, and to make the issue move into the world of my reader. Even if one wishes to define rhetoric as more than the art of persuasion, even if one wishes to dignify rhetoric by describing it as a means for discovering contingent truth, still discourse is carried on between and among people, and implicitly all discourse argues the acceptance of the writer's way of understanding. It is social, and social acts are based on an identity of interest.

"Since feeling is first / who worries about the syntax of things / will never wholly kiss you." Cummings may have been right in his poem, yet one is not free of syntax until one has mastered it. Spontaneous relationships are fun, but most of the business of the world is not quite included in that metaphor of kissing. And, although I'll concede some of Cummings's point that worrying is self-conscious egotism, I've observed that people who say whatever comes to mind without either plan or revision cause trouble and pain to others. Even my free letters and poems are silently censored by a private self—ah, yes, the apparent freedom is often merely an effect—and business requires calculation because it is social and usually involves relative strangers. Fussy revision is based on a concern for others. Although a startling amount of business is still carried on by means of trust—ethical proof—still logical appeals govern the surface of the text and social awareness governs the subtext.

Another variation on the conventions of the bureaucracy is the academic paper. Sometimes school teachers make "the paper" seem to be all of writing rather than a specialized form for a specialized sub-group of the society. In fact, each kind of academic group has its own subset of rules, and as a sometime teacher of writing I have to take that into account in my classroom, but mostly I write by the rules of my own friends who use the conventions of the Modern Language Association. To be sure, I thumb my nose periodically, but only within a context that suggests I am an insider mocking myself. An outsider in violation is judged to be ignorant; the insider gains the protection of irony by suggesting her or his own limits. An ironist usually can keep the eaten cake.

Still, an academic who doesn't write academic papers quickly slips off the academic slope altogether. One can be an honorary academic in English by writing novels or poems or even commencement addresses, any of which may be much more difficult to write, but good standing requires "the paper." Perhaps it is like the compulsory figures in skating competitions in proving a basic competence. I write as few as possible because the imp is always in me, sneaking out with a pun, or a paradox, or an alliteration, or a wayward allusion. My official self will usually manage to conceal such primitive figures in the proper clothes of Western Thought, but a whimsical reader will discover the hidden sally.

I revise academic papers more than I revise the morning mail, even though the forms are often just as mechanical, because some people I like and respect enjoy rereading papers. They like the predictability of the form, the efficiency of communication, the explicitness of assumptions, the openness to evaluation. Virtues, I suppose, if one believes that mastery of abstractions, models, and theories constitutes knowledge— and one *should* believe in that a little, at least on Monday-Wednesday-Friday. Even I like reading papers, and I'm usually short of time, so I appreciate the writer's care for my living in a world of academic business, but part of me still likes Cummings, the forever-adolescent, as some of his critics have suggested. Efficiency is not the first virtue of prose.

My procedure for generating academic papers doesn't quite fit the usual textbook description. I don't start with a systematic gathering of materials from the library. Of course, I don't ordinarily choose to write on subjects I haven't already ruminated on. I begin in the middle of my learning. Looking-up is different. I look-up on a hit-and-run basis when I want specific information for a specific task. I write on subjects I've chewed a bit, to make sense of what I already know. To be sure, after I've completed a good bit of preliminary exploration, I establish systems (imitating the social sciences) for examining carefully and testing a theory or a body of material, but that sort of rational effort is likely to follow a long subconscious bit of speculation. The basic question or fragment or hypothesis that will generate writing comes from puzzling through metaphors or incomplete but substantial information. For me, it is not likely to be a rational process. I set myself up mentally to receive a notion from some other part of my mind. Or perhaps I make a soup of life-generating observations, apply some heat, and wait for the one-celled creature to emerge and reproduce.

When the question or hypothesis comes—and it usually has its answer or proof trailing along behind—I'm likely to write a draft, in my mind at least. It has no footnotes. In college I viewed footnotes as a decoration applied to a paper to make instructors happy. Sometimes I collected footnotes in advance of drafting; I knew an oral version of my paper and could guess where footnotes would be pretty, so I'd go hunt for some. I had to become a real member of the academic club before I could imagine myself actually discussing ideas with the people I read, and thus could have a real reason for acknowledging their existence. Even yet, the footnotes themselves are often an addition, a concession to politeness, for most of my academic writing has its basis in sensory experience.

My paper, thus, is independent of its "academic" sources, although the ideas doubtless come from the whole range of my memory, including academic sources. I am a product of the collective past of my society. My procedure for assimilation probably had its origin in a number of my weaknesses. My handwriting is terrible; my fingers often don't produce the requested letters, and the lines wobble. I draw the same way. My typing is only marginally better, but it is much faster and less physically demanding. I can recall the irritation of scratching a steel pen point across the paper with ink from a well, but pencils did little better. Although I was impatient in learning to type, for thinking in letters was a bother, still eventually the speed made it possible for marks on the page to come reasonably close to the speed of composition. I disliked the labor of making a script, though, and I suspect that is why I tended to write short lyric poems. I cultivated rule systems for writing poems that would force the quick completion of a pattern, so then I could write less and still be done. The pleasure was in being intricate. I also wrote rather short and concentrated papers in college, so my instructors had to infer a lot. Fortunately, my high school required almost no writing, so I didn't have the frustration of having to produce lots of manuscript at an age where acquiring fluency was more important.

In fact, I developed alternative means of composition in competitive debating and in other speaking activities. I rarely took notes but listened carefully to my opponent, assigned each point to a category in my own system of thought, and then proceeded to blend my own remarks and those I opposed. I developed all sorts of heuristic structures for controlling information. I rarely quoted, for I translated and digested the ideas of others, but I became very fluent. I also read weekly newscasts on a local radio station, acted in a modest way, and performed poetry quite vigorously, so I learned to pay attention to style and audience reaction. In short, I adopted all sorts of oral systems for developing ideas fluently.

I was thus spared the labor of making multiple manuscripts. I was not committed to a script, so revised easily. I was facile. As a result, given the rigidity of academic forms instead of the rigidity of debate forms, I can produce the frame of a paper quite quickly. Probably the "first" draft represents in some sense a fourth or fifth draft, but it ordinarily takes its final shape at once. After that, revisions are tinkering.

Recently most of my papers have been speeches. Sometimes I speak in my preferred way—extemporaneously from a plan, the technique I mastered while I was still in high school. But in a world of timed addresses and printed proceedings, I have found myself required to produce a text. Oral writing is different from speaking, as anyone who has examined a transcript of a meeting knows, but writing for oral delivery is also different from writing that seems to be talking. People who listen have different needs from people who read. As one who is hard of hearing, I am especially aware of the need for redundant systems in actual speech. Say the same message two or three or four times, with variations, so what is half understood at first can be mastered before the argument must continue. Recognize that minds will wander. Admit that if you offer a good incidental jest, the next line will be lost to those who are amused and the jest itself will be lost to some others, who then will be puzzled about what is happening.

The same redundance in an oral-seeming bit of writing will become tedious.

When I write to speak, I usually am revising an often-spoken message. Ordinarily the intended audience is quite clear, I can predict the circumstances of delivery, and I'm dealing with an assigned topic—or at least one determined by circumstances. Probably I wouldn't have been asked to speak at all were it not that I have already made comments on the same topic before, so I am like a candidate in a political campaign giving variations on the basic stump speech. Unlike the candidate I have an interest in real variation as well as in polite situational variation, so I try to rethink whatever my basic message is. It's not enough merely to adapt my greetings to fit a different city, or a different interest group, I must really consider the rhetorical edge in social relationships as they make one rethink statements. The various rehearsals allow me to try alternatives in a context and to perfect my timing in relation to points being made. The eventual written version is often merely a final choice among the trials.

The test comes in making the script for delivery into a text for publication. I find it so interesting that I have now come to attempt to make almost all of my writing seem to emerge from a very direct conversation in language redolent with patterns of speech.

The problem of reducing speech to writing is difficult. I become enchanted by the sound of my own voice. I recall the reaction of the audience. Oral by-play, planned ad libs, and local allusions are fun; a few are useful in creating a sense of context and situation. Cutting seems like self-destruction. I find that if I plan to eliminate *all* situational references, I usually get down to not-too-many. I also find it helpful if my delivery script is prepared in very large primer type catering to farsightedness and leaving room for notes and changes. Then, when I have a fresh typescript absorbing the handwritten revisions made for delivery and the later ones based on audience reactions and questions, the whole paper looks new, as though someone else did it. The choice tidbits look less choice.

Unfortunately one rarely has enough time. Just as class papers and office reports have inexorable deadlines, so also the delivered speech has a date, and the sponsors ordinarily are very eager to get the proceedings published; so one rarely has a chance to look at a text with the perspective of time. Perhaps, though, some marks of haste may preserve the flavor of the immediate delivery.

The illusion of speech more nearly beguiles me than actual speaking, although it is pleasant to have an immediate audience reaction. Illusion is a challenge, for it is the home ground of meaning. Meaning is made in the mind; it does not simply lie in the object. How does one make things into ideas? The writer must produce a piece of architecture in language. A reader can contemplate the whole text at one time even though the original reading is done serially. A reader can jump back and forth, can change speeds, can stop to admire or puzzle out a meaning. Then, in retrospect, the interpretive reader can contemplate the whole as pattern and even reconceive the text. The writer, then, presents an arrested moment in the flow of existence, an illusion of stability giving meaning to brute fact.

The speaker is immersed in the flood of sensation. Everything is present and transient. The fly buzzing, the back-row cough, the lawn-mower in the yard are part of the speech and draw the listener away from the abstractions of language. The phonology of dialect and often the vocabulary as well indicate that a particular person with irrelevant allegiances is on the platform. Every moment offers the potential derailment of a line of argument. Some startling aside may reveal truth hidden in a carefully planned treatise. The tune is modified when the audience dozes. At its best speech wraps people in a moment of life, but much of any speech exists in ways not represented in our systems of script, and probably a written text never recreates the pressure of the moment. Even now we cannot hear FDR's fireside chats quite as they were because those issues have changed, are no longer immediate. The tapes create an illusion of the speeches, but perhaps a less satisfactory illusion than the performance by a contemporary actor reading edited versions. The good actor creates a substitute context; the tape reminds us that the right context is gone and that we are reviewing history.

I want the best of both worlds—speech and writing. I want the architecture and the music all at once, the permanence and the transience, the immediacy and the distance. I do not aspire to the transparent style, a form of prose in which a writer seems to disappear. That is an effort to find the ineffable voice and demeanor of God. Or of the mid-century scientist. In the passion of human flesh we will find the truths we must live by, the mortal, fallible, fragmentary insights that carry us to another dawn.

How does one make the written voice live? Having lived among people, I try to imagine talking to a person. One or two, a knot at a party. Even when I know that I am writing for several separate individuals, the separate paragraphs—or even phrases—are written to one at a time, as though I turned to appeal to the person on my left instead of the other before me. When I write for a genuine group, an undistinguishable mass, I write for one of the group. Sometimes I find that I am writing for another version of myself, but only for one version at a time. When I forget in the drafting and muddle my audience, I try to edit out one or more of my readers. In a way all readers are but fictions created by writers. The examples, the vocabulary, the syntax are governed by what I imagine as the need of a reader in a situation I construct, and a person who reads tries to become a suitable reader. We aspire to understand each other.

At the same time I try to recognize the rules of economy. I have no outline as such, but I have a strategy, often rather severely structured. Although I usually add examples and definitions in revision, I try to find shorter structures with a colloquial flavor. I use asides, literary figures, and fragments to pack in material which may be noticed only in second or third readings because I want a trim line even as I cultivate the illusion of haphazard conversation.

Of course, I have a packet of rules about writing. As a teacher I avoid imposing those rules on others because they are mostly my game. Solitaire. They soothe me with a sense of order. I think writers should play games as complicated as possibly can be mastered, but only some rules should show. Catch the long fly ball so it seems to be routine, but give the easy hopper a little razzle-dazzle. Borrow anyone's rules for a while, even the ones in the tiresome textbooks. Everyone should fuss at something. In the end, though, the only rules that have to be followed are the limits of the mind and the customs of whatever society one chooses to be a part of. By choosing to join one group, one usually opts out of other groups. Since society and language both change, one is never wholly in touch even with one's most immediate friends, so we are forever learning how to write, how to reach other groups, but that is part of the fun.

These notions about writing turn up in my classes not as theory but as a guide to experiments. I think theories about language are fun. I read about them and even create a few, but writing is to be done by the feel, for it is a tacit craft. The audience changes, the subject changes, the circumstances change. The scope of language so far exceeds any-one's complete control that we might as well think of it as tentative. I ask myself and my students to seize the moment in writing, to make a try. Then we all read together to discover what wild beast we have captured and hope to tame. So it goes until we all get a little better and have more courage. Then we are ready to write our way into the next tangle of the unknown. Although we talk a lot about technique as we look at particular texts, we say little about technique in the abstract. We talk about theory only when we need to explain something we've seen happen—or not happen. Just as we are explorers together, we also are crafters. If I don't look like a master, at least I am a coach, and they are apprentices. My theories become theirs only when they have earned them in experience, and what they earn may change my theories.

I came to this view of writing while learning to write poems and occasionally to read poems. I began teaching business writing and tech-nical writing and was immediately confirmed in my sense that writing serves people. "Great poets need great audiences." I'm not sure what that means for advertising, but clearly writing for business and industry is tested by utility. When the manual supporting a computer is badly written, the computer company goes broke. We read in the writing what kind of people share it, and we discover a good many divorces where the writing has no audience. Through writing we learn of the world, so it is good to have writing filled with fact—good concrete stuff of existence—but we also learn of people, a stay against the inevitable loneliness of the conscious mind.

But finally writing is fun, the game the mind plays to celebrate itself —it is, you are, but also *I AM*. For a moment.

*Sue Lorch is associate professor and head
of the English Department at the University of South Carolina at Aiken. At present
she is also associate director of the South
Carolina Humanities and Writing Program, a project funded by the National
Endowment for the Humanities. She
holds a Ph.D. in Renaissance literature
from the University of Louisville, where
she served as director of the writing clinic.
Lorch's text* Basic Writing: A Practical Approach *is in its second edition; she has authored various articles on composition
and literature; and she regularly presents
papers at national and regional conferences.*

CONFESSIONS OF A FORMER SAILOR

Sue Lorch
University of South Carolina

What could be improved? I had sixteen years of almost solid As on written work, and the smattering of Bs I had received came, I firmly held, from my own inattention or disdain for the task at hand or from the ignorance or animosity of the benighted individual assigning the grade. How could one improve upon perfection?

I do not like to write. Most people to whom I reveal this small, personal truth find it exceedingly odd, suggesting by their expressions that I ought either to repair my attitude or develop the discretion necessary not to go around telling people about it. Apparently these people hear my confession as an admission of fraud. Because my professional life centers on the written word—on producing it, interpreting it, teaching it, and teaching others to teach it, people assume that I should enjoy writing. Not at all. I inevitably view the prospect of writing with a mental set more commonly reserved for root canals and amputations: If it must be done, it must be done, but for God's sake, let us put it off as long as possible.

It has not always been thus. It has, in fact, been very much un-thus. While I will not claim ever to have written eagerly, I once wrote willingly, putting pen to paper, if not with glee, certainly with aplomb. From elementary school on, I launched myself into writing assignment after writing assignment without blushing or blanching. While my classmates bit pencils, twisted hair, chewed lips, and despaired, I sailed smoothly down the page, serene and sure. I wrote of Dick, Jane, and Sally, of Spot and Puff. I wrote of my summer vacation and my favorite places. And as the years passed and the pencils changed from fat and red to thin and yellow, I wrote of Ionic columns, *Julius Caesar,* the Kennedy assassination (Jack), and Chaucer's *Prologue.* Number two pencils gave way to blobbing ball-points and I rolled on, writing of reproduction in single-cell organisms, the Kennedy assassination (Bobby), Vietnam, and *Othello.* Whatever the subject, I sailed forth on an endless sea of words, undaunted, unafraid. And my classmates bit pencils, twisted hair, chewed lips, and despaired.

Now as I sit here gnawing my pen, twisting my hair, chewing my lip, and despairing of ever getting this essay done to my satisfaction, I look back on those days with a faint nostalgia. I no longer write with ease. The words do not flow, and I have lost my capacity for sailing down a page. I have left the smooth waters of confidence for the rough roads of doubt, but I have become a better writer thereby.

The good ship *Easy Writer* did not go down until my senior year in college. My arctic iceberg appeared on the horizon in the person of one Maurice Hatch, professor of English, destroyer of dreams. Had I known what was to follow, I feel sure I would not have plead so ardently to be admitted to his already closed advanced composition course. But I had no spyglass into the future, and with all the eloquence I could muster and only a fleeting regard for the truth, I begged to be allowed in the class. I cited the imminence of my impending graduation (true), the sterling reputation of the professor (true) and the course (true), my dedication to scholarship and learning (hmmm), and my sharp desire to hone my writing skills to a scalpel's edge in preparation for the rigors of graduate school (hah).

This last was an outright lie. I did have plans for graduate school, although not within the instant, which is what I implied. I did not, however, even for a nanosecond believe that my writing skills needed a keener edge put on them. What could be improved? I had sixteen years of almost solid As on written work, and the smattering of Bs I had received came, I firmly held, from my own inattention or disdain for the task at hand or from the ignorance or animosity of the benighted individual assigning the grade. How could one improve upon perfection? My true reasons for wanting in the class were three: It met at a time that fit my schedule; it was required for the teaching certification that I had decided to pick up as a practical complement to my lovely but increasingly unsaleable B.A. in English; and, most important, it would be an easy A. Or so I thought.

Today, after having myself turned a deaf ear to many similar pleas, I'm unsure why Professor Hatch admitted me to that class. At the time I was certain that he made an exception for me because he perceived my astonishing abilities. He knew that he would not have to take time and trouble teaching me to write, that my papers would not require laborious marking, extensive commentary. I did not make mistakes.

Hadn't Miss Ruth, who was my twelfth-grade English teacher as she was my daddy's before me, always spoken highly of my command of The Rules (a command I gained cheaply, having heard the language correctly used from the cradle)? Hadn't my high-school friends turned to me for additional help in penetrating the mysteries of who and whom? Didn't my college suitemates seek me out for the answer to that great imponderable: "Do I need a new paragraph here?" That Professor Hatch could know none of this never occurred to me. I had grown up, or more accurately, had spent my first seventeen years in a very small town, one whose population was a fraction of the university's I now attended, and I still expected everything about me, good or ill, to be public knowledge.

Today, I would guess I gained my seat either because the student who left his office as I entered it had just dropped or because Professor Hatch felt sufficient obligation to his profession—I had announced my intention eventually to join it—to save it from an insufferably arrogant sort who couldn't perceive that the wind filling her sails was only so much hot air.

Had I listened carefully on my way into the Fine Arts building, there to knock out with grace, alacrity, and ease my first paper, I might have heard the soft strains of "Nearer My God to Thee." I was about to go under. Deaf with confidence, I heard nothing. I was concentrating on spotting the buoy signaling the location of the painting I was to describe, and sure enough, there it was—a tight knot of pencil gnawers. My classmates. I sailed up, sat down, and let the words flow. What could be so difficult about describing an oil on canvas depicting a few cows standing in a field surrounded by trees, I wondered. As I left some thirty minutes later, my one-draft, sure-fire A paper stowed in my knapsack, I hope I refrained from smiling smugly at the gnawers, twisters, and chewers. I doubt that I did. Arrogance has a way of turning the milk of human kindness to clabber, particularly in someone twenty-one. Near-rer tooo Theeeee.

When the papers were returned a scant two days later, I opened mine confidently in class, my eyes searching the pages for the familiar letter acknowledging my prowess of pen. In the world according to Lorch, only the timid, unsure, iffy writers, the gnawers, twisters, and chewers, waited until they reached the privacy of their homes before checking their grades. I had nothing to fear, and sure enough on the last of three pages there was my . . . no, wait, this can't be right. There's a side missing from my A; it looks like an, it is . . . oh, no. I quickly decided that the few words following the F didn't require reading until I got back to the privacy of the dorm. To say that I was shocked is to mince the matter exceedingly fine. I could not have been more stunned had the paper I held metamorphosized into a mule and kicked me in the face.

It took me quite a while to garner the strength to reopen that paper and peruse the unthinkable, but I did so with a fierce determination to go and sin no more. I would take the good professor's remonstrances to heart, look up whatever rules of good writing I had inadvertently violated, observe them, like Horatio, with the very comment of my soul, and then get back into my boat, steering forever a more carefully charted course. I suspected a problem with semicolons, or perhaps my who's and whom's were slipping. These matters had been the bane of many of my classmates in freshman composition (a course wherein we had discussed two books—*Franny and Zooey* and Cassirer's *An Essay on Man*—and no one had ever said a single word about writing except that we were to do it). But no, the comment scratched there said my paper was boing. Boing. BOING? Now what did that mean? I was puzzled but rather relieved, actually, to discover that my paper was boing. I was not committing crass errors; this was something I had never heard of, a violation of a rule that perhaps even Miss Ruth didn't know. Then the fog lifted. That word wasn't boing; it was *boring.* My paper was boring.

During the painful process of revising that paper—the words following *boing* indicated that I must do just that—I became an uncertain writer, a slow writer, the hair-twisting, lip-chewing concentration of concern that I remain today. Every time I set down a sentence, a phrase, a word, there rose before me the specter of Professor Hatch, bored and baleful. I tried to imagine what would interest him—an effective use of colons perhaps, more adjectives, maybe an allusion to classical myth. What was the name of that cow Jove courted in the form of a bull? Crumpled wads of yellow paper soon littered the floor around my desk. I saw no need to return to the Fine Arts building to view the painting again as I had the most complete, albeit boring, description of it that anyone could wish. I had described it in meticulous detail, top to bottom, left to right, down to counting the spots on the cows. What did Hatch want?

Not for life, love, or sacred honor (a concept intimately tied in my mind with the need to make As) could I conceive of the means whereby I could make my description more interesting. The painting wasn't interesting; it was, after all, of a bunch of cows standing in a nondescript field, and images of pastoral perfection and bucolic bliss did not accord with my view of the world in 1968. As the pile of yellow paper at my feet grew deeper, my mood grew darker. I was going to have to take myself to see that so-called art again, through the rain this time, and I didn't want to. I was bored into a near coma by the thing the first time I saw it, and the second time could only be . . . . Whoa. Wait. What had I just said? Could it be that my paper was boring because I had been bored? Had something of *me* inadvertently crept into a paper about a picture? Now I was in deep trouble. Not only did I have to go look at it, I was going to have to become interested in it. Professor Hatch may have been Scylla, but apparently I had served as my own Charybdis. I began to conceive of writing as something of a tricky business.

Standing again in front of Bossy, Elsie, and rest of the lowing herd, I felt a faint but nagging guilt. I feared I might be cheating; I was fairly sure I was skirting the edges of the unethical; I knew I was violating the laws of the sea. On my way across campus I had devised a radical plan: I would abandon ship. Not only had my paper failed to pass muster, my trusty sit-right-down-and-write-myself-an-essay technique had failed along with it. I intended to give up both, at least temporarily, whatever the cost to my sense of personal integrity or to my vision of what the composing process of a competent English major should be. The captain was not going down with the *Easy Writer*. It was now my firm intention not to rewrite the essay I had, but to start over, and to start over not by writing, but by staring, staring with the fixed purpose of discovering something of sufficient interest about that painting to convey to Professor Hatch.

Planted squarely in front of the canvas without pad and pen and viewing it *in toto*, I immediately noticed something that had escaped my attention during my initial inch-by-inch, left-to-right, top-to-bottom, pen-to-paper tour. One of those cows, the one center canvas and (presumably) closest to artist and viewer, had rather an odd look about her. While her sisters placidly chewed cud and cropped grass, their expressions registering blank, bovine contentment, this old girl stared straight out, eying the observer with a look that suggested you were quite close enough, thank you, and if you ventured another step, she was prepared to take action. This painting didn't promote an image of the world as pastorally perfect or bucolically blissful; it suggested the tenuousness, the fragility of such tranquillity and peace. With a deft stroke of the brush, a single line above a cow's eye, this unknown artist had managed to convey the old Virgilian truth: *Et in Arcadia Ego.* Nothing perfect endures. That, I thought, was interesting. That I could write about. Land, ho.

My sailing days were over, but my travails were not. Back at my desk I soon found that, on land anyway, discovering one's destination and figuring out how to get there are two very different things indeed. Finding the subtle irony of that painting had given me direction and purpose. I knew where I wanted my paper to go. How, though, was I to get there? By what route? By which conveyance? My all-purpose sea chart for getting through a description—begin at the upper left of whatever and move clockwise until you come round again to the starting point—was not going to get me where I needed to be. Should I begin with the cow? Her eye? The herd? The field? Should I focus first on what the painting initially seems to be or on what it actually is? It was not that I could not find a path, but that I could see so many of them. Which was most direct? Which would require detours? Where were the dead ends?

My problems were complicated by my constant awareness of someone following me—Professor Hatch. It was his arrival, after all, that would signal the success of the trip. I must lead him to the prospect from which he could best see the painting as I saw it; we had to reach the same destination. To lose him along the way would surely be worse than boring him. That complicated the matter further. In addition to deciding the route at every crossroads, apparently I was also responsible for leaving a trail of crumbs for those coming behind to follow. This business of land travel was burdensome, but it seemed the only way to travel. Eventually, I earned my A.

In the doing and the redoing of that paper I learned more about the writing process than I had in the previous sixteen years of my education. At the time I lacked both the vocabulary and the theoretical basis for understanding precisely *what* it was that I had learned. Not until several years later, after I had read Kinneavy, and Winterowd and Emig and Moffett, would I have the terms to analyze my own experience and discoveries. In 1968 words and phrases such as *rhetorical situation, audience, communication triangle, prewriting,* and *editing* were not a part of my lexicon. I had, however, at last become aware at an intuitive level of the concepts those terms represent, and I knew that, for me at least, writing would always be hard work. Correctness, conformity to rules is a simple matter; communicating effectively to another human being is not.

I travel down the page today in the style I developed that semester after my sleek little sloop went under. My progress is now that of a '39 Ford negotiating hard terrain, a Ford operated by a slightly dim twelve-year-old child lacking entirely any experience with a stick shift. I have trouble getting started. I move by fits and starts. I lurch. I shudder. I come to screeching halts only to leap forward again. I bump; I scrape; I rattle. Sometimes I get lost. Other times, I get where I'm going only to discover I'm not where I want to be. Occasionally I arrive—only occasionally. And when I do it's so awfully nice to be there that I decide to stay put, postponing further road trips until sheer necessity forces me out again.

I do not like to write; it is an always slow, frequently difficult, and sometimes painful process. Few things, however, offer the satisfaction of having written.

*Ronald F. Lunsford is associate professor
of English and director of composition
and rhetoric at Clemson University. He is
also director of the Clemson Writing Project. He has published articles in* College
Composition and Communication, Language and Style, *and the* SECOL Bulletin.
With Charles W. Bridges he has written
Writing: Discovering Form and Meaning
*(1984), and with Marvin K. L. Ching and
Michael C. Haley edited* Linguistic Perspectives on Literature *(1980). He has
more recently edited, with Michael G.
Moran,* Research in Writing: A Bibliographic Sourcebook *(1984).*

CONFESSIONS OF A DEVELOPING WRITER

Ronald F. Lunsford
Clemson University

Every attempt that a writer makes to capsule advice about the writing process must be taken as an attempt to capture reality in language. And like all such attempts, it can be true in general without being true in the particular case.

My writing process varies according to situation and purpose. For example, in responding to a letter of inquiry about our freshman English program, I usually know pretty well what I need to say before I begin. The same is true when I write a memorandum to members of our composition staff. In these situations, I often find myself rehearsing in my head what I am going to say. By the time I sit down to write, I know what is going to be in each paragraph and the writing consists of fleshing out, in words, the thoughts that I have already formulated.

After generating a rough copy of the letter or memorandum, I have only to go back and polish—find the exact word instead of an approximate one I may have settled for, and make my sentences smooth and efficient. This may be accomplished in the second draft. However, I can nearly always see ways of improving upon this second draft—if only by improving the rhythm of the sentences or by avoiding the same word three times in the space of three lines. If time permits and if the letter or memorandum is sufficiently important, I will compose a third draft.

This type of writing is relatively easy. Harder are academic pieces (articles and books) which I am called upon to write: The content is certainly more open-ended than that in letters and memoranda.

The process by which I compose such expository pieces has developed continually since I began to study writing seriously in working on my Ph.D. and, particularly, in the writing of my dissertation. Oddly enough, I had never realized I had a writing process before. I had assumed that "the" writing process consisted of outlining what you were going to say, writing a draft of your paper from the outline, and making the necessary editorial changes as you recopied or typed that draft.

This view of the writing process had shaped my teaching of writing as a young instructor, prior to doing Ph.D. work. That I did not realize I did not use this process is strange. I had only to reflect upon the four drafts of my master's thesis to see how I wrote. But somehow I persisted in believing that I had gotten off on the wrong foot in that "assignment" and that it had taken me three drafts to get back on track; that I would not have needed those three "wrong" drafts if I had been a better writer. I could not see those drafts as the "scaffling" (to use Peter Elbow's term) necessary to get to what I wanted to say.

In studying the writing process for my doctorate, I worked my way to a more realistic concept. By the time I had completed my dissertation, I had pretty much settled upon a writing process consisting of pre-writing (brainstorming, free writing, heuristics), rough outline, and multiple drafts of the essay. That overall process has continued to work for me, but I am always adapting it to the various writing situations I find myself in.

While I was writing a composition textbook, I took the occasion to pay particular attention to how my writing process developed. I began the project following the process described above as faithfully as I could. About midway through the project, however, my coauthor and I decided that we could produce more quickly and with less effort on computers. My writing process underwent several changes as a result of this move.

At first, I simply typed into the computer drafts that I had already handwritten, revising words and sentence structures where necessary. Since revising on a computer is much easier than revising with a typewriter, I found immediately that the computer would serve its purpose of helping us produce our book more quickly. However, I assumed that I would have to return to longhand to compose chapters that had not yet been drafted, since I had only very rough outlines for these chapters at this stage and needed to do much pre-writing to move to outlines I could write from.

Free writing was, and is, an important part of my pre-writing. It occurred to me that the computer would be perfect for free writing, since the purpose is to get as much onto paper as quickly as possible. This free writing on the computer led to a second, not-so-rough outline, and I was faced with a dilemma: It was now time to compose a draft in longhand, but I was reluctant to give up the computer—it was just too easy to work on.

Before recounting how I began composing drafts on the computer, perhaps I should mention an incident in my writing career that may have had some impact. I had always composed first drafts in longhand, with one notable exception. When taking my Ph.D. written examinations, I found myself in an office with an IBM typewriter. As I looked at the questions on that exam and was beginning to compose an outline for the first answer, I decided to see whether the outlining process wouldn't go faster on the typewriter. The outline came quickly and I was ready to begin drafting the essay. But then I found myself in the same dilemma I was to face in writing the composition text. I knew I should begin drafting in longhand, but I was reluctant to do so. Since I knew pretty well how I was going to begin that first essay, I decided to write on the typewriter until I found it hard to continue. I never did. That is, I never reached a point at which I felt I would do better in longhand. I wrote the entire examination on that typewriter, and while my examiners had some fun with my typographical errors and letter reversals, they seemed rather pleased not to have to read my handwriting.

I was certainly pleased with the process and its outcome, but I discounted it as a special instance, a certain type of writing. I reasoned, correctly to a point, that the process had worked because I was presenting material that had been given to me in an ordered, somewhat predigested form in class notes and textbooks. I had little confidence that keyboard composing would work for me in most of the situations I faced as a writer, and I returned to longhand drafts in writing my dissertation.

Things remained pretty much unchanged, then, until that day I sat staring at my computer keyboard and at the rough chapter outline I had written. Once again, I put off going to handwriting as long as possible, reasoning that I knew pretty well what I wanted to say in the first section of that chapter and that I could return to longhand when things became less clear. I never returned to longhand.

I had been partially right, however, in feeling that this writing would not flow as easily as the writing had when I was taking my examinations. I soon faced difficulties that caused me to modify my writing process.

I had started with a very rough outline of each of the chapters of the text. Then by free writing, I had generated a more detailed outline. (Actually, the free writing here was guided by a heuristic that my coauthor and I were introducing in the text itself, a set of questions based on Kenneth Burke's Logological Analysis.) Having generated as much information as possible in this manner, I hammered out a more complete outline from which to write. At this point, I began composing the chapter on the computer keyboard.

I was able at the beginning to flesh out the outline rather easily. However, as I wrote the draft of that first chapter, I soon became aware that what I was writing was changing my concept of what was to follow. In some cases the material going onto the page would make clear to me —give me specifics for—what had been conceived in only the most general terms in my outline. In other cases, the material would make me see that radical changes in the outline were necessary. Sometimes, what I was writing in this chapter made it clear that I must change my concept of another chapter.

At first, I moved away from the draft and began free writing as these insights came to me. However, I soon realized that with the flexibility of the computer I did not have to shift from the composing mode to the pre-writing mode in any official sense. I had only to stop composing, draw a line, and give a heading such as "Thoughts" to my pre-writing. When the insights that had led me to begin free writing had been developed, I could draw another line and reenter the composing process confident that I would not lose those thoughts; that when I was ready to move to a finished draft of the chapter, I had but to delete those "Thoughts" from the manuscript.

Once I had composed a draft of the chapter in this fashion, I was ready for official revision. My first step at this stage was to attempt to get a sense of the whole I had created by extracting something like a formal outline out of it. That is, I outlined the chapter as if I were studying it for a test. This stage was quite helpful in showing me places where I had moved off at tangents and places where I had not developed my point sufficiently. Problems in finding a "1" and a "2" under a heading often indicated a need to develop that section more fully or a need to drop the section entirely. Problems in parallelism might reveal a lack of unity in a section.

After rewriting the chapter to make the improvements suggested by the outlining process, I was ready to begin polishing the text. In addition to correcting spelling and punctuation errors, I attempted at this stage to make word choices as exact as possible and sentence structures economical and rhythmical. Of course, the computer made these kinds of editorial changes very easy.

Finally the draft was ready. Not the final draft, however. My writing process was not over. The next step was to send the draft to my coauthor. In many cases, his responses sent me back to the revision stage, to deleting whole sections of the chapter, to restructuring and developing other sections. Revision was again followed by polishing and a second submission to my coauthor. If the changes worked—and sometimes they did not—the manuscript went on to the editor, who sent it in turn to his readers. After that, it was back to the revision stage, to the polishing stage, and to the editor again.

This, then, is the writing process that developed as I was writing a composition text. The process has obviously evolved over a period of time, and it will continue to do so as I gain experience to develop as a writer. I am particularly interested to see how it will change as I continue to write on a computer, as I am sure I will do. But as things stand now, this is the way I write.

HOW A SECOND ESSAY EMERGED

The preceding essay on my writing process proved to be much more difficult to write than I thought it would be. Those interested in writing processes may find some discussion of this difficulty as helpful as the essay itself.

In beginning the essay, I faced a problem common to all writers in every writing situation: finding something of worth to say. I was intimidated by the fact that many excellent teachers of writing were going to offer their writing processes. I felt somehow that my essay was going to describe how they write. I did not listen to the advice I have repeatedly given to students, namely, that the worth of a piece of writing derives from the way a writer puts things together, not from any strikingly new ideas he or she may present.

I was also troubled by the fact that no explanation can capture all the in's and out's of a particular writer's process. It must necessarily falsify, as all generalizations do. I was unwilling, then, for my explanation to serve as a model for students.

A third difficulty was provided by my computer, which figures prominently in the essay that finally did develop. It decided to break down before I could get around to writing, and by doing so upset my entire process of composing. I tried longhand and then the typewriter, but nothing seemed to work. Finally, I was able to find a computer in another department.

In retrospect, I see this as an excuse, not a reason, for procrastinating. I do like to write on a computer now, and I think I can write better and more efficiently on one. But that is not the only way I can write. If I had not already been experiencing difficulties, I probably could have made myself write the essay without the computer. When I finally did get to the computer, and after the essay was overdue, I faced the real problems that were keeping the essay from coming.

As I have said, one difficulty in this assignment was my feeling that I had to say something strikingly original about a subject on which much has been written. As I struggled with this problem, I wrote two essays. The first, having to do with my writing process, was embedded in a second, having to do with the difficulty of saying anything that would hold true for all writers in all situations. I wrote this second essay (which originally formed the beginning and end of the first one) because I felt that what I had to say about my own writing process was not important enough in itself. Ironically, this second essay turned into a comment upon itself. That is, it explained why I was having so much difficulty in writing the first essay.

That this second essay happened explains some important things about the writing process. First, it shows that we sometimes have to write something before we can see that it does not belong in the piece we are composing. Second, it shows that these "misfit" ideas may have merit in themselves and be appropriate in another writing situation. Finally, my difficulties are illustrative of the fact (stated in this second essay) that there are no formulas for good writing or for an easy writing process, that writing is always hard work, and that all writers encounter blocks that they simply have to work through.

ESSAY TWO

I'm as suspicious of someone who has easy answers for writing and a formulaic writing process as I am of someone who has simplistic answers to life's important moral questions. There are no simple formulas. What works for one writer will not necessarily work for another. Indeed, what works today for a particular writer in a given writing situation may not necessarily work for him or her tomorrow in another situation.

This is not to say that one cannot become a better writer and develop a more efficient writing process. However, one should be very cautious in offering one's writing process as a model. Every attempt that a writer makes to capsule advice about the writing process must be taken as an attempt to capture reality in language. And like all such attempts, it can be true in general without necessarily being true in the particular case. For example, it is usually a good practice to free write, to put ideas down on paper in rough form and then to go back and sort them out to see what they mean. It is generally true that this will be a more productive activity than sitting pencil in hand waiting for words to come. However, there are times, and the experienced writer will come to recognize these times, when it is good to sit and wait, times when ideas will seem to take shape in the mind.

One does have to be careful of generalizations, but that does not mean that they may not be of some use. I think I can sum up what I have learned about my writing process and what I feel to be true of "the" writing process in general (as far as any generalization can be said to be true) in positing two traits that I see as characteristic of writers whose processes are successful. When my writing is bad, when I have great difficulty, I can usually trace the problem to a lack of one or both of these traits.

First, I have become a better writer and my writing process has become more efficient as I have developed *confidence* that I have something of worth to say. This confidence empowers my writing in several different ways. It frees me to write in an honest voice. I write badly when I don't believe in the "me" who is trying to write. In such cases I will attempt to make up for what the "me" lacks in knowledge about the subject, or in commitment to writing about that subject, with overly ornate language or with strikingly original content.

For many years, now, I have been impressed by the fact that the leading authorities in the various literary fields I have researched seem to write the "tamest" kind of articles. As Pope has said, they seem to be content to say "What oft was thought but ne'er so well expressed." I have often come away from reading their articles chiding myself for not having written something like what they wrote.

But could I have done so? Do I have the knowledge and confidence in myself to make the points that person made so elegantly? I have often damned such a person's work with the faint praise of "at least he/she can write well." As I think back on these comments, I see that I was praising the person much more highly than I realized at the time.

As a young writer, I have often felt that I have to discover something about a particular writer or work that no one else has ever seen. I have to be strikingly original and creative to catch the attention of people who would not otherwise listen to what I have to say. I have often gone so far as to hold to a theory or interpretation longer than my evidence warrants and in the face of counterevidence to which I should have paid attention.

In contrasting what noted scholars have done with what I have done, I do not mean to suggest that originality is unimportant. The best writers are always original. However, their originality derives from the way they put things together rather than from their attempts to find "new" insights. They have the confidence to relax and trust that their way of seeing things will be worthwhile, that someone else will benefit from seeing things as they have seen them.

Second, my writing has improved as I have become more willing to accept the *responsibility* to make my writing better. This trait is integrally connected with the first one, in that I have been more and more willing to put the time into writing as I have become more and more convinced that the product will be worth the effort. I have learned that regardless of what I know about a subject, I often—most times—produce bad writing about that subject before I produce good writing. But I can work through this bad writing and do the necessary preliminary work when I have the confidence that the "bad" writing is going to help me find what I want to say.

If this confidence is lacking, it is difficult to work through this stage.

When I accept an assignment simply because it seems something I should do, with the unexpressed fear that I really don't have anything of worth to say on that subject, I usually find my schedule too crowded to work in any time for the assignment. I am often surprised to find, when I finally face the deadline and put in the work, that I really did have something to say. If I had only known that before, I would have begun the task much earlier. But at other times, I find my fears justified. Nothing comes, or if I am committed to offering something for publication, I produce knowing that the product is not worth my time and certainly not worth the readers' time. If I had made myself do the work earlier, I might have developed the commitment necessary to do research that would have given me something of worth to say. Or I could have backed out of the project while there was time to do so gracefully.

How much of our writing would be better and how many times would we find the writing process easier if we had the courage to do what I have just suggested? If we don't have anything of worth to say on a subject, we should decline to write about it. At first, this statement might seem an easy way out for students in required writing classes. They could argue that they have nothing of worth to say. I can accept the fact that there are many subjects about which students may have nothing of worth to say. However, any thinking human being can develop worthwhile ideas about hundreds of topics. The ideas do not exist ready-made in students' brains, but if they have the confidence in themselves to put forth the necessary effort, the ideas will emerge through the writing process.

In addition to a Ph.D. in English from the University of Nevada—Reno, where he studied with Robert Gorrell and Charlton Laird, William Lutz also holds a J.D. from the Rutgers School of Law. He is currently associate professor of English and chair of the Department of English at Rutgers University—Camden. He is author of numerous articles on rhetoric and language, author or coauthor of five books on rhetoric, and editor of the Quarterly Review of Doublespeak.

HOW I WRITE

William Lutz
Rutgers University—Camden

Before I write, I write in my mind. The more difficult and complex the writing, the more time I need to think before I write. Ideas incubate in my mind. While I walk, drive, swim, and exercise I am thinking, planning, writing. I think about the introduction, what examples to use, how to develop the main idea, what kind of conclusion to use. I write, revise, rewrite, agonize, despair, give up, only to start over again, and all this before I ever begin to put words on paper.

We woke to find ourselves snowed in. Overnight a severe blizzard had deposited over eleven inches of snow, all of it on my doorstep it seemed. Harry Brent, my coauthor and good friend, was staying with me for a few days so we could complete a manuscript on which we had been working for some time. We both thought the snowstorm was a stroke of good luck. Now there would be no distractions. Now we would have to concentrate on our writing while we waited for the snowplow to free us from our winter prison. I settled at the dining room table while Harry took up residence in the living room.

I surrounded myself with the necessary tools of writing: lots of Pilot Precise Ball Liner pens (black ink only) and stacks of yellow legal-size writing pads (each one new with no sheets missing). With these essential elements in place I could begin. I gave Harry plenty of pens and pads of paper so he could write also.

While I was busy writing in the dining room, I could hear mutterings drifting out from the living room. When I stepped into the living room to confer with Harry, I found the carpet covered with crumpled balls of yellow paper as Harry would write a few lines, tear the sheet of paper from the pad, throw it on the carpet, and then begin writing again, only to repeat the process. Harry was accustomed to writing on his word processor. Pilot pens and yellow legal pads were no longer his tools of writing; they were my tools of writing. Until then I had never realized just how important the tools of writing are to the writer, and even more important, how personal the tools of writing are to each writer.

Over the years, my preference for writing tools has changed. I own an IBM Selectric typewriter, which I once used for all my writing. Indeed, without that typewriter I could not write. But over the years I slowly changed, using the typewriter less and less, so that today I write everything—articles, essays, book manuscripts, wills, legal briefs, letters, memoranda—by hand with my Pilot pen and on a yellow legal pad. As I look back I can see why I changed my writing tools.

I write with my pen and legal pad because I feel closer to my writing. I can touch it, feel it. I can pause, write fast, write slow. My writing speed seems to be the same as my thinking speed. Moreover, writing (that is, penmanship) is an automatic act for me, unlike typing, which for me is anything but automatic. I have discovered also that I write visually; I must see my ideas blocked out in paragraphs and how the paragraphs relate to each other. Writing with my pen and legal pad allows me to see my writing, to see my ideas take the concrete form of words on paper. I see my ideas flow from my hand through my pen onto the paper. My words are close and still a part of me. They do not leave me; they do not take on a life of their own until they are typed in the final manuscript. When my words appear in print I look at them and say, "Did I write that? Are those words mine?"

Writing with pen and legal pad also allows me to rewrite and revise both as I write and after I complete the first draft. I feel free to cross out words, phrases, sentences, whole paragraphs. As I write I will pause to consider the choice of a particular word, perhaps changing it once or twice. For me, the typed word represents the finished product, while the written word is the draft, to be worked upon and shaped before it is turned into the final copy.

It was a bright, sunny, winter afternoon. I was sitting in Harry Brent's living room writing furiously as we strained to meet a deadline for a manuscript. As I was rewriting and revising pages of material I had just written, Harry walked into the room and asked if I would like a cup of coffee. I had to say no; there was no time for coffee. How could Harry think of coffee at a time like this? For Harry it was easy; he had finished his writing. Using his word processor, he had written, revised, and polished his part of our project. After checking the spelling of the words he had written, the computer would type out the final copy error free. While the computer was doing all that, Harry would have coffee. I, however, was busy revising and rewriting. The next day I would give my handwritten sheets to my secretary to type. After she had typed them I would proofread and correct them, so she could do the necessary retyping. Harry's copy, of course, had long been completed, and with far less drudgery.

Clearly a word processor is efficient. My tools for writing are not as efficient, yet they are the only tools with which I am comfortable.

And this is my point: How anyone writes is a very personal matter. Each writer must discover for himself or herself the most comfortable tools for writing. Each writer will have a preference, whether it is a battered old typewriter, a sleek new electronic typewriter, a word processor, or a yellow legal pad and special kind of pen. No tools are wrong, as long as the writer is comfortable with them.

The tools of writing are the how of writing. Equally important are the where and when of writing. At first these seem to be minor aspects of the writing process, not really related to the writing process, as we define it, at all. But it is the little things that count. Before we can discuss the writing process, we must begin at the beginning and examine those little things that are so important to any writer: where, when, and how.

All writers have idiosyncrasies that are essential to their writing process. For example, writers usually have special places for writing. A good friend of mine, a novelist, can write only at her kitchen table. When she moved to a new apartment, the kitchen was the first room she organized so she could write. Another friend writes only at his desk in his study. I can write only at my dining room table. Place is crucial for many writers. Place provides not just the physical means for writing (table, chair, light), it provides the atmosphere for writing. For many writers, writing occurs in a context and this context helps them write. Granted there are some writers who can write anywhere; but for many writers, it is important to have a specific place for writing.

Equal to place is time, or when writers write. One writer I know can write only in the early morning. She will write until noon, but then she is finished for the day, no matter what. Another writer I know can write only after midnight. He will write until five or six in the morning, then go to bed, his day's work of writing finished until the next night. For these writers, these hours are their writing times, the hours during which they are productive. While they may write at other hours of the day or night, they usually find that the writing they do then is not their best nor their most serious. As one of them said, letters and other kinds of writing are written in the off-hours. I write in the late morning and early afternoon. The early morning is for coffee and waking up, the late afternoon is for reading mail and catching up on daily chores and business. I write my best and most productively in the late morning and early afternoon. No other time will do.

Teaching writing then is more than teaching the writing process as we know it. We must help students discover the where, when, and how of their writing. We must recognize that writing is a very personal, idiosyncratic act. Students must be encouraged to discover the where, when, and how of writing that best suits them, with which they are most comfortable. Writing is difficult enough without creating an uncomfortable environment using awkward tools at inconvenient times.

Having said how important time, place, and means are to my writing, let me now contradict myself. If I were to write only in my favorite place (at my dining room table) at my favorite time (late morning and early afternoon), I would never get all the writing done that I need, indeed am required, to do. Since there is some writing I cannot do where and when I want, I have, like most writers, developed a kind of competency writing.

All writing is not equal. In my personal and professional life I do many kinds of writing. That writing which is most important to me is done under my ideal circumstances and conditions. That writing which is less important to me is done when and where I can most conveniently do it. I take care with everything I write, but my most important writing is done at my dining room table, with Pilot pen and legal pad, in the late morning and early afternoon.

What is important writing for me? That, of course, depends on the audience and purpose of the writing. This essay is important to me so it is being written under my ideal conditions. The purpose of this essay is to explain to graduate students and teachers of writing (and to myself) how I write. Both the purpose and the audience of this essay are important to me. When I write an article, a paper for presentation at a scholarly meeting, or a manuscript for a book, I do so under my ideal circumstances. All these are examples of important writing. But there are other kinds of important writing for me: a formal argument for tenure for a member of my department, a letter to my parents telling them how much I love them and appreciate all they have done for me, a letter to my son expressing my love for him and my pride in his accomplishments, a letter expressing my condolences to the wife and family of a dear friend who was killed. There are other instances of important writing, but these are a few.

Writing that is of less importance, that is a kind of competency writing, fills much of my life. I do not mean to suggest that I do not take care with this writing; I am careful with all that I write, even a note to the mail carrier. Competency writing is that writing which I can produce quickly, clearly, and even stylishly. Competency writing includes daily letters and memoranda, letters of recommendation, reports, legal briefs, and wills. The crucial difference between competency writing and important writing is the complexity of thought and planning that each kind of writing demands.

Before I write, I write in my mind. The more difficult and complex the writing, the more time I need to think before I write. Ideas incubate in my mind. While I walk, drive, swim, and exercise I am thinking, planning, writing. I think about the introduction, what examples to use, how to develop the main idea, what kind of conclusion to use. I write, revise, rewrite, agonize, despair, give up, only to start over again, and all this before I ever begin to put words on paper. Important writing demands this of me, and I can give it nothing less.

Important writing demands that I understand everything about the topic before I write. To reach this understanding takes time and a great deal of critical, analytical thought. Once I have conquered the subject and made it mine in my mind, I can write. Writing is not a process of discovery for me, for I have discovered everything already in my mind. Writing then becomes for me an end product, a distillation of hours of thought, a conclusion. The writing process takes place in my mind. Once that process is complete the product emerges. Often I can write pages without pause and with very little, if any, revision or even minor changes. The words and ideas just flow, but they flow only because of the large amount of time I have spent thinking, writing, and rewriting in my mind. Writing of this kind is a relief, for I can finally move the text from my mind to the paper.

Competency writing demands far less of me as both writer and thinker. At one time, competency writing was important writing, but because it consists of writing that is repetitious it has become almost automatic. Many of the letters and memoranda I write require only competency because I have written so many of them. So too with the various reports and letters of recommendation I write. Even grant proposals become competency writing after a while. This is a significant point to note: important writing can become competency writing through repetition. The fifth grant proposal can become fairly automatic to write. But competency writing is important in the sense that it is the basic writing of my working day. Competency writing is not careless writing; it must be careful writing, done as best I can. Yet I know that I have a high degree of proficiency with competency writing; the letters and memos flow all day long because they must if I am to do my job.

We make a mistake when we teach students that all writing is equal. We may teach that writing varies with purpose and audience, but writing varies more than that. Obviously I will work much harder on writing an article for publication than I will work on a memo to my departmental colleagues on changes in the class schedule. All writing is not equal. Students know that, and they expend their time and energy accordingly. What we really are aiming to achieve in most writing courses is a kind of competency in writing. We hope to have students develop into solid, competent writers; writers who can write with clarity, and perhaps just a touch of style and a pinch of grace. If we were to add to this course goal the idea of communicating to students the need to judge the kind of writing they are called upon to do and respond accordingly we would have gone a long way to restoring credibility in the writing course.

Writing is like cooking; the quality of the food depends upon the situation and the audience. When I cook for myself, I am competent in preparing the food, but I do not fuss. When I cook for guests, I fuss, and I fuss a lot. The ingredients of the salad are fresh and carefully arranged, the pasta fresh and precisely *al dente,* the breast of chicken boned then cooked to a golden brown in fresh olive oil with herbs and spices, and the gelato carefully presented and served in dessert dishes. When I prepare an important piece of writing such as an article or book manuscript, I fuss, and I fuss a lot.

What we are asking students to develop is competency writing, a skill that we possess but think little about. Once they have developed competency writing they can move on to important writing, for important writing has competency writing as its base. But students need to be aware of when to use competency writing and when to use important writing. It is not an easy choice; for competency writing is far easier to produce than important writing, which comes not just from the hand and mind but from the heart. Important writing demands that a part of the writer be put on the page for all to see. It is a public act that reveals part of the private self. It demands risks. Competency writing is safe, comfortable. But we fail as teachers of writing, and as writers, if all we teach our students is competency writing. We must teach them also important writing.

Carolyn B. Matalene is associate professor of English at the University of South Carolina. After four years as director of freshman English she needed to get away, so she spent a semester teaching writing to senior English majors at Shanxi University in the People's Republic of China. She teaches graduate courses in the composition and rhetoric program at South Carolina as well as undergraduate writing courses. Her course Classical Rhetoric: Theory and Practice, based on Ed Corbett's text, is extremely popular with students in the university's honors college; last year they named her "The professor who was the greatest influence on us."

THOUGHTS ON THE OPENING AND THE BARRING OF THE DOOR

Carolyn B. Matalene
University of South Carolina

We are culturally averse to a shared understanding [of the composing process] because we value doing it differently; we sincerely hope that we are weird. No wonder then that as Emig and Flower and Hayes have concluded, individual accounts of the composing process are idiosyncratic, more concerned with feelings about writing than with the act itself.

What joy there was in all this, the joy which
  sages and worthies have coveted.
He was taxing Non-Being to produce Being,
  calling to the Silence, importunate for an
  answer:
he was engrossing the great spaces within a span
  of silk, belching forth torrents of language
  from the inch-space of the heart.
Words were expanding the theme, the more as it
  proceeded: thought was bringing it under his
  hand, as it became the more profound.
He was scattering a fragrance of delicious hanging-
  clusters, putting forth a profusion of
  green-budding twigs.
A laughing wind was flying by and whirling up
  a solid shape, a mass of shining cloud was
  arising in the garden of letters.
  —Lu Chi, 302 A.D.

Lu Chi's lines, describing the composing process as we would all like to experience it, come from the "Wen Fu" or prose poem that he wrote on "The Art of Letters."* Here he tried to "put on record the superb artistries achieved by the writers before us, and follow on with a discussion of the causes of good and bad writing." His sense of the incomparable joy that the act of writing can provide rings true through the centuries. So does his understanding of the difficulty of writing well, "Either he found himself on even ground and advance was easy, or the ground was rock-bestrewn, and he hobbled along in misery." And so does his experience of confusion and frustration, "Always dissatisfaction remains when the end / is reached—dare we then be complacent and / cherish our conceit?" In the final lines of his great poem, Lu Chi resigns himself to knowing nothing about his own creative powers, "This thing which is in me but which no efforts / of mine can slay! / Wherefore time and again I stroke my empty / bosom in pity for myself: so ignorant am I of / what causes the opening and the barring of the door."

We know little more than Lu Chi did about the opening and the barring of the door. But undoubtedly facing the blank paper is much more difficult for us, post-Romantic Westerners, than it was for Lu Chi. Every literate Chinese has spent years memorizing thousands of characters, set phrases, maxims, analogies, and allusions and thus approaches any writing task with a huge memory bank of acceptable expressions, patterns, and models. Furthermore, manipulating these well-known elements to produce a text is not only acceptable but desirable. The more one depends upon and refers to the tradition, the more educated, cultivated, and scholarly is one's prose adjudged. As Lu Chi explained, "When we writers come to grasping axes and hewing axe handles, we do, after all, select models which are near at hand." The Chinese writer is and always has been encouraged to imitate and praised for achieving a voice that sounds like everyone else's.

For us, however, the Romantic revolution and the deliberate separation of rhetoric from poetry meant the elevation of the individual imagination, and thus, as writers we are saddled with the terrible burden of being original. We must ever make it new, say it differently, and sound unique. To be truly creative means to achieve a radically original, individual style. The artists we have canonized in the twentieth century are the great stylistic innovators, and we can recognize them on museum walls and on pages without even seeing their names. But what this "tradition of the new" means for ordinary, everyday writers is simple terror, the fear of sounding like the person at the next desk or in the

---

*The quotations from Lu Chi are taken from E. R. Hughes, trans., *The Art of Letters: Lu Chi's "Wen Fu," A.D. 302, A Translation and Comparative Study* Bollingen Series 29. Copyright 1951, © renewed 1979 by Princeton University Press. Excerpt pp. 98–99. Reprinted by permission of Princeton University Press.

next office, the humiliation of being boring, the grayness of the inau-
thentic voice.

The Romantic values of individuality and originality greatly prejudice academic writing instruction and continue to inform classroom
practices. We of the academy want to encourage each student to
achieve and to value individual expression. That the world of business
and government values something else, clear and concise prose that is
collectively useful and subject to a single interpretation, constitutes a
great gap between the world of work and the world of belles lettres. But
as James Kinneavy, Ross Winterowd, Merrill Whitburne, and many
others have noted, it is a gap that most English teachers, trained in the
literary tradition, prefer to ignore. Being original and being valued for
being original are, after all, our basic motivations for doing what we do.
As Western, post-Romantic academics and writing teachers, we must
judge and be judged according to the criterion of originality. It is a
cultural given, but not a universal truth. And we might do well to admit
how profoundly the burden of originality affects us as writers, teachers,
and students, and how profoundly it affects our sense of the composing
process.

Consider, for example, the contributors to this volume, each required herein to be original about being original. An unsettling assignment indeed and one likely to be fulfilled in extraordinarily diverse
ways. Thus, even from such a highly self-conscious and homogeneous
group as this, collectively attuned to the rhetorical tradition and to its
most esoteric terminology, it is unlikely that the collected accounts will
yield a consensual view of the composing process. We are culturally
averse to a shared understanding because we value doing it differently;
we sincerely hope that we are weird. No wonder then that as Emig and
Flower and Hayes have concluded, individual accounts of the composing process are idiosyncratic, more concerned with feelings about writing than with the act itself.

Rather than offer one more weird, or perhaps—alas—only slightly
weird, account of one more idiosyncratic composing process, I want
instead to focus on the delicate and perilous interactions that occur
between teacher and student, eventually between editor and writer,
and that seem to have a great deal to do with the opening and the
barring of the door.

We all teach writing in an academic and cultural setting in which
originality is the measure. Every description of letter grades, every
explanation of grading criteria, features the word *original* as a primary
descriptor of the A paper. The B paper is also original, but somehow less
so; somewhere between a B and a C originality is lost. Excellence in
prose unquestionably means originality. It also inevitably means that
the writer must go it alone, solo, depending only on "the inch-space of

the heart." Unlike the Chinese writer, however, the Western writer cannot match his prose—its words, phrases, maxims, metaphors, analogies, allusions, sentences, paragraphs, and forms—to an unchanging external standard, to a corpus of what all agree is acceptable prose. For us, uniqueness is the standard. Originality is the outward and visible sign of individuality, and individuality is all.

When a Chinese writer sounds like everyone else, she knows she has got it right. When an American writer sounds like everyone else, she knows she has a C at best. If she is my student, she won't have a letter grade but instead a collection of comments ranging from the gentle, "cliché" and "pre-used language," to the brutal, "ugh" and "yuck," to the symbolic, a wavy underline to be translated as "You've got to be kidding" or "Go back to the drawing board." No real approval can be garnered by fitting in, by drawing upon a fund of stock phrases or practiced techniques. Revision then means making it new, newer, newest.

The psychological effect of the aloneness we impose on the writing process is, of course, a paralyzing insecurity and an intense, sometimes pathetic, need for approval, praise, affirmation. Grown men and women weep at hearing the meagerest of compliments on their prose. When no praise is forthcoming, writers rage and drink, take dope and quarrel, abuse their spouses and children and pets. Struggling in terrible loneliness to meet the awful requirement of originality, we must have what our therapists call "strokes." Never quite knowing whether our struggle has yielded "a solid shape, a mass of shining cloud," or inchoate trivia, we must be told. We must be reassured. If we are not, we do not write.

Recently, I have asked writing teachers in my graduate class to write brief accounts of their own histories as writers, a sort of portrait of the teacher as a young writer. Such a group is of course made up of the survivors, those who have weathered their language training, gathered enough reassurances, and amassed enough strokes not only to continue, but finally to make linguistic originality their profession. Not surprisingly, the common theme in all of their stories is that from someone somewhere along the way they received enthusiastic affirmation of their abilities to manipulate language. That good writers receive praise for writing well might seem the most obvious and simple-minded tautology. Actually, given our lack of agreement about what constitutes good writing, it is more like a self-fulfilling prophecy. Only those who are praised and stroked and encouraged, or who at least perceive the responses they get as affirming, have the heart to struggle with the opening of the door.

As I talk informally to my undergraduate writing students, especially when we are in our cups after the work of the semester and they tell me how they really felt about the remarks on their papers—"great" and "terrific" and "wow!" as well as "ugh" and "yuck"—I am forced to admit the impact that serious comments have on serious students. They remember exactly what I wrote, where I wrote it, and how it affected them. A vertical line with "yes" or "good" in the margin often marks passages I consider praiseworthy; I make such swipes with extreme haste in order to maintain my reputation for returning papers at the next class meeting. But one bright young man told me that he longed for those decisive lines, that he knew the approval stopped and the disapproval began exactly at the end of the line. I was too stunned to tell him otherwise.

If Chinese students have a memory bank of elegant phrases, American students probably have a memory bank of nasty remarks. "This is an excellent topic, but. . . ." "Although your argument starts well, . . ." Most of us can, with some Proustian recall, not only remember but even visualize the comments our professors wrote on our great works. I can, from a generation ago. Professor Frederick Faverty wrote in large, drooping pencil, "Brilliant apperçus"; Robert Mayo typed a single-spaced page beginning, "Your paper is like one of those ice cream parlors where we are offered thirty-one flavors, but never allowed to indulge fully in just one"; but the most devastating came from Richard Ellman's grader, "I can only suggest that you be more tactful." Even worse was the single sentence my friend Elizabeth received on the fifty book reports she had written for a graduate seminar in Shakespeare, "Don't correct typos with a pencil." Imagine the comments we have scrawled on papers and the brains they are emblazoned in. Imagine the number of cryptic instructions we have offered, like the wonderfully abstract, "Be concrete." Think of the nitpicking editorial corrections we once endured that we then elevated into our own pet purisms. If we were chastised for writing, "centers around," so too will each of our students be chastised. (If you can't beat students with a rule, how do you know you're real?)

The truth is, comments that seem like verdicts on our individual papers are actually lifelong intrusions into our composing processes. Like the apocryphal child in the behaviorist's lab, sensitized to fear white fur and never desensitized, we go on forever trying to write by a patchwork prescription for being original, pieced together from the directions, negations, affirmations, and humiliations we have received.

The longer I teach writing and the more I listen to students talk about their setbacks and advances, the more convinced I am that a writing teacher's real function is simply to require students to write and write and write and then to respond to that writing with praise and praise and praise. Having to be original is after all so terrifying, anxiety-producing, and soul-destroying (even Shakespeare quit as soon as he made some money), that surely our major responsibility is to offer support and encouragement and affirmation. We know that children who have been read to in their parents' laps become readers because of pleasurable associations. Our job is to establish an atmosphere of understanding and kindness in which positive strokes are offered lavishly; then our students will associate writing with affirmation instead of with the composing neuroses that we unwittingly bequeath them, and then they will eventually teach themselves as they try—all alone but with courage and hope—to open the door.

Or perhaps this is overly dramatic for the stuff of everyday prose.

The composing process, like courtship, may be based on universal human urges, but its surface forms are the result of cultural practices. The act of writing is indeed lonely and ineffable and risky, but perhaps the anguish, the despair, and the romantic agony need not be painted in quite such florid hues. Demystifying the composing process has for me depended upon two unromantic but becalming redirections as a writer and a writing teacher. The first is to deemphasize the individuality-originality syndrome and to give up on "the writer as culture hero" going it alone. Being original doesn't have to mean total solitude or editorial isolation. Writers need help—and company. The Chinese writer has help, a whole headful of formulas ready to flow through his brush; since we eschew repeating or imitating the canon, we need another kind of help—the help provided by an editor. "Take a lover who can spell," I tell my students, or who can punctuate or paragraph or organize. Editors are the seldom-sung heroes and heroines of literature, as the professionals know. *Il miglior fabbro,* said Eliot of Pound with gratitude and without embarrassment. Every writer, which is to say everyone of us, needs a good editor, one who is discerning where we are blind, critical where we are satisfied, cool where we are feverish, uncomprehending where we are facile, fastidious where we are slovenly, strong where we are weak.

That we are strong at some tasks and weak at others leads to a second redirection, also demystifying. The ancients divided rhetoric into the five arts of invention, arrangement, style, memory, and delivery. In our emphasis on process, we have linked them sequentially. But thinking of these arts as stages in the composing process is to impose a misleading temporal metaphor. The five arts, it seems to me, are not so much stages as they are different sets or bundles of cognitive skills. Different writers have different combinations of them, that is different strengths and weaknesses; they also have different combinations available to them for different writing tasks.

Some writers can present brilliant ideas in highly structured texts but torture us with appalling sentences. Others offer us the weariest of ideas but do so with the most elegant syntax. Some speakers compose moving and important addresses but put us to sleep with their inept delivery. Some tasks seem impossible at some times, easy at others; hard for him, easy for her.

Self-appraisal means analyzing where our own strengths and weaknesses lie as writers and as teachers, and then making them explicit, matching our talents to our tasks, getting and giving help according to our gifts. After many years, for example, I have learned that for invention I need time, time away from the keyboard to let ideas percolate in my head; but for arrangement, I usually need an editor, especially in the blind period right after finishing something, when the result of all my effort now seems both silly and obvious, that moment when Lu Chi wondered, "dare we then be complacent and cherish our conceit?" My answer to this question at that moment is no. So I get another opinion, and give it to a friend. Being such a friend—a serious, critical, but highly subjective editorial friend—is the best I can do for students. And letting them know my strengths and weaknesses as a writer and an editor is an important part of that friendship.

At present, our sense of the composing process is extremely limited, about as limited as our notion of intelligence, which is still defined very narrowly. But progress is being made in demystifying the opening and the closing of the door. Recent work directed toward defining "multiple frames of mind" is paralleled by the recent work of Flower and Hayes in which they present their "multiple representation thesis" as a fuller explanation of the invention stage. They suggest that writers use a number of different ways to represent meaning to themselves. We still have a long way to go, however, before we can accurately discriminate among the different skills that coalesce to produce writing, before we can achieve, for example, a placement procedure so refined that all the poor organizers could be put together in a classroom with a teacher whose talent is structure. Our best techniques for evaluating writing skills are still extremely crude.

So we'll have to muddle on, analyzing as best we can for ourselves and for our students which sets of skills we have, which we lack, where we can offer help and where we need it.

"Wherefore time and again I stroke my empty bosom in pity for myself: so ignorant am I of what causes the opening and the barring of the door," said Lu Chi. But at least and at last I have learned that there are many doors that open onto creating a text, and I needn't struggle with all of them alone.

Louis T. Milic was born on September 5, 1922, in Split, Yugoslavia, served in the USAF in World War II. He is currently professor of English at Cleveland State University, where he has served nine years as chair of the Department of English.

Milic has authored numerous texts on stylistics and rhetoric, including A Quantitative Approach to the Style of Jonathan Swift *(1967) and* Stylists on Style: A Handbook with Passages for Analysis *(1969), and he has published over forty professional articles, ranging from the entry for "Gender" in* Encyclopedia Americana *(1958) to "Theories of Style and Their Implications for the Teaching of Composition" in* College Composition and Communication, *16 (1965); from "Computer Programs and the Heroic Couplet" in* Think *(May–June 1968) to "Eisenhower's First Inaugural Address: Composition and Style" in* Style, *16 (1982).*

HOW A
STYLISTICIAN
WRITES

Louis T. Milic
Cleveland State University

All writing . . . has the feature that it is difficult, lonely work, and satisfying mainly when finished. I face writing with enthusiasm when I am rolling the topic around in my mind and I enjoy the attendant research, but I genuinely dread the moment when I have to put pen to paper—or, for that matter, put fingers on the keyboard in front of the green screen.

Before the age of word processors, I was the sort of writer who writes a draft, corrects the typescript, has another version typed, studies and corrects that one, and so on until the conviction sets in that nothing more can be done or, more likely, until the deadline has expired. Before I ever had any secretarial help, I had a wife who could type, or a graduate student, or my own ten fingers—though this last possibility was unsatisfactory, not because I am not a good typist, but because I cannot stop myself from editing while typing, which produces careless repetition errors. Now that I have a word processor, I can do endless editing without subjecting my associates to heavy typing burdens. Nonetheless, unlike my students I find it difficult to *compose* at the keyboard, although I have been trying. What I do now, in this new machine age, is not very different from what I did then, except that the IBM PC performs as the typist used to. Now I correct each printed-out draft with one of two writing implements (a Kimberly 2B—very soft— pencil or a black Pilot Razorpoint pen) and then enter the corrections on the screen previous to printing out a new draft. One reason I cannot easily edit on the screen, apart from my long habit of using pen or pencil on paper, is the restricted number of lines visible there at one time. I need to be able to see the whole piece simultaneously, so as to be able to assess the relative length of sentences, to ponder the amount of emphasis placed here and there, to inhibit the unnecessary or careless repetition of words, and so on, practices that derive from my notion of writing as being in great part editing.

As a stylistician, I believe, unlike the novelist Anthony Trollope (who liked to write a thousand words every sixty minutes, with his watch on the table, and who had trained himself not to need to rewrite) that the process of composing goes something like this:

1. A topic is thought of or assigned.
2. A period of time elapses during which the topic and its ramifications are whirled around in the mind and ideas about it are accumulated. This process may last for hours, days, or even years, depending on interest, pressure, and other factors. This stage of the composing process includes the period during which actual primary or library research is performed, in the course of which the original topic or idea may be considerably altered. Sometimes as a result of this process, the topic is abandoned, either temporarily or for good.
3. A structure for the piece is designed, which may be set down on paper, with more or less elaboration, depending on its complexity, or merely kept in mind as a sketch or rough outline.
4. A draft is attempted, with a maximum of attention to substance and organization and only the slightest care for polish at the sentence level. The important thing at this stage is not to be distracted by a search for the *mot propre* or the fine example.
5. The draft is revised and structural changes, organizational re-arrangements made (i.e., parts interchanged, a new beginning considered). Frequently, at this stage, the draft is still incomplete.
6. The complete draft is subjected to rhetorical and stylistic revision (sometimes called "polishing"). Depending on the audience and the time available, this may be the briefest or the longest part of the procedure.

Although research papers are not the only kind of papers that I write, they are the most complex and they readily illustrate several of the stages I have described above. It may be useful to trace the history of a particular topic as an example of what happens as an idea matures.

While studying eighteenth-century texts, I had made it a habit to collect quotations containing the word *style* from both British and French writers. For me this had a particular significance because of my interest not only in stylistics but in its history and in the development of the idea of style during the eighteenth century, when style was considered either correct or not, and high, middle, or low, but never valuable because of its individuality. I arranged these citations in a kind of order, mainly chronological, and with framing commentary made the whole into a paper entitled "Towards a History of Applied Stylistics in the Eighteenth Century," which I delivered at the annual meeting of the American Society for Eighteenth-Century Studies in Victoria, Canada, in 1977. By the time I submitted the paper for publication in the proceedings of the society *(Studies in Eighteenth-Century Culture)*, I had discovered that the difference between the eighteenth-century's and later views of style was conveniently summarized in the change of meaning that occurred in the terms *singular* and *singularity.* Whereas to us, these words merely refer to unusualness, to the contemporaries of Swift and Johnson, they meant "unusual and therefore objectionable." The idea that a style such as that of Ernest Hemingway or Tom Wolfe, for example, is attractive because of its unusualness, its extreme individuality, is a relatively new one. It is probable that it developed around the time of the French Revolution and may well be associated with the far-reaching convulsion in values and ideas that accompanied it. Consequently I revised my paper so as to include the emphasis provided by examples of these terms, retitled it " 'Singularity' and Style in the Eighteenth Century," and submitted it in that form to the editor of the Proceedings of the Society. It was severely criticized by the reviewers and was not printed. I intended to revise it once more, but time passed and I was unable to give it my attention.

Two years later, in 1979, I was approached by the editor of the Japanese English-language journal *Poetica* and asked to contribute something in my specialty. Since I had a paper nearly ready—or so I thought—I offered him the "singularity" paper, subject to further revision. I believed that some of the criticism directed at me by the ASECS reviewers was based on misunderstanding, which was partly my own fault for having failed clearly to explain my intentions and my presumptions. I would now have the opportunity to make everything much clearer. In addition, I reasoned, the paper was already in existence and revision would be a relatively brief affair. As is nearly always true, however, the revision was very complicated and took much longer than I allowed. The paper, under the title "Singularity and Style in Eighteenth-Century English Prose" finally appeared in 1982, more than six years after the original conception. In the course of these revisions, the original idea had changed considerably and the expression and presentation of the idea had also changed.

For me, finding a topic has never been difficult. In the course of reading, teaching, talking to students or colleagues, listening to papers at conferences, walking, driving to work, or even shaving, ideas cross the threshold of consciousness and are recorded at first in one's memory and eventually on a scrap of paper or in a journal and filed—nowadays no doubt in a data base management system. A difficulty arising from this method—as opposed to the more businesslike one of keeping only one topic in mind and working on it until finished—is deciding which topic deserves the highest priority, to allow time for the necessary research, an activity that may be infinitely variable in duration. Often topic priority is determined by external considerations: a promise to deliver a paper or contribute to a book edited by someone else (such as the present effort), a contract deadline, or a desire to publish while the topic is timely, relevant, or exciting to others. Of course, an agreement to accept a deadline involves a decision about priority.

The second stage of composing, the accumulation of ideas, or the research into the data that will yield the substance of the work, is in many ways the most satisfying, but it can also be the most time-consuming. It can go on so long that it becomes autotelic: the researcher forgets that the purpose of research is the eventual presentation of the material to the community of scholars. I am one of those who can luxuriate in the pleasure of looking through old books, works that were previously only items in a bibliography or summaries in a history, and find that contact with the genuine article delivers a different message, reveals a truth previously hidden. What is both fascinating and seductive about the process of research is its uncertainty. One heads in a certain direction, but the facts determine whether that direction is the one that will be followed or another itinerary substituted for it. It is the deviations from plan that stimulate the intellectual curiosity associated with the distracting power of research.

Research, unfortunately, tends to be unstructured when it is as I have described it. One begins with a plan, but it is often abandoned as new facts are uncovered and new insights formed. Hence problems of structure are postponed to the writing process, though an outline sometimes precedes the research, seldom at the initial stage. In a complex task such as the writing of the "singularity" paper, I use an outline, sometimes quite an elaborate one (see Figure 1). By the time I was writing the first revision of this paper, I had developed quite a different outline (see Figure 2), from which, however, I deviated quite a little in writing the actual revision. For the final version,[1] I began with the belief that no new outline was needed, but that a cut-and-paste job would suffice. My files reveal that the final paper was redrafted four times and that much of the material was new, including a number of the citations. It is hardly possible to go into detail about the specific changes that were made, but a look at the introductory paragraph of each of the three versions will reveal my desire to establish at once what the paper is saying.

---

[1] *Poetica*, 13 (1982), 91–112.

DRAFT OUTLINE—VICTORIA PAPER

I.   Sciences and their names in the 18th century
       The advent of linguistics and later of stylistics
       Definitions concerning the current practice of
       prose stylistics

II.   Purpose of the current paper: to provide some
       materials which taken altogether may serve as
       the basis for an idea of the history of the sub-
       ject in the 18th century in English and French
       only.

       There is no attempt to achieve completeness or any
       kind of distribution.

III.   The several kinds of statement which were made
       about style during the given period
       a. instructions about how to write
       b. statements of ideals
       c. comments about the writings of individuals
       (provide examples of each kind)

IV.   Chronological list of French, English, and
       American examples of Type C

V.   Interpretation of the data with specific respect
       to:
       emphasis on deficiencies
       deviation from an absolute standard
       obliviousness to the value of uniqueness
       failure to distinguish between stylistics and
       linguistics

VI.   Counterarguments could include the interest in
       the individual genius of writers like Shake-
       speare, Dante, Cervantes, Chaucer, Milton, etc.

       In each case however the praise is diluted by a
       criticism of their deviations from the standard
       of the period.

VII.   Conclusion
       Interface between the general nature of the 18th
       century and the emphasis on individuality of the
       Romantic period.

       Therefore a search for genuine instances of sty-
       listics in the 18th century is a search for devia-
       tions and aberrations.

Figure 1

OUTLINE

1. The history of stylistics is very thin.
2. There is no coherent account of the progress from singularity to originality.
3. There are a few articles and parts of books that treat ideals, key words, and some matters of theory, for example, Abrams, Mann, etc. But even they distort the evidence in the service of a thesis.
4. The modern distortion and reversal of Buffon's famous remark indicates the distance that has been traversed.
5. An examination of a series of remarks about style written during the eighteenth century reveals the consistency with which writers held to the uniformitarian view. The following examples suggest as well a number of other preoccupations characteristic of commentators of the time.
6. It is convenient to suppose that this important change took place during the French Revolution or the early Romantic period when so many other things changed. But nearly every citation reveals not the modern notion but a version of the earlier one concerning individual stylistic uniqueness.
7. The modern view is based on concepts of psychology, language acquisition, and psycholinguistics unknown in the eighteenth century or for that matter in the nineteenth century.
8. To a great extent our notion partakes of an amoral relativism that has its unfortunate aesthetic consequences. Individuality, even if repugnant, achieves an aesthetic effect. Perhaps the gradual impoverishment of writing in our time can be traced to the growth and development of this concept.

Figure 2

Original Oral Version

The task I have proposed to myself in this paper—bringing together some materials for the study of the applied criticism of style in our period—requires some preliminary stipulations and definitions. Strictly speaking, there was in the eighteenth century no study of the language of individual writers based on the assumption that each writer had (and inevitably must have) individual peculiarities of expression. First, there was not a general consciousness of a language as a repository of synonymous options available to express a given meaning, though there was a great deal of discussion of style in a semi-linguistic context.

Second, there was no widespread belief in the value of "singularity of manner" in expression. Thus there was no place for stylistics.

First Revision

Although the history of stylistics is marked by disagreements—of theory, definition, and method—and even during the most recent period some skepticism about the very existence of an entity called "style," a consensus appears to have formed concerning the nature of statements about style. Such statements seem to require both the inclusion of the name of a writer and some characterization of his individual manner of expression. Anything lacking these elements is considered a statement about something other than style. [Examples follow.] ´

Final Version

To the student of stylistics, the profuse critical writings of the eighteenth century offer a strange mixture: much talk of *style,* many works on *rhetoric,* but very little of that applied *stylistics* (which I take to be the study of the peculiarities of language that distinguish one writer from another), to which we are now so accustomed. Today, a great deal is written about style; stylistics is active, assisted by the heavy guns of modern technology and science: linguistics, computers, and statistics, among others. To look to the idea of progress for the causes of this difference would be simplistic, for the change was not at all progressive. We write less well than did our predecessors, we read less and we are less concerned with certain ideals of good writing than they were. The rise in our interest in applied stylistics resides in the sharply different attitudes toward style held by critics of that time and ours, attitudes I shall call "generalist" and "individualist," respectively. I propose to illustrate this distinction of theory, which is a chapter in the history of applied stylistics, with citations from critics of the period, which together constitute an anthology of eighteenth-century stylistic criticism, not without its own interest.

It is easy to observe that the last version gets to the point more quickly, provides enough historical background to make clear the relevance of the study, and introduces the main technical distinction (generalist and individualist). The paragraph that follows summarizes the argument and offers a refutation of the most obvious counterargument—the one that was prominent in the comments of the referees who examined the paper for the ASECS. I cannot take credit for this effective arrangement, which was already standard in the time of Demosthenes and that of Cicero. But I must take the blame for having failed to avail myself of it the first time the paper was reviewed.

A paper of this kind is more difficult to organize than might appear at first. One cannot simply string the citations in chronological order with some bridging matter in between. For one thing, the citations were of paragraph length and needed to be introduced and explained both before and after in order not to appear to be extraneous to the argument. Several had to be divided so that each part could fit the section of the argument it was relevant to. One could not merely say, for example, "as Burrowes said in 1797," and then quote a page, and expect readers to make out for themselves the point of the quotation. That this applied even to very sophisticated readers I am in a position to testify. Thus the structural problem for this kind of paper is finding an appropriate form for the argument such that the citations may be inserted seamlessly or wrapped in such a way that only the relevant part protrudes.

As for the actual drafting, I believe and act on the principle that the important need is to get the ideas down on paper, in some sort of logical order, but without particular attention to the language, except insofar as it must be indicative of the intention one has when one puts it down. The finish can be applied as part of the last stage of work. Of course, this description is misleading, for it implies that something is being laid on top of what was there, style as it were applied to substance. A better analogy is drawn from sculpture: the figure is roughly cut out of the block of stone, meaningful only to the sculptor, who provides the actual image, the careful details in the statue that will have meaning for the spectator. Thus it is during the last stage when in addition to cosmetic changes, such as fixing up of idiom, removal of crossed metaphors, correction of spelling, substantive changes of lexis and taxis are made, which will provide not only a more accurate meaning for the reader but the appropriate emphasis to aid understanding. Such changes are more than mere polish.

A disadvantage of the "dirty draft" method, one that I have often encountered, is the ineradicable influence that first drafts have on what follows. For writers, everything on paper has a reality, even a sanctity, which creates obstacles when what is on paper needs to be discarded. I could hardly have written this paper if I did not have file cabinets full of the various drafts of all my papers. I am often tempted to discard them, but I do not. Similarly, when I find that my first throw on the paper will not take me where I want to go, I tinker with it instead of simply deciding to start over again. And the cut-and-paste method is only theoretically attractive. Anyone who is at all careful in his or her writing knows that the process of moving from one part of the argument to another, from one paragraph to another, requires a simultaneous consciousness both of the two parts of the arguments and of their role in the total design. This consciousness results in the development of what in music is called a modulation, a gradual shift from one key to another. If a paragraph is moved from one part of a paper to another, these transitional threads are missing or become misleading and the work of repair is more arduous than beginning anew, because in a new beginning the modulation process goes on more or less automatically. The result of the tension between the desire to cast words on paper with speed and the realization of its dangers is writer's block—the tendency to postpone writing as long as possible, something that every writer is afflicted with at some time and which can be total and disabling or disguised, as when the "need" for more research delays the beginning of the drafting stage.

Whereas the drafting stage is tense and meets resistance, the revision stage is generally pleasurable. It signifies that the work is nearly completed and it is relatively easy by comparison with the original process of creating sentences where none have been before. Sometimes, miraculously, there is very little to do and it seems that the drafting process was working at very high efficiency. It is also true that the more time elapses between draft and revision, the more unsatisfactory the draft seems and the more revision there is to do. Every writer knows that "being too close" to a draft blinds one to its defects. The alternative to giving oneself time away from it is to secure the help of another pair of eyes, an editor in effect. There are a few people on whom I rely for this sort of help, but only when it is absolutely necessary, because it is an imposition on them and it is not without its delays. So I am generally my own editor. To illustrate the process, I shall draw on some material dating back to a time when I was writing a freshman English textbook.[2]

In Figure 3, you can see the first paragraph of Chapter 29 of *The English Language: Form and Use*. This text was prepared during a period when language-oriented books for freshman English were thought reasonable, or at least publishable. Of course, they were considered dangerously difficult. Hence, the chapters had be short, and the pace slow, adapted to the supposedly minimal attention span of the students. Compare this final version with Figure 4, the original first draft (written in blue ink using a Parker cartridge fountain pen). You will notice only a small number of revisions in Figure 4. It is essentially a first cast of the thought on the paper, stimulated by the ever-nearing publisher's deadline. But it is on the pages shown in Figures 5a–c, that the work of revision was done.

On the first page (Figure 5a), it can be seen that several sentences near the beginning have simply been deleted, necessitating a transitional adjustment in the sentence following the deletion. Several other syntactic changes can be seen on this page, along with another deleted sentence. The three sentences deleted near the beginning of the paragraph were left out because they seemed redundant and condescend-

[2]With William S. Chisholm, Jr., *The English Language: Form and Use* (New York: Longmans, 1974). Copyright © 1974 by Longman, Inc. All rights reserved.

Section Four:
ENGLISH WORDS

29 EMPHASIS AND THE IDEA OF CHOICE

When you know the rules of grammar in any language, you can produce well-formed grammatical sentences. But no mere series of grammatical sentences, like those turned out by a computer, can make a composition. What makes sentences into a composition is the connection of meaning that runs between them, what might be called their "logic." And the main quality that makes connected sentences into an *effective* composition is the choice of the right kind of **emphasis** to make the connection stand out for the reader. Every time a sentence is framed, a large number of choices is made but the speaker or writer is not always aware of them. It is only when he stops to consider why a sentence is not clear or not effective that he becomes consciously aware of choice, of choosing this word, those forms, and that order. What makes one choice effective and another not is emphasis. Emphasis attracts the attention of the reader or hearer to the particular sense intended by the speaker or writer. It is not possible to avoid putting some emphasis in any statement that one makes. When you pronounce a sentence, you normally place a heavier stress on one word than on the others. The following sentence would normally be pronounced with a heavier stress on the italicized word:

1a. I can't see the *birds* in the tree.

When you choose to stress *birds,* you are choosing normal emphasis. But you could choose differently:

Figure 3

Emphasis and the Idea of Choice

When you know the rules of grammar of any language, you can produce well-formed grammatical sentences. What more can there be to learn once you have [the mastery of] that skill? If you are learning conversational Spanish, sentences may [well] be all you [will] need. But if you are going to be more than a talker, let us suppose a speaker or writer, being able to write grammatical sentences is only the beginning of the job. No series of grammatical sentences, like those turned out by a computer, [can] make a composition. What makes sentences into a composition is the connected meaning that runs between them, what might be called [this] "logic." And what makes connected sentences [(composition)] *effective* is the choice of the right kind of emphasis to make the connection stand out for the reader. The choices that are available run from sounds, spellings, inflections, words, constructions, word order, arrangement to imagery and other poetic resources. Every time a sentence is framed, a whole number of choices are made but the speaker or writer is perhaps not aware of them. It is only when he stops to consider why a sentence is not clear or not effective that he becomes consciously aware of choice, of choosing this word, those forms and that order. What makes one choice effective and another not is emphasis. Emphasis is what makes something more attention-getting than the things around it. The problem of emphasis, however, is not always solved, by making everything emphatic — it doesn't work that way. Emphasis is relative: it depends on what is around it.

Consider the way people dress. Some kinds of clothes are appropriate for certain activities ("contexts"): bathing suits for swimming, cap and

Figure 4

Part II
Chapter 29

Emphasis and the Idea of Choice (all caps)

When you know the rules of grammar, in any language, you can

produce well-formed grammatical sentences. ~~What more can there be~~

~~to learn once you have that skill? If you are learning conversational~~

~~Spanish, the mastery of sentences may well be all you will need. But~~

~~if you are going to be more than a talker, let us suppose a speaker~~

~~or writer, being able to write grammatical sentences is only the~~

But no more
~~beginning of the job.~~ A series of grammatical sentences, like those

turned out by a computer, can make a composition. What makes sentences

connection of
into a composition is the ~~connected~~ meaning that runs between them,

the main quality that
what might be called their "logic." And ~~what~~ makes connected sentences into an

composition
~~(composition)~~ effective is the choice of the right kind of emphasis

to make the connection stand out for the reader. ~~The choices that are~~

~~available run from sounds, to spellings, inflections, words, constructions,~~

~~word order, arrangement to imagery and other poetic resources.~~ Every

time a sentence is framed, a whole number of choices are made but the

Figure 5A

ing. But the sentence that was deleted near the bottom of the page was left out for another reason, one having to do with direction. If it had been left in, the natural expectation would have been a discussion of each of the items in the list, something I was not ready to do at that point while still engaged in making general approaches to the subject. On the next page (Figure 5b), there are several lines blacked out with interlineations above them. The two sentences that were replaced seemed too informal and to be oversimplifying the matter, which required more explanation than I had given it. Hence an insert (Figure 5c) was written in which an additional explanation was given along with a set of examples. The pages constituting the stage of revision shown in Figures 5a–c were again retyped and very minor adjustments made before they were sent to the publisher. My colleague and I constantly struggled between being offensively simple in our explanations and examples and going in the opposite direction. We may have erred in the former direction. Those of our students who understood us and passed the course said the book was condescending. The others said the course was too difficult.

These two kinds of writing typify the range. Like any academic, I also write memos, reports, letters, talks. I have also written some popular articles about my computer work and I have even done administrative ghost-writing. During the past half-dozen years I have written openly autobiographical short stories, none of which I have even tried to publish. I have written poetry, computer programs, and computer poetry. All of these genres involve more or less the same stages as those outlined above. All writing also has the feature that it is difficult, lonely work, and satisfying mainly when finished. I face writing with enthusiasm when I am rolling the topic around in my mind (Step 2) and I enjoy the attendant research, but I genuinely dread the moment when I have to put pen to paper—or for that matter, put fingers on the keyboard in front of the green screen.

If writing is so strenuous and difficult, why do it? The answer is not clear or obvious. Dr. Johnson's remark (that no one but a blockhead ever wrote except for money) does not apply to the writing of academic papers, nor to any of the other writings that I have mentioned except textbooks, and even these are seldom very remunerative. I calculated once that all the money I had received from writing amounted to a good deal less than an average year's salary. So there must be another motive. It has to do with the desire to record one's opinions in some permanent form, which oddly enough paper is and magnetic traces on a small disk are not. If what I wrote were never printed, I don't think I could continue to write. When I think of the reader, I visualize a browser in a distant eon stumbling across some words of mine and finding in them something to make him pause for a moment.

2

speaker or writer is ~~perhaps~~ not _always_ aware of them. It is only when he

stops to consider why a sentence is not clear or not effective that he

becomes consciously aware of choice, of choosing this word, those forms

and that order. What makes one choice effective and another not is

emphasis. Emphasis _attracts the attention of the reader to the particular sense_ ~~is what makes something more attention-getting~~ _intended by the speaker or writer. It is not possible to avoid_ ~~than the things around it. The problem of emphasis is not simply solved,~~ _putting some ~~stress~~ emphasis in any statement that is, unless, one makes._ ~~however, by making everything emphatic—it doesn't work that way.~~ (A)

Emphasis is relative: it depends on what is around it. _What is stressed depends on what is not stressed._

Consider the way people dress. Some kinds of clothes are appropriate

for certain activities, _(normal in certain contexts)_ ~~("contexts")~~: bathing suits for swimming, cap

and gown for graduation, bib overalls for farming, full dress for

orchestral music~~ians~~, fatigues for Army field duty. ~~impermeable pressure~~

~~suits for going to the moon.~~ When you choose to wear the appropriate

clothing for the given _occasion_ ~~context~~, people don't especially notice your

clothes. The emphasis is minimal. To achieve emphasis, merely wear

the wrong clothes: ~~for the given context~~ _fit. or ills_ ~~bathing suit~~ to graduation,

~~full dress for rocketing to the moon,~~ cap and gown for Army field duty.

Figure 5B

Ⓐ

~~In a simple sentence~~

When you pronounce a sentence, you normally place a heavier stress ~~on~~ one ~~the~~ word than on the others. ~~The words~~ ~~You~~ The following ~~sentence~~ would normally be pronounced with a heavier stress on the underlined word:

1a   I can't see the ~~~~~~~~ birds in the trees.

When you choose to stress *birds*, you are choosing normal emphasis. ~~Let me~~ But you could choose differently:

1b.   I can't *see* the birds in the tree.

By putting the stress on *see* you are doing two things: removing the normal emphasis from *birds* and placing it elsewhere. By placing the stress on *see*, you are actually saying something which is not in the sentence, so that the sentence becomes something like this:

2a   I can't *see* the birds – the tree (I can hear them)

2b   I can't *see* the birds in the tree (but I know they're there)

2c   I can't *see* the birds in the tree (but I feel their presence)

It is as if the sentence included the words ~~enclosed~~ in parentheses.

Figure 5C

Donald M. Murray, professor of English at the University of New Hampshire, publishes fiction, poetry, and nonfiction. He won the Pulitzer Prize for editorial writing, and his books on the writing process and the teaching of writing include Write to Learn *(1984),* Learning by Teaching *(1982),* Writing for Your Readers *(1983), and a complete revision (1984) of* A Writer Teaches Writing *(1968).*

GETTING UNDER THE LIGHTNING

Donald M. Murray
University of New Hampshire

Writing is easy; it's not writing that's hard. The writing comes in a bolt, one moment there is nothing and the next there are a thousand words or more, an always unexpected burst of language that is frightening in the power and complexity of its connections, in the sudden clarity where there was confusion a moment before. It's easy to receive a bolt of lightning when it strikes; what's hard is to create conditions that cause lightning to strike—morning after morning—and then wait for the bolt to hit.

Writing is easy; it's *not* writing that's hard. The writing comes in a bolt, one moment there is nothing and the next there are a thousand words or more, an always unexpected burst of language that is frightening in the power and complexity of its connections, in the sudden clarity where there was confusion a moment before. It's easy to receive the bolt of lightning when it strikes; what's hard is to create conditions that cause lightning to strike—morning after morning—and then wait for the bolt to hit.

Every six weeks or less I get drawn away from the writing—too many interruptions, too much traveling, too much talking about writing, too many meetings, too much nonwriting writing: letters, memos, handouts—and I have to reteach myself the conditions that allow me to receive writing. These include:

SITTING

· *Waiting.* Lightning hits twice, thrice, a thousand times in the same spot. Flannery O'Connor teaches and comforts me: "Every morning between 9 and 12 I go to my room and sit before a piece of paper. Many times I just sit for three hours with no ideas coming to me. But I know one thing: If an idea does come between 9 and 12, I am there ready for it." She was a magnificent sitter; I wish I could sit as well as Flannery O'Connor.

But sitting has its price. Watch writers waddle across campus and you'll notice they grow broad in the beam, their spines shaped like a question mark, their necks crane forward as they peer at you. Writers are sedentary hunters. They wait for the lightning and keep making New Year's resolutions to sit better a dozen times a year—each resolution is aimed at getting the rump in *the* chair on a regular basis. My present resolutions:

· *Only* write before lunch.
· *Never* write after lunch.

If I write in the afternoon and evening—when I don't write very well anyway—I put off all those things that interfere with writing but have to be done. Soon they build up and steal my mornings. Then I don't write and become mean. As Simone de Beauvoir says, "A day in which I don't write leaves a taste of ashes."

· *Immersion.* I am involved with the subjects I write about long before I know I am going to write about them. And I am involved to a degree I cannot demand of my students. I am on duty 24 hours a day, reading, observing, absorbing, connecting, thinking, rehearsing. The subjects I write about are never far from me: the death of my daughter, the questions about my family and myself I am still trying to answer, the war in which I learned I could kill, the way I see others and myself behaving toward each other, the process of learning to write.

Of course I suffer all the guilts that my students admit and my colleagues usually try to hide. I do not read enough, I do not read effectively enough, I do not read what I should read. I'm not up on the latest work—or I do not understand it. And yet I realize that never a day goes by that I am not grabbing hold of new information about the subjects on which I write. I am a continual student, and that is the resource from which all my writing is drawn.

· *Need.* Writing for me is more than a vocation; it is a need; it is the way in which I make meaning of my world, the way I collect and relate, explore and comprehend, speculate and test in a dialogue with myself that never ends. If you don't have to write, don't.

I don't (and didn't) write to win tenure, to get promoted, to make money (with this energy and commitment I could have made eleven killings in real estate). I don't write for fame since I had a teaspoon of fame early and found it was both irrelevant—the process of doing the writing was long gone and I was doing new work—and unsatisfying— win one award and you want a dozen more.

I write because I have to write. Meet writers and they look ordinary because they are ordinary. It's important for students to become familiar with that ordinariness. We have many writers in our department and our students learn from their ordinariness. "Gee, I look more like a writer than Murray, perhaps I . . . ."

But you'll never know writers as well in person—even lovers, wives, children?—as you'll know them from their writing. And you won't know them from their writing either. The more open and revealing writers are, the more they may be hidden, the more successful at camouflaging their necessary loneliness.

Writers are here and there at the same time, living while observing their living. Talking to you we are also often talking to ourselves in an interior dialogue that discusses—silently, secretly—what is being done while it is being done. Writing, for the writer, is an essential kind of talking to oneself. You may like what you hear, be amused, stirred, stimulated, angered, encouraged, startled, comforted, but what you are hearing is only part of the conversation by which the writer lives. If you don't have to talk to yourself, if you have no need to teach yourself by writing, then writing may not be essential to you. Talk, play the flute, paint, build a bridge, do business, bake, hammer, and do not worry that you're not writing. Society has never said it needed writers. We are all self-appointed and rise to speak without being called upon.

I have no choice. I must write to answer questions I am asking myself, to solve problems that I find interesting, to bring order into an area where the confusion terrifies me. Donald Barthelme said, "Write about what you're most afraid of," and I nod, smiling. I write to hang on.

· *Readers.* I also write from an external need, to share what I am thinking with that tiny audience of intimates whose respect I need and with whom I am learning. I need to share my writing with my wife, my daughters, Don Graves, Chip Scanlan, Tom Newkirk, Jane Hansen (Carol Berkenkotter who makes science of pauses, hesitations, and what is left out), and a changing audience of readers, always small, mostly writers themselves, who may respond or not.

If hundreds or thousands of other readers tune in later, that's nice, but I really can't see that vague, distant audience who will not see the work until I am two or three projects down the road anyway. Publication is nice but it is not significant enough to motivate me to place my rear end in the writing chair each morning. I write mostly for myself —and a handful of patient friends.

· *Critics.* I must confess those friendly readers on whom I depend are appreciators mostly. I am too immature to enjoy criticism; more sadist than masochist. I hunger for appreciation, and my writing takes its largest steps forward after praise, not criticism, no matter how much the constructive—or even destructive—comments are deserved. As a teacher I try to remember that.

I find little criticism relevant to the work in progress. Critics usually have their own idea of what I should say—based on their own beliefs —and how I should say it—based on their own ideas of good writing. Even the praise of nonwriting critics has little relationship to the writing in progress, and it can even be destructive—if that's what they think I am saying, I'm really in trouble.

· *Invitations.* When I receive an invitation to write a chapter such as this, to produce a journal article, to give a talk, I try to combine an internal need—how *do* I write—with an external need—maybe students *do* need to know what their teachers practice—and I have a condition for receptivity. The lightning may strike again.

· *Innocence.* I have the advantage in being undereducated for my trade. I'd like to be well educated but I am surrounded by people who are too well educated, who know too well what has been done and what can't be done. If you have the disadvantage of a fine and complete education, move out from that center of comfort to where you don't know everything, where there are dark forests, looming mountains, shadows that move, strange noises in the night.

I write out of what I don't know, not what I know, and that exploration of my ignorance makes each draft, the failed ones even more than the successful ones, fascinating, a challenge for another morning. Of course I keep discovering what others already know—but I have the challenge and the joy of exploration.

ACTING

· *Fragments.* I need something to say—an idea, a subject, a theory, a thesis—but what the lightning bolt leaves is usually just a fragment, a puzzling piece of information, a question without an answer, an answer without a question, a detail, an incomplete observation, a partial pattern, an image, a phrase (a fragment of voice), a problem not yet defined, a feeling of anxiety that may be relieved by writing. Writers have learned to pay attention to fragments that others do not even see lying at their feet.

· *Concentration.* Well, yes. Perhaps stubbornness is what I mean, a dumb determination to finish what is started. But that isn't all of it— a good deal of it—but not all of it. With all the necessary distraction and all the unnecessary interruptions, I need to be able, at the time of pre-writing and writing, to concentrate on one task over all the others —at least for an hour, an hour and a half, two hours, half an hour, fifteen minutes, ten, less but still a moment when I fall out of the world, forgetting time, place, duty, and listen to the writing flowing through me to the page.

· *Deadlines.* I have to have deadlines that are self-imposed or imposed by others and, I confess, the deadlines of others are more powerful than my own. I have to be patient, to wait, to listen, not to force the writing, but the day-by-day, hour-by-hour, and louder and louder and louder goose-step march of an approaching deadline is one of the most powerful lightning rods on my study roof.

· *Planning.* I spend most of my time planning what I may write, making lists, making notes, making more lists, talking to myself in my head and in my Daybook. I try not to be too formal about how I plan —planning should be, above all, play—and I try not to write too early but wait as Virginia Woolf counsels: "I am going to hold myself from writing it till I have it impending in me: grown heavy in my mind like a ripe pear; pendent, gravid, asking to be cut or it will fall." I will not force the writing—forced writing sounds like forced writing—but hold back until I have to write. The draft must demand to be written. I want to write when I can *not* not write. When the writing will come easily, without effort.

· *Drafting.* I write fast. I rush forward, writing so fast my handwriting becomes incomprehensible even to me, typing beyond my ability so that the letters and words pile up on the word processor like a train wreck, or dictating so fast I can produce 500 words or 1,000 in an hour; 1,500, 2,000, 2,500, 3,000 in a morning.

The speed itself is important. The best accidents of phrase or meaning—or meaning illuminated by phrase—occur when I am writing too fast.

· *Rewriting.* I'm doing it less and less. Rewriting means the creation of a new draft with major changes in subject, focus, order, voice. These days I plan more and rewrite less. But when I rewrite, I start back at the beginning, seeing the subject anew, not through the vision of the past draft. Rewriting is mostly replanning.

· *Revising.* Of course these first drafts—or third or fourth drafts— will have to be fussed with, cut, added to, re-ordered, shaped, and polished so they appear on the page with the effort hidden, all the spontaneous touches neatly in place. That's fun, once you have a draft in hand.

· *Voice.* Most important of all, voice. I do not begin to write until I hear the voice of the writing, and when that voice fades during the drafting, rewriting/replanning, or revising, I stop, make myself quiet and listen until I hear it again. The music of the writing, more than anything else, teaches me what I am learning about the subject, what I am feeling about the subject, how I must write to make those thoughts and feelings clear.

And when the writing doesn't go well, the most effective tactic is to listen, quietly, carefully to the writing. If I listen closely enough the writing will tell me what to say and how to say it. As Jayne Anne Phillips says, "It's like being led by a whisper."

BELIEVING

· *Acceptance.* Of what I am, not what I wish I were. Acceptance of the writing I am receiving, remembering that intention is the enemy and surprise the friend. William Stafford reminds me:

> I can imagine a person beginning to write up to that standard he imagines the world has set for him. But to me that's surrealistic. The only standard I can rationally have is the standard I'm meeting right now . . . you should be more willing to forgive yourself. It really doesn't make any difference if you are good or bad today. The *assessment* of the product is something that happens *after* you've done it.

The way I write today is the way I can write today. I must accept what the lightning delivers and make use of it. I can't imagine another text, written by someone other than myself, into being. I must accept myself to write—and accept the fact that writing reveals not just what I say, but who I am. Of course, I am afraid I will be found out—and I will.

· *Self-consciousness.* I used to worry that my compulsive study of my craft—"Don't think" we used to tell the goalie, knowing that if he thought the puck would be in the net before the decision was made—would paralyze my writing or at least cause terminal constipation. Perhaps it hasn't helped, but I had no choice; long before I taught or made a profession of studying the writing process, I was a student of my craft. Aren't most writers?

Writing is luck but writers are repeatedly lucky. They hit the lottery number again and again. To be a writer, you have to be unselfconscious enough to allow the writing to strike, to allow it to surprise you, to accept the gift. But you have to be prepared—calculatingly prepared—to be lucky, and you have to have the cunning to allow what is written to appear spontaneously in the reader's mind. William Shakespeare: "The truest poetry is the most feigning."

· *Escaping Craft.* Skill is our goal and our prison. We have to learn the tricks of our trade. We apprentice ourselves to our craft to learn to write better—and we do. Our words are surer, stronger; our sentences grow lean; our paragraphs are packed by a professional. We learn to turn a phrase, to shape, to polish until our writing becomes professional, polished, slick. Our pieces are so well constructed they say what we have already said—better and better and better until we are hidden within our too well constructed pages. We are safe. Skilled. Craftpersons. Publishing scholars. Pros.

We have constructed a prison around ourselves with our own carefully crafted words, and we can't see out, can't hear out; can't see what needs attending to; can't hear the voice of what we might write on the outside. So we have the obligation to break out, to push beyond our skills, to try and write what we cannot yet write but what needs writing in ways that we have not yet found so that we write with less polish and craft and learn the craft of not finishing the writing too much, to make it rough enough, (to leave the roughness in) (to remember what Amiri Baraka wrote, "Hunting is not those heads on the wall"), to let our writing be finished enough so that it helps us do our thinking but not so finished that our readers can only stand and gaze in awe at our clever thinking when we should invite them and allow them to do their own thinking, messing around with our drafts so they will not respect the text too much.

would I stop and mess around with a finished text, unpolish it, unshape it, incomplete it?

you know it

if I can learn how.

know your craft

yeah—that's the complicated thing. Exactly. If I get to know how to do that too well, then I'm crafty again, blinded by my carefully unfinished drafts.

But we *do* want to allow the reader to get into the writing with us, so that the writing doesn't get in the way of the experience of writing/reading reading/writing, so we aren't blinded by the conventions, deafened by the traditions, made dumb by our own hard-earned craft.

unfinishing a text

it is necessary and will be necessary again

as we learn how to get out of the way—how to write rough—when we become crafty enough to allow the writing to appear spontaneous. Even when it is really spontaneous, when we have not got in the way, then what we have done is to learn a new craft, a new skill, a new way of digging in where it is safe and the lightning can never find us. So . . .

· *Incompleteness.* This is a new draft but it isn't the last word on how writing is made or even how I make writing. It contradicts some things I've said about how I write, and what I say in the future will produce more contradictions. I just wrote a new version of *A Writer Teaches Writing* without opening the previous edition; I am writing a novel without referring to the last draft. I don't want to be imprisoned by my own ideas and my own words. I don't want to be either consistent or proudly inconsistent. I want, each morning, to find out what I have to say that day. Each publication is nothing more or less than an entry in my Daybook where I talk to myself about what I don't know and need to know, imagining answers to questions that really can't be answered: How do people stay with us after they die? Why did my family do what it did to itself? Why are we able to make war—and to be proud of it? Why did I survive? How do people take experience and recreate it in the minds of others through some squiggles on paper? How do we learn from writing? How can we help others learn to learn from writing? I don't want any questions that have answers—they aren't any fun.

· *Faith*. Hardest of all for me. Faith that I can write, that I have something to say, that I can find out what it is, that I can make it clear to me, to a reader, that I can write so that the reader is not aware of the writer but the meaning.

Faith enough not to read what is written until the entire draft is done and then not to compare it to what might have been or what others have done, but to listen to the writing, to see in it, its own meaning, its own form, to hear its own voice. Faith enough to stand out there all alone and invite the lightning.

Patricia Y. Murray is director of composi-
tion at DePaul University, where she has
also acted as coordinator of the Common
Studies Program. With W. Ross Win-
terowd she has authored English Writing
and Language Skills *(1983), a major six-*
volume textbook series in composition and
language skills for grades 7–12. She has
served as presenter, speaker, or workshop
leader for the Conference on College Com-
munication and Composition, the Na-
tional Council of Teachers of English, the
Conference on English Education, the
Michigan Council of Teachers of English,
the California Association of Teachers of
English, and many other professional
conferences. She holds a Ph.D. in linguis-
tics and literature from the University of
Southern California.

DOING WRITING

Patricia Y. Murray
DePaul University

Writing is acting. It is choosing, shaping, arranging, rearranging, shifting, adding, deleting, discovering. To write is to perform, to reveal, to show. The performance may sometimes be perfunctory, but it is a show, nevertheless. A writer can "do" a paper in the same sense that she can do a dance, do a magic show, do a rope trick.

DOING

The starting point in doing an essay or report is choosing a suitable subject. By "suitable" we mean one that is manageable, suitably focused so that we can find enough to talk about sensibly. Our subject for now is the conflict in Central America. Immediately we know that "the conflict in Central America" is too broad, for it concerns a complex, many-faceted problem involving several nations and factions within those nations. So our next step is to narrow the subject to a topic, something such as "the role of the Sandanistas in Nicaragua" or "the significance of Duarte's election." We may find, later, that we need to

What a fiction this is! You don't believe in this, do you? Did you ever compose anything in this orderly fashion? Where's the chaos that really exists when you write?

A typical freshman topic—too big, too deep, full of traps. Better than abortion or the death penalty, however.

Steps are neat things. Logical, sequential, steady, permanent. There's security in one-two-three. You're describing a procedure that ignores the times you stumble or stub your toe, or doesn't admit that a board is loose here and there.

225

focus even more narrowly, depending upon how much information we can find about the topic. But we have completed step one.

Is the reason for focusing on a limited topic utilitarian only? Is it dependent upon how much or how little information you can find?

Our next step is to find information about our topic. While this will take a little time, it shouldn't be difficult, for the *Reader's Guide to Periodical Literature* will point us in the right direction. Mr. Strunk, the librarian, will show us where to find the Guide. We will take a stack of 3 x 5 cards with us and jot down information in note and paraphrase form, not forgetting to note bibliographical detail. Once this is accomplished, we are ready to return to our desk and prepare our paper.

How often does going to the library by-pass any original generation of ideas? Where does the "invention" stage come in?

Should you comment on the impoverishment of student resources?

Are you guilty of sending students first to the *Reader's Guide* on the grounds that a little predigested, reported information will get their projects off the ground? What have you done for them before this?

Look in any handbook for the system. Does one digest any of the original material, or is it merely committed to paper?

After sorting our note cards into meaningfully grouped units, our next task is to write an outline so that our paper will have coherence. The outline will aid us in several ways as we write: It will provide a "roadmap" to follow, so that we don't go off on a tangent; it will help us see the relationships among the sections of our discussion; it will provide our instructor with evidence that we have planned our paper carefully and thought-

At least this is a heuristic of sorts: seeing relationships.

Tangents are taboo, of course. They foul up your coherence rating.

Another reflection of the utilitarian view of doing a paper. What will it get you? How do you get it? Through "evidence" that is "planned" and "gathered" to be developed "adequately."

fully and have gathered enough information to develop the topic adequately.

We have five major sections in our outline, two of them obligatory: the introduction, where we will place the thesis statement, and the conclusion, where we will sum up our findings or argument, or restate our thesis in a slightly different way. Of course, we could have more than three sections in the body of the essay, but three is about the right number. The pattern fits the five-paragraph essay pattern we have learned to write so skillfully. At this point, it is crucial that we write a well-phrased thesis statement. It should state the narrowed topic, assert something about it (from our special perspective, of course), and give some indication of how we will develop or arrange our ideas in the following paper. It should probably be a periodic sentence, too, containing at least one noun clause.

Now that we know what particular point of view we want to argue, or what perspective we want our information to reflect, we must consider our audience. Who will

A framework—a first "container."

Do you mean that "forming" is "filling a form"? Berthoff raises more questions about "forming," questions that don't appear in your handbook. What you've got here is the standardized approach to organizing and developing a paper, a standardized length, and a standardized format. Like "steps," standardization is neat.

Produces empty writing, but mastery of a formula. What's wrong with a little mastery?

Every handbook says so. Is it true?

read our paper? What is she/he likely to know or want to know about Duarte or the Sandanistas? What argument is the audience likely to fall for? Finally, what level of diction is called for? If this is a paper in response to an assignment, formal language is required. Our tone should be reserved, reasonable, respectful of the authority of facts. The progression of our argument should be syllogistic, and we should avoid emotionalism while at the same time demonstrating that we are sincerely committed to our thesis.

Our note cards in their groupings provide us with subtopics to develop. If we write an argument, we will put our strongest argument first (or last). If we inform and explain, we will arrange the subtopics from most to least important (or vice versa). We will choose appropriate transition words and phrases to move the ideas from point to point. There's a handy list of them in our handbook, arranged by function.

Topic, outline, thesis, audience, language, form—these components of our writing procedure decided upon, we are ready to write. A few rituals to

If you pose this description against the argument Fort makes in "Form, Authority, and the Critical Essay," what do you have?

This isn't the same as "earning the thesis." Where's your commitment?

Why?

This sounds like simple plugging-in, pulling from a bag of tricks. You run the danger of writing a superficially cohesive essay.

get out of the way first—sharpening pencils, cleaning the typewriter, fixing the coffee, arranging notes and outline handily nearby—and the rest almost takes care of itself. We will, of course, leave time to go over our finished paper to edit out any grammatical or typing errors and to check the spelling of foreign or commonly misspelled words. We'll type up a neat cover page, attach the bibliography (after checking to see if the form fits the new MLA guidelines), and be done with the job.

The perfect draft approach. Admit that you do some of this yourself.

So much for revising.

. . . .

Going south on I-94 now. A rainy, windy drive into work. Three semis up ahead jockeying for lead position—watch out for those crazies. Car knows his way, so I can think. Seeing the semis lined up side by side, I know suddenly how I want to begin this "essay." I mean those quote marks because I want to do something a little different. A description of how I compose has no inherent organization. Why not write crot-like, the way the pieces have presented themselves to my mind over the last several weeks? This piece has been writing itself in my head since

I have talked this part through with myself, first by asking questions, then by defining what began as inchoate non-sense. I agree with others who have noted the interior dialogue as the voice that keeps dialectic going. My interior voice brings to the surface those things in my imagination that will eventually be written down. It abstracts my meaning and gives it structure in language that I can transmit to others. The voice is an editor, too. It cajoles, scolds, derides, blue-pencils, and occasionally gives its approval.

March, column inch by column inch. Some of the marks have already faded. Probably just as well, for I wouldn't want to commit to print everything I've thought about this topic. "Writing itself in my head" is a precise phrase. It describes the action taking place visually, for a picture appears magically but mechanically on a colorless screen about two inches behind my eyes. I watch as the words, phrases, sentences, paragraphs take shape. This phenomenon isn't unique; some of my students have described similar processes in their "How I Write" papers.

Driving allows me the leisure and, apparently, the atmosphere necessary for writing. While the actual typing of my composed piece takes time, the composing has been done before my fingers hit the keyboard. Not entirely, for revising and editing are going on during the typing. A year ago, the typing-revising-editing stage required several bottles of white-out and a change or two of ribbon. Now the process takes less time because the word processor allows—even encourages—more extensive revision. A major difference in

See Winston Weathers on alternate grammars of style: *An Alternate Style: Options in Composition* (Hayden, 1980). Crots, cataloging, double-voice, collage, disjunction, conscious borrowing of technique from visual and aural fields, suggest ways of breaking away from the rigid "boxes" into which we have been taught to put our writing. Some of my students (and I) have found that breaking out of the mold is so liberating and energy-giving that writing becomes a joy again and our creativity is rediscovered.

In retrospect, this time-saving factor isn't true—yet. Like others new to the computer, I spend too much time fiddling with the mechanics of the process: setting up margins, saving and losing files, looking up the commands for various typefaces, etc. Until the process becomes second nature,

working with the word processor is that infelicitous expressions and gross errors loom physically larger on a screen than on paper. There they are, staring directly at me, vivid black letters on rich blue background surrounded by a deeper magenta frame, the errors themselves almost a work of art. In contrast, the writing on the screen in my head is always in black and white, probably because I learned to read before I learned to view a television screen.

. . . .

INVENTING

As I suspect many writers do, I talk-write. This essay is intended to demonstrate that process, so far as I know how to demonstrate it in print. A monologue takes place, from topic-given or topic-conceived, to completion of the written piece. A voice tells, describes, narrates, dictates, explains what it is the writer "knows"— the substance, organization, and style of the essay or story. No it's not a monologue exactly or entirely, for the writer talks back, confirming, refuting, arguing, questioning the first voice with a second. A dialogue

as typing is, my attention is too frequently focused on the mechanical features of writing. This must be similar to the problem young, inexperienced, or "basic" writers have—simple attention to the mechanics of fashioning letters, spelling the word, drawing the shapes that make up words, sentences, paragraphs. I better understand their problems now.

What about the conscious application of heuristics?

Which questioning system works best? For me, the tagmemic grid fits nearly every subject and purpose except literary analysis. Clustering helps when I'm stuck. I promote the learning of heuristic-using in my classrooms, but must confess that my inner dialogue works better than any schema I've studied. My dialogue is an inner-directed Chatauqua, much like Pirsig's in *Zen and the Art of Motorcycle Maintenance*, but on a smaller scale.

232 · Patricia Y. Murray

between (or among) voices provokes ideas, provides the dialectic necessary for developing
those ideas, serves as a testing
device to refine ideas and arguments, and above all supplies
an initial audience who mea-
sures, assesses, and reacts to the
thing being composed.

FORMING

I dance-write. (I know I'm
in trouble here, but there's no
better name for what hap-
pens.) What I'm discussing,
perhaps, is form. I image the
form my composition will take
while conjuring up the words
that will fit that shape. Words
take their position just offstage;
groups of them cluster in the
wings, poised to enter stage
left; groups assume patterns or
figures once onstage, forming
and reforming until they
please the choreographer;
movements progress through
short and long, rough and
smooth, solo and ensemble, in-
terlude and finale. Or perhaps
I'm talking about style. Chris-
tensen-like, a combination of
movements moves right or left,
to the rear or center front, arranging and rearranging themselves in evocative patterns.
Sentences are staccato or le-

Not many writers mention the kinetic nature of writing, though they talk about rituals of seeking comfort, the physical fatigue
that follows hours of working on a manuscript, and of eye-hand-brain coordination.
Dance serves me as more than metaphor.
Familiar dance forms provide ways to
shape my sentences, paragraphs, and
longer stretches of prose. Rhythm, cadence, emphasis, repetition, motif, sound
effect, and other elements I can't name in
sentences and paragraphs take on the look
and feel of body movement. Sometimes
music supplies the metaphor, but even
then music as stimulus to movement.

gato, truncated or extended. There are amazing lifts, bravura passages, and welcome pauses.

. . . .

INTENDING

Typically, my writing is related to my profession, teaching. Consequently, audience is my major consideration. Not just "audience" in the abstract, but individual students—Joe, Mary, Karen, and Igor—determine the way I write, my purpose for writing, and the shape my writing takes. Even while writing a textbook for anonymous students-out-there, I enter a dialogue with students I've known or will know. I write to their idiosyncrasies, their personalities, their capabilities. I know that each lesson must include a task that Igor, with his limited command of English, can do. Likewise, there must be tasks that will challenge Mark, who plans to enter MIT in the fall, and Kate, who needs her AA degree for a job in June that is waiting for her. My lesson material, my written directions and explanations, are *aimed* at these students as if they were present during the writing.

Don't you ever write just for the fun of it? or for yourself? Once upon a time you tried poetry, a direct influence of reading Dylan Thomas and T.S. Eliot for the first time. I don't think of the instructional kind of writing I do now as non-creative, however. It is interesting to me, involving emotionally and intellectually, and personally satisfying. I care about how my words might affect a learner-writer just as I would care about the aesthetic response I would seek from readers through a novel.

But "aim" means purpose as well as direction. What purpose does a teacher have? To show, to lead, to provoke reactions, to elicit questions, to help students think, to share, to shape, to love. And more: to entertain and create. Even exam questions ought to be creative "positive learning experiences," as the jargon goes.

Students' facility with language, their intellectual abilities, their social and cultural backgrounds, their home and school environments, their beliefs and expectations—all these considerations figure into the writing a teacher does. No wonder teacher-writing is a slow, often painful, time-consuming, excruciatingly cautious, frustrating process. No wonder the obstacles so near-impossible to overcome. No wonder we turn to someone else's textbook, whether it is appropriate for our students or not.

I write for my colleagues as well, an audience more difficult than the student one. Its members are anonymous for the most part, harder to imagine except in a familiar academic background. Of course, there's Dr. X whose friendship

I write for students
 texts
 tests
 directions
 lessons
 explanations
 demonstrations
 comments
 evaluations
 recommendations
I write for colleagues
 summaries
 reports
 proposals
 arguments
 pleas
 justifications
 rationales
 syllabi
 recommendations
I also write for friends, husband, Mom and Dad, the kids
 summaries
 comments
 explanations
 supplications

I seek; Professor Blygh, upon whom I want revenge; fellow teachers who will accept or reject my performance. But this audience assumes *roles* in my imagination, and I write to those roles rather than to individuals with names and shapes. This audience sits in judgment of my writing in a way qualitatively different from that of my students. Both audiences judge, evaluate, and respond, but the student audience is far more predictable and forgiving than the professional one.

directions
proposals
justifications
stories

· · · · · · · · · · · · · ·

Walking along the parkway now, Panama dashing off to chase rabbits, I squeezing out two more paragraphs. Literally-figuratively squeezing, the sponge in my head oozing the words out drip by drip. Move this word to the end of the sentence; replace *form* with *forming;* add an absolute phrase to the end of the "Christensen" sentence. There! Set type!

VALVERT: Poet!
CYRANO: Yes, sir, I *am* a poet, as I'll demonstrate by composing an impromptu ballade while I fence with you.
VALVERT: A ballade?

CYRANO: You don't know what
that is? Allow me to explain.
VALVERT: But . . .
CYRANO: The ballade consists of
three eight-line stanzas . . .
VALVERT: Oh!
CYRANO: . . . with a four-line
refrain at the end.
VALVERT: You . . .
CYRANO: I'm going to compose
one as I fight with you, and
when I come to the last line,
I'll draw blood.

. . . .

CYRANO: Wait, I'm thinking of
how to begin . . . There, I
have it.*

Writing is like that: se-
lecting and choosing, thinking of how to begin, is part of
Invention. Arranging my
words, my lines, into three
stanzas of eight lines each,
followed by a refrain, is
Form. Delivering them with
panache while fighting a
duel at the Hôtel Bourgogne
is Style. And think of the context in which the message
takes place: the crowds an-
ticipating the outcome, taking sides in the dispute,
cheering the performance
on.

Would that I could say this: "Wait, I'm
thinking of how to begin . . . There, I have
it." What writer other than Cyrano com-
poses with such certainty?

On the other side of this coin is the writer's
block. When I read *Dubin's Lives* some
time ago, I was going through a long, dry
spell, unable to finish a writing project by
deadline. Malamud perfectly describes the
agony of writing, better than CCC articles.

*From *Cyrano de Bergerac: Heroic Comedy in Five Acts* by Edmond Rostand, translated
by Lowell Blair. Copyright © 1972 by Lowell Blair. Reprinted by arrangement with New
American Library, New York, N.Y.

Writing is not like that.
Selecting and choosing what
to say seldom comes as easily
as Cyrano suggests. Perhaps
the difference is that Cyrano
is more practiced in his art
than my students and I. Arrangement is more likely to
suggest itself than it is subject to my deliberate manipulation of a procedure
planned and outlined beforehand. The context is less entertaining and lively, certainly less dramatic and
visual, than a romantic poet's
imaginativeness.

· · · · · · · · · · · · · ·

LEARNING HOW

Q. How did you learn to write?
A. I both do and don't know. School writing was the bulk of my
writing for some years, except for the occasional story or poem I
jotted down in secrecy and hid in the bottom drawer of my dresser.
Once I tried keeping a diary, but the entries soon bored me, so I
gave it up. There was a grammar book in high school and work-
books in elementary school. I was quite good at usage exercises and
diagramming. Diagramming, like plane geometry, was pleasing in
form—both were the only graphic arts I ever mastered. I enjoyed
diagramming for its own sake, as I did grammar lessons. Neither
had anything to do with writing. More likely I learned to write by
reading widely and mimicking the style of those writers I liked. No
remnants of my school writing exist, so I can't say whether imitation worked for me or not. Many of my students tell me they
learned to write in the same way.

I had no formal college instruction in writing. My fellow students and I learned what was expected and acceptable in college
writing by trial and error. If one were perceptive enough and
sensitive to the professor's peculiarities, one could satisfy require-

ments. No professor assigned papers in classes other than English. Even then, nearly every paper was a critical analysis of a work of literature. Sometimes one was asked to argue the merits of one writer over another, or to compare two styles. Opinions were allowed, but they must be "informed" opinions, not mere assertions. What was expected was writing that offered evidence to prove a thesis, sounded appropriately authoritative, and displayed the writer's credentials by citing the right references. It must also show evidence that the writer had read widely in the field and could synthesize what she had gleaned into a cohesive whole. The process became a game with rules that seldom varied. As a game, it soon was enjoyable, and I found self-satisfaction in the gamesmanship itself, as I would in playing basketball or chess.

Q. But surely you've learned something about how to write since your college days. Hasn't the present introspective piece produced an insight or two?

A. Yes, but a limited Yes. Thinking through my own writing process crystallized a notion I've had for some time—that I approach writing as action, that is, to write is to act in some specific, purposeful way. Not an original idea, of course, but one that seems to guide what, why, when, where, and how I write. Results never please me. The writing itself is body- and mind-wrenching, very physical.

Q. What do you feel when you write? Do you enjoy writing?

A. Enjoy? No. But there's a certain satisfaction from having created a piece, even a well-constructed essay assignment or an exercise for my students. What do I feel? In order: resentment, frustration, fatigue, relief, satisfaction, peace. Frequently the order ends with simple relief.

Q. What or who has influenced your writing?

A. My writing changed as I learned from reading or from attending courses and workshops. An NDEA institute in curriculum development showed me the need to learn to write more than the college critical essay so that I could teach my students to write with variety. You might think "How obvious," but for an inexperienced young teacher, it is a crucial lesson.

Soon after, a workshop for English teachers at my university introduced me to the Nebraska curriculum materials, where I first learned about Francis Christensen's work. Here were the ingredients, spelled out and exemplified, of the kind of writing I admired and had been trying to master. Now I had guidelines and theory to go with them. Later I would discover sentence combining as method and find its usefulness in my own writing but particularly in teaching.

As a graduate student in rhetoric, I found a body of articulated theories that both confirmed what I had intuited about the composing process as a result of teaching it and opened up new areas to explore. To mention them here would require a lengthy bibliography. Some of those influences appear in this volume.

But I learn most from my students. The daily exchange, the conferences, the struggle to communicate that takes place between me and my students have been and are my greatest resources. I have learned, am learning, to write by trying to teach others to write.

· · · · · · · · · · · · · · ·

DOING WRITING

Writing is acting. It is choosing, shaping, arranging, rearranging, shifting, adding, deleting, discovering. To write is to perform, to reveal, to show. The performance may sometimes be perfunctory, but it is a show, nevertheless. A writer can "do" a paper in the same sense that she can do a dance, do a magic show, do a rope trick. The benefit for both the performer and her audience lies in the creative process and its resulting satisfaction. As performances vary, so do their benefits and satisfactions.

Inventory time: have you covered the topics you intended to? said enough? too much? the right things? established the tone and point of view you wanted? have "shown" more than "tell"? listened to me carefully and critically? Is there a sense of an ending? Then do what you tell your students: put a period at the end and stop.

Louise Wetherbee Phelps is assistant professor of English at the University of Southern California, where she teaches in the rhetoric, linguistics, and literature programs. She is the author of journal articles and book chapters on the psychology of composition, coherence, and other topics, as well as guest editor of a special issue of Pre-Text *on Paul Ricoeur and rhetoric. Her current projects include a book of philosophical essays on composition as a discipline and a study interpreting student writing.*

RHYTHM AND PATTERN IN A COMPOSING LIFE

Louise Wetherbee Phelps
University of Southern California

The naive commonsense conception of "writing a paper" so powerfully dominates one's consciousness that only by trying to set it aside can I feel clearly, and thus articulate, the slow, deep rhythms and texture of the composing life. Ultimately, this decision leads me to conceive composing as constructed from a more diffuse and confused experience—as much the products of a composing life as the texts themselves.

An experience, a very humble experience, is capable of generating and carrying any amount of theory (or intellectual content), but a theory apart from an experience cannot be definitely grasped even as a theory.

—John Dewey

When I perform I'm transformed into something else. Once you start to touch on yourself you touch other people. But it has to have fire. It has to have meaning. It has to have living—all the things that I've gone through and that I'm sure everyone else has.

—Dwike Mitchell, jazz pianist

THE MUSIC IN MY HEAD

Sometime early in my marriage I discovered the tune in my head. My husband informed me that I had an irritating habit—quite unconscious —of tapping my feet or hands incessantly, especially while reading. Following the rhythm back into my mind, I found the tune there, or rather many tunes. Occasionally I sit down at the piano and find it at my fingertips, but mostly it just runs along quietly below my thoughts and sets my foot swinging. Recently, I read in Howard Gardner's account of musical intelligence that according to Roger Sessions my tune marks me a composer:

> As [Sessions] explains it, a composer can be readily identified by the fact that he constantly has "tones in his head"—that is, he is always, somewhere

near the surface of his consciousness, hearing tones, rhythms, and larger musical patterns. While many of these patterns are worth little musically and may, in fact, be wholly derivative, it is the composer's lot constantly to be monitoring and reworking these patterns.

Composing begins at the moment when these ideas begin to crystallize and to assume a significant shape.[1]

Whatever little talent I might have as a musician is exploited only in the pleasure of playing the piano and listening to music. But I am another kind of composer, with a different and predominant tune in my head —the music of my worded thoughts. Like the musician, I lead a composing life, and the sounds and images of language in my head crystallize periodically into texts. This essay is about the rhythms and patterns of my composing life, and how my writer's imagination works and elaborates them constantly toward finished discourse.

I have been struck for a long time by the embedding of so-called "composing processes" in the continuous language experience of the literate person. Every human being is immersed in a sea of discourse that permeates the cellular membranes of the self with a ceaseless flow of talk, writing, and verbal thought. These currents form the semiotic environment or cultural context for my understanding and using language in a given instant. In this great interchange of symbolic energy I experience myself distinctively as a central source of language, through the symbolizing function of my human brain, which continually transforms my experience into a personal stream of verbal activity. That ongoing process of symbolization forms the innermost context for my specific language experiences and the situational matrix for all my composing activities.

Composing, as distinct from the practical literacy of signing one's name or writing a grocery list, or from the fluent spontaneous improvisation of conversation, is a process of channeling and consciously working some of this dynamic linguistic material into discursive form. Being a verbal composer by nature, choice, and training, I am attuned to the discursive possibilities in my inner and outer language, which appears to me tacitly as intrinsically composable, inviting craft to shape and elaborate it as wood or stone invites the sculptor's hand. This situation engenders distinguishable composing acts, not when I pick up a pen, but whenever I direct my mind attentively toward a particular event, thought, or utterance as potentially textual and begin to play with it and work it over in composing ways. At any moment in my daily round— fixing dinner, playing ping-pong, listening to music, talking with friends —such moments of composing attention may crystallize in my consciousness as images, fragments of text, shadowy patterns: sometimes

[1]Howard Gardner, *Frames of Mind: The Theory of Multiple Intelligences* (New York: Basic Books, 1983), p. 101.

transient, merging smoothly back into the verbal background; sometimes fixing themselves in notes or talk or memory; sometimes pursued
effortfully throughout long periods of sustained composition.

But I may also be composing without knowing it. Much of my
language and thought is not consciously oriented to text, yet later I will
perceive, use, and refer to it as a precursor of achieved writing. More
significantly, like other nervous activity much of my ongoing composing process is submerged below consciousness and only occasionally and
partially rises to the level of intensity where it can be felt. Even less
often does it result in observable language behavior. But in my life as
a writer part of the stream of my language is continually being directed
in all these ways toward multiple, vaguely anticipated or possible textual events, some of which are gradually discriminated from their matrix and realized as individual entities. I see this enlarged, holistic "composing process" as the primary reality to be explained.

This is quite a different perspective from that of most empirical
research, which takes discrete, time-limited composing events to be the
molecular elements of literacy and does not really try to account for
their contextual source in the verbal life stream of the individual. If you
try to extend the model for that purpose, it quickly breaks down. My
composing life is a texture of discursive ideas that cannot easily be
referred to in particular texts. Looking ahead, I cannot fully identify
which strands of my composing will result in texts, and how they will
get braided or separated into specific bundles of written language.
Looking back from the finished text, I cannot clearly trace its history;
its beginnings and sources are fuzzy, its development entangled with
the threads of other compositions. Because my texts are relatively long
(up to book length, some of them), deeply felt and thought through;
because I write slowly, often painfully, and develop ideas discontinu-
ously over long stretches; and perhaps because I am composing theories
of discourse that depend on a reflective understanding of my own
language experience, my personal life, work, and writing intersect in
changing but always intimate ways.

The peculiar reflexivity of being a writing theorist means that I am
always examining my own composing with a detached and ironic eye.
What I am trying to do here—a beginner's effort—is to intensify that
self-reflective attitude to approach the level and quality of phenomenological description, which involves not only intuiting, analyzing, and
describing particulars of composing in their full concreteness, but also
attempting to attain insight into the essence of the experience.[2] A
primary obstacle to this goal is the conceptual baggage I carry—the

---

[2]See Herbert Spiegelberg, *The Phenomenological Movement: A Historical Introduction*,
3rd ed., rev. and enl. (The Hague: Martinus Nijhoff, 1982), pp. 681–719, on essentials of
the phenomenological method.

labels, concepts, distinctions, and assumptions I have absorbed from existing rhetorical or composing theory and the teaching tradition. In order to clarify my intuitions and open myself patiently to the truth of my own experiences, I need to bracket or hold in abeyance two aspects of my composing that carry a heavy burden of such prejudices. Formulating and maintaining those brackets has been the most difficult and rigorous task in composing this account, requiring constant vigilance. As in perceiving one of those ambiguous visual figures, my mind slips constantly even now into a different gestalt.

The first bracket involves postponing the question of how specific composing activities attach themselves to particular texts so that I experience them as coherent and bounded events. This bracket is implied in the distinction I took as a premise, between composing episodes and a composing life. The naive common-sense conception of "writing a paper" so powerfully dominates one's consciousness that only by trying to set it aside can I feel clearly, and thus articulate, the slow, deep rhythms and texture of the composing life. Ultimately, this decision leads me to conceive composing events as constructed from a more diffuse and confused experience—as much the products of a composing life as the texts themselves. More immediately, it requires me to observe and describe my composing from a middle distance, close enough for detail but not zoomed in to the molecular level of, say, protocols, which follow thought and inscription minute by minute over brief intervals. What is grasped from middle distance is called by psychologists "molar activity," meaning events perceived at a normative level where, though dispersed in time and space, they cohere holistically and acquire names such as walking the dog or going on a diet.

The second bracket suspends consideration of the temporal nature of composing experience, even as molar activity, because of the irresistible association of sequence with the history of particular texts. When dealing with such an integral yet intricately interlaced tissue as a composing life, one cannot grasp it through componential analysis, which involves cutting up a whole into its irreducible atomic elements, examining them in isolation, and determining rules of combination and transformation. Rather, I want to abstract from the ongoing vital process itself the dynamic principles that govern its continuities and change. Hence the unit of analysis here is a stretch of experience— approximately three summer months—sliced at convenient junctures from the continuum of my composing life, during which I studied introspectively these processes and their patterns. Those which I can identify as textually pointed present a dense, busy pattern of simultaneous and interconnected intellectual work.

Here are some of the more distinct activities, in no particular order: writing a prospectus for a book of philosophical essays; reading for and planning three remaining essays for that book; much professional and personal reading that is less textually directed; imagining a graduate course on literacy development and a writing course to be taught next year; writing an abstract for a convention paper; preparing and giving two lectures for a seminar on rhetoric and composition; making notes for future projects of various kinds; preparing a commentary on a pair of essays; working on this account. I talked with family and friends, wrote letters, journals, notes, abstracts, outlines, essays, kept a reading journal, filled three daybooks with notes on my composing, elaborated all these in further notes, annotations and commentary, sketches and maps, drafts, on the computer screen. In the chaos and multiplicity of these composing activities I discern finally an underlying simplicity in my composing life: two deeply rooted impulses whose conjunctions and opposition construct its fundamental rhythm.

Quite late in the composing work on this essay, in a marginal notation to my daybook, I wrote the charged phrase "resistance to form." There followed quickly a wave of annotations whereby I gathered together under this rubric dozens of diverse and hitherto unrelated behaviors, observations, and reflections. These words signal my first clear intuition of a motive underlying the fluctuations of surface patterns in my composing, almost immediately suggesting a dialectic of opposing and complementary impulses: the *generative,* a desire to link information and feeling into more and more densely connected and layered networks; and the *discursive,* a drive to formulate meaning in precisely articulated, highly textualized, and rhetorically addressed sequences of meaning.

My composing nature motivates me powerfully to formulate knowledge and feeling in the discursive order of written language. But this drive encounters at every step the pressure of the generative impulse to wait, to postpone form indefinitely: instead to remain open to the inexhaustibly changing patterns of connection within the stream of experience. My notes, journals, discourse maps, drafts, inscriptions of all kinds short of finished texts—all these display an extraordinary resistance to order, hierarchy, selection, definition: they are scrawled in every direction on the page, in layers of inserts and annotations, in various colors, with an impatient illegibility. I feel compulsively reluctant to follow the conventions of outlining, to write or think in terms of thesis statements; I proliferate redundant words and phrases rather than choose one form over another and, especially on my computer screen, multiply and juxtapose alternate versions of whole stretches of text.

Yet in the very abundance of these wild and anarchic scribblings there is an insistent desire to articulate distinctions, find the precise and true word and image, develop lines of thought that can arrow through the jumble of ideas toward some satisfying closure. In one place I write in my notebook of the danger in outlines of thinness—loss of depth and richness of meaning; in the next breath I write of the danger of muddle and disorder in my loosely scripting ways, in the piles of paper that rise around the house in little puddles concentrated around couch, chair, desk, bed. Between these two (I write finally) I am drawn back and forth irresistibly, as in breathing. The push and pull of generative and discursive impulses is not just a brute force struggle; they enact a true dialectic rhythm. Without the generative urge the drive toward form would be empty; without the possibility of writing them out these patterns of understanding would remain mute and unrealized.

It is tempting to suggest here such classic oppositions as metaphor and metonymy, or to invoke the specialized functions of right and left hemispheres—staples of composition theory. I will acknowledge these cultural resonances and their undoubted channeling of my thought even as I insist on bracketing these theoretical constructs along with others. I am trying here to train and to rely on my own introspection, largely via the medium of a daybook always at hand, repeatedly reread and examined, annotated, expanded in separate notes, elaborated in layer upon layer of reflections. Here is the direct source of the distinctions drawn so far, and the basis for pursuing them further.

The deeply figured interplay of motives that I have described runs along below the rhythms that play across the surface of my everyday composing mind: the ebb and flow of power and fluency; highs and lows of feeling; repetition of themes, breaks in continuity, turns of feeling; the symmetries and contrasts of form. From these patterns I want to abstract three "moments" of composing as action. Much earlier than my intuition of the dialectic of generative and discursive impulses, I recognized "generating," "structuring," and "focusing" as the three most distinctive molar experiences of my composing life. The trouble was that their meaning as concepts shifted constantly (even throughout the drafting of this essay), largely because it is so hard to detach these notions from the temporal evolution of a given text in "stages" (i.e., the planning, organizing, drafting, revising, editing sequence we attribute to composing events). By rigorously striving for the suspension of textual particularity and temporality I succeeded in conceiving these as abstract, unordered phases or "moments"—composing ways of the mind in the sense that David Sudnow describes the ways of the hand in playing jazz piano.[3] I am using "moments" in the phenomenological sense, not as temporal points (though they have complex temporal implications) but as contextual elements of a concrete experience that can be conceived separately only by abstraction. They may be thought of to begin with as attitudes or modes of attention in terms of which I think composingly, with characteristic feeling tones, objects, purposes, textual expression, pace, structure, and problems.

[3]David Sudnow, *Ways of the Hand: The Organization of Improvised Conduct* (Cambridge, Mass.: Harvard University Press, 1978).

Through abstraction and contrastive analysis these moments will appear at first pure and distinct attitudes, but even at this point they must be defined relationally. Their complex interpenetrations and mutual affordances will unfold as the description proceeds, until finally I must remove the brackets and deal with events of concrete textuality. For now I will put their relation in this tentative formulation: *generating* is the moment of connectivity, an open-ended exchange between myself and the ideational environment; *focusing* is the moment of tunnel vision, single-mindedly coming to grips with meaning at the fine-grained levels of textuality, sacrificing many latent possibilities for the lesser actuality; *structuring* is the work that mediates these modes, translating open radial patterns into closed, linear, teleological ones.

GENERATING

Throughout my daybooks I have tried repeatedly to capture the feeling of the generative moment. It is not a cool, cerebral experience but a joyous state of physical excitement and pure power felt in the stomach and rising up in the chest as a flood of energy that pours out in rapid, explosive bursts of language. It is a pleasantly nervous state, like the feeling of the gymnast ready to mount the apparatus who is tuned tautly and confidently to the powers and capabilities of her own body. Ideas compel expression: I write in my daybook of their force shooting and sparking through my fingers onto the paper.

The generative power both draws on and affects everything in my environment. It means being wide open to stimuli from every direction and source. In this state any experience, no matter how trivial, may suddenly seem strikingly relevant, funneling into the expanding connective web of my thought. My mind transforms everything around me —the concentration of an Olympic athlete, the spareness of a Japanese house, the self-consciousness of an adolescent son—into ideas for writing about writing. When most intense this attitude makes the entire stream of daily life nutritive, to the point of overstimulation. The transforming power of the generative state is generous, contagious, unselective in what it affects, ideas touching each other off like firecrackers almost simultaneously. Ultimately composing power spills over from writing to other dimensions of my life, creating everywhere possibilities for action, order, transformation.

The essence of the generative moment is experiencing the human power to connect. The small power of my composing is perhaps a very shadowy expression of the unity of being that is felt in profound religious experience—what Freud called the oceanic feeling. It is by nature both an enormous and a diffuse power, because it understands or presents everything I know in terms of (ultimately) everything else I know

or learn. Nothing is excluded and therefore nothing is selected or directed—except, as we shall see, through the mediation of the structuring moment. Hence to be in the high generative state is to be uncritical,
naive, playful, and unfocused. Typically I might wake up from a dream,
rush out of the shower, or return from my hour-long commute with my
head crammed with inchoate ideas, fragments of phrases, titles, vague
patterns that I try quickly to capture in free, telegraphic, idiosyncratic
text and, often, little icons—sketches, diagrams, lists. This brings me to
what I call the observables of my composing, a technology of physical
forms, formats, tools, places, and ways of inscription.

Technology creates an external memory without which I could not
compose because of the transience of the word music in my head. I store
in this safety net traces of the vast verbal matrix from which my texts
will emerge: in a homely image, like the French stockpot simmering on
the back of the stove, to which nutritious bits of bones and meat are
regularly added, forming a base for various stews, sauces, soups, and
other dishes.

My basic stockpots are two more or less continuous notebooks, one
called "The Third Basket" and the other "Reading Journal." The Third
Basket takes its name from Sir Isaiah Berlin, who wrote that human
questions fall into three baskets: the empirical, for questions whose
answers depend on data; the formal, for questions whose answers require calculation (deduction); and the third basket, for everything else,
including questions of ordinary life, art, craft, and philosophy.[4] The
Third Basket is mainly a dated journal where I write down any thinking
that seems to point toward texts, typically philosophical writing about
discourse. Near the beginning I simply list, and periodically update,
titles or key words that trace the course of my projected writing. I have
added other sections at times, on teaching or large projects, but my
journal works best when I throw everything into one pot. Although
apparently a sequence of pages, it is actually constructed in layer upon
layer of annotation, producing an enormous, inchoate mass of observations and commentary; any page may contain ideas that end up in four
or five different texts. Recently I have been working on systematizing
these layers through ink colors and tags written in margins and on
facing pages. I try to keep the Reading Journal physically independent,
but it has the same texture of notes upon notes: paraphrase, quotation,
commentary, and response merging into text planning—more about
what I am going to write than what I've read.

This prediscursive, partly iconic analogue to my memory presents
similar problems of tagging, filing, and retrieving information. I am

[4]Isaiah Berlin, *Concepts and Categories: Philosophical Essays*, ed. Henry Hardy (New
York: Viking, 1979), pp. 1–11.

peculiarly incapable of detail memory and find myself having to read and sort through both my journals and subsequent notes repeatedly in order to produce a particular text, going back to this chaotic source even though I have made a long series of abstracts and outlines that are supposed to reduce and organize it. I sometimes wonder if I am relying more heavily than most people on the global, fuzzy, holographic aspect of memory, as represented in notebooks that, like a radio set, can only be tuned in all at once. If I do not work continuously on a piece of writing, most of it disappears from my head and I must rely on my notebooks, not so much to remember what I planned, but to stimulate a new, similar but not identical train of thought. This method (not really a choice, but my nature) is undoubtedly slow and inefficient, but it also holds off the premature closure of form and keeps my mind more flexible to adapt to new information. To think freshly it is often useful, even necessary, to forget what I (or someone else) has already thought. I thus notice in my composing a texture of recognition and surprise, innovation and continuity, which marks the reinvention in different terms of half-forgotten themes. Over a writing life this texture is how I come to know and project my identity as a theorist and composer.

How do I make up my stockpot and what are the ingredients? Basically I am always generating patterns of two kinds: patterns that connect events and objects and abstractions in the world I am writing about, and patterns of discursivity. Searching for such patterns is not a matter of applying "heuristics" in the textbook sense. Over the years I have acquired heightened sensitivity to abstract connections of ideas in my field and to discourse patterns generally, constantly enhanced by studying writers I admire, students' work and my own. Like other composers, I have a conceptual style, a habit of noticing certain kinds of connections and constructing them discursively in typical ways. Probably the coherence of my work as a theorist depends as much on these preferences (which have many cultural roots) as on specific content. For example, I often develop a distinction that is mediated by a third term. I almost always turn a straightforward analysis or description of something in the world into a self-reflexive and ironic consideration of thinking and writing about it. I am fascinated by the particle-wave-field distinction in two interpretations. First, setting in motion an apparently static object and, its reverse, freezing a flux in space or time so as to perceive it as a simultaneous whole. Second, the precipitation of a perceptually real "particle" from a dance of energy through the interaction of an observer. The reader can discern some of these patterns in this discourse; over the years I have become self-conscious of their appearance and learned to recognize and elaborate them deliberately.

My power of creativity is subject to a natural ebb and flow accompanied by extreme swings of mood. I have described the flow, a state of high excitement; the ebb is an affliction of spirit that I have not learned to accept easily. I call it a slump, to suggest the inexplicable alternation of slumps and streaks in the baseball player's season, defined as a sustained period of discouragement, depression, confusion, loss of confidence and competence. Typically, I went through one long slump this summer of several weeks, much of it spent worrying futilely because I could not restore my energy and work when I needed to. I wrote in my daybook: "listless, lethargic, no ideas, no new ideas, all ideas seem worthless. Nothing connects or reminds or leads anywhere." (I knew, of course, that it would pass; but that was an intellectual conviction, not truly felt.) I marveled at the descriptions I had written earlier of the generative moment; later, when I had passed out of the slump I could not remember how it felt or how one could ever feel that way.

Trying to exorcise that feeling, I looked for explanations and, finding no rational ones, blamed myself for sloth and a failure of will. After a while I discovered that there is a natural rhythm to creativity that cannot be altered simply by will power. When I chart the ebb and flow of generativity in my composing life, there are broad, slowly changing tides representing my power to compose over a period of time, and little waves and swells day to day, minute to minute. I am particularly susceptible to the ebb of creative energy in transition periods between work activities that are differently paced.

At the same time, this intense lethargy is not arbitrary, because whatever its mysterious source it becomes attached to genuine intellectual and ethical problems that have to be worked through. The most profound of these has to do with the abstract nature of philosophical writing and a related dependence of my work on analogies to work in other disciplines.

The abstractness of writing philosophically about discourse and teaching is a constant threat to the experiential richness of connectivity that constitutes the generative moment. Abstractions empower connection because they relate concrete experiences and feelings through concepts; but they also empty those realities of their content. I write over and over again in the daybooks about my fear of losing the richness behind the abstraction and forgetting its concrete meaningfulness. When this happens, the codings in my journals and notes—lists of comparisons, titles, fragments of text—suddenly appear to be nothing but words, and I can't imagine how I could ever have expected to flesh them out in consecutive text. They are empty, thin, sparse (I complain to myself); the problem is not too few connections but too many, too vague, too general. In contrast, when my concepts are charged with generative power they carry a penumbra of concrete possibility layered down to my own actual experience of discourse or teaching or growth. This structure supports and anticipates the detailed working out of a concept and constitutes an image of achievement for eventual text, like those which athletes project with closed eyes to set in their muscles the patterns they are about to enact. When I lose that image, my ability to write is paralyzed and I must restore it by reexploring the relationship between my abstraction and the realities it represents or derives from. (At least, I console myself, I cannot deliberately write abstractions false to my experience.)

One reason for losing this contact is that I draw many ideas for understanding problems in my own field by analogy with other disciplines. This necessitates adapting concepts and terms to a new technical use and producing connected step-by-step arguments. It means that work starts at a high level of abstraction, relying on a strong intuition of relevance that is based on my own experience but has not been directly referred to it. An example is my application (in the lecture to the Purdue Seminar in Rhetoric and Composition) of concepts drawn from the analysis of women's ethical development to composition as a field. After drawing together a number of points about the status of the discipline, I was inspired in reading Carol Gilligan's *In a Different Voice* to interpret these in a developmental framework, specifically to see composition as experiencing the same developmental crises and espousing the same "ethic of care" as the women she describes.[5] The typical work of composing following this intuition involves analyzing and following out the implications of the concept rather than illustrating or detailing the experience it is based on. Thus my musings explore the various ways that philosophical discourse makes itself real to readers while trying to make sure I myself do not lose the sense of experience that charges my concepts and analogies with meaning—a problem that is not solved by giving examples in some simple sense.

FOCUSING

Focusing is the mood or mode of fierce concentration that funnels thought from its diffuse matrix into fully discursive form. Literally, it is the attitude necessary for me to draft a single text per se, as distinct from producing written thought in fragments and clusters unattached or only loosely attached to possible discourse. Here it is necessary to explain what I mean by fully discursive, and how text differs from the writing of daily life—a kind of deposit or trace of the constantly composing mind.

Text creates the virtual experience of a train of thought for a reader or audience to whom it is addressed in a situation defined by occasion and purpose. It does not, like the composing life reflected in my notebooks and their extensions, simply go on indefinitely; it has distinct

[5]Carol Gilligan, *In a Different Voice: Psychological Theory and Women's Development* (Cambridge, Mass.: Harvard University Press, 1982).

scope as an episode. Thus it begins, moves, ends. As I have suggested, composing is the tension between the effort to turn mental life into event and the correlative resistance to the closure of form as false to experience. For me, to produce text as event it seems necessary to construct it eventfully: on a single impulse held with intense concentration from beginning to end of the inscription process.

Here is what I imagine, desire, project as I write—discursive form in the large. It is patterned in many ways, but gathering up all these patterns is a great sweep or movement to carry the reader irresistibly through the text from start to close. I conceive it most often as a path I must find, and create for the reader, through a nonlinear network of patterns. As a path it reveals the topography of thought as felt, with a distinctive rhythm, pace, points of intensity and relaxation, surprising turns—an experience something like skiing a particular trail. The point of departure is crucial, and my most difficult task in focusing is to find my way onto a path that feels right and flows smoothly. I am constructing something here entirely different structurally from the verbal matrix—what I call the "narrative line" for a given text.

Two decision points fix my intention to focus. The first is a resolve to plan, and the second to write out (draft and complete) a particular text, defined as particular by title, audience, occasion, and a process of collecting relevant material that has gradually accumulated in my various storehouses of composing ideas. Each stage of intent has a textual analogue: at the planning point, setting up a folder to contain any further writings for this definitely anticipated text, separating these sharply from the notebooks (I will use these now as a stimulus and source of plans); at the drafting point, titling and numbering a page as first in a consecutive sequence. No matter how many times I throw away that page, I will always begin again by titling the whole piece and (usually) identifying or titling an introduction.

By the time the second decision is made, I have put myself in the focused state, usually gradually and at considerable cost. By definition focusing excludes composing in the usual diffuse daily ways since it requires attending exclusively to one text and (because of the difficulty in holding concentration) producing it as rapidly and continuously as possible. (In the case of very long texts, this is a severe problem, only partly alleviated by chunking them into parts.) I describe this process in the notebooks as one of closing down, shutting out stimulation, tightening and screwing down my attention through an exertion of will, sinking deep into a trance of concentration. It is a self-contained, inward, absorbed state. When the composing is difficult or the text long I work almost continuously for days if possible (to the degree my family and circumstances will tolerate it), resisting interruption and scheduling meals and rest around the rhythms of my thought and writing. During such a period I must deliberately avoid intellectual stimulation such as reading, which might throw me into a generative state, incompatible with focusing because it destroys my control over the connectivity of my understanding.

The primary means of control, or the top level, is a set of patterns that has emerged, usually tentatively and somewhat confusedly, from the verbal matrix and structuring process. This includes a rather unstable anticipation of the narrative line that will eventually dominate the text. All these patterns together constitute what I think of as the harmony of the text, within and against which I improvise a melody, the spinning out of ideas from word to phrase to sentence to paragraph. I call changes in the harmony "deep revision" and in the melody "shallow revision," the latter including both language and content (inseparable at this microscopic level). As in the improvisation of jazz, the melody is the most labile and free element of what is created; harmonic changes, that is, restructuring the conceptual patterns, are less drastic and frequent; the most enduring, and in discourse, least definable, qualities are the rhythm of thought and the identity or essence of intention that persists through all the changes.

I am going to say little of the actual improvisation, the detail of drafting, because it must be described at a closer distance than the molar one I have chosen. Broadly, it is a recurrent cycling between maps or abstractions of meaning, freely written loose approximations, and carefully formed text, which involves a pulsing of attention between a participatory and a critical focus. In the first case I indwell my language and experience my meaning as intention. In the second, I withdraw to a critical distance and experience the text as reader. Control, the essence of the focused moment, depends on this critical eye to make two comparisons and judgments. On the one hand, I must compare an image of achievement (the shadowy anticipations and projections of my intention) to the meaning I actually read back out of the text. More profoundly, I must test my meaning for its truth, by going back to memory or verbal matrix and reexperiencing in imagination the truth that I claim. Whereas the generative moment suspended both tests to allow imagination free play, the moment of focusing sternly demands of me both a faithful clarity of language and a rigorous integrity of conceptualization.

My resistance to form derives partly from the impossibility of satisfying this discursive ideal, which cannot capture through its linear, teleological, sharply articulated disciplines the holistic network of understanding and feeling that is elaborated partially in my notebooks and more generally by the composing life. My exquisitely poignant awareness of this inadequacy creates the pain of the focusing moment, which at times intensifies to the point of blocking. Blocking (quite distinct from the slump that marks the low ebb of generativity) occurs when the critical function overwhelms the power of the patterning imagination to control and yet free the forming impulse to improvise text. It creates a negative force of inertia and fear that results in my making repetitive formulations of alternate choices—the same idea in different language, different orders or patterns for a sequence of ideas—and feeling unable to choose among them. The resistance to form that is productive in generating is destructive in this instance, reaching its height at the second decision point when, writing a title and the first sentence that is not free-floating but addressed, I balk at committing myself to event. Not only must I give up the fluid dynamic of my composing life for the controlled path of text, but I must enter into a relationship only dimly apprehended up to now, a dialogue with another whose demands make themselves felt most intensely at the beginning of text.

I can overcome blocking with patience and blind faith, slogging through the repetitions until finally I break out of the vicious circle and begin improvising fluently. As I proceed I encounter another problem, particularly when the focusing moment must be sustained over days or weeks. Such concentration is a fragile thing that must be selfishly protected from the interruptions of daily life. What I am doing as I write is to stabilize and intensify my holistic sense of the controlling patterns in my text until they are both so simple and so compelling that I can pack them like suitcases with layers of richly textured development. Once such a texture is laid down, it becomes accessible to craft, and it is relatively easy to prune, sharpen, and heighten impact through editing.

If I lose concentration before I gain this degree of control, I usually have to begin again on a new impulse. I am always surprised, therefore, to realize how differently a text would have developed had circumstances varied slightly: how unexpected and dependent on chance is its actual content. This is my compensation for the discipline of form, the manifestation of the suppressed generative moment in improvisation. Composing even in focusing must remain for me an open system, as John McDermott remarked about modern art:

> Order is maintained, but at the service of novelty. The future is anticipated not as a codification of our intention, rather as a harbinger of surprise. Indeed, intention itself emerges with clarity only when we are far into the creative process, and is often retrospectively reconstructed when our work takes a surprising turn.[6]

STRUCTURING

In the process of describing the generative and focused moments, I have gradually disclosed the role of structuring and opened the way to

---

[6]John McDermott, *The Culture of Experience: Philosophical Essays in the American Grain* (New York: New York University Press, 1976), p. 90.

understanding how the composing event crystallizes in relation to text from my composing life. The essence of the structuring moment is *work*, the working of weblike patterns of meaning into discursive ones. Here let me reintroduce, or rather recognize, the aspect of temporality in the nature of each moment. The generative moment is a rhythm of ebb and flow that underlies composing at any temporal point, but is most quintessentially realized when I am able to relax into this productive state over a time of my life, often a vacation with lots of personal reading, varied experiences, a change of place, a renewal of relationships. During such a time no pressure compels me toward focusing, and my composing energies disperse themselves fruitfully in many directions, attached loosely to shifting and shadowy potential texts. In contrast the focused moment is sharply delineated within my life as an intensive episode during which my composing mind is concentrated exclusively on one text in a purposeful, determined movement toward completion.

In one sense structuring enters into both these moments. Structuring may be defined more specifically as the process by which discursive features arise and persist in clusters of ideas, so that looking backward from an actual text I perceive that text as having evolved from a few key words through notes, lists, outlines, sketches, and other pre-texts to its drafts and final form. From this perspective focusing appears as a refined mode or final stage of structuring, during which such features as sequenced, grammatical sentences, cohesive devices, paragraph indentation, and so on are introduced or stabilized. On the other hand, in the generative mode what I create are connections that are the seeds or material of structures. What I want to think about now is how these patterns develop simultaneously but at varying pace toward focusing moments, through a differentiation of the verbal matrix.

My composing life produces a verbal stream that is partially captured in a dynamic matrix of written materials (for which the Third Basket and Reading Journal can stand). This production of written thought continues at all times except when I am focusing, when it becomes the object and source of further writing. In fact, the typical activity of my composing life is not a pure generative state (rare) or focusing (relatively short and intense) but a sort of normative structuring work that goes on intermittently through the medium of my notebooks. When I look at these chronologically, I discover a series of generative points each representing a high point of creative energy, followed by the working out of these ideas in increasingly discursive ways. Frequently the first move in this process is to title a possible text. Titles function as nodes or hooks on which to hang my ideas; and my constant titling changes represent the fine-tuning of a discursive intention. This work differentiates the matrix into pattern clusters (although they still intermingle up to the moment of focusing), some of which ultimately devolve into individual texts.

A particularly clear example of such differentiation occurred this summer when I worked simultaneously and interactively on the plans for a book prospectus and for three of the essays in the book. I perceived this work as a process of discovering principles by which I could sort many closely related ideas into piles of strands and braid them into distinct essays—in the case of the prospectus, combine them. This work went on at the same time as, and indeed by virtue of, my creation of new patterns, not simply connecting ideas but connecting them in discursive ways. This means that they began to acquire such features as these: discrimination of segments or parts; order; hierarchy; holistic unity (keyed often to a title); specific relations such as opposition or similarity. As I worked on the three essay plans, eventually through a focusing mode tied to writing the prospectus, I noticed that the work proceeded by decision points in the same sense that I spoke of in focusing, except that here the decision applied to the whole matrix rather than a single text. Each decision point was a choice that opened other choices and led to experiments with their structural implications and possibilities. For example, I might decide to collect many ideas under the notion of theme and variation or hermeneutical interpretation, or to relate them through dynamic principles such as a pendulum swing or sudden reversal.

Eventually this structuring work moved from notebook (verbal matrix) to folders (in the case of planning the essays, no further than this first decision point in focusing). As structuring progressed I tended to focus more and more urgently on the narrative line, that is, a plan that would set in motion (and address to a reader) the various distinctions and relations I had sketched out. I displayed distinct preferences for particular designs and rhythms, often dissolving a knot in my thinking by turning to a favorite one. Choices such as these examples have a strong aesthetic motive: a distinction mediated by a third term; parallelism or symmetry; analogies; and surprising turns and moves within a drama of thought.

REFLECTION

An ironic reversal has occurred in this effort to describe the three moments of my composing life as the mediated relation of generative and discursive impulses. In articulating my composing life I reveal composing events to be not raw experience but constructs of anticipation and memory that are precipitated from the continuity of my composing life just as texts are from the verbal matrix. The very notion of a "composing process" seems paradoxically dependent on that of fully deployed text. In my experience the event appears to be constructed by making focusing the temporal center for a pattern of decision points that is only fully realized in memory, but unfolds through anticipation. Thus prospectively, I differentiate the matrix through structuring and gradually, moving toward the point of separation or birth, create intentionality; retrospectively, I revise memory to reflect more cleanly and coherently the historical evolution of an achieved text—here is where it began, this is when I realized . . ., this goes back to. . . .

In the same way reflection layers yet another moment into the melange of thought and language—the moment of self-consciousness embodied in this essay. Through reflection I reconstruct and rationalize the composing life in order to understand how it shapes my being as theorist, teacher, person. I discover in doing so how intimately tangled are my composing energies, my work, and my personal growth, daily life, and relationships. The composing life seems sometimes to me a burden, almost a geas; in the focusing moment particularly it is fiercely self-absorbed and narrowing, asserting its imperatives in competition with the pleasures and responsibilities of family and public life and forcing me to agonizing choices. In compensation, there is a symbiotic relation between my composing life and the experience that it interprets, because the power to connect not only feeds on the vitality of life but illuminates and changes its possibilities. My work as a theorist ultimately develops that symbiosis, relating the composing of meanings through writing to the ways individuals grow and develop in personal contexts.

The use of language to compose meaning must, like any universal human act, have both great commonalities and incredible idiosyncrasy and individuality. For theorists of discourse, reflections such as we write here on our own composing experiences clearly have subjective value and indeed are simply intensifications, as I have described, of a sustained attitude and habit. Intensifying to this level of description tears away the conventional sedimentations that frame my composing behavior and leads to understandings that change it—for example I am newly aware of the ethical nature of conflicts that had appeared technical or psychological. But I also think there is an objective value in these accounts, because they at once reveal a human practice, in which literacy or composing always grows out of and expresses a life and a personal identity, and remind us unforgettably of the endless multiplicity of the concrete activity of making meanings, which in the end is what the teacher or the composer must confront. As Clifford Geertz puts it, in an old African proverb, "Wisdom comes out of an ant heap."[7]

---

[7]Clifford Geertz, *Local Knowledge: Further Essays in Interpretive Anthropology* (New York: Basic Books, 1983), p. 91.

D. Gordon Rohman is professor of English and lifelong education at Michigan State University, where he has served in a variety of roles for the past twenty-six years. A native of upstate New York, Rohman received a Ph.D. in English from Syracuse University in 1960. Previous to that he had worked on newspapers in Utica and Syracuse. He joined the Department of English at Michigan State University in 1958. With a grant from the U.S. Office of Education, he developed the concept of "pre-writing," a term he coined to describe the idea-forming stage of the creative process of making meaning with words.

Since 1975, Rohman has directed his attention to adult and lifelong education. For four years he was a consultant to the president of Michigan State to help develop the new idea of lifelong education. He regularly teaches adults in the university's Evening College, in such courses as Mindplay, a program in creative problem solving, and Writing for Your Life, a new kind of adult composition course.

THE INS AND OUTS AND UPS AND DOWNS OF WRITING

D. Gordon Rohman
Michigan State University

Whenever we write we search both for something to say and for a way of saying it. Others may find it helpful to separate these two things. I don't. To me they are two ends of one journey. I discover what I want to say by saying it and resaying it. For I believe that writing is a means of inquiry as well as of communication, and wording is a powerful way of thinking ideas up as well as a good way of putting them down.

Whenever we write we search both for something to say and for a way of saying it. Others may find it helpful to separate these two things. I don't. To me they are two ends of one journey. I discover what I want to say by saying and resaying it. For I believe that writing is a means of inquiry as well as of communication, and wording is a powerful way of thinking ideas up as well as a good way of putting them down.

Depending on which end of the process I am on, I use words differently. At the beginning I want to *see* with them, at the end to *say* with them. Along the way—if I find a way, I don't always—my essay transforms itself from something I write for myself into something I write for the reader.* My relationship to the words changes also. At the end I find myself striving as hard as I can to lead these recalcitrant horses into the harness of good form. But at the beginning I try as best I can to follow my words to see where they might go, unleashing them as the hunter his dog to see what game it can scare up off the beaten track.

*I shall use "essay" as a generic term for all the forms of prose I write.

If, as is usually the case in the sort of writing I do, the occasion challenges me to see as well as say something new, then when I begin I intentionally and deliberately move away from everything I have always known about the subject—more precisely away from every *way* I have known about the subject—and into a cloud of unknowing. I do not treat this stage of unknowing as the necessary evil of all beginnings but rather as a necessary good. For two reasons.

First, I believe that any idea worth more than trivial pursuit doesn't know where it's going until it gets there, and furthermore, the "getting there" is the way to find out where "there" is—even whether there's a "there" there at all! When I am writing for the reader I must be as clear as I can from the start about what it is exactly that I have to say. With words I seek to bridge the gap between my head and his. No clarity in me, none in him. But when I am at the stage of writing for myself, I seek to span a more puzzling gap, that between how I now know something and how I might know it. Clarity is not where I begin but only (with luck) where I end. With one foot planted firmly in midair, I lend myself to an involvement with the mystery of my yet-to-be-discovered insight. My writing at this point becomes an essay in the original sense of the word, a continual weighing of alternatives, a very trying affair, as with words I blaze varying paths of purpose into the dark woods of possibility.

The quarry I stalk in this trying fashion is not a new idea to think *about* so much as that most elusive of all game: a new idea to think *with*. Like an adolescent in search of a personality, my essay begins as words in search of a meaning. Just as the life of our years, so also does the life of our words consist not simply of what happens *to* us as what we *do* with what happens to us, what we make of it. And so in the initial groping stage of my essay, I hunt with words for the words that will become the map of my territory, the menu for my meal, the music for my notes.

And that brings me to my second reason for treating "unknowing" as a necessary good. In order to hear new music, I must escape from the boom box of my culture to a silence where I can hear myself think. So that I may have freedom *for* speech, I must first find a freedom *from* speech. Hearing a fresh word to think with is difficult because our semantic space buzzes with our culture's thrice-told tales that plot the play of my understanding before I enact it. Years of teaching creative problem solving have taught me this at least. To every problem we bring a problem: ourselves. The way we perceive/conceive a situation is precisely how we define/confine it as "the problem." A "problem" is a point of view, a plot, a map. To the extent that we are unaware of that and of how, as the kids of the sixties used to say, we are "making the scene," just so much are we the prisoners of our own play, or more likely, just so much are we merely cultural instant replay. We need to get offstage, into the darkened audience, and become spectators of our own performance.

Our voyage to the moon symbolizes what I mean. The conventional way we are told to tell "The Moon Story" is this: "For the first time, mankind set foot on the moon." But Norman Cousins reminded us—literally "re-minded" us—that we can replot this story so that it reveals an entirely different meaning: "For the first time," he said, "humankind set eyes on the Earth." His retelling makes a world—a worldview—of difference in how we understand the adventure. Furthermore it illustrates the necessary good of the cloud of unknowing. In order to see something in a new way, we need to stop seeing it in an old way, we need to get "outside" and "above" the old way. In order to see the world, literally, we had to go to the moon. In order to have a new worldview, we have to get outside our old view. For in either case, it's hard to see the picture when you're inside the frame.

I get out of my worldview worlds with the spacecraft of words, with *other words*. Words name life to life; *other words* rename life to new life. So when I begin my essay, I try with other words to—as the creative problem-solving system known as synectics puts it—"make the familiar strange." In the same old words, the world looks like the same old place. But in *other words*, it looks "funny," "illogical," "incorrect." With other words I can always escape from the invisibility of my commonplace world. With other words, I can sometimes spring a new world from the wilderness of uncommonplaces.

One of the most powerful ways of *other wording* I know is metaphor, using it not to upholster prose but to rename the world. With metaphor we call things by their "wrong" names—and thereby enable ourselves to see the familiar world strangely, from "outside and above." Sometimes—and these are the best times of our writing lives—we are by such other words able to *say* a new way of seeing into existence. With such other words, we sometimes can discover a better map for the same old territory, a better menu for the same old food, new music from the same old notes.

If and when I can do that, my essay reaches a turning point. I can stop writing it for myself and start writing it for my reader. I have reached the end of my beginning and the beginning of my end. There is an old trick question that asks, "How far can a dog run into the woods?" The answer is: "Until he reaches the center. At that point, he is running out of the woods."

TRUE CONFESSIONS

Gary Tate
Texas Christian University

Composing is painful and slow, and although some good sentences may be the result, the overall structure suffers. If you have your nose down in each sentence as you write, you won't have much sense of larger elements. You may find the right word but the paragraph will probably be a mess.

[The following is an edited version of an imaginary interview that took place in June of 1984 somewhere in Texas. The scene: the cheerful but messy office of an aging, overweight teacher of English. Next to his desk sits a serious young person, obviously a graduate student.]

GT: I'm pleased to meet one of Tom Waldrep's students, but I'm not quite certain why you're here.

GS: Well, as I said on the phone, I'm a graduate student in English at South Carolina and I've just finished taking Tom's 701 course, Theory and Teaching of Composition. At the end of the course some of us felt that excellent as the course had been there was too much theory and too little practical advice.

GT: Ah, yes. I hear that same complaint from my students.

GS: I guess we're all the same. Anyway, Tom and I were discussing this problem the other day and he found out that I was coming through Fort Worth on my way home for the summer, so he suggested I stop over and chat with you, ask you about your own writing and teaching. Try to get a more down-to-earth sense of what really happens.

GT: Good old Tom!

GS: He said that if you were busy or out of town I should talk to your lovely wife.

GT: I'll bet he did. But enough of that. So you want to talk about "real" life instead of theory, do you? Fine. But I want to come back to that distinction before you leave today.

GS: I'll try to remember. Now, shall we begin at the beginning, with invention?

GT: I'm not sure that's the beginning, but sure, go ahead.

GS: Where do your ideas come from?

GT: I haven't the faintest idea most of the time. It all seems very mysterious. It *is* mysterious, in spite of all our attention recently to invention. I know that this is blasphemy, but I have never had much luck using formal techniques of invention in my own writing.

GS: Do you realize what you're saying???

GT: Now just a minute. Calm down. All I'm saying is that I haven't found these procedures helpful. Others evidently do. One of the things you must keep in mind is that *my* way is *my* way. Not your way or anybody else's. The worst mistake you can make as a teacher (or writer) is to assume that your way is the best way and to try to force it on your students. Always be suspicious of teachers who have found THE WAY.

GS: Well, sure. But you have to have *some* convictions.

GT: Of course. But one of those convictions should be that there is more than one way to write and to teach writing. Your way is only that. My way is only my way. That's one of the reasons that teaching writing to large groups of students at the same time is not effective.

GS: I'd like to come back to the problem of finding ideas. If heuristic devices don't work, what does?

GT: Sorry that I disturbed you about that, but let me try to explain. Most of what I write has to do with the teaching of writing. Now, I've been teaching writing and reading about it and writing about it and talking about it for almost three decades. Under these conditions, I think that it's natural for me not to have to engage in formal search procedures. But I mustn't try to put my students in the same boat. They certainly have not been involved with anything for thirty years—at least not most of them. So I mustn't assume that what works for me will work for them. I think that formal search procedures are valuable primarily when you are writing about a topic that you've not been immersed in, a topic that you're struggling with.

GS: So then the more a student is familiar with a subject, the less likely she is to need help finding ideas?

GT: That's probably true. But not always.

GS: You're very cautious.

GT: I've learned to be.

GS: Do you have a strong sense of audience when you write?

GT: Almost always. I think most writers do. Most writing is done because somebody has something to say to someone. Certainly writing helps me clarify my thinking, indeed, it gives rise to ideas

I would never otherwise have had. It's very generative, but this doesn't mean I sit down and say, I'm going to write something so as to generate ideas. The writing begins, for me, when I have an idea, or when I am asked to write something. That sort of thing starts the writing and then the ideas start to come. I seldom start writing without a purpose.

GS: But does your sense of audience determine how you write and what you write?

GT: Only to a certain extent. It doesn't affect the ideas as much as the style, but even here there is very seldom only *one* way to say something, one appropriate way. The options are almost always numerous, more so than we sometimes tell students.

GS: Right. But students in the classroom don't have real audiences to write for.

GT: Of course they do! And they write for the one audience that matters. The teacher. They know it and I know it, and I take advantage of it by trying to be a real audience, not a fake audience, a marker of papers who doesn't care what's being said. I know that it's popular to have students work in groups so that other students become the audience, but that has never worked well for me. A student writer doesn't really care what another student thinks, and the student audience usually doesn't much care what other students write.

GS: But that sounds terribly old-fashioned, Dr. Tate—may I call you Gary?

GT: Of course not.

GS: Sorry. But lots of teachers are doing imaginative things to give students a sense of audience.

GT: Splendid! I'm all for them. All I'm telling you is what works best for me. It has nothing to do with you or other teachers.

GS: How much do you usually revise?

GT: Quite a bit, much more than I once did. You see, in the bad old days when I sweated over every sentence until I got it "right," the revision took place line by line, word by word as I wrote. That's a terrible way to do it. Composing is painful and slow, and although some good sentences may be the result, the overall structure suffers. If you have your nose down in each sentence as you write, you won't have much sense of larger elements. You may find the right word but the paragraph will probably be a mess.

GS: So how do you do it now?

GT: Well, I try not to polish each sentence as I go. I feel myself wanting to, but I try to resist it. And the more I try to write freely and quickly, the easier it becomes. Of course there are often some terribly rough sections that need lots of attention later on, but, you know, I'm often surprised that things turn out as well as they do when I write fast. Sometimes, when everything is working, what comes out is almost as good, sentence by sentence, as when I worked in the old, slow way. But revision is a way of life. For me, at least.

GS: And what do you find yourself "fixing" as you revise?

GT: Well. I'm not sure about the word "fixing," but more often than not I find myself revising for—well, tone, I guess you'd call it. If I'm trying to write something informal, which I like doing, then I revise to make it sound natural, relaxed, and so forth. But that can involve everything: word choice, punctuation, sentence structure, everything.

GS: What about revising for elements other than tone?

GT: That happens, of course, especially in pieces in which the writing itself has generated new ideas. These new ideas don't always come to mind at the appropriate moment so far as the structure of a piece is concerned, but I find that if I don't put them in when they present themselves, I will just plain forget them. This means that later restructuring is necessary.

GS: Do your students revise much?

GT: Not as much as they should. But I've changed my thinking about that recently. I once thought they were just lazy. Revising is hard work, much harder in some ways than the original act of composing. But recently I've begun to learn that students don't revise much because they don't know what in their papers needs revising. And they don't know this because they are poor readers of their own words. Often, of course, they are poor readers period. The point is this: It takes a good reader to know whether a piece of writing is working or not and if it isn't, what's wrong with it. That kind of judgment, which is, after all, pretty complex, is just not one that a poor reader can make.

GS: So we must help them become better readers?

GT: Yes, but that's no easy task. Many times, I suspect, it's not even possible. People who have read very little during their lifetimes are not likely to suddenly become avid readers at age 18 or 19. Some do, thank God, but not many. What does *not* help is having freshmen buy a collection of "readings" when they take Freshman English. When we say that most good writers are readers, we mean that they have a lifetime of reading to draw upon when they write. Marching a class through twenty or thirty essays in a four-month semester is not going to help.

GS: You say a lifetime of reading to draw upon. Draw upon for what?

GT: Everything! Most of the decisions that you make and that I make when we write are influenced, whether we realize it or not, by the sounds of English prose that have become a part of us as a result of years and years of reading. Now, imagine that you had not "internalized" some such sense. What would you draw upon when you wrote? Rules from handbooks and rhetorics? Advice from teachers? The reading of a few essays? Helpful comments by fellow students? It's the difference between having read scores and scores of authors as they moved from one idea to the next—that is, having really experienced the whole process of transition in prose—and, on the other hand, memorizing a list of transitional words and phrases so that you might remember one when you decide that a transitional device is needed.

GS: So what's the answer?

GT: There's no simple answer, no quick fix. And it's certainly not a problem that colleges can solve. We can probably do a better job than we do to get students to read more, but any real solution must start much earlier in a student's life. Most people who are readers start very young. And they often seem to turn to reading because they are lonely or unhappy children. But I think we'd better not pursue the implications of *that* observation.

GS: I agree. So let's move on. What bad habits would you like to break?

GT: I take it you mean bad writing habits. Well, my worst "habit" is not having a habit at all, a habit of writing regularly each day. I promise myself I'll do it, but something always seems to interfere. Actually I allow it to interfere. There are always plenty of things around to intrude if you allow them to. Discipline is the key. But it's more than that. When I first started teaching, not many people—not even writing teachers—talked much about the necessity of writing if you were a teacher of writing. I never thought of myself as a writer. I was a teacher. You must remember that it's only recently that we've insisted that writing teachers must be writers and that to be a writer means to write more than just the occasional piece that we used to compose.

GS: So your teaching has influenced the way you write or at least the way you think about writing?

GT: Both. But not only my teaching. My reading, my experience as a writer, and so forth. I'm not even certain most of the time where my ideas have originated. I think I've just discovered something new and then I realize that I saw it in a journal or heard it at a meeting several years ago. But anyway, I have profited immensely from my teaching of writing and of courses about the theory of teaching writing.

GS: How would you characterize your writing?

GT: It's been called a good many different things, not all of them complimentary. I don't know that I have a word for what I often seek in writing. What I try for, I think, is an informal, relaxed plain style. The "formal" essay—whatever that is—bores me. I don't do it well, maybe because I'm never quite certain what it is I'm trying to compose.

GS: But isn't it difficult to get published, especially in academic journals, if you don't write formally?

GT: That's not been my experience. I think many editors welcome relaxed pieces that sound as if they had been written by real human beings. But the informal essay is rare, the good informal essay. Most journals don't publish them not because they object to informality but because so few people attempt that style—and of course some who do shouldn't.

GS: Speaking of editing, what has been the effect of your editorial work on your writing?

GT: Disastrous! Early in my career I discovered I had a knack for organizing editorial projects and getting people to contribute. Ed Corbett and I have edited three books and I have edited three on my own. Then for eleven years I edited *Freshman English News.* One of the results of all this is that I've spent a great deal of my time reading, criticizing, and making value judgments about the work of others. It has been enjoyable—most of the time —but it hasn't left me enough time for my own writing. But even as I say this I realize that it's a cop-out. I've had the time—we *all* "have the time." What happened, I guess, is that my editorial work became my excuse for not writing. It's not difficult to find excuses, and I had hit upon one that was halfway respectable.

GS: But your editorial work has certainly provided you with an opportunity to keep up with what's being written.

GT? Oh yes, certainly, but that's a mixed blessing. I often think that the best way to discourage yourself about writing is to read what everyone else has written. Before too long you begin to think that there's nothing left to be said. And also, when editing *FEN,* I became discouraged, especially toward the end, about the state of the profession. So many bad articles by so many people desperate to publish! So I gave up the journal and I'm just now beginning to recover from the experience. But of course these have been only ways that I excused myself from not writing more. Had it not been for the editorial work, I imagine I would have found other, equally compelling reasons.

GS: I know what you mean. I think all of us are inclined in that direction. Why is it, do you think?

GT: I don't know about other people, but I have lots of reasons for not writing more. One important one is that I am insecure about displaying my ideas for all the world to see. I'm always certain that someone will find them trivial or, even worse, just plain wrong. A certain amount of success helps with this problem but not much. I'm convinced that just as there are people who never get over the terror of speaking in public so there are people who never get over the fear of writing for the public.

GS: I appreciate your honesty. And I'd very much like to continue this but I've got a plane to catch. I do remember that you wanted to say something about theory.

GT: Yes. Just this. New teachers of writing often complain about so much emphasis on theory—in their classes, at meetings, in journals, and so forth. And I understand some of what they feel. They are often anxious about the day-by-day teaching of a class, the marking of papers, and all the details of teaching a successful course. The problem, however, is that we too often don't know *why* we are doing what we do when we perform all the many tasks required of us as writing teachers. We don't know why we do what we do because our actions are not undergirded by a clearly delineated theory.

GS: For instance?

GT: Well, take grading papers for example. Why do we put one set of marks on a paper rather than another set? Why do we put (or not put) marks at all? If we don't have a well-thought-out "theory of marking papers," what we do will be random, sometimes confusing, and may even send signals to our students that we would regret were we to understand what was happening. Or why do you assign these topics for writing rather than others? Why do you assign topics rather than allowing students to find topics? You see, theory has enormous practical consequences. That's why one of our most important tasks, if we are seriously interested in composition, is the constant effort to make connections between theory and practice.

GS: That makes sense, I guess. I'll have to think about it.

GT: That's all I ask.

GS: Thanks so much for your time, Dr. Tate. I've really enjoyed it.

GT: So have I. And, please. Call me Gary.

Stephen Tchudi is professor of English and director of English education at Michigan State University and has also taught at Northwestern University and at the University of British Columbia. He served as president of the National Council of Teachers of English during the 1983–1984 term. Tchudi is the author of a number of books on aspects of teaching, among them The ABC's of Literacy, Explorations in Teaching English, Writing in Reality, *and* An Introduction to Teaching Writing. *He began his career in Chicago's public schools.*

HOW I WRITE

Stephen Tchudi
Michigan State University

There is a crucial moment in my composing process when I get what I call the Write Idea. This is more than just a "good idea" for a piece of writing. . . . A Write Idea extends beyond the limits of a flat sheet of paper and involves seeing connections between my past experience, the writing task at hand, and the impact of some writing on an audience, known or imagined. A Write Idea centers on *having a sense of the possibility of managing and completing a piece of writing.*

When writing on such a potentially narcissistic topic as "How I Write," one needs to keep in mind Wallace Douglas's distinction between the writing *process* and writing *behaviors.* Douglas, who was a pioneer in describing the writing process,[1] has remarked that much recent research which describes itself as studying the process has merely examined the idiosyncratic behaviors of student and professional writers as they compose. He would argue that although it might be interesting to know that Jacqueline Susann wrote successive drafts on different colored sheets of paper or that Norman Mailer claims to isolate his writing carrel with a wide gap that he must cross—sober—on a six-inch plank before writing,[2] such information does little to elucidate the mysteries of the composing process itself. Douglas suggests that the *process* of composing—conceiving a paper, drafting, revising—is essentially similar for all writers, even though writing *behaviors*—mannerisms, tricks of the trade—vary considerably from writer to writer.

Like many writers, I enjoy describing my writing behaviors, and I will share some of my habits and tricks before I end this essay. However, I want to concentrate first on describing the writing *process* as my

---

[1] Wallace Douglas, "An Introduction to Some Lessons in the Basic Processes of Composition" (Evanston, Ill.: Northwestern University Curriculum Center in English, 1963). It is to Douglas that I owe my interest in studying the writing process, my own and that of other writers.

[2] Bruce Felton and Mark Fowler, "Our 60th Anniversary Salute to the Wackiest in American Writing," *Writer's Digest*, January 1980, pp. 23–35.

experience as a writer and teacher of writing and teacher trainer has led me to perceive it.

I am convinced that the most crucial and mysterious part of the writing process is the moment of conception[3] of any piece of writing. As a teacher, I have been troubled for many years by that perennial question raised by the novice writer, "What shall I write about?" I find it fascinating to flip through the pages of a ninety-year-old composition textbook and discover a writer/teacher lamenting writing block in his students. George Butler of the Lawrenceville School in New Jersey observed in 1894:

> Doubtless many young people have often experienced this sudden chill and paralysis of the powers of expression.[4]

Like many nineteenth-century teachers, Butler decided that the solution was to supply young writers "matter for thought" in the form of poems, stories, and essays by established writers, which students were to summarize, abstract, and reproduce in their own language. His theory was that supplying the ideas beforehand freed writers to develop language fluency. Their powers of invention would presumably be developed later and grow to match their verbal adroitness.

We know now that Butler's practice ignores the complex relationship between perceiving, thinking, and expressing, that he was not teaching *composing* in any real sense. As John Dixon summed up in his report of the Dartmouth Seminar,

> Language is learnt in operation, not by dummy runs. In English, pupils meet to share their encounters with life.[5]

Language learning cannot be separated from the *stuff*, the *substance* of discourse. Still, I am not certain that the composition research of the past several decades has moved teachers much closer to solving the sort of writer's block observed by George Butler.

There is a crucial moment in my composing process when I get what I call the Write Idea. This is more than just a "good idea" for a piece of writing. It certainly involves more than simply responding to

---

[3]In this paper, I will freely mix metaphors about the writing process. I will make allusions to birth, carpentry, and musical dissonance before I am finished. No single metaphor adequately encompasses the writing process, so that rather than beating a dead metaphorical horse or making it travel that extra mile, I will shift gears as necessary.
[4]*School English* (New York: American Book Company, 1894), p. 160.
[5]*Growth Through English* (London: National Association for the Teaching of English, 1967), p. 13.

an "assignment," whether that assignment be writing an article for a book of essays or sending my department chair an evaluation of a program. In fact, a Write Idea extends beyond the limits of a flat sheet of paper and involves seeing connections between my past experience, the writing task at hand, and the impact of some writing on an audience, known or imagined. A Write Idea centers on *having a sense of the possibility of managing and completing a piece of writing.* It involves some sort of "message" or expressive idea, but it also includes a sense of *how to do it:* how to cast the content (or how to learn more so content can be cast), how to focus it for an audience, how to take a tone or stance with that audience. It involves having a vision of the piece of writing as a whole, complete thing: a product. Prior to the moment of the Write Idea, I may have a head or briefcase full of notes and ideas, and I may have a pressing manuscript deadline, but I will not be able to write.

The arrival of a Write Idea often has elements of the "Ah ha!" or "Eureka!" experience for me. (At this point I am discussing my writing behavior as a means of getting at the process.) One moment I'll be intellectually struggling, saying (just like a student), "I haven't got anything to write about" or "I just can't get a handle on this." The next moment, I am, like a battery-powered radio or robot, ENERGIZED, either ready to write or ready to prepare directly for writing.

I'll illustrate the Write Idea with two examples from my own work, one from nonfiction, one from fiction.

In 1972, I knew that I wanted to write a "methods" textbook for secondary English teachers. Wallace Douglas, my mentor at Northwestern, had suggested it was time for me to do one, and I, the diligent former student, was trying to take his advice. I was staggered by the idea of the task: a methods book was a compendium of every bit of wisdom about the teaching of literature, language, and composition known to humankind (or so I imagined). Such a book was to be exhaustive, the work of a lifetime, a book to publish on one's deathbed while sighing, "It is finished." Although I probably had enough material in my notes and files to write a book on teaching English, I had no vision of a way into the project.

About that time I restructured my undergraduate methods course at Michigan State (without a thought of the book). I wanted my students to experience new directions in English teaching rather than simply reading about them, so I created a series of "explorations," where they read, wrote, dramatized, and generally "Englished" in class instead of studying text chapters and journal articles.

One day, I can't recall just when, a title popped into my head, *Explorations in Teaching English.* This turned out to be more than a title; it was a Write Idea. I suddenly saw how I could build a methods book around the idea of explorations. Instead of writing that awesome compendium, I could simply write about what I knew, putting what I *didn't* know into explorations for teachers. The whole concept fit my philosophy of teacher training, since I have always argued that "methods" are a matter of personal discovery anyway.

Once that title and the Write Idea had come along, the project was under way. Although there was still an enormous amount of planning, information gathering, and note writing, the basic direction for the book was settled.[6]

Then, in 1981, several books and monographs later, I was beginning to write fiction. I had done one novel, *The Halls of Poison Ivy*, which was (and remains) unpublished. I wanted to try another novel, and my wife had suggested that I consider young adult fiction. (Obviously I am receptive to and grateful for suggestions from others about what I should write.) I had one idea for a book called *David and Goliath*, and it was nearing Write Idea stage. But one evening I saw a television commercial that changed my plans: It showed a high school band, its members dressed in maroon and yellow uniforms, piling into a Burger King restaurant. Almost instantly I asked myself a series of questions:

Who were those kids?

Were they hired actors or real kids?

If they were real kids, what was the effect of being in a commercial
on their daily and school lives?

and

Wouldn't that make an interesting idea for a young adult novel?

That chain of questions led to the basic Write Idea for my first published novel, *The Burg-O-Rama Man*,[7] in which an advertising executive comes to a small-town Midwest high school and announces that he will be filming some slice-of-life television commercials with the high schoolers as the stars.

As I describe my writing behaviors, the Write Idea may sound suspiciously like "inspiration," that stereotypical light bulb in the brain that nonwriters lie around waiting for. However, it is clear that considerable incubation takes place before the Write Idea emerges. For *Explorations*, I had been teaching methods courses for over half a decade and thinking about a methods book for perhaps a year. For *Burg-O-*

---

[6]*Explorations in the Teaching of English* was published by Dodd, Mead in 1974. Dodd, Mead was acquired by Harper & Row, which published a second edition in 1981. A third edition is under way, and at this point I still find the basic Write Idea for the book comfortable and appropriate.

[7]New York: Delacorte/Dell, 1983.

Rama, I had been thinking about fiction in general and young adult novels in particular for some time.

The pre–Write Idea incubation often appears random and unfocused, rather like the files of "interesting" newspaper clippings I maintain, thinking they may be useful sometime. But when I examine my clipping file, I can recognize patterns, tastes, and interests; I clip purposefully, not at random. The incubation period before a Write Idea is similarly guided and focused, even though it may not be or seem particularly systematic.

The key point about Write Ideas, I believe, is not so much how and when they come (I know writers get them by various routes), but that they engage the imagination of the writer with a sense of possibility. The concept of the Write Idea also helps me understand why so many bits of professional advice about finding topics for student writers turn out to be partial truths. "Write from your own experience," we tell students, only to see them succeed at writing outer space fantasies that catch their imagination and that of their readers, while the same writers fail at "My Summer Vacation." "Always limit a topic to manageable size," we say, teaching a textbook process of narrowing, and then we see students tackle astonishingly broad topics successfully because they get a Write Idea. "Write about anything you want," we say in looser moments, giving freedom of expression to our students, and we see them lost for lack of a sense of possibilities.

One cannot teach students how to generate Write Ideas, but the teacher can encourage the process. In my own writing classes, then, I spend a considerable amount of time trying to alert students to the possibility of writing something successfully, showing them how ideas can be developed in writing myriad ways. In my own writing, I have tried to cultivate my receptivity to Write Ideas, keeping the doors to my mind open. The result is that I now have a file of perhaps twenty Write Ideas for books. I probably won't write many of those books, but I know, with certainty, that those books are possible; they are writeable.

I have dwelt on the Write Idea and its formation because I think it is such a crucial stage in the writing process. Post–Write Idea, but prior to drafting, the pre-writing is much more focused and purposeful. I have recognized in my pre-writing Jung's concept of synchronicity: When I am preparing to execute a Write Idea, *everything fits.* Daily newspapers are suddenly filled with articles that relate to my writing; professional journals conveniently appear with thematic issues on my topic; my neighbor makes an offhand remark that is a perfect line for the mouth of one of my characters.

For example, when I was planning *Explorations in Teaching En-*

glish, post–Write Idea, I found all my new class notes and handouts pointing directly to chapters and activities. (When I revised the book for a second edition, the same thing happened.) During the planning for *Burg-O-Rama,* I kept synchronistically stumbling across material that fit the novel: the trip to the grocery store that led to a subplot; my daughter's ballet recital which gave me a new character and a whole story.

This process, too, sounds suspiciously like "inspiration" or just plain good luck. However, it has happened to me often enough, and I have spoken with enough writers to whom it has happened, for me to be persuaded it is a legitimate part of the writing process, not just an idiosyncratic behavior. It may, however, be a phenomenon that happens primarily to the *committed* writer, the person to whom executing a Write Idea seems important, even vital. In teaching, it is often difficult to obtain that kind of commitment from students, especially if they see no real value in learning to write or if their writing course is required rather than elective.

As I move closer to writing a piece, I begin to do some framing. The framing metaphor is borrowed from carpentry—the roughing out of the outline and basic structure of a building. However, that metaphor seems somewhat rigid, so perhaps it is better to see framing as similar to the process of the movie director, who frames a scene with a thumb-and-forefinger rectangle, shifting the frame here and there to get a glimpse of what a scene will be on film. Framing is emphatically *not* the cut-and-dried process of outlining described by nineteenth-century rhetoricians such as Brainerd Kellogg and their twentieth-century followers:

> Facts forming the subject-matter of the theme must be found. They must be grouped under the sub-topics into which the general topic, or subject of the theme is resolved.[8]

I do not outline my "themes" in advance, but I do try to write some preliminary notes about what will come first, second, and next in a paper. Often these frames turn into spaghetti maze diagrams or collections of "balloons" with clusters of related ideas. Although writing is said by some media advocates to be sadly "linear," I find the difficulty of writing down a frame clear evidence that writing actually invites all sorts of nonlinear excursions, both for writer and reader.

Eventually, after meditation and collection of materials and writing down some sort of framing notes, I begin the actual rewriting and

[8]*A Textbook on Rhetoric* (New York: Effingham, Maynard & Company, 1892), p. 68.

revising. Here again Brainerd Kellogg presents a useful negative example:

> [The facts are now] wrought into thoughts, then thoughts are expressed in sentences, then sentences formed into paragraphs, and these paragraphs arranged upon the page.

Would that drafting were that easy and mechanical, merely rendering thoughts into sentences and paragraphs to be "arranged" on the page.

Many other writers have described the pleasures and pains of drafting. Suffice it to say, I find this stage as exhilarating and painful as many. I've had many bad moments of writer's block (despite the Write Idea), good times of discovering I knew something I didn't know I knew or of having characters take over a scene and virtually write it for me.

The research of Leonora Smith has helped me understand how I go about this part of the process. In "Rewriting and Revision in the Work of Versatile Writers"[9] she discovered through interviews and draft manuscripts that writers focus on different matters in successive drafts. A first draft (there may be several) is a place where writers hammer out the basic form of a piece. I choose the hammer metaphor deliberately to mesh with the concept of framing a piece of writing. My first drafts consist of slapping on the siding, sometimes quite hastily and sloppily, but it gets the frame covered.

Second drafts, Smith found, tend to focus on adjusting the structure of a piece or, in my metaphor, making some changes and corrections in the framing and siding. A friend once told me that the difference between a professional and an amateur carpenter is not in their skill at sawing straight or pounding nails true, but in knowing how to fix things gone askew. The professional will see that a door jamb is out of alignment and know how to shim it into place. The amateur lives with a door that's hung crookedly.

Gabriel Della-Pinna describes this skill in the writer as that of being able to sense *dissonance* between what was intended (the Write Idea) and what has emerged (the first draft).[10] Some writers can see discrepancies themselves; others need to rely on outsiders. I feel as if I have a reasonably good sense of the dissonances in my own work, but I rely heavily on my family for help: my wife for professional writing (she is in the same field as I am), my wife and kids for young adult fiction and nonfiction.

[9]Doctoral dissertation, Michigan State University, 1983.
[10]"Revision in Writing Poetry," in Charles Cooper and Lee Odell, eds., *Research on Composing* (Urbana, Ill.: National Council of Teachers of English, 1978), pp. 105–134.

I have discovered over the years, however, that not all dissonances or crooked doorways can be resolved or straightened, even if I have the technical skill to do so. Once the central frame of a piece has been set, it's not always possible to make adjustments.

More concretely: When I had completed the first draft of *Explorations*, I realized that there were a number of places where I wanted to insert more of my own opinion, to tell teachers what to do, not just pose questions that would help them discover things on their own. Yet I quickly realized that I couldn't insert those opinions and be true to the book I had framed and drafted. (I did find a way around the problem: inserting quotations from writers whose work I respected as a way of nudging teachers to my own way of thinking.) After reading the first draft of *Burg-O-Rama*, an editor suggested that I have my heroine discuss her problems with her mother. That couldn't be done, I discovered, without wrecking the book. (I solved the problem by changing a teenage character into a confidante for my heroine.)

Some current research into composing talks about the recursiveness of the writing process, implying that writing, like humankind, is infinitely revisable and perfectible. My experience with first and second drafts suggests that the Write Idea, the frame, and the first draft increasingly place limits on the author's freedom to revise, although there is some give and take between the conceptualization of a project and the writing, revising, and reconceptualizing.

Leonora Smith's research supports this view. The second draft (of which there may be several, she found) tends to focus much more on language and style than on content and structure. The second draft shingles the sides, puts windows in the window frames, and hangs the doors. My second draftings find me concentrating much more on language: accuracy, tone, style, appropriateness.

The third draft, Smith found, is the paint job, the final spit-and-polishing of a manuscript, including handling matters of correctness. This phase is the least interesting of the writing process, though by no means the least important. In my teaching, I emphasize to students that it must be saved until last, for many of them have, through previous teaching, become so error conscious that they confuse proofreading and "recopying" with revising.

To recap my experience with the writing process, then, I see it *not* as a fully circular, completely recursive process, but as a kind of narrowing, beginning with apparently undirected incubation, finding focus through the Write Idea, nearing a stage of commitment with framing, hacking out a rough structure with the first draft, sensing dissonance between the draft and the Write Idea, refining within the framed limits in the second draft, and polishing the whole thing in the third draft.

My writing *behaviors* have been developed over the years as a way of helping me implement this process as easily and comfortably as possible. Briefly, here are some of my behaviors that may be of interest to readers of this collection of essays:

1. I can, on rare occasions, condense all the stages of the writing process into one and sit at the typewriter and create final copy. I confess this, not because I'm particularly proud of it or because I think it leads to my best writing, but because it demonstrates (again) the process/behavior distinction. Two things are necessary to bring about that condensing of the process: panic over an impending deadline and sheets of high-quality typing paper (usually Neenah 20-Pound Baronial Ivory) that make me especially cautious about making errors in typing. I learned this skill (for better or worse) in college, where my freshman course placed a premium on producing error-free impromptu writing. Actually, freshman English worked for the worse with me, because it gave me an error consciousness that for years pushed me into writing in the plainest of plain styles. Turning to fiction has helped me considerably in adding a little jelly to my bread-and-butter style.

2. I write almost every weekday, year round, usually not more than five pages of manuscript at a time. I take weekends off if at all possible and prefer to do my writing during working hours, between 8 A.M. and 5 P.M. I adopted these work hours after reading the biography of Conrad Hilton (a complimentary copy supplied by the Pittsburgh Hilton along with its Gideon Bible); Conrad urged a philosophy of working nine to five and reserving the rest of the time for important matters such as going dancing. That makes sense to me. Writing five days a week usually proves to be enough anyway. Woody Allen once observed that if someone writes as little as a page a day, after a couple of years he or she is regarded as prolific.

3. I think about my writing a great deal, often evenings and weekends, and thus I "cheat" on my avowed work day. Much of my incubating, framing, and even drafting is done as internal monologue. Where a Peter Elbow[11] apparently free-writes his way to a Write Idea, a frame, and a draft, I subvocally mumble my way. I talk to myself while mowing the lawn. I've crashed into the wall of the YMCA swimming pool while rehearsing lines of nonfiction. I recently tumbled off my bicycle into the path of an oncoming train while monologuing a potential line for a short story.

4. I do most of my drafting on a typewriter (Smith Corona Memory Correct II). I've been fascinated by typewriters since I was a kid,

[11] *Writing Without Teachers* (New York: Oxford, 1974).

especially since I learned early that writing by hand was literally painful (I'm a pen clencher) and led to unreadable scrawls. I like the looks of a typed first draft and find it makes revision easier. I also don't mind retyping manuscripts several times, provided there's time, and get a surprising amount of satisfaction from simply seeing a complete manuscript I've typed myself. (Leonora Smith found, by the way, that many so-called "versatile" writers had this sort of attachment to a physical manuscript. Seeing the manuscript, whether typed or handwritten, helped them "see" their work in print.)

5. Perhaps that explains why I'm not enamored of computer word processing. I own an outfit (Radio Shack TRS 80 with Scripsit and Telewriter 64 word processing), but after several attempts to draft and prepare final copy of manuscripts on it, I've gone back to the Smith Corona. It may be that I never practiced enough on the computer to become adept at it. I certainly never became comfortable with all the steps and procedures required just to load the computer, type something, and get it printed in the proper format. More important, however, is that I feel that the alleged virtue of the word processor—making revision easy—also forced me to focus more on the additions, deletions, and rearrangements than on the frame of my writing as a whole. Further, I found that despite the alleged ease of revision (which sometimes involves a lot of complex button pushing), once a piece of writing was safely on disk, I had a tendency not to revise. Word processing encouraged me to save and perpetuate some garbage. When I retype a manuscript "by hand," I'm more inclined to see the whole piece of writing in perspective and to cut the crap.

6. Although I prefer to draft on a typewriter and seek out a machine for writing when I'm away from my office or home study, I have recently trained myself to write any time, any place, with any available combination of paper and writing implement. My inspiration here is the prolific western novelist Louis Lamour, who boasts on the dust jackets of his books that he could write anywhere, including in the middle of Sunset Strip at rush hour. After reading that, I dropped my prima donna addiction to typewriters. Portions of this manuscript were written in my awful longhand in pen and ink at a McDonald's restaurant while a three-year-old and her cronies celebrated her birthday at the next table.

7. I often have several books in the works, fiction and nonfiction, adult and young adult. However, I can only work on one project at a time.

8. I believe the writing process is the same for both fiction and nonfiction. Fiction absorbs me more, especially when I am monologuing

to myself about it, but the essential process seems to me the same for both forms.

9. Publication of a piece of writing is very satisfying, but typing the final page of a third draft is more satisfying.

10. Whatever I am writing at the moment seems to me the most interesting thing I've ever done (including this essay).

Formerly director of the Writing Center at the University of South Carolina, Tom Waldrep is now director of Freshman English. He has served on the editorial boards of several professional periodicals, including College Composition and Communication *and* Teaching English in the Two-Year College. *He is president of the Southeastern Writing Center Association and has served as chair of both the regional executive committee of the SCETC and the freshman English section of SAMLA. Before moving to the University of South Carolina, Waldrep had taught in two-year colleges in Alabama and South Carolina. He is a frequent leader of writing and teaching writing workshops for businesses and public schools in Alabama, Georgia, and South Carolina.*

OH, TO SEE THE SMILES ON THOSE SHADOWY FACES

Tom Waldrep
University of South Carolina

Realistically, I guess I am always trying to "become" a writer; I think a writer "becomes." That person "becomes," I am becoming, as a result of my experiences: my observations, my perceptions, my training, both formal education and at-home rearing.

On a warm morning in late May of 1980, Dr. George Geckle, chair of the English Department at the University of South Carolina, called me at home and said, "Tom, can you come up here, up to my office; I want to talk to you." At first, I thought some freshman student was challenging a final course grade, as I had taught two courses of freshman English as an adjunct professor that spring semester. I replied yes, but it would be a few minutes: I was cuttin' grass in the back yard and weedin' my flower beds. After a shower, I walked the two blocks to his office.

George asked me if I would like to direct the Writing Center the next academic year. I was surprised, excited, and began wondering what I could do with a university writing center. After a couple of weeks of considering we decided I should take the job as a visiting professor for one year. He wanted me to "build the writing center" and teach writing courses. I said I could and would enjoy "visiting" for one year; after that, I knew I would want to go back to my secure position in South Carolina's largest two-year technical college.

That fall went by rapidly, and the next spring the department advertised for a "composition specialist to direct the Writing Center." Dr. Geckle encouraged me to apply formally. I did, and the New Appointments Committee hired me after some deliberation.

However, I was told by a friendly colleague that a senior member of the department, a committee member, questioned my credentials as a "composition" person. He knew I could direct a writing center (after all, I had proved that), but he warned, "You know, he's a *talker*, not a *writer.*"

After hearing that comment, I was irritated; but after much thought I knew there might be some truth in the statement. After all, I had learned the language through acquisition and use at home and in the rural public schools of Alabama. I had in fact started *talking* before I started *writing.* I had in fact taught over 150 sections of freshman English in thirteen years of college teaching. And I, like many others, believed if you can teach writing courses, you can write. So I couldn't understand this pronouncement. Why did he want to shock the other committee members into thinking more carefully about the decision they were about to make?

I haven't forgotten that pronouncement, and now, five years later, I think it has merit. Many of us are *talkers*, not *writers* as the senior professor defines "writer." So when we do write, we write like we talk. I am not a writer, in that I have *no* short stories, only a few bad poems, and *no* novel to my credit. I've always been afraid even to attempt to write a short story, much less a novel, 'cause the Lord knows not even most *senior* professors can write novels. Most novels are written by other people, people "out in the world" who come into our universities in the spring and "read" to these professors in the Writers' Series.

But, even though I have no short stories or novels on my vita, I *can* write, *do* write, that is, *talk* to myself or to some other audience on paper. I write letters, evaluations for graduate instructors, class notes, speeches for professional meetings, and sometimes grocery lists. I write editorial commentary on students' papers, but I always *talk* out the commentary to the student in the conference. I always *talk out* a paper for a professional meeting, *talk out* a letter to a company I'm really irritated with, *talk out* a letter of recommendation or evaluation. I have *talked* through this paper in all of its various stages from the note-taking, list-making stage through the revisions, which I have *talked* out animatedly, seeing and engaging you, the listeners, all the while. I am a *talker*, not a *writer*. I'm always listening, too, to see if what I'm saying is "right." And I will try to develop that later.

In one sense, then, I have learned to write because I learned to talk. And I'm still learning. I have learned to write the way I do because I have listened to others talk, watched others as they talk, listened to myself talk, and know when a "talk" or a piece of writing is "right" or when it simply won't work. I know that when I talk I must engage the audience, and that when I have finished writing a piece my audience will read it, know, understand. The audience and I will be *engaged*, will be working, knowing, understanding together. Therefore, sometimes I have to talk and retalk, write and rewrite, until I see the smiles on those shadowy faces. And, realistically, I guess I am always trying to "become" a writer; I think a writer "becomes." That person "becomes," I am becoming, as a result of my experiences: my observations, my perceptions, my training, both formal education and at-home rearing. But to write, to produce discourses, verbal or written, I have to be in the mood.

THE MOOD

Mood is synonymous with *force*. There must be a mental force, a mental nudge that lets me know that there is no chaos, no disorder, no distractions. All must be well. If I'm worried about balancing my checkbook, my sugar level being out of whack (I am diabetic), or my aging father who is ill, I can't write. I'm preoccupied. I'm not in the mood. Any one of these can become a more important consideration than writing a speech, a letter, a professional paper. Any distraction prohibits my writing. In the foreground of my brain must be my writing subject. There must be peace in my head and in my dining room.

THE SETTING

When I'm writing or when I'm talking, give me space. Usually I compose at the banquet-size table that seats twelve in my dining room, all spread out. It must be quiet, as *I'm talking.* The room is either full of people, mythical people, dozens of them, or maybe just one, maybe two. I write on a subject I know about and I know the audience is quiet, listening to me as I go on. I move forward. Stop. Go back and reiterate a point. Move on. Stop. All the while I'm watching their faces. As long as their faces are smiling, pleasant, I move on. When frowns appear, I stop. When *I* don't understand what I have said, they don't understand what I've said, and faces become contorted. I stop. Go back. I try again. But since I talk so much, I know that what I say/write usually comes from an initial *observation* or observations. What I say is usually a *perception* or perceptions of these observations. Many times those spoken perceptions come from a very careful *enumeration,* a listing in my brain, a recall as it were; this enumeration has these perceptions classified or categorized, thus *related,* before I make the *assertion,* the analysis of the perceptions. Therefore, I think of my writing/talking process as what I have come to call an *OPERA:* an *o*bserving, *p*erceiving, *e*numerating, *r*elating, *a*sserting.

OBSERVING/PERCEIVING

OPERA provides for me a framework for writing. This acronym, Latin for *work,* indeed frames my process well. Writing for me is work! Writing—as good as it may be or as bad as it may be—comes only after work. Before beginning the physical process though, I must have observed. No matter what the topic, I must have probed. Observing is probing, looking closely at experiences, objects, people; sometimes asking questions to others and myself. I must make solid, honest observations. They may have no meaning at the time I observe, but later a dull, lifeless observation may take on new meaning. Sometimes my observations are associated with "dark spots," skeletons in my closet so to speak. I may push these observations away—perceiving, yet too afraid to perceive for long, to analyze and associate—I observe, but I repress the perceptions. Sometimes courage—much courage—is required to observe, to probe, and later to reflect on these observations. But, I'm always observing, making perceptions from these observations, using the perceptions instantly or storing them in the memory bank, relating, classifying, categorizing these new perceptions to old ones stored in the bank. Some of these perceptions I know I'll use again; I'll draw them up from the well of perceptions from past observations, but others I might repress and never use. I probe by looking closely at my environment, those in my environment, and in so doing I know I sharpen my contact with life. Sometimes even clumsy observations, those that I just "hit upon," sharpen my contact with life. And when I write, just as I am now, I realize that what I'm writing comes from observation, observation since birth I guess. Perceptions from these observations, thoughts I retain in the memory bank, I use or lose. But my writing is a flow of these perceptions, a jelling, a coagulation of those that I comprehend, that I understand. I think I would become a better writer, a better, more sensitive person, if I were a better observer, one who looked more closely, more carefully. Observing well and perceiving well have dual purpose. First, I feel more alive, more sensitive. I can articulate, explain, clarify, argue, justify *better.* Second, the people in my environment with whom I am communicating see *my world* my way; they have access to my ideas when I'm talking/writing. They may or may not agree with my explanations, justifications, or arguments, but they comprehend, they know from where I am coming, what I'm thinking.

ENUMERATING/RELATING

Up to this point, my writing process has been physical/mental: observing (seeing, hearing, smelling, tasting, feeling) and perceiving (thinking, relating, categorizing, classifying). After observing/perceiving my topic, then I begin the *physical* step of writing. I make notes, lists that may be words, sentences, or paragraphs. I draw from the memory bank of perceptions and list randomly as many as I can. Sometimes as I list, new perceptions are generated from ones pulled up from the past. Relationships are made, new thoughts added to old thoughts. In relating these, I often delete as well as add to the list. This enumeration is a mixture, a grand English flower garden like the ones at Chelsea, where the gardener gathers carefully the many varieties of flowers, the many colors, all the shapes, the different lengths of stems, the "filler" greenery. All these items on the list—like the various flowers—may go into the piece of writing—the bouquet, the arrangement, and that arrangement can be full, rich, superbly textured or lean, lank, thin, a "live arrangement" so to speak. The lists, the enumeration, with all the various classifications, reflect the ideas and thoughts for the piece of writing.

ASSERTING

Asserting my ideas is the next stage in my composing process. Asserting occurs as I write on yellow pads, usually talking aloud to the mythical people in my presence. I'm watching them; I want agreement—nods, smiles, an occasional "Yes-yes." I want an audience engaged with me as I produce my "talk," one that gives me some sign of its comprehending what I'm trying to communicate. In this stage I finally produce a written copy, a draft, of *many* of the observations/perceptions that have been enumerated in a classification or categorization system in the previous stage. This is the stage that allows me to communicate in some framework, a letter, memo, speech, or professional paper, the knowledge that I have gained from earlier observations and perceptions. While the framework is usually predetermined before the physical act of enumerating begins, it is this stage where the building begins. Maybe "building" is a misnomer here, for what I actually do is "modeling" and "remodeling." I write words and sentences, "remodeling" them as I write, adding them to my framework. Changes are made in almost every sentence. My pieces of writing are always rewritten dozens of times: Words deleted, added, substituted; sentences and paragraphs deleted, added, moved, placed, and replaced. The staff assistant, somehow or other, makes sense of it, and after a fresh typewritten copy is made, more revision occurs. More often than not, this revision undergoes even more "remodeling," and finally through all of this the framework has been filled in, the model is complete. But somehow, I always feel it could be "remodeled" again, remade, revised, *re-talked*. I'm never quite satisfied; therefore I talk/write as long as time allows and until I see the smiles on those shadowy faces.

John Warnock is associate professor of English and law at the University of Wyoming and director of the Wyoming Writing Project. In the summer of 1984 he directed the NEH Summer Seminar for College Teachers entitled "The Writing Process: A Humanistic View." He has worked on writing with many different groups, from elementary-school students to judges. Warnock has published fiction, poems, and academic essays, and has recently authored an essay for "The Writing Process," in Research in Composition and Rhetoric: A Bibliographic Sourcebook, *to be published by Greenwood Press.*

HOW I WRITE

John Warnock
University of Wyoming

To write at all under [certain] circumstances, you have to accept that the best way you can is good enough, though it will never be good enough, not even for yourself. What a business this writing is! What cartwheels it has us turning!

I am going to tell you the story of how I wrote three things. I'm not going to try to tell you how I write everything, because that is too much of a story for me to pretend to know. The story of how I wrote these three things is too much of a story for me to know, but I can pretend to know it at least.

WARNING: Do not read this account as if it presents a shining example of how to write. I am anything but a shining example for writers. I take comfort, however, from a belief that when it comes to writing, most of our shining examples are not good examples. Writing, Mary Savage says, is an impure act.[1] I agree. So don't, if you don't see anything for yourself in it, think of the process you see portrayed here as something to be emulated or admired.

Since I don't believe I can tell you how you should write, the best I can hope for is to let you see some possibility for writing that you might not have seen before for yourself. I am going to tell you how I wrote some poems. One reason I have chosen to tell you about poems is that I am not known as a poet (though I sometimes know myself as one). Furthermore, these poems were written mostly in situations not usually thought to be "normal" writing situations—not in a writing class, not in my study or den or office or other such official writing room, and not because it was in any way my job to write them. In other words, this isn't writing that was "supposed to be done," or that was done in the "right place," or done by someone with any special qualifications for

[1] In a draft written in the NEH Summer Seminar for College Teachers entitled "The Writing Process: A Humanistic Perspective," Laramie, Wyoming, Summer 1984.

doing the kind of thing that was done. You might call it off-the-wall, if-I-can-do-it-you-can-do-it-too writing.

All three pieces were begun and mostly written in writing conferences where I was meeting with teachers to think about how to teach writing. As it happens, I was set up as the authority in these sessions: The one who was supposed to know something about how to teach writing.

If I do know something about the matter, it is that writing—in certain kinds of circumstances—is what best teaches how to teach writing. So in setting up these institutes I made sure that we all had time in which we could write. None of us, however, was told what to write, and many different kinds of writing were produced. I had no plans to write any particular piece. What I wrote was these poems, and some other stuff too, which I'll show you.

The first of these institutes was held in June of 1983 at Sam Houston State College in Huntsville, Texas. My assignment for this institute was to help teachers see how one might use literature in a writing class.

This was not an easy assignment. Literature is often used in writing classes but not usually, as I see it, to teach writing, rather as a way for literature professors and graduate students to teach more literature, or more accurately, for these people to teach literary criticism. Most English teachers are trained in a tradition established and controlled by literary critics, and they have a devil of a time escaping some of the assumptions of that profession.

There is virtue in reading literature and writing literary criticism. What rankles me and other writing teachers is seeing writing reduced to just those things. In my own writing-with-literature classes, I had often felt that people were trying to get me to work on *their* problems, *their* literature, instead of letting me work on mine, or even letting us work on *ours*.

So what I thought I would do in this institute was read everyone a poem, ask them to write afterward (without giving them any direction about what to write, but making sure that they knew it would be all right to write something other than official, interpretive criticism). Then we would talk together about the writing, write some more, repeat this process a few times, and see what came out. After we did this, I thought we could talk about how literature might operate in a writing class, using our own writing from literature as a touchstone.

The poem I read them (I didn't tell them who wrote it) was Richard Wilbur's "The Writer." Here it is. I invite you now to read it aloud, twice, as we did that day.

The Writer

In her room at the prow of the house
Where light breaks, and the windows are tossed with linden,
My daughter is writing a story.

I pause in the stairwell, hearing
From her shut door a commotion of typewriter-keys
Like a chain hauled over a gunwale.

Young as she is, the stuff
Of her life is a great cargo, and some of it heavy:
I wish her a lucky passage.

But now it is she who pauses,
As if to reject my thought and its easy figure.
A stillness greatens, in which

The whole house seems to be thinking,
And then she is at it again with a bunched clamor
Of strokes, and again is silent.

I remember the dazed starling
Which was trapped in that very room, two years ago;
How we stole in, lifted a sash

And retreated, not to affright it;
And how for a helpless hour, through the crack of the door,
We watched the sleek, wild, dark

And iridescent creature
Batter against the brilliance, drop like a glove
To the hard floor, or the desk-top,

And wait then, humped and bloody,
For the wits to try it again; and how our spirits
Rose when, suddenly sure,

It lifted off from a chair-back,
Beating a smooth course for the right window
And clearing the sill of the world.

It is always a matter, my darling,
Of life or death, as I had forgotten. I wish
What I wished you before, but harder.*

After I read the poem, I sat down with the rest of the teachers to
write. Though I didn't have any clear idea of what I *would* write, I
suppose I knew what I didn't want to write. I didn't want to write a
conventional critical interpretation. I guessed that many of the teachers
would think that was the only kind of writing response permitted, so
I had told them that they didn't have to write "about" the poem, but
that they could also think of writing "from" or "through" or "against"
it. I believed that many different kinds of writing would follow from
hearing the poem, one of which might be conventional critical interpretation. Though I think I would have let myself write some academic
criticism if I'd had an impulse to do so, in these circumstances I was
biased against it to begin with.

At any rate, the first thing I seem to have done as a writer[2] is mark
the places in the poem where I had responded strongest. Here is what
appears in my notebook:

drop like a glove: how that moves
clearing the sill of the world: not so much

I started with what I liked, then noted something that I didn't, or
rather that I had ambivalent feelings about: "clearing the sill of the
world." The line seemed a little overstated, or something.

Then I seem to have wanted to explore that area of ambivalence
some. I started talking about those feelings, or perhaps I should say that
the writing started talking about them:

I'm not sure the heroic quality of the starling's flight is all that
pleasing to me. Yes, heroic. But, my God, we can't be expected to fight
that way, unless driven far past the point . . .
a lucky passage: Well, that is what writers rely on. They're always
saying that. "It may not come. But if does, I'm ready."

*Richard Wilbur, *The Mind-Reader* (New York and London: Harcourt Brace Jovanovich,
1976), pp. 4–5. Copyright © 1971 by Richard Wilbur. Reprinted from his volume *The
Mind-Reader* by permission of Harcourt, Brace Jovanovich, Inc.
[2]There are some very big mysteries here. In an important sense we simply do not know
how we do things, not when they are things as complex, as many-layered as writing is.
A growing psychological literature argues that we can be aware of only a small portion
of what is involved in any skilled act. And another problem is that our memories of what
we *were* aware of are faulty. So when someone tells you "how I did it"—how they learned
to spell, or to be responsible for themselves, or stay married, or teach, or write—it is best
not to trust them too far.

Blind instinct, fly out of the house—I'm talking myself into not liking this poem. The starling is a dreadful bird, with a lovely name.

William Stafford talks about the "nibble" he can feel while sitting in front of a dark window, in his writing place, waiting for a poem. I was writing, but I was waiting too, because I knew I wasn't yet writing the kind of thing I wanted to be writing. (This is complicated, isn't it? I *was* writing what I wanted to be writing while I waited . . .)

Well, then I started trying to make a poem. I'm not sure what idea of "poem" I started with. But you can see some poemlike idea in what appears on the page of my notebook:

A lovely name for such a dreadful bird:
Starling.ᴧ It wobbles as it walks.

Stubby tailed The reptilian eye.

In what spirit does it throw itself
                    that light?/
Against ~~that window~~ᴧ. In the same
            his
spirit that ~~the~~ daughter throws ~~itself~~ herself

against meaninglessness?

Daughter is hauling anchor

and will leave home. Soon she will carry
                    away
her ~~own~~ chainsᴧ and leave/
    old and
Anᴧ grieving father who will write
                    stay
how hard it is to ~~live~~ in the world.

I don't remember if I looked back at "The Writer" as I did this. I probably did some, though I don't remember it. Clearly I had it "in mind". You could almost say that I was arguing with it, or arguing with a voice I heard speaking through it.

At this point, I might have gone back to writing prose, to criticism, or to more expressive stuff of the kind I started with. But in my experience, there is a kind of irreversibility that sets in once you start a poem. Poems don't seem to evolve into anything else, except more poems. Maybe that is part of what people are talking about when they say that poetry is the highest kind of expression, though I often am curious just why people would need to make the argument.

But deciding that you are writing a poem doesn't simplify matters any, if at all. When you start writing it, you may be nowhere near where you want the poem to start finally, and nowhere near the idea of a poem that the writing of this poem will take you to. Of course you can always start writing out of some definition of "poem" that you refuse to budge from, no matter what the writing is telling you about what a poem might be. But that is like writing from an outline that you refuse to change, even when your ideas change. That doesn't seem to be any way to get real writing done or to find any joy in it.

Was I somehow misreading Wilbur's poem? If that had been the question set for me by myself or through my English professor, I would have next had to do something other than what I did do. I would have had to reread the whole poem, paying special attention to the possibility that things were being said ironically, that something was being said other than what appeared to have been said. I would have had to look for ways in which I might have been led astray, or might have allowed myself to be deceived in my initial reading. In short, I would have had to act like a scientist, one whose primary commitment was to being right instead of to being, discovering, and creating who one was.

But by now I wasn't primarily concerned with searching out what Wilbur's poem actually said. Something about the poem had led me to worry about the relation of fathers to daughters, to see how they could be sentimental, and thus dangerous, and to raise my guard against that kind of fathering. At the same time I saw the father-poet's relation to his daughter and to writing as in some way admirable. What I wanted to work on now was that problem. Of course I was anything but off the hook and free to do just what I pleased.

Undertaking to write a poem frees you from the need to be faithful to some things in some sense, but it brings on the obligation to be true to a whole bunch of other things that may be harder to be faithful to than what you started with—such things as your actual experience (including the experience of reading this poem and other texts), your feelings, life. Language, too. And when you finish a poem, you have to finish not just some of the things the language starts, but everything the language starts. The best way you can.

To write at all under *these* circumstances, you have to accept that the best way you can is good enough, though it will never be good enough, not even for yourself. What a business this writing is! What cartwheels it has us turning!

Well, obviously a lot of revising had gone on as I wrote through the version of the poem set out above. More revising was to come. I drew a line on the page under draft one, and started again, recopying the first line.

Now I was remembering a line from Wilbur's poem that hit me, though I hadn't marked it at first: the words "humped and bloody" used to describe the fallen, witless bird. They seemed to stand out, darkly, in a poem that made much of the heroism of trying for the light.

Then it struck me that both words had strong connotations of sex and sexuality. Something having to do with sex was going on in "The Writer," though at the time it was not at all clear to me just what it was. Father thinking about his young daughter-bird, coming of age, trying to grow up-escape to the light: I added a line to my poem which said that the starling was "trapped in her bedroom." It seemed to add something right.

Looking back now, I could say that there is a tension in Wilbur's poem that comes from the fact that the daughter is clearly growing and wanting to grow into mature sexuality, while the father wants her, and himself, to fly away from it, so to speak, through writing to the light. Luckily neither Wilbur nor the father kids himself about the nature of this escape to freedom. He realizes that it is a matter of life *and* death and "lucky" passages. If he really asked us to believe that all we had to do was "try, try again" until we made it over the hump, I think we wouldn't like the poem so much, or we'd like it for bad reasons, for the way it collaborates with us in our efforts to fool ourselves.

The paragraph above probably looks like literary criticism to some of you, and in a way it is. It is here in this paper about how I write because it gives me a way now of talking about how I wrote this poem, what was in it for me as I tried to make sense out of my experience in the writing.

But I worry that as I talk about "having written" something, I might make the description have too much sense, more than the situation had at the time. I wasn't reasoning and making sense so much as I was listening, feeling, throwing it up there to see if it would go in the basket, not figuring things out so much as having inklings and acting on hunches.

After the second draft, I seem to have wanted a title. That could mean that I thought I had at that point something that "deserved" a title, or that I thought that trying to write a title would help me find what it was I wanted to do. At any rate, for a while, I had at the top of the page "His Daughter Also Writes." Then I crossed that out and wrote "Father of the Writer." My interest seemed to be in the father's end of the relationship primarily. Also I wanted some implication that the humped and bloody bird was father to the writer. Or rather, after I wrote the title, I saw that implication in the words, and welcomed it.

I had two days with the teachers in Huntsville. At the end of that time we all published (i.e., posted on the bulletin board) something of

what we had written during that time. Here is the version I published
to them:

Father of the Writer

A lovely name for such a dreadful bird:
Starling. Stubby tailed, it wobbles as it walks.
The reptilian eye.

Trapped in her bedroom,
does it throw itself against the light
in the same spirit that his daughter writing
throws herself against meaninglessness?

Daughter is hauling anchor
and will leave home. She will carry
her chains away, and behind her leave

a grieving father, old, who writes
how hard it is to live in the world.

John Warnock
June 16, 1983

The name and the date mean something, don't they? They mean
you have brought this artifact to the point where you think it has some
sort of identity. It doesn't mean you think it's good, or as good as it can
get: It doesn't mean that you have stopped revising.

I think this poem is not so good, though it has its moments. It isn't
as good as it could be either. Since June 16, 1983, I have made some
other changes in it. Unfortunately, I'm not sure they make it better.

But since this is a book about process, not product, let me invite you
to take this "final" version as in process, if not in progress, and make any
changes you like, and then compare your changes with someone else's.

It is of course possible that the poem has come as far as it can, and
that it should be left alone, left behind. Each of us will decide that one
for ourselves.

But I wasn't through arguing with "The Writer." Or it with me.

The next poem I want to show you was written at another institute
for teachers, this time at Clearwater Beach, Florida, and sponsored by
the Conference on College Composition and Communication. I had
been asked to make some kind of presentation on Alternatives to Freshman English. (The principal consultant for the session was Don Murray,
whose excellent essay appears elsewhere in this volume.)

One of the things I decided to do in my session was read "The

Writer" again in the way I had at Sam Houston State, and see how this group of college teachers wrote in response to it. Again, I wrote along.

Again, I had no idea what I would write, except that I probably would not write critical interpretation. I had no inclination to work on "Father of the Writer" just then. So I just started writing, as I did at Sam Houston State, about my responses *this time* to having read the poem. (I try not to wait too long, or at all, to start writing since I find that I get further writing than I do "just thinking" without writing. But I'm always tempted to wait until I have "something worth saying." I know others who are not hung up by this problem, though they of course have other problems: Writing is a certain way of "having" problems, isn't it?)

As I wrote this time, I was thinking hardest about the starling, and demanding an answer to the question I had asked in "Father of the Writer" about the spirit in which the starling throws itself against the light. In "Father of the Writer" I didn't have to answer the question beyond implying that there was an important difference between the spirit of the bird and the spirit of the daughter. Now I found I wanted another kind of answer.

I can't report the stages of composition of this poem as specifically as I could "Father of the Writer." So I'll give you the poem and tell you what I remember about what I was working on when I made it.

Starling
The brightness drew me on and I fell through
into this cool dark, where I feel nothing alive
where flying to the brightness throws me back
battered. Since I don't know how to be careful
about brightness, I fly again and am through
into this dark world where the brightness beckons.

I liked finding "brightness" as the word for what drew the starling on: It was attractive but noncommital. It allowed me not to have the bird yearn for freedom, or have some other emotion that humans like to attribute to birds (but not to spiders and snakes), but which most likely birds don't have, or don't have in anything like the same way humans do.

I also liked finding "fell through" to describe what happened when the bird flew into the house: something of the underworld there, and something of one's "ground" giving way, among other things.

Now that it was in the house, my question was: What was wrong with being in the house? This is a version of the question of what is wrong with a comfortable prison, one in which you have all the comforts of home? But I had decided that I couldn't let myself talk about freedom here. So what could be the problem? "I feel nothing alive" seemed to let me say enough about the predicament, without saying too much. And its being a place where "flying to the brightness throws me back/battered", a place where following one's natural inclination got one (almost automatically) battered, added a motive, together with a nice string of "b" sounds.

Now a line in which I give myself a little slack and give the bird some self-consciousness: "Since I don't know how to be careful about brightness . . . ." It feels now, and it felt then, like an important line. It is the line that most strongly invites us to feel some kinship with the bird in its inability to be careful about something it knows damn well it ought to be careful about. We all would have our lists.

I like the line because it motivates the attempts of the bird without giving them too much of an intentional quality: It keeps me (pretty much) out of that "humanizing" domain I am trying to avoid. I didn't want to have the bird "deciding" anything, for the same reasons I didn't want it to "yearn for freedom."

So the last attempt of the bird is *enacted,* by switching to the present tense ("I fly again") and the escape is understated as much as I was able to understate it ("and am through"), since the bird ought not to be expected to have experienced "a sense of relief," or "ecstasy," not in a human way, at any rate.

And so the question that was left me was: What kind of a world is the bird's "normal," "free" world? A world of light and delight? Not bloody likely. A world full of cold and cats and scrounging for food. And yet . . . "A dark world where the brightness beckons": It is a dark world, but there is brightness in it, and the brightness beckons ("b's" again), maybe to another prison, but maybe not. Not all brightness is a snare or delusion. Maybe not.

So I think this poem was written not so much in an attempt to argue, finally, as in an effort to imagine a world in which a starling's attempts to escape from a room could be seen, and experienced by a writer/reader, as motivated by something more interesting than instinct and something more valid, more believable, than a desire for freedom, life in the wild blue yonder, and the rest of that stuff.

I sent this poem to a friend who wrote back that he liked it best of the batch I sent him because it seemed to try for more.

When I send stuff to friends or teachers or publishers, I am grateful for any specific, authentic response. It is hard to offer this, much easier to dodge the thing, or give some general, prefabricated response. It takes more than just time to come up with the kind of response I want, and none of us really deserves it.

I used to want my readers to like my stuff. I'm sure I still do. But whether they like or don't like it has become much less important than any information they give me about how they read it. That is information I can use in a way I cannot use the information that they like or don't like something. (Of course, if we are having a hard time just keeping going, we can use what helps us do that . . .)

I wasn't sure how to use my friend's response, though. I wasn't aware of trying for any more in "Starling" than I was in "Father of the Writer." I do think that if I had to choose one of the two to support my application to be Numbered Among the Poets, I would probably choose "Starling," but if it did come out better, it didn't come out better because I was trying for more. If it did, I don't know why it did.

Not knowing why doesn't bother me. I'll just keep writing what I can write. I think I have no other choice.

One more story, and one more poem. Another of the consultants at this conference in Clearwater Beach was Andrea Lunsford, and her topic was how to give good assignments for writing.

Now I have real difficulty with most of what I read and hear about how to give good writing assignments. I think most of this talk misses the point. The point is that the only good assignment is the one a writer takes as his or her own, and that while some assignments make it *easier* to produce certain kinds of writing, the very best you can hope for from the very best of all possible writing assignments is a love-hate relationship between it and the writer as the writer tries to find what it is he or she can make out of the occasion.

Whether or not I am right about this, as I sat in the audience listening to Andrea—who is a most engaging and informative speaker —I felt she wasn't making "the point" about assignments strongly enough.

At one point, she offered us one candidate for the worst writing assignment ever. On her first day in Freshman English, her professor had walked in, written "the bluebird in Aunt Jane's hair" on the blackboard, told them a paper was due on Friday, and left.

Andrea took the leap, submitted a paper, and it came back marked D−, not on the grounds (as I recall the story) that it didn't say anything worth saying, nor that it made any mistakes, but on the grounds that it violated certain canons of propriety for academic writing.

Now what this story shows me is not a bad assignment but a bad professor—a rascal who wants to have it both ways. I suppose the worst assignments we might imagine are those given by the Zen masters: What is the sound of one hand clapping? And yet in the relation between the master and his not-yet-enlightened pupil, such assignments seem to provide a means of getting some place important. The profes-

sor in this story was obviously anything but a Zen master, though he
might have had some erroneous idea that he could justify his assignment by the analogy.

Well, again I was feeling argumentative, and so, with a vague feeling that this might be a way of making what to me was the point about
assignments, I decided to try to make something out of that assignment.
The job, as I saw it, was to find a place, or make a place, where the words
"the bluebird in Aunt Jane's hair" would have meaning. So I thought
about Aunt Jane "at home," so to speak, and suddenly there was Uncle
John:

> Uncle John could have told
> the bluebird in Aunt Jane's hair . . .

(Well, what? Asking what might rhyme with "hair" gave me an answer,
and more of an answer than I had expected.)

> about the snare there.

(Surprise! Aunt Jane wasn't a batty old lady; she was a lady so lovely and
so loved that Uncle John thought she had a bluebird in her hair.)

(Well, that seemed somehow to finish one thing, but in another way
it seemed only to get things started. So I wondered: What if someone
actually believed there was a bluebird there. They'd have a hard time
convincing us hard-headed realists . . .)

> Yes. There was a bluebird
> in Aunt Jane's hair.
> (Oh? Did you see it?)
> I couldn't see it
> but I knew it was there.

(Something still needed. Find something in the sound? "Ear?" Okay.
Our expositor realizes that a bluebird couldn't come from nowhere:
He's that much of a scientist at least. And maybe his audience will be
convinced if he can give them a causal account . . .)

> It must have come out of her ear.

(This line sent me back upstairs: Here was the voice of this one. It was
a child speaking here, pleading a little for belief. So a child's voice:
Change "Yes" to "Really!")

(Hey, I like this. Try another one. No child this time. Someone very far from childlike belief, defeated, perhaps, by the skeptics.)

> could not care
> for what I should
> nor even for what I would
> care for.

(That's world-weary all right: Can't even care for what he *wants* to care for. But what about the bluebird?)

> What saved me
> was the bluebird
> in Aunt Jane's hair.

(You *could* be saved by such a thing, couldn't you? Or even by imagining such a thing, as the child might have done . . .)
(One more. The world is not all just skeptics or fantasizers.)

> A bluebird in Aunt Jane's hair?
>
> That's nothing much.
> In the Dali museum

(Just can't get that painting I saw in the museum yesterday out of my mind . . .)

> I saw a piano
> coming out of a man's neck.

(I mean, what an idea! And he had several paintings with that image. You could say that Dali is always wanting you to see more than you can, more than you even think you can. The reference seems appropriate.)
Well, what do we have here? Time to number them, I guess.

I.
Uncle John could have told
the bluebird in Aunt Jane's hair
about the snare there.

II.
Really! There was a bluebird
in Aunt Jane's hair.

I couldn't see it
but I knew it was there.

It must have come out of her ear.

III.

I could not care
for what I should
nor even for what I would
care for.

What saved me
was the bluebird
in Aunt Jane's hair.

IV.

A bluebird in Aunt Jane's hair?

That's nothing much.
In the Dali museum
I saw a piano
coming out of a man's neck.

By now I didn't care much whether I had or hadn't made my point about assignments. I had a powerful sense of having made something for myself out of that bad professor's assignment anyway.

After Andrea's session I saw Don Murray. It turned out he had started a poem too. We showed each other what we had done. His was a wonderful thing about a young man who was sternly reminded by his mother not to make fun of Aunt Jane, who had a habit of saying she had a bluebird in her hair. One day the boy's mother told Aunt Jane that he would soon be "flying away" to college. Aunt Jane looked alarmed and later leaned down to whisper to the boy that there was no bluebird. . . .

As I recall, Don didn't like his draft as much as I did. He asked me for a copy of mine, which made me feel good.

Of course, the fact that I found my work satisfactory, and that someone else wanted a copy of it, doesn't mean the bad professor would have found it satisfactory. Knowing Andrea, I'd bet she made something out of the assignment too. But that wasn't what the man wanted. In such a situation, we have a number of options. We can try to give the man what he wants; we can try to convince the man that he missed something good in his reading of what we made out of the situation; we can forget the whole thing and try to start over; we can go throw ourselves under a train (if we can find a train). . . . The thing I wouldn't like about that last one is that it would stop me writing, among other things. And I'm not at all inclined to give up the delights (they come with disappointments, fears, and frustrations, of course), the surprises, the joys of writing.

Tilly Warnock has been at the University of Wyoming for the past ten years, where she has directed the Writing Center, given courses in composition and rhetoric, taught in the Wyoming Writing Project, and directed school-university projects funded by the National Endowment for the Humanities and by the Wyoming Council for the Humanities. She has published articles on rhetoric, literature, and literacy theory, and she is presently preparing a manuscript on Kenneth Burke for publication.

HOW I WRITE
Tilly Warnock
University of Wyoming

How did I take the plunge? How am I still learning to write? How do I help students begin writing and join the community of writers? How am I learning to overcome the excuses of time, busywork, head-tripping, and hems of [poets'] garments to avoid writing? Most important, I believe, I am learning to write, not alone, but with others.

One cold July night several years ago at Vedauwoo, during the Wyoming Conference on Freshman and Sophomore English, several people were talking beside the fire when one man began explaining how exhausted he was from revising his textbook. We asked how he writes. He described his writing process in detail but seemed particularly pleased with the stage when he passes his draft to his wife, who is not in English, so that she can detect the b.s. in his work. Because I was delighted by his account, I asked if he included such collaboration as a common stage for writers in his textbook. He drew himself to full height, a large shadow against the flames and silhouettes of the mysteriously shaped mountains, and replied indignantly, "Every word I write is my own." The conversation ended.

I want to admit right away that no words I write are my own and that I never write alone. I also want to confess that I spent many years of my life with the golden dream of having a book dedicated to me, not of writing one but of inspiring one. I wanted to be the power behind the throne, or, in the words of Ernest Hemingway, to be that "most essential gift for a good writer, a built-in shock-proof shit-detector." I did not want to take risks myself: I wanted to be "the one without whom not."

At a certain point, I began to want not the upper hand but the writing hand to be my own. Instead of motivating someone else to write, I wanted to relax—in an important sense of that word which I will try to develop later—and write for myself.

With this change in attitude toward myself and toward writing, I began scrounging around to find words to help me write and to see myself as a writer. I had been teaching writing for many years and had published several articles on composition and literature, but I could not call myself a writer. I still cannot, but I can now say confidently that I am writing.

I feel presumptuous, though, describing how I write. The rat in the basement—as a colleague, Fred Homer, refers to writing fears—creeps up to remind me that I cannot write, not real writing. Of course I write articles for publication and talks for conferences. I have become a whiz at writing abstracts for conference papers, before-the-fact-writing; and through two humanities proposals I have learned to bureaucratize my imagination, as Kenneth Burke says. I also write letters, grocery lists, and class notes, and I am presently revising a manuscript on Burke's rhetoric of the symbol. I do not like to write reviews of books I do not like, although I enjoy writing reviews of books I learn from. I began writing poems only last summer during a Wyoming Writing Project institute in Gillette, Wyoming, and I have never finished a work of fiction. But I will. (Having written this, several days later I finally finished a short story, which certainly needs revision but which I pushed through to the end.)

In one sense, then, I have learned to write, but my attitude is that I am still learning. Past tense is inappropriate. The biggest rat in my basement remains the definition I still have of writers as people who have published several novels, several very good novels. I strongly encourage students to name and erase such destructive rats, but my excuse for believing the rat who says I cannot write is that I grew up in the land of Carson McCullers, Flannery O'Connor, Alice Walker, and Eudora Welty. I am like Mary Anne Bocquin, English Department chair at Green River High School, who says she never wrote a poem because she felt she was not worthy even to kiss the hem of a poet's garment. We talked about how most poets don't even wear robes anymore; she has begun writing poems. The early drafts, early works, and comments about writing by Welty, Walker, and others have helped me understand writers primarily as people who write and work hard at it.

How did I take the plunge? How am I still learning to write? How do I help students begin writing and join the community of writers? How am I learning to overcome the excuses of time, busywork, head-tripping, and hems of garments to avoid writing? Most important, I believe, I am learning to write, not alone, but with others.

TAKE A DEEP BREATH, REACH OUT, AND WRITE

William Stafford gives me a gentle push in *Writing the Australian Crawl* when he explains how swimmers must have faith that the water will keep them afloat and how writers must have faith that the writing will keep them afloat. The only way to write is to write, not to spend hours, days, and years talking about writing.

Stafford also suggests how to take the plunge when he describes how he sits daily beside an open window, with pen and paper in hand, waiting for the nibble. He says that on any given day nothing may happen, but he knows for sure that if he is not ready and waiting, he will not get the catch. I try to write daily, but I do not have a certain window, scheduled time, or enough confidence yet to claim such time and space for myself. Those are some of my excuses, but I now recognize them as excuses, and I now realize that I need to write daily, so that I won't feel frazzled. I constantly struggle with the feeling that I am not worth the writing.

Of course, I do write daily in another sense. I write lists that I then rewrite throughout the day. The only time earlier when I was a list-maker was when I was pregnant. Then I made lists of things to do, so that when I awoke, I could cross "nap" off of my list and feel a sense of accomplishment. I put away lists when my children were young because then there was no question about what I had to do. As they grew older, I realized that I was making lists again. Although I feared the meaning in my messages, I knew I was not pregnant with a child: I was pregnant with ideas and images. Now I keep lists of titles, ideas, images, and people to guide my writing.

While the lists are bait for the hook, I also like to wait with pen and paper—at present a fine-point black Bic and narrow-ruled paper—not having any notion of where the writing will take me. Don Murray writes so compellingly about writing for surprise and discovery that for several years I have tried to give myself the pleasure of beginning with blank mind and paper at least for a few minutes a day.

Murray's own writing, as well as his ideas about writing, also help me to become more patient with myself and with writing. I have often wrestled with my writing as it would turn into something alive that I could not control, like the slime children play with that oozes out of cupped palms. As I begin to have faith that the writing will keep me afloat, not that I have to make it happen and control it, my interaction with language is changing. Kenneth Burke discusses how we do to language but also how language does unto us, and for Burke, symbolic action is the dancing of attitudes. I am beginning to relax, in that important sense of the term which I alluded to earlier. I knew from sports and from dancing that fighting the water or the music only prevents motion. Ideally, we cannot know the dancer from the dance as we are performing.

In addition to keeping in shape through some form of daily writing, with faith that the writing will keep me afloat if I let it, I also let my head fill with writing. In graduate school, my head was always working on a current project as I drove the Los Angeles freeways to and from classes. Because of time constraints, I had to write in my head as I drove, and I would arrive home and race inside to get down on paper what was spilling out of my head. This writing in the head was not figuring out what I wanted to write before clothing thoughts in words; it was letting ideas happen, letting them spark each other, and letting voices speak in dialogue.

On about the second day during writing project institutes, teachers often comment of their embarrassment at writing in strange places, during dinner, during the middle of conversations, even at traffic lights. We assure ourselves that as long as two writing project teachers aren't at the same light, others are safe. Teachers confess that they are no longer listening to family and friends in the same way; even though part of their minds seem to be writing all of the time, their attentiveness seems to be heightened. As the writing continues, teachers discuss how writing begins to enter their dreams.

Writing in the head is not scary, at least not yet. There is no loss of identity or concern for others, and voices in the head do not distract from voices outside. In fact, inner writing seems to make life richer. I have also realized that I was exerting enormous energy keeping the writing out. Again, I am learning to relax and letting the writing happen and the ideas nibble. In a recent writing project institute, when Bob Burk, a biology teacher at Green River High School, created a new term —relaxive writing—a variant of reflexive and expressive, he gave the name for something I have been feeling for some time.

As I listen more attentively to myself and to others, I realize that in my teaching I am guilty of the do-what-I-say-not-what-I-do approach. Although I profess that writing teachers must be *writing* teachers and that people who write can call themselves writers, I teach what I want students to believe and act upon, but what I do not fully enact myself. I repeatedly say that people don't have to play in the NBA in order to call themselves basketball players and that people don't have to publish novels to call themselves writers. That applies to students but not to me. What helps is for me to write regularly and to read widely. I also remember Stafford's gentle nudge to reach out and write. What else helps?

LOWER YOUR STANDARDS

When Stafford was asked if he ever gets writer's block, he replied that he doesn't: he just lowers his standards. This may sound like blasphemy to teachers but not to writers. Lowering standards is a way in to writing, a way in to raising standards ultimately. Stafford's phrase has generated numerous other rag-tag theories and mixed metaphors that have helped me and my students learn to write.

In addition to the paltry draft fear, the I-have-nothing-to-say syndrome, which can be alleviated by lowering one's standards, the dry well theory has also arisen in my classes. Many writers are afraid that if we write what's in our heads, we will run out of words and ideas; therefore, we tend to write without disclosing much until the conclusion, where we place gently the golden egg. Of course, few readers want to wait until the end to find substance.

I encourage writers, myself included, to replace the dry well image with the belief that writing can prime the pump, instead of draining it. The more the well is pumped, the greater the yield. If that variation doesn't work, we use another, the squeeze play image, which encourages writers to write what they have in mind right away, instead of waffling around, with the belief that the more they say specifically the more they will have to say. By boldly casting the line, to use another image, the writer elicits numerous nibbles. Students comment on how a writer is like a magician who draws a long string of colorful scarves from a seemingly empty hand, or who releases numerous clowns from a miniature car. All of these scraps of images and mixed metaphors are reflections of my own fears as well as of students' fears; we are all writers together.

The drafts produced by the dry well fear may look like discovery drafts, in which writers write to discover ideas that emerge at the ends of sentences, paragraphs, and papers. Writers learn to read both kinds of drafts critically in order to locate the watershed moments. One revision strategy for such drafts is to flip-flop the sentence, paragraph, or paper, so that the main point is put up-front. We have named another strategy for such drafts, the pluck it method, by which the writer extracts the gem or kernel and begins again.

Donald Graves has suggested, although in other words, that the dry well fear is taught by teachers. In his article, "Break the Welfare Cycle: Let Writers Choose Their Topics," he explains that when we give students topics we teach them that they don't have anything to write. He advocates also that we *let*, not make, students write, with the confidence based on research that children do have subjects to write on and that they want to write—when the writing means making meaning.

Another variation on the dry well fear also has developed in classes, which helps us lower our standards. Perhaps because of living in mineral-rich, yet dry, Wyoming, we developed the oil well theory. In classes I noticed that some students write freely, without stopping to look up or read, filling a page quickly, whereas others write hesitantly, stopping frequently to think and reread, getting very few words down on paper.

Gushers became our name for those who can't seem to stop writing, and eekers became our name for those who can't seem to start. Gushers write without shifting to the role of critical reader of their own text, while eekers shift immediately to the role of critical reader, sometimes even before they have written a word.

These two terms describe extremes in writers; neither is good nor bad, and neither fully describes a particular writer. But with these terms, people begin to see themselves as writers and to recognize tendencies in their writing processes, as specific actions, attitudes, and textual features begin to cluster around the terms. For example, gushers tend to work whole to part, while eekers work part to whole. Gushers focus on the overall feel or gist and tend to omit letters, endings, words, sentences, and transitions. For them, everything seems to flow together, and so there is no gap between themselves and their readers. Gushers tend to write run-on sentences, omit specific details for development, and omit markings of tense, possession, and punctuation. In contrast, eekers focus on specifics, such as words, a sentence, an image. They seem acutely aware of the distance between them and their readers, and so they seldom omit a word, ending, letter.

The oil well theory has become common in my writing classes, and students who begin to see themselves in terms of certain tendencies seek strategies that will compensate. For example, gushers often seek a strategy that gives order and control, such as a cluster or outline, whereas eekers benefit from free writing, and brainstorming. Writers who tend in one direction, but not too far, often seek strategies that give a balance of freedom and restraint, such as list-order-label and questions.

As I watched my students use these terms to help them lower their standards and write, I began to recognize my own tendencies. I am a gusher in that I like the initial bursts of writing, but I have difficulty pushing through to the end. Assembling footnotes and polishing irritate me. But I am a gusher only when I am writing freely, on my own to get started. Less and less, I like to write an assignment. I remember vividly the tall pile of yellow legal paper beside my desk after a psycholinguistics exam, when I could not for forty-five minutes get started because I wanted the first paragraph to be just right. Certainly tendencies in writing are affected by rhetorical contexts, purposes, and audiences.

As a gusher, I have learned to recognize and name the various ways I revise. My most common strategy is the rolling dough method. Ideas pour out very quickly and fully, often the initial burst being a condensed form of the final paper. What I then do is roll out the mass of dough many times—rolling out, reforming, rolling out again to gain the right texture. The physical act of rolling out the ideas seems to help me fill in gaps. The method is time-consuming in that I start from the top many times, but the revisionary actions are very satisfying, unlike the actions that produce the layered look. I recognized in D. H. Lawrence's drafts that he rewrites by the rolling dough method—for example, beginning *Lady Chatterley's Lover* in full several times. In contrast, James Joyce's manuscripts reveal him to be a writer of the layered look school of revision. A single page of the drafts of *Ulysses* is a palimpsest. Several other revision strategies that have also emerged in classes are the collage method, in which small chunks of writing are assembled; the poker hand method, in which written pieces are arrayed like cards to determine which will work best for the particular game and players; and the cut and tape method.

All of these strategies are ways for me and students to lower our standards so that we can begin to write and rewrite. Naming our strategies helps us to integrate them, as it creates a code language for our particular community of writers. Most of these strategies, however, are text-centered; they are essential but not sufficient. What else helps?

LET THE LAWN DIE

Annie Dillard has said that in order to write, people have to let the lawn die. This dictum reflects the importance of the writer's relationship to the surrounding situation. Virginia Woolf has made us aware of the importance of a room of one's own, but we also know how difficult it is to claim time for writing—since life must go on and we feel it cannot without us. She has also helped us kill the Angel in the House. Although Agatha Christie has said that "the best time for planning a book is while you're doing the dishes," if one does dishes more than one writes, the book never is written.

Unless we are in a place where writing counts most, letting go of other activities is difficult. Teachers, for example, are often afraid that if they write with their students someone might think they are not on the job. Many writers share the experience of having been asked what they are doing. When they reply that they are writing, someone responds, "Well, since you aren't doing anything, would you mind doing this chore for me?"

But letting the lawn die means more than claiming time and space for writing, letting go of other duties. It also means taking more risks and responsibilities in writing. One way of letting the lawn die is to identify theories and rules that inhibit writing. I remember a student who came into the Writing Center several years ago with a draft of her review of *The Ugly American*. As usual, she first talked about her review, which sounded exceptionally clear and convincing. At that time, instead of asking her to read it aloud as I do now, I looked at the draft and was horrified by the contorted syntax and indirection. I asked her a question and once again she talked clearly, but she wrote again with the same contorted writing. After several talk-write sequences, I finally realized that in writing she did not use "I." When I asked why, she said that she was not supposed to, at least that's what she had been taught. The unreadable text was a result of her ingenuity in expressing her views on the book without using the first person pronoun. Once free of the forbidden "I" rule, she wrote clearly and intelligently.

Often I discover that I am holding on to a rule as if for life. I might have acquired it as a warning but have since concretized it. I have found myself trying to avoid "and" at the price of clarity, and for a time I wrote as if every other paragraph had to include someone else's authoritative voice. Certainly I, and students, are operating with numerous tacit rules that inhibit writing, but the more we talk about the ones we can identify, the more we reveal.

Two useful variations on the let-the-lawn-die theory are the chuck it and tuck it methods. Learning to throw away writing is often painful, and it has to be taught or encouraged. Bob Boba, a junior high teacher in Big Piney, gets his students on the first day to ball up a piece of paper and throw it in the trash can. Then everyone retrieves a piece of crumpled paper and begins writing. For many years I would worry a piece of writing to death, but I could not throw it away. I learned, though, that nothing I write has such importance. Whenever I have a clipping that won't sprout but which I think might, I tuck it away for a while, like bulbs in the winter. Don Murray says that whenever he likes a sentence particularly well, he knows it will probably have to go. In classes, we learn to distinguish ideas, metaphors, and private terms that help the writer get started but that have no meaning for the reader.

Ironically, letting the lawn die usually does not mean that the lawn will die. Having been raised in Georgia, I know that lawns grow on their own and that kudzu thrives on isolated back roads. Although the Laramie perspective has made me doubtful, as I cultivate with care the blue flax and yellow daisies that grow as weeds elsewhere, I try to let the lawn die. What else helps?

LISTEN TO THE VOICES

One night after dinner, as we were all talking about how we write, my son, Walter, tried to exit unnoticed as he juggled the three oranges and two ice cream sandwiches for his after-dinner snack. We asked how he writes. He paused, put down his nourishment, and replied, "Oh, I just listen to the voices," indicating the general area behind him between his left shoulder and ear. He continued to explain that he sometimes writes from his forehead, especially when a teacher tells him what to write, but he knows that the writing is good when he writes the voices.

From Walter and others, I am learning to listen to the voices, the disembodied voices in my own head, who speak not always one at a time but often as in a chorus or shouting match. Instead of trying to control the voices in my head, I try to listen to them as to a dialogue I am overhearing. I also have begun to listen to the voices around me: family, friends, students, radio announcers, and television characters.

For several years, Kenneth Burke's image in *The Philosophy of Literary Form* of how people learn language has been very important to me, but I have lately begun to see it as an image of myself participating in the conversations in my head:

> Imagine that you enter a parlor. You come late. When you arrive, others have long preceded you, and they are engaged in a heated discussion, too heated for them to pause and tell you exactly what it is about. In fact, the discussion had already begun long before any of them got there, so that no one present is qualified to retrace for you all the steps that had gone before. You listen for a while, until you decide that you have caught the tenor of the argument; then you put in your oar. Someone answers; you answer him; another comes to your defense; another aligns himself against you, to either the embarrassment or gratification of your opponent, depending upon the quality of your ally's assistance. However, the discussion is interminable. The hour grows late, you must depart. And you do depart, with the discussion still vigorously in progress.
>
> (*The Philosophy of Literary Form*, pp. 110–111.)

I also find it helpful not to enter the inner conversation sometimes but just to listen.

Listening to voices does not mean only listening to internal voices. I hear my students in writing give voice to themselves and others, and I learn. Mike, who is now a graduate student in biology with several publications, wrote the following in a freshman English class several years ago:

> I don't know why in the hell I am here. I hate to write. I have flunked English four times in three different states. I don't want to be here. My palms are sweaty and I am mad.

I heard Mike that day, and I am still listening to him as he writes in various voices.

Throughout last semester, I heard Rhonda voice her perspectives on returning to school and my own writing grew:

> As I loaded my two-year old daughter, Elaine, into the old Ford truck and drove up the country lane, I tore our family apart, leaving my five-year-old

son, David, behind with his father and grandmother on the small ranch that had been my home for nine years of a troubled marriage.

Judy also gave voice to herself in writing and helped me to hear myself and others:

> I was a junior in high school when my mother sank down on the freshly vacuumed suburban home. Her size five shoulders shook as she passed a hand over her carefully mascaraed eyes. An absurd, tight smile stretched to grimace proportions. With dread resolution my mother announced, "I just can't do it anymore."
>
> But my mother did go on. She rose the next morning as if last night's scene was someone else's property. By eight in the morning she had already made breakfast, put the house in order, showered, dressed and was ready for an eight-hour day. At lunch she would do the grocery shopping, at five she would attend exercise class, by seven supper would be on the table and then the remaining evening would be devoted to laundry. That was seven years ago and I have yet to see my mother erupt in anger and bitterness. But it is still there, smouldering in coals until fanned by a wisp of discontent when it will flame hot and consume itself again.
>
> I am becoming a woman now. And I am angry.

Gary is an older student who, after being an accountant for many years, has returned to school. Through a series of drafts he experimented with various voices. The first appeared in an in-class, short writing about a job:

> I wonder what they do with wool these days—bet it isn't handled like it was in 1946—one of the jobs I had during part of a summer when I was in high school.

He wrote on this job again for an in-class free writing four days later:

> I worked as a laborer in an old warehouse for a part of one summer between my freshman and sophomore years in high school. The job was working with wool.

A month later he returned to the piece:

> The wool sacks stood on end, slightly sloped, each leaning against its neighbor, holding one another from falling. They appeared as a ghost-like army, row on row, separated by narrow aisles, in the shadowy darkness of the long warehouse.

At this point, Gary decided to let the writing become fiction, and he allowed the voices of the other boys with whom he had worked to speak in his writing.

Our voices seem to come when we stop and write—lower our standards, let the lawn die, and listen. I am glad that my son, Walter, trusts the voices that he hears. I am also glad that Alice Walker wrote *The Color Purple* with its chorus of voices, and I am glad she described in her collected essays, *In Search of Our Mothers' Gardens,* how she moved around the country, so that her characters could feel at home and speak clearly.

I am glad also in this writing to give voice to the many professional and student writers whose words encourage me to learn to write. While this clutter of rag-tag theories, images, and metaphors has helped me in the past, by writing them in this form they allow me now to move beyond them to a new language. I am not sure what the new language will be, but I am fairly certain that it will be a language already well used by others. I am also fairly certain that I will never learn to write but that I will continue learning, with the help of others.

Winston Weathers is professor of English at the University of Tulsa. His books on writing include An Alternate Style: Options in Composition *and* The New Strategy of Style, *and he is coauthor of* The Quintilian Analysis, *a software program for the computerized analysis of prose style. He is also the author of* The Broken Word: The Communication Pathos in Modern Literature; The Lonesome Game, *a collection of short stories;* Messages From the Asylum, *a sonnet sequence;* Indian and White: Sixteen Eclogues; The Beethoven Meditations; *and* Mezzo Camin: Poems from the Middle of My Life. *His recent creative work appears in* The Kenyon Review, Sewanee Review, Southern Review, Poetry, *and other literary magazines.*

THE WINSTON WEATHERS WRITING WAY: A SELF-EXAMINATION

Winston Weathers
University of Tulsa

A great deal of my writing time is spent building a storehouse of writing material. I squirrel away passages of writing, anything from a short sentence to a long character sketch. Not generated by particular projects, these writings are, rather, "savings" put aside for the future.

Intro: How do I write? (Let me count the ways.) Various ways, actually. (As in most of our affairs.) Various scenarios for "the forthcoming movie *Writer at Work.*"

(Just as I have various styles in which to write any given composition, so I have various processes, methods of getting words down on paper, of making my journey toward the completed composition.)

(**Invention:** Often I turn to literary invention as a way to begin. Not to *passive* invention (waiting for the Muse to strike, q.v.)—but *active* invention—playing word games, doodling, a host of other tricks and devices to unlock the unconscious and start the creative juices flowing. Invention is an important part of the pre-writing process for me: If my attempt to write a sentence with the words in alphabetical order—"After Bill caught David eating fresh

The Situation: So much depends. Each writing situation is special, unique. Those ancient determinants of rhetorical situations still play their part. (Let me see if I remember: subject, audience, occasion, purpose, authorial identity, the rhetorical profile . . .)

But other determinants, too: How much time do I have? What's the state of my mind? my mood? What equipment do I have on hand? Pencil, type-

317

grapes . . ."—starts me down a re-
warding path of thought I'm certainly willing to play the game. Yes,
invention has to do with games,
tricks, artificialities, exercises—see
Raymond Queneau's *Exercises in
Style.* The immediate invention
product may eventually be discarded, but the process may have
generated thoughts, even copy, that
may lead to a finished text. Invention is the game I play to get from
"nothing to say" to "something to
say" to "something more to say" to
"something said." I call it game/
writing. And it works for me.)

Writing Instruments: Pencils first, of
course. Well-sharpened. No. 2 lead.
A good eraser. For notes, rough designs, ideas, lines of poetry. But also
pen and ink. (I've always enjoyed
black ink on white paper; something
sharp and visual.) But pen and ink
are for shorter things even so.
Poems, sketches, miniature essays.
For longer things, obviously the
typewriter. I've typed nearly all my
life. And it makes sense to me to
move to the electric, correcting
typewriter: It opens a door to more
extended production, greater
sweeps of narrative, the longer flow
of ideas, several pages of writing at
one sitting. And now, in recent
years, I've discovered the word
processor, the miracles of which
continue to amaze me, making
more revision possible, making a
dreamed-of perfection more feasi-
ble. Now I find the word processor
absolutely necessary for final or
near-final drafts. (And the computer
will proofread my writing for me,
will check my spelling, will—via the
Quintilian Analysis—analyze my
prose style, and do a lot of other
time-saving tasks.) I actually like to
play one writing instrument against
the other. Moving a particular composition from pencil, to pen, to type-

writer, word processor? What resources
are available? A lot of books on the
shelves in this room? How far am I from
a decent library? No books at all, only
memory? is this going to be published?
Am I getting paid for this? In other
words, what's going on? what's the
deal?

Grammars of Style: One of the most important decisions I try to make, early
on, is whether I shall write in Grammar
A or Grammar B. Grammar A is, of
course, the syndrome of style I use
when I'm planning to be very orthodox,
rational, logical, orderly, coherent in
my composition. Grammar B, on the
other hand, is the syndrome of style I
use when I wish to create a verbal experience just as much as I want to transmit
information; when I'm trying to be disjunctive, provocative, synchronic, etc.
Often I decide to use one grammar or
the other on the basis of the material
itself: This very article, for instance,
dealing as it does with my own writing
process, is being written more in Grammar B than in Grammar A—since I'm
not sure my writing process (or anyone's writing process for that matter) is
as orderly and reasonable as Grammar
A would suggest. I think Grammar B
gives a better idea of the synchronic relationships that exist in composition,
the complexities, etc. Grammar B (or as
I also call it, *An Alternate Style: Options
in Composition*) permits me to speak
more appropriately about the mysteries
of writing.

Basic Writing Methods: Usually, I follow one of three basic writing scenarios,
realizing as I do that I may have to
make minor adjustments. But most of
the time I can tell—once I have deter-

writer, to word processor makes the composition seem always new to me, permits me to be more objective than I would be otherwise; I understand my writing better; the writing seems more serious.

(This very article has been written with (a) lead pencil, in my University of Tulsa office; (b) ball-point, on a Delta Airlines flight; (c) an IBM Selectric at Texas Woman's University in Denton, (d) my TRS80-Mod III, 48K, two disk drives, here in my Tulsa apartment.)

Outlines: I'm not too keen on formal outlines, the kind I learned in school. I do, however, find value in a kind of rough outline, at least a list of matters to be dealt with in a composition. If I am writing in Grammar A (q.v.), the rough list of topics guides me as I move from one idea to the next. If I am writing in Grammar B (q.v.), I think of the list more as a map whereon I have tried to locate parts of a composition. In either case, I use the list, or rough outline, or map simply as tentative guide. If in the process of composition I find the outline not working, I drop it; if I find it in need of change, I alter it.

Actual Writing. I distinguish between pre-writing and actual writing, between preparatory writing and the actual task of putting ideas into sustained discourse, into sentences and paragraphs, etc. That is, I do a lot of bits-and-pieces writing before I come to the actual preparation of a draft.

Draft writing is always linear (q.v.), even if I'm only drafting a block of writing (q.v.) to be included in a

mined the writing situation—which of the three scenarios will serve me best. Sometimes I make a mistake and have to start over again. But I never really deplore this. So much of writing is a kind of trial-and-error experience; one learns even by false starts, false paths.

Which path first? Well, usually,

The Short Linear Romance Co-Starring the Muse and the Inspired Author

One word after another. Don't look up until you're done. Like floating down the river, rapids and all. You either make it or you don't. Or, to mix a metaphor: You turn on the mind, say "go," let it take hold of the topic, the subject, the thesis, and run. When most people say "writing," I think they usually mean linear activity; writing words in the same sequence that will be read.

I, like everyone else, write a great deal in this linear mode. I find it works fairly well for briefer compositions—letters, short essays, short statements, even for blocks of writing (q.v.) that may eventually be incorporated into longer works. The linear method draws upon knowledge and skill already in place, already functional in the mind. And when all goes well, linear writing is a beautiful demonstration of the mind's ability to search, integrate, synthesize, articulate quickly and smoothly: the microcomputer of the brain purring away with a flawless program up in the head. But I have found that the linear run can only last so long. After so many words, it peters out. At least it frequently does for me. I come to an abrupt halt. And either I have to sit back and wait for some renewed inspiration or I have to aban-

larger composition. In draft writing, I let some "inner pilot" take over, some inner awareness that moves ideas into words, sentences, paragraphs. In draft writing, I try not to think; rather I let my mind, unimpeded by too much conscious decision making, do the work. My general rule is: Think *before* preparing a draft, think about the draft *after* it is prepared, but while in the actual throes of composition, try to be uncritical, put down what seems necessary at the time, what seems to connect, what is being drawn up to the conscious mind from the unconscious at the very moment you're busy putting words on paper.

The Muse/Imagination: Yes, Virginia, there is a Muse. And she does visit writers. And she does a lot of the writing for which human writers receive the credit. She has certainly done a lot of writing for me. And yes, she comes at odd hours, at the most unexpected times. She can just suddenly appear, carrying her great quill pen and her set of matched luggage full of wit and wisdom. I have discovered, however, that when she does show up her visit is much more pleasant if I am prepared to work with her. I've learned not to tell her I don't feel like working today or that I'm not ready or that I haven't done my homework. I've known her to leave a message something like this: "I'm not coming back until you're ready to play." Which means: Try to be ready, any time of the day, with your writing instruments ready to go, with your desire to write alive and aflame. If you aren't ready, she'll simply depart—and she may wait a long time before she returns. She certainly deplores getting all dressed up and making the trip if, when she gets to the writer's studio, the writer's vocabulary is no larger than it was her last visit; the writer's

don the linear method altogether. The linear method is rarely a successful method for composing long texts: Only for a brief time can I row the boat, hold my breath, court the Muse—all at the same time! Yes I write letters home, brief reports, brief reviews, mini-essays, essay examinations, and the like in a generally linear way. But I realize I'm flirting with danger if I continue on the linear path after about the fourth or fifth page.

One problem with extended linear writing is that it becomes difficult to see the "whole." And certainly this on-going, down-the-line method has a way of breaking down in the middle of chapters, in the middle of books. It has a tendency to break down cross-country.

A second way to write is

The Extended Engagement Co-Starring Lefty Cerebrum and the Methodic Author

A lot of my own writing involves something other than linear activity (q.v.). A lot of my writing has to do with research, getting material, gathering and organizing material, ordering material, constructing a composition, building and rebuilding. It certainly isn't a matter of sitting down and writing from first word to last.

For nearly all nonfiction pieces (articles, papers, reviews, reports), especially if careful reasoning is involved, I have developed the habit of writing down incidental thoughts, ideas, expressions, observations on pieces of paper (or cards, or what have you) that can later be organized into categories, into a sensible sequence, and incorporated into a finished text.

journal is no thicker than it was before; the writer's wastepaper basket is as empty of writing efforts as always.

And one last point: I know, of course, that all goddesses and muses and fairy princesses love gifts, little tokens from their supplicants. And I know that what the Muse likes best of all is a nice stack of words on paper, evidence that I have worked on my own. The Muse loves to see that I'm doing my part, that I'm a serious courtier. She once told me that she really hates frivolous little writers who can't get their act together and who expect her to do every bit of the work. She also hates writers who simply stare out the window all the time. A little window staring, O.K. A little wool gathering, O.K. A little meditation O.K. But I know that my relationship with the Muse depends primarily on my having some words on paper, on the desk in front of me, at all times. I know I must give her proof that I want to write, that I *am* writing. Otherwise, she doesn't seem to be of much help at all.

Polishing: Yes, I have to give every text I create a final polishing. No matter which scenario I have used, I must polish—after revision—all the joints, cracks, connections. I must edit to ensure consistency of tone and style. I don't really mind editing; in fact, I find it one of the more pleasant parts of composition. Not that it isn't sometimes laborious; yet, by the time I get to the editing, I know I have a composition with which to work. By the time I get to the editing, I know that the bulk of writing work is behind me.

Usually this kind of composition is identified well in advance of writing—and it isn't usually written overnight. Many times I write toward a deadline—a week away, preferably a month away, perhaps even a year away. And in the time between knowing that I have the task to perform and the completion of the task, I proceed steadily, somewhat methodically, gathering appropriate material—some drawn from my own thinking, some arrived at in traditional research ways. I accumulate a stack of cards or slips of paper—all of them related, some way or other, to the topic at hand.

What I really do is tack up the "theme" or "topic" or "thesis" on a wall in my mind. I start walking around it, pondering, thinking. This is a ritual of gestation for me. And as ideas, images, words, sentences come to mind I jot them down. Sometimes I become very physical about it all—I write out the topic on a piece of paper and place the paper at the center of a table; then I literally lay cards all around the topic, watching the raw material grow. Admittedly, at some time during this "collection" process, an outline (q.v.) also begins to appear, but the outline is always tentative until the "research" is done, until all the evidence is gathered and my basic thoughts have been articulated. During this gathering process, I keep checking evidence against outline, outline against evidence. And at some propitious moment, the "outline" jells. I then begin to write a draft (q.v.). I simply set the cards or slips of paper by my word processor and begin to write copy, incorporating card or slip, one by one, into a text. If some card or slip seems

Building: I use the building metaphor a great deal of the time to describe my own writing processes. Writing, for me, is a kind of building, building a text—even a linear text—out of words, sometimes out of blocks and pieces and hunks and incomplete passages. I figure I spend at least two-thirds of my time in the construction business.

Building blocks, frames, connections, fasteners. And even though the final composition may be read sequentially, viewed sequentially, its sequentiality is probably one of the last things it has achieved.

An Interview:

Q. Do you listen to music while you write?

A. No. I find it a distraction.

Q. Do you write in the morning or evening or when?

A. Whenever I can find the time. I believe, of course, in having a set time for writing, a schedule to follow. But sometimes circumstances deny me a schedule— and I have to write whenever the opportunity presents itself. If I have my wishes, I write in the morning from eight until noon.

Q. Do you ever ask anyone— friends, family, colleagues—to read your work while you are in the process of writing it?

A. No. I suppose every writer would like some kindly reader on hand to respond instantaneously to the words, yet responses-midst-proc-

obdurate and cannot be incorporated easily or effectively, I set it aside for later evaluation.

Finally a draft is produced. In all likelihood it is a rough piece of writing, with some rather finished sections, but with a good many sections, paragraphs, passages suffering either from overwriting or undue brevity. This draft must now be submitted to careful revision (q.v.).

I consider this kind of writing to be very much an act of construction. Though it involves at certain points "actual writing" (q.v.) (linear, perhaps even inspired), it is not the outgrowth of spontaneous, flowing articulation. It is a writing that pieces together, then polishes.

A third kind of writing is

The Miraculous Pot Luck Payoff Co-Starring Fortuna and the Don't-Throw-Anything-Away Author

This kind of writing is more speculative, a kind of "tomorrow" writing, not done on special assignment. This is writing done without knowing, at the time, exactly where or when the writing will be used. It's writing in advance of specific need. A great deal of my writing time is spent building a storehouse of writing material. I squirrel away passages of writing, anything from a short sentence to a long character sketch. Not generated by particular projects, these writings are, rather, "savings" put aside for the future.

I try to have a good supply of such material always on hand. And it is from this supply of already written material that I often turn to build a composition. I

ess don't really help. Anyway, why impose on people? I believe a writer should be his own worst/best critic. Besides, I'd rather make my own mistakes than the mistakes that someone else has advised me to make.

Q. Do you read very much?

A. Not as much as I should.

Q. When you were a student in college what course or courses did you find most helpful to you *in re* writing and composition?

A. Classical Greek.

know that if sometime in the future I need to write on a particular topic or thesis, I may well find in my storage closet a good deal of writing already in existence related to this thesis/theme. I may have a poem, a chapter, a sentence. I dig these out and ponder how I might integrate them into the composition I want to build. I know, of course, that what has been saved as a poem may well have to be rewritten as prose. I know that a list of this or that may have to be transformed into a serial sentence.

Sometimes I go through my "saved" writings and simply look for some common denominator that will bind some of the savings together. New composition ideas are generated this way. And I have had happy success with this method: piecing and patching, bringing together diverse pieces of writing, done over a long period of time, tacking them onto a common idea. This kind of potluck writing depends, of course, upon what's in the cupboard when I go to fix supper. That's why I never worry about writing something that turns out not to work; I save it. Maybe tomorrow it can become a part of a greater whole.

Revision: Revision for me involves a very careful reading of a draft, noting in particular (a) the structure and arrangement of the material and (b) the flow and sound of the words.

Looking first at structure, I edit toward design and form. Ideas usually appear to me, in the first place, as structure— in structured sentences, in balances, tricola, tetracola. I'm eager to find patterns and designs in my work.

I look first to the overall structure, the form in general. Timing and spacing are important to me at this point. A composition should have its own kind of balance, its own kind of structural stability. I look at the big sections: Are they equally treated? Are there disproportions anywhere?

After dealing with the big picture, I turn to smaller things. I turn to the actual phrasing of the material. In general, I have a tendency to overwrite, so I'm on the lookout for places to cut. And I keep an eye out for the usual editorial matters—usage, spelling, punctuation, ambiguities, etc. Especially important to me is the conclusion of a piece of writing. I fear abrupt endings; I don't want to write compositions that just "stop." I work hard for closure, for some sort of rhythm, cadence, denouement, descent. My mind goes into slow motion when I come to the final sentences. And I probably spend more time on the last few words of a text than I do on any other similar quantity of words.

Another important aspect of revision to me is the auricular aspect of the composition—that is, the way it sounds. And I spend a great deal of time reading a draft, giving full attention to the sound of it. I listen. I listen again. Sound is very important to me—and it involves all such things as rhythm, fluidity of sentences, sequences of sounds, the readability of the text in general. As I read —not aloud (though I might read a text aloud on some occasions) but silently— I mark those parts of the text (a word, a sentence, a transition) where I find a rough auricular spot. I then go back and try to polish each such place. Then, of course, I must listen again to the text. Sometimes I have repeated "listenings" before a manuscript sounds just right.

Even if a text will never be read aloud, the text should be written so that it *would* read out loud very well.

I have one rule as far as my "listening" to the text is concerned. It must be an uninterrupted listening. If I am interrupted, I always start the listening process all over again; I go back to page one and start over. So much of the sound of a text depends upon all that has come before; the sound of one sentence depends upon the sound of all previous sentences. Because listening is so important to me, I am more concerned about my privacy as a writer when I'm doing this listening than I am at any other time in composition. Even the actual writing (q.v.), when I'm in the throes of composition, requires no greater privacy.

Structure and sound. Paying attention to those two things in particular, I sometimes revise a manuscript, one way or the other, twenty to thirty times.

In Conclusion: Any description I might give of the writing process will be incomplete, partially false, perhaps misleading. Whatever I say about writing—whatever anyone says about writing—always misses the mark to some degree or other.

Writing is, alas, more mysterious, miraculous, unpredictable than we pedagogically say it is. Yet, on the other hand, writing is far simpler actually than pedagogy would often have it be. A paradox? Yes, it is.

Writing, on the one hand, is a skill, craft, art that one can indeed learn from others; in fact, writing is an "unnatural" activity in comparison with the naturalness of language and speech: children do not have to be taught "speaking" very often; at a certain age, children begin speaking, without much tutoring, their "native tongue." But they do have to be taught writing/reading. One learns writing from others. One learns writing from formal education—in elementary school, in middle school, whenever it is one first learns about sentences and paragraphs.

But, on the other hand, writing is a skill that can only be learned through one's own practice. As with so many skills— riding a horse, flying an airplane—formal instruction only goes so far. The rest of the skill must be learned solo: the writer facing the page by himself.

That's why, in my own writing life, so much attention is given to my own trial/error activities, my own dry runs, my own dry holes, my own experimentations, my own playing with words to see "what if . . ." I've found that actually I never write the same thing twice, at least rarely so. Every writing task draws upon prior knowledge, prior skill—yet every writing task also calls for a certain amount of "learning on the job," the job that this particular writing task happens to be. I think I usually know more about writing at the end of each new composition than I did before. That is, I not only write any given composition for the usual reasons—to communicate, to entertain, to reach others, to reveal myself, etc.—but I write to learn about writing. What I have learned in writing this very article, I will carry over to the next writing task I may face—next week, next month, yet this evening perhaps. And in that new writing task— later on—I will use this knowledge, but if I am lucky I will also generate new knowledge about writing that, in its own turn, will be carried over. . . .

So it goes. Learn. Write. Learn. Write. A circle.

Now let me see. I think I'm about ready now to go back to the beginning of this text and start reading it with an eye and ear toward revision (q.v.). . . .

W. Ross Winterowd is currently Bruce R. McElderry Professor of English at the University of Southern California, where he established a graduate program in rhetoric, linguistics, and literature. Since the early 1960s he has been interested in written composition, but the scope of his work has broadened to include the whole range of literary studies. Since 1975, he has done extensive work with the public schools.

Winterowd is author of Rhetoric: A Synthesis *(1967), author-editor of* Contemporary Rhetoric: A Conceptual Background with Readings *(1975), and author of* The Contemporary Writer, *the third edition of which will appear in 1985, as will* Perspectives on Composition/Rhetoric. *With Patricia Y. Murray, he has written a grades 7–12 series,* English Writing and Language Skills *(1984).*

THE COMPOSING PROCESS PAPER

W. Ross Winterowd
University of Southern California

An exquisitely simple fact about composition is that every teacher can be—should be—a researcher. Before us in every class are the data: the composing processes of the students we teach. If we are observant, we can learn worlds about what happens when writers are successful and unsuccessful. We should rely more heavily on what we can discover for ourselves and less heavily on the dogma of composition textbooks.

And every writing teacher should do his or her own composing process paper.

For at least ten years, I have been asking both my graduate and my freshman students to write accounts of their own composing processes, and my colleagues in the public schools have used the same assignment, *mutatis mutandis.*[1] In fact, I suspect that I may have invented the specific genre, which is now appearing more and more frequently.[2]

In the composing process papers, I ask students to do "ethnomethodology" on themselves, and such research demands hermeneutics, not mere eyewitness reporting.

One content that is typical of the composing process papers is discussion of attitudes toward writing.

> This morning I had a half-idea about how I might make this a paper about writing this paper. My prewriting stage has involved preparing myself for an intuitive leap. (I keep wanting to turn this paper into one about me and writing instead of about me and my composing process. That's what I'm really interested in.) That is, in prepping lit crit papers, I've tended to read and reread a text, waiting for ideas while making notes.

[1] See W. Ross Winterowd and Barbara Crane, "Eureka! An Assignment: Heuristics in Theory and Practice," *Freshman English News,* 8:3 (Winter 1980), 19–23.
[2] For example, Barbara Wright, "How I Wrote 'Fat Chance,'" *College English,* 44:3 (March 1982), 258–264.

SP kept giving me grief about the distance of my voice. I've alread talked about this—mentioning it again was a way of trying to get at something else—got it. I feel uncomfortable about the fact that I feel uncomfortable about writing, that I feel I don't know enough to say anything about X— except, of course, there are all those articles in professional journals which have made me say, "Why didn't I write this? I've already figured it out for myself." (Student Number 307.)

Intimidation and fear are attitudes most commonly expressed by graduate students:

To begin with, I have a fear—something ridiculous and crippling— of saying the obvious. This means worrying at length about what I will say. This worry is the first stage of the whole process. (Student Number 136.)

"The Composing Process Theme" . . . Shudder . . . I had heard of this famous assignment two weeks before our class began and even then the thought of writing it made me cringe. My sense of dread was even stronger than what I usually felt when faced with a writing task. The subject was painful to me: I had been pleased with very little of the writing I'd done in graduate school so far, and I didn't want to think about the reasons why. Yet if there's anything I'm learning in my seemingly never-ending trek through academia, it is that the truth, once discovered, feels good. In this spirit and buoyed up by the anonymity my social security number so humanely provides me, I am finding the courage and even a certain enthusiasm to write this paper—truthfully.

I will reluctantly begin by admitting that most of the critiques, interpretations, and sundry essays I've written for graduate school were not products of "my best," but products of fear and even, at times, panic. This leads me on to an ever more soul-shattering evaluation: my ability to teach. How could I propose to instruct others in something I didn't enjoy myself? The more I painfully introspected, the more I realized that an examination of my composing process was essential if I wanted to gain insights that might liberate my "hung-up" writing style and generate firsthand composing advice I could pass on to my students. (Student Number 457.)

One of my students, working with a collaborator, had some success with television scripts. In her paper, she reported the Eureka phenomenon:

Working on a boring, nonspontaneous scene physically and mentally exhausted us, so we decided it was time to take a break. We took off to Marie Callender's Restaurant—our favorite change of environment. Of course, we took our legal pad with us in case we came up with any ideas for Scene Two. Suddenly inspiration struck over the strawberry pie. Gags started pouring out of our mouths faster than we could shovel in the pie.

Unlike the first scene, we didn't feel straightjacketed by the plot, and our imaginations were able to wander freely. We stayed at the restaurant until we had worked out the entire scene, and we were quite pleased to find it up to our usual standard of wit and ingenuity. (Student Number 152.)

Here is a typical statement in regard to pre-writing:

> I generally try to let my mind play with my subject for a time before I actually begin writing. Sometimes this involves a period of concentration with pencil and paper; others times it involves keeping a page or series of pages on which I make notes as ideas occur to me, often while I am working on something else. Frequently, both are involved. At some point in that process, there usually comes a notion about the shape in which I can cast what I have to say. I jot that down as well. (Student Number 307.)

In doing a survey of the composing process papers that I have received from graduate students, I find that the following themes arise again and again:

attitude

easy and hard writing (Easy writing usually involves some kind of algorithm.)

the Eureka phenomenon

heuristics (Students report having developed their own before studying composition/rhetoric theory.)

instruction in writing (high school and undergraduate college)

the journal (Certainly more than half of my graduate students keep some sort of journal.)

notes (on slips of paper or cards that can be arranged and re-arranged)

pauses (to read over what is already written)

planning (Very few students use formal outlines; many use informal scratch outlines.)

pre-writing

process (The two general methods might be called "inch-by-inch" and "all-at-once.")

purpose "This dynamic [the writer-reader relationship] changes depending on my purpose and motives for writing. I write for three reasons—I have to, I want to, I need to. Although these are not mutually exclusive categories, they are motivations that produce different kinds of writing and writing processes" (Student Number 442).

rewriting (Some of my students, like D. H. Lawrence, rewrite by starting afresh from the beginning. Others make changes almost sentence by sentence.)

rituals (such as elaborate preparations, using music to get in the
   mood, and so on)
scene (Many students report that they work best in a given scene;
   others are unable to work outside the proper scenes.) "Every
   writer, playwright or prose essayist, serves his idiosyncrasies. I
   have several. First, I demand a familiar, comfortable place.
   Only two places work: at my desk at home or at a long wooden
   table in a library reading room. Home can be almost anywhere;
   I once wrote the better part of a play in a series of bed-and-
   breakfast places along Scotland's east coast. I was only in each
   place a week, but I felt settled" (Student Number 469).
starting
structure
talk-write
time (morning, afternoon, evening, late night)
typing versus handwriting

An exquisitely simple fact about composition is that every teacher
can be—should be—a researcher. Before us in every class are the data:
the composing processes of the students we teach. If we are observant,
we can learn worlds about what happens when writers are successful
and unsuccessful. We should rely more heavily on what we can discover
for ourselves and less heavily on the dogma of composition textbooks.

And every writing teacher should do his or her own composing
process paper.

As I said, I have assigned the composing process paper for years,
yet—and I am reluctant to admit it—I had never written my own until
two days ago. Doing the paper was educational and exhilarating.

*

Feb. 7, 1984, 8:30 A.M.

On January 14, 1983, I wrote this in my journal:

> Calculating people are never as clever as people who act openly on in-
> stinct. The human situation is far too complex to be manipulated by cold
> calculation alone. Impulse and instinct finally work better than scheming.
> People whose every move is based on prudence are slightly less than
> human.

I had in mind two acquaintances, one of whom I care for deeply. I was,
in fact, preoccupied with the attempt to explain her motives, to my own
satisfaction at least, and in my journal entry I had said everything and
nothing; I needed to fill in the details, work out the "argument," satisfy
myself that I had grasped at least some aspects of a complex and fascinating person.

I had been rereading *The Ambassadors,* a novel that was perfect for me at that time, and I suppose, in a way, I had begun to think of myself as a Strether in regard to the charming but calculating young woman who meant so much to me. The resonances of James's great masterpiece preoccupied me as intensely as my concern regarding the young woman. And I went on from *The Ambassadors* to *The Wings of the Dove,* where, of course, I got to know that fascinating schemer Kate Croy. When I found this, regarding Kate Croy, I knew that I had discovered something tremendously important:

> . . . every one who had anything to give—it was true they were the fewest —made the sharpest possible bargain for it, got at least its value in return. The strangest thing, furthermore, was that this might be, in most cases, a happy understanding. The worker in one connection was the worked in another; it was as broad as it was long—with the wheels of the system, as might be seen, wonderfully oiled.

On May 7, 1983, I made the following entry in my journal:

The Charming Lady, a Jamesian Tale

"She isn't really beautiful," Lambert had said, "not beautiful at all, though something else, of more worth than beauty: she's attractive, certainly one of the most attractive women I've known. When it comes to a choice, attractiveness outdoes beauty every time."

Chad sipped briefly, tentatively, and then, with a voluptuousness uncharacteristic of thin persons, slowly and deeply nodded his approval of the sherry and doubtless of the charming lady who was the subject of Lambert's remark.

Late afternoon in harvest time, season of mellow fruitfulness: Professor Lewis Lambert, known widely for his definitive study *Ronald Fairbanks, the Conscientious Pixy,* Professor Lambert, ensconced and senior, reaped meticulously during these afternoons with very junior colleagues. Sherry, declining light, the beginning of an academic year, the careful deference of untenured colleagues such as Assistant Professor Martin Chadwick, desultory conversation, not quite gossip and tinged with literary allusion, the almost deserted campus, the obligatory ivy and books, even the barely audible whirring of the freeway and the oily tinge of exhaust in the six-o'clock breeze that blew through the open window of the professor's office—the makings of a perfect scene for discussing Lambert's preoccupation: the charming lady.

"You've noticed, Chad, that one of her common phrases, almost a tic, is 'bringing it off.' 'If I can just bring it off,' she says to me repeatedly. Her whole life is devoted to 'bringing it off,' as if everything she does is a plot, all her successes, coups."

What, then, was the motive behind this story—which ultimately became a chapter in a novel, *Academy Awards?*

In the first place, I was writing fiction for utilitarian conceptual purposes: I wanted to explain one of my life's great puzzles, and I had to use a dramatistic method to accomplish my end. On a deeper level, I probably wanted to live psychically with my main character, who had meant, and who still means, so much to me. Furthermore, as the story develops, I am clearly taking human (and thus cruel) vicarious revenge on my character, for in the tale, she is a user, wounding those with whom she associates.

"Ja, ja, Her Doktor, but I sink dot's kvite enough pscyhoanalysis."

I certainly agree. Do any of you have further questions?

"Tell us, Professor Winterowd, do you think that your reading of James had anything to do with the story that you are discussing?"

Yes, I think you might say that. We writers, you know, have an interest in craft; in that sense, we're very much like cabinetmakers, blacksmiths, machinists. I wanted to create a fiction that, to the trained eye, would look "Jamesian," that to the trained ear would convey the tones and cadences of the Jamesian voice.

"And, Professor, would it be presumptuous to ask, 'Did you succeed?' "

Modesty prevents me from answering. However, I might say that a colleague, internationally respected as a student of James, told me, "Hm, yes, there are Jamesian elements here, quite decidedly."

*

Let me talk about my "representative anecdote" a bit more.

Depending on your point of view, you can take "The Charming Lady" as emotive, referential, poetic, phatic, or conative discourse. (And since I have resolved in this essay to avoid the footnote tic, I'll say right here, without a garland of ibids, that I'm using Roman Jakobson's categories, which shouldn't surprise anyone who is familiar with my work.) Certainly it's emotive, in that I needed to get my tangled web of motives and emotions, not necessarily untangled, but laid out against the white of paper in the sharp, black tracery of writing. The tale was genuinely cathartic, allowing me to live with an ambivalent situation that my values, commitments, cowardice, selfishness, and, I think, a saving modicum of human decency had gotten me into. I could sublimate my hostility with metaphor:

> Glowing Kate was, at her best, the romantic flicker of a candle or the sociable warmth of a blaze in a fireplace, but all too often she was the scrambling green phosphorescence of a computer.

In another way, from another angle, however, "The Charming Lady" is, as I said earlier, referential, a faithful representation of my attempt to conceptualize, to understand a complex situation. And I think this point is worth underscoring: "poetry" can be—and probably most often is—an instrument of rational thought in the strictest sense. In the dry language of cybernetics and artificial intelligence, in fictions, we are able to construct elaborate possible worlds and live through their consequences.

Here is the interesting point: the two main characters, Kate Reese and Lewis Lambert, are decidedly not my friend and me—or perhaps not so decidedly. In any case, the tale is not autobiographical, but analogous, allowing me, therefore, to stand back and weigh the evidence impersonally before I reached a judgment. The story ends with that judgment. Lewis Lambert has died, and Chad and Kate attend the memorial service. Kate says,

> "Lewis was our friend and mentor, wasn't he, Chad?" And she radiated gratitude for the past, expressing by intonation, slight gesture, and a barely perceptible move toward Chad her sincerity. "I did love him, you know. He was an important part of my life."

As Kate scurries away from him, Chad says, to himself, "I do love her . . . and so did Lewis. Yes, and she has loved us truly. I'll invite her for sherry next week."

The judgment is, then, sweetly, benignly fatalistic: you must make no conditions for love. In more personal terms: by my own choice, I'm stuck; hence, it is foolish to fret, fume, and fuss. "The worker in one connection was the worked in another; it was as broad as it was long—with the wheels of the system, as might be seen, wonderfully oiled."

I have tried to show something about how my story came to be and why I wrote it—that is, I have attempted to deal with purpose and process. More important, I think, I have explored the uses of one genre of writing—at least the uses to which I put that genre, arguing specifically that "poetry" is an extremely powerful agency for conceptualization and argumentation. (Without doubt, persuasive or conative motives also fueled my work on the story, but I choose not to deal with them here.)

*

And you, you faceless wraiths, you throngs who will eagerly imbibe my essay for its heady wisdom, elegance, grace, wit—you who wait, though unknowingly, for the appearance of this writing, be not your wonted lurid selves. In the foregoing discussion of my story, I was not alluding to a love affair, an extramarital romp. Love *does* have *other* meanings, you know.

*

TO: Professor Whatsyourname
FROM: W. Ross Winterowd
If I understand your objection correctly, you accuse me of being an arrogant ass for parading my own unpublished fiction through this essay. You further question my authority to discuss composing fiction since I have never published any of it.

I can only respond thus: you are perfectly right on both counts.

Thank you for your concern and your insightful, though acerbic, comments.

*

Derrida argues that texts are merely occasions for further textuality, commentary upon commentary *ad infinitum*. As I said, "The Charming Lady" provoked a novel, *Academy Awards*, which is now in process. Whereas the story allowed me to get things right with myself, the novel in which it is embedded is allowing me, primarily, to vent my spleen. One of the main characters, Professor J. Melongaster Druse, has become progressively more despicable as the tale progresses, while his wife has become more and more admirable. It will undoubtedly be the case that Druse will suffer an accident or find that he has an incurable and rapidly fatal disease. I'll simply not allow a wonderful person like Beulah Druse to be stuck with Mel.

"Uh, Professor Winterowd, might I point out that authors we admire do not manipulate their characters. If you want to control puppets, why don't you ask for a position with the producers of 'Sesame Street'?"

[Laughter ripples through the audience.]

My answer to that, sir, is straightforward. It's my novel, and I'll do anything with it I damn well please.

I shall now read you a brief section from *Academy Awards*, so that you can get the "flavor" of this, the longest work of fiction that I have undertaken since I was a junior in college and wrote *Blunt Thou the Lion's Paws*, which remains in MS.

In his tan warmup suit and Adidas jogging shoes, Mel was listlessly puttering around the yard, snipping a branch here, pulling a weed there, making, really, no difference whatsoever in the domesticated flora of 1415 Dimple Dell Drive, when Beulah called him to the phone.

"Yes, Les. . . . Certainly, Les. . . . Couldn't agree more, Les. . . . Certainly, Les. Monday at three. I'll be there, Les," Beulah heard him say.

"Who was that, honey?" she asked.

Snarling, Mel answered, "Who do you think it could be, huh? Do we know anyone named Les? Lester? Do you know anyone named Lester?

Have you ever heard me mention Lester? 'Les,' you know, is short for 'Lester.'" And in utter disgust, Mel took a diet Dr. Pepper from the refrigerator and, popping the top, drank deeply.

"It must've been the dean—Lester Amore," said chipper Beulah.

In response, Mel hissed, "Yes, Lester Amore. Lover Boy. The sonofabitch."

"But I thought you liked Dean Amore."

"But you thought I liked Dean Amore," mimicked Mel, his scorn thick enough to butter a pretzel. "You think I like all of those assholes over in the administration building. You think life at that lousy, third-rate university is like . . . is like"—and literary Mel was groping for the appropriate simile—"is like the bowling alley."

Failing to make the tropic connection between the university and the bowling alley, Beulah was momentarily silent, thinking.

Dr. Pepper in hand, Mel flopped on a chair at the dinette table and soliloquized: "They call me at home—on Saturday. And I'm supposed to run around for the bastards and do their dirty work on their damn committees. Well, they can go fuck themselves, that's what they can do. I'm not good enough for their parties—oh no!—but I'm sure as hell good enough to sit on their curriculum committee."

From long exposure to her husband's moods, Beulah was adept at finding salient clues and following their leads to the explanations of Mel's vagaries. And, of course, Mel's growlings had provided such a clue to his current funk. A party to which he had not received an invitation—that was the answer.

"What party's that, Mel? What party didn't the dean invite you to?"

"The goddamn party for the new goddamn graduate dean, that's what party. Oh yes, I'm good enough to edit the faculty newsletter. You bet your sweet life. I'm good enough to chair the commencement committee. Sure. Sure. The only thing I'm not good enough for is their goddamn snooty social life."

"Well," said Beulah soothingly, "I've never liked those faculty parties anyway."

"You've never liked those faculty parties, anyway," echoed Mel whiningly. And, throwing his Dr. Pepper can clatteringly into the sink, he shuffled into the backyard, there to snip and clip and, like the good physician, do no harm to the patient.

[A scattering of half-hearted applause throughout the audience.]

Where's the gentleman who accused me of manipulating my characters? Ah, yes, there you are. Sir, after having received this brief introduction to him, wouldn't you now agree that Professor J. Melongaster Druse must die before the novel ends?

*

I'm relatively prolific and have been for years. The least charitable judgment that anyone, to my knowledge, has made on my work is this: "Winterowd types faster than he thinks." Since I myself have made the most charitable judgments of my work, diffidence prevents me from stating them.

But I do type fast. It is now 2:00 P.M. (Feb. 7, 1984), and I am at page 10, line 48 of the current essay—which I began this morning at 8:30, a period of five and a half hours, with two timeouts: one thirty-minute break while I did calisthenics and watched a game show and another of equal duration to shop for country ribs, which I intend to prepare this evening.

At this point, I have the impression that I will do little revising; the essay is coming out pretty much as I wanted it to. When I started it, I had a grand scheme in mind, and it looks as if the circumstances of writing will not change that scheme significantly. To be sure, I've incorporated some happy notions that popped up—for instance, addressing an imagined present audience or a presumed future audience, as I did in the previous pages. But these are local details that have not as yet skewed the blueprints that I had in mind when I started.

On the other hand, I have on my desk fifteen pages of MS. titled "Other Knowledge." It is a series of false starts, new beginnings, confusions; a farrago of citations that don't really add up.

Relating to the fifteen is one notepad page with the following inscriptions:

A critique of verbal knowledge
  (1) phatic-referential speech-writing split
  (2) discounting purpose and mode
  (3) "episodes" as conceptual pivots
  (4) felt sense
  (5) structure and event
  (6) semantics

[An interesting thing is happening right now. At the last asterisk, I switched to a discussion of my scholarly writing, and at this point, hardly more than a page into the topic, I'm bored. I am, then, violating my cardinal rule for writing. *Make sure that you, the writer, enjoy the stuff, and all else will follow.*]

To dispel the miasma of ennui, fol-de-rol-de-doo-dum-day, I'll get right to the point, which, is, after all, probably worth making, at least to graduate students who are faced with the need to write dissertations.

"Other Knowledge"—the sheaf of MS. that I mentioned—is the first chapter of a book, *Representations of Consciousness in Prose and Poetry,* that I've been thinking about and assembling ideas and data for since 1980. I'm now ready to write—overready. In a sense, I am over-tired of the great harvest I myself desired. Somehow, though, I must get direction, impetus, momentum, and the only way I can do that, in this and similar cases, is to type, almost indiscriminately, letting the ideas tumble out in apposition, not logical succession, forgetting connections and sequences. Once I reach a certain critical mass, I am ready to go back and begin shaping, connecting, arranging—creating, in short, the kind of discourse that fits the genre "scholarly writing."

In fact, I have another start. The file is labeled OTHERREV for "Revision of Other Knowledge." Through the magic of IBM and floppy disks, I let you compare the beginning paragraphs of the original version, OTHER, and OTHERREV:

Other

That admirable poet and irascible critic Yvor Winters enunciated a view of literature that might fairly be called archetypically rationalistic:

> The theory of literature which I defend . . . is absolutist. I believe that the work of literature, in so far as it is valuable, approximates a real apprehension and communication of a particular kind of objective truth. . . . The poem is good in so far as it makes a defensible rational statement about a given human experience (the experience need not be real but must be in some sense possible) and at the same time communicates the emotion which ought to be motivated by that rational understanding of that experience. *(In Defense of Reason)*

In fact, I have just encountered a technical problem. To give an idea of the drift of OTHER, I would need several more pages, followed by the first few paragraphs of OTHERREV. The business of tracing semantic intentions from their first glimmerings through their realizations in successive drafts demands enormous documentation and infinite patience, hardly the sort of exposition demanded in an occasional essay such as this one.

Two other problems arise. In the first place, it would bore both you and me stiff to follow the evolution of the text. Second, I find myself "fictionalizing" the moment I begin to account for the evolution—fictionalizing, in the first place, because I don't know exactly what happened between draft one and draft two and, in the second place, because I want to present the drama of generation, not the dry facts about the texts.

Both of the latter two problems are, to be sure, temperamental. I don't have the patience and assume that most of my readers won't—at least in the context of the volume for which I'm composing this essay.

Let's back off to generalization then. (Anyone who wants the "data" can write to me, and I'll send the successive drafts, for I'm a compulsive printout keeper. Before I revise a file in my computer, I "save" and print out. Just think of the possibilities. Long after my wife and I have retired to our air-conditioned tomb in Forest Lawn—with eternal muzak to soothe our troubled spirits—a volume will appear: *The Successive Rough Drafts of W. Ross Winterowd: The Triumph of Quantity, the Failure of Quality—an Inquiry into the Composing Process of a Proficient Typist.* Ah, hubris!) Unsurprisingly, *I write to get my ideas straight.* (I have italicized because, my mind for the moment on posterity, I feel that we have here a real quotable.)

There is an interesting point to be made. After intensive work, massive reading, unsystematic mulling, I get the sense that I have come to a conclusion, that I have arrived at an insight. The point, then, is to develop a presentational strategy that will give that insight salience for someone other than myself. I agree with Kenneth Burke and Morris Raphael Cohen, among others, that we reach our conclusions by extralogical processes and then use "logic" rhetorically to establish them. In my own case, that logic takes place only when I begin to write, to sort categories, arrange hierarchies, develop arguments. There is no way that I could make sense without the tedium of "illogical" drafts that spill ideas out almost as they occur to me.

And yet my last statement, like all that have gone before it, is at least part fiction. (How can any statement be else?)

When I am clattering away on my IBM—and for years on my balky, badly designed Olivetti—my wife asks me, "Are you typing or writing?" (The import is something like this: "Do you know pretty much what you want to say, so that I can interrupt you?" or "Are you conceptualizing as you type?") The distinction is important to me (and, I suppose, to our marriage). By and large, I have "typed" this essay. (It is now 5:39 P.M. I started the essay at 8:30 A.M. In the interim, I would remind you, I have done calisthenics—a euphemism for a good deal of grunting and groaning that doesn't seem to improve my figure—while I watched "The Price Is Right"—an exercise that doesn't seem to improve my mind; I have shopped for our supper; and, by the good Lord! I've cooked the whole thing. (I know you're curious. Thus: country ribs from a recipe devised by John and Tilly Warnock; wilted lettuce, an old family favorite; yams to be baked in the microwave when my son arrives. And Norma made the pumpkin pie.) Yes, I've spent a good deal of the day typing, about seven hours, to reach page 15, line 40 of this computerized MS. I wish that I could estimate the number of hours that I have spent generating OTHER and OTHERREV.

The difference, I think, can be traced to what might be called a sort of appropriation. I need somehow to make the subject of my book mine, not in the intellectual sense, but in a way that has much to do with love. I need to contextualize my work and make it relate to my world, to the people, quiddities, activities, scenes, smells, sounds, customs, textures of what I take to be me, not an intellect or an intellectual, but a fifty-four-year-old rotund husband, scholar (yes, I appropriate that title), father, jogger, sherry drinker, cook, sloth, manic, curmudgeon, lover, crossword puzzle addict, Henry James addict—a person whose philosophy of life has been shaped at least in part (and probably large part) by Mark Twain and D. H. Lawrence.

You see, I know for a fact that I cannot intellectualize until I live through.

That, I think, is one of the main points about writing. Writing is the most human of actions; it forces you to live through your ideas and your experiences, and to realize that the two are not strictly separable.

*

I've never been able to swear off anything. Upon occasion I have resolved to give up cigars. I solved that problem of will and moral stamina by proposing a counterresolution: I will never, I solemnly swore, give up cigars. And, by all that's holy, I never will. I will keep that resolution. I swore that I would not drink sherry during the week. Then my physician, an infinitely wise and humane soul, suggested that sherry in the afternoon would be extremely beneficial. I reluctantly take his advice, and though I suffer moral pangs, I do drink my sherry every afternoon—for my health's sake, you understand.

I think, however, that I may be able to keep one resolution that I made three or four years ago. *I will never again produce impersonal, gritty scholarship, from which the personality that I have grown to love and admire is effaced.* If I do statistics, they will be laughingly or liltingly presented; when I do logic, it will be tongue-in-cheek.

I have just completed a scholarly discussion of the state of the art in composition/rhetoric, 250 pages of manuscript. The tome is, I hope, respectable or even exceptionally well executed and useful, but my own current passions would not allow me to turn out good khaki scholarship. So I began the discussion of form in discourse thus:

> More deeply into the swamp; more intriguingly into the mysteries of our profession. Image with me for the moment, analogize, somewhat cornily, to be sure (but, then, every writer should have franchise to indulge in corniness on occasion).
>
> On the firm ground of style, among the romantically mysterious oaks with their shrouds of Spanish moss—we will pause to hear Robert Penn Warren, reminding us that our concerns are not only with basic writers and the plain sense, but with a good deal more than "the basics" or, more properly, ever with the basics. Let the poet set our scene:
>
> **Bearded Oaks**
>
> The oaks, how subtle and marine,
> Bearded, and all the layered light

Above them swims; and thus the scene,
Recessed, awaits the positive night.

So, waiting, we in the grass now lie
Beneath the languorous tread of light;
The grasses, kelp-like, satisfy
The nameless motions of the air.

Upon the floor of light, and time,
Unmurmuring, of polyp made,
We rest; we are, as light withdraws,
Twin atolls on a shelf of shade.

Ages to our construction went,
Dim architecture, hour by hour:
And violence, forgot now, lent
The present stillness all its power.

The storm of noon above us rolled,
Of light the fury, furious gold,
The long drag troubling us, the depth:
Dark is unrocking, unrippling still.

Passion and slaughter, ruth, decay
Descend, minutely whispering down,
Silted through swaying streams, to lay
Foundation for our voicelessness.

All our debate is voiceless here,
As all our rage, the rage of stone;
If hope is hopeless, then fearless fear,
And history is thus undone.

Our feet once wrought the hollow street
With echo when the lamps were dead
At windows; once our headlight glare
Disturbed the doe that, leaping, fled.

I do not love you less that now
The caged heart makes iron stroke,
Or less that all that light once gave
The graduate dark should now revoke.

We live in time so little time
And we learn all so painfully,

That we may spare this hour's term
To practice for eternity.
                    —Robert Penn Warren*
          Among the oaks of style, we are mysteriously in repose,
for our methodology is clearcut: we can teach syntactic
fluency, editing, accessibility. The "software" is powerful
and easily applied. The consolation, however, is a
will-o'-the-wisp, for we are ever confronted with the
inspiriting problem of purpose.
          Beyond the eternal grove where style is all—where
students could play their sentence games, syntactic Pan
songs, lilted to the nymphs of sentence combining—lies the
alligator-infested morass of making sense.

     Such is the scholarly manner that I now choose. My new strategy
makes scholarship a considerably less gritty business for me. And, after
all, it's my life to enjoy. The kind of personal writing that I now choose
to do makes life a good deal more pleasant for me.
     As the sun sets in the west, you can hear me crooning, "I want to
be me. What else can I be?"

                              February 7, 1984, 8:13 P.M.

*"Bearded Oaks" from *Selected Poems, 1923–1975* by Robert Penn Warren. Copyright
1942 and renewed 1970 by Robert Penn Warren. Reprinted by permission of Random
House, Inc.

AN AFTERWORD FOR GRADUATE STUDENTS

Michael Ray Taylor

This afterword is for graduate students and teaching assistants only. If you are employed as a full-time professor of English composition and/or hold a Ph.D. in composition, linguistics, or English or American literature, do not read beyond this point. I mean it.

There's nothing here for you. I am not a psycholinguist, a tagmemicist, a generative grammarian, a bibliographer, a deconstructionist, a textual critic, a textbook author, or even a rhetorician; I am a student with barely a year of teaching experience under my belt. No essay I produce can compare to the works of those illustrious professionals who have, through the honest revelation of their writing processes, graced this volume. My comments are included here only because of Tom Waldrep's concern for graduate teaching assistants.

Specifically, this essay exists because a group of students in Waldrep's class for new graduate instructors—a group with a vested interest in the inner workings of successful rhetoricians—first suggested he investigate the actual methods employed by contributors to the field of writing instruction; for the sake of these and similar students toiling in the nation's departments of English, stuttering in cruel isolation before their first freshman classes, Professor Waldrep has solicited the works that make up this book, and he now allows me this opportunity to address these student readers, my colleagues.

Alone. Without supervision.

Now, for the rest of you, this is how it all started:

It was a dull, damp October afternoon, midway through the fall semester at the University of South Carolina. We were sitting in English 701: The Theory and Teaching of Composition, a course designed to introduce first-year graduate instructors to every theory of rhetoric from Aristotle to Winterowd, with a little time left over for tips on catching plagiarists, grading freshman themes, and getting nominated for departmental teaching awards. I'm sure you have the equivalent at your own school. (God help you if you don't, if you're stuck in one of those institutions where they throw you at freshmen unprotected!) Anyway, we were sitting there in 701—about fifteen of us plus a guest, a local high-school teacher who had come to watch—and we were discussing Francis Christensen's "A Generative Rhetoric of the Sentence." Perhaps it would be more accurate to say that we were sitting in 701 listening to Waldrep discuss Christensen's work.

We were not having fun. Some of us were merely bored, were dutifully shifting about and taking notes in that time-proven method employed by all graduate students about to nod off, while others of us —and I like to think of these as the more "serious" students among us —were downright mad. We had had it up to here with heuristics for invention. We were sick of rhetoricians. We were not about to sit idly for this "syntactical ingenuity" stuff. The little red lights on our shit detectors were lit up.

Here we were, halfway through a course supposed to equip us to teach freshman composition, and yet all we had done was read a lot of high-minded, jargon-ridden essays excerpted from professional journals, essays whose authors had often seemed more concerned with refuting someone else—usually the Aristotelians, the cognitive psychologists, or Ann Berthoff—than with advancing whatever new pedagogical device it was that their essays purported to advance. Sure, some of the theory had been interesting. Some of it had certainly been well written, even entertaining. But enough was simply enough. Now we were being told that, according to Christensen, good writing necessarily contains long, multilevel, complex sentences (it had been statistically proven), that such writing could and should be taught to freshman students, and that in fact whole writing programs had been shaped around this proposition; we were not going to swallow all of this without a fight.

Now Professor Waldrep's standard method of operation after introducing a new piece of composition theory was to ask the class for comments or questions; if this failed to generate discussion, he would ask one or two individuals for their personal reaction to the theory and then try to draw out their noncommittal answers Socratically, narrowing and pointing his questions in such a way that the answerer was forced both to demonstrate knowledge and to take some sort of stand on the subject. It was always great fun to watch, so long as you were not one of the individuals called upon. After all, this was a three-hour, once-a-week class, and you had to take whatever entertainment you could get.

But as I said, this time we had had enough. Waldrep had asked his perfunctory "Any questions or comments?" and was already running his fingernail down the roll sheet, searching for a victim, when he glanced up and saw the sea of hands. There were at least eight of them waving at him, certainly a 701 record. Even Ellen Steadham, who had spent most of the semester sleeping on her desk, had raised her hand and looked half awake.*

"Well," said Professor Waldrep, "My, my."

The room pulsed with righteous indignation. There may have been a faint smell of ozone. Everyone present felt a sense of historic moment: The revenge of the theory weary was finally under way.

Professor Waldrep maintained his composure. "Mr. Glover, why don't you begin? Tell us what you think of Christensen."

"I think he's full of crap," Tim said. Tim had never been one to mince words. "I mean, look at this first sentence he quotes, the Hemingway." He paused to glance down at his textbook. " 'George was coming down in the telemark position, kneeling, one leg forward and bent, the other trailing, his sticks hanging like some insect's thin legs, kicking up puffs of snow' and so on and so forth. I don't much care for it, but I suppose that it worked in its context. But my God, what's going to happen if I try to get a student to write a sentence like that? Instead of vivid communication, won't it lead to the kind of pretentious, false academic style that characterizes poor college writing? Why is Christensen trying to kill the simple declarative sentence? I mean, where does he get off?"

"Well," said Professor Waldrep, one eyebrow arched, "My, my. How do you respond to that, Ms. Korosy?"

Mary Korosy was a bright, timid A student who in the past had always sided with convention. "I agree. At least to a certain extent. I'm sure these exercises might be helpful for some students, but I think there would be a danger in depending on them too heavily. Good writing, I think, should vary, should have a rhythm made of long, medium, and short sentences, not just one kind."

"Yeah," interjected Ellen from her corner, one side of her face still bearing the red imprint of her spiral notebook, "What about Hemingway? He never used that kind of sentence. What about 'A Clean Well-Lighted Place?' Hemingway never could have made Christensen's survey, because . . ." she paused to see what was in the text that Mark Gregory was waving so frantically before her. "Oh." The other side of her face reddened. "Never mind."

Mark rescued her from the embarrassed silence that followed. (This later caused speculation about those two, but that's another story.) "Okay," he began, "so what if these novelists and professionals do use complex sentences? How does that help us teach 101? Doesn't Chris-

---

*Note: Names have been changed to protect stipends.

tensen's whole thing—sentence-combining, T-Units, all of that—defeat the concept of writing as process? How can you reconcile this method —producing complex, layered sentences at the invention stage—with the heuristics we discussed earlier, like free writing? It seems to me that this device will lead to two or three well-written sentences in a paper that has no structural unity, no coherence, if it's ever finished at all."

Harold Flythe and Wanda Parke both nodded from the back of the room. They were now the only students with unraised hands. Harold and Wanda were two of those pure-Lit types who come to graduate school to massage the classics. Here at USC, their kind tended to massage only the Southern classics, but still, they thought of themselves as defenders of Western culture against the Yahoos. Composition, which they would *never* teach after receiving their degrees, was like mucking out the stables: necessary for riding, but best done by others. Thus, their attitudes in the required 701 course had been unveiled contempt, hauteur, ennui, malaise, and general bloody-mindedness. Now they were perfectly beaming with looks of "I told you so."

Wanda could contain herself no longer. Before Waldrep could call on anyone else, she blurted out, " 'O'er step not the modesty of nature: for anything so overdone is from the purpose of playing, whose end, both at the first and now, was and is, to hold, as't were, the mirror up to nature. Now this overdone, or come tardy off, though it make the unskilful laugh, cannot but make the judicious grieve!"

"Quite," echoed Harold.

Terri Olson, who had studied linguistics and sat in the front row, disagreed. She assured us that there was indeed linguistic validity to the concept of generative rhetoric. I would quote her exactly, but I hadn't yet taken LING 780, and didn't understand the lingo. But those who had and did nodded their approval, and the rest of the class might have been willing to take her word for it, to give up and move on, had not our guest, veteran high-school teacher Harley Quackenbush, picked that moment to speak up.

"Look," he said, "You people are discussing this theory without any knowledge of its foundations in real life. I've used Christensen's methods at Heathwood High and they do work, and work quite well. I've a number of students who would never produce *any* type of complex sentence if it were not for sentence-combining exercises. It seems to me, and I hope you'll take this in the right way, that you people take an entirely too simplistic view of the purposes of composition theory. You expect to have everything laid out for you, right down to the lesson plan." The animosity the class had directed at Waldrep began drifting toward a new target. Quackenbush kept speaking. "What you fail to take into account is the *experience* that practiced rhetoricians bring with them whenever they sit down to write. The people who drafted the essays that make up your textbooks—people like Christensen and Winterowd and Corbett—they know from careful observation what student writers need, but more important, they know how to express their observations in a scientific, analytic manner. To understand theory, you people need to adopt a more professional approach to it."

Cries of "Bull!" "No way!" and "Come off it, Harley!" echoed through the small classroom. Waldrep tapped a pencil on the lectern until things calmed down. There were now twelve hands in the air. "Folks, let's remember that Mr. Quackenbush is our guest. Now Mr. Gregory, would you care to respond?"

"Okay. Number one: If rhetoricians are so scientific in their approach, why do they always seem to be in disagreement with each other?" Mark held out his hand to indicate that the question was rhetorical. "The answer, obviously, is that writing is no exact science. There is no 'right' or 'wrong' way to write or talk about writing; I don't think anyone would disagree with that. There may be better and lesser ways, but there's no right or wrong way. Okay. So number two: In order to lend weight and credence to whatever methods *they* have found successful, to whatever writing or teaching methods they wish to share with the professional community through the various writing journals, contemporary rhetoricians adopt, some I would say affect, a 'scientific, analytic' writing style." Quackenbush started to respond, but Mark kept going; when Mark Gregory got on a roll, he got on a roll. "Number three: The very essays in which rhetoricians propound their theories often give those theories the lie. How many essays in this book"—he lifted his text and waved it to the class—"were *actually written* using cubing or tagmemics or sentence combining? Certainly none of the best ones, the articles you see reprinted everywhere, that seem to somehow touch the essence of composition, were written with such artificial devices. Truly good writing is too complex for that. Some of the 'scientific, professional' devices we've discussed in this class make me wonder whether their creators were most concerned with their profession, literally, as in tenure and travel money for conferences."

Again there was an outburst, this time one of support.

When he had us quieted down, Professor Waldrep shook his head and said, "You all are being entirely too harsh on these people. Rhetoricians are wonderful people. Absolutely wonderful. You just need to go to four Cs and have drinks with a few of them. After all, they were once graduate students like you, and you all—well, some of you, anyway—are eventually going to become professionals like them."

But the damage had been done.

Quackenbush got up and stormed out, and we plodded on through the period and then the semester wary of rhetoricians, suspicious of the notion that they were real people who ate and slept and taught and watched TV, who had to sit down and struggle with writing like the rest of us. Once someone in class suggested that they were all frauds, that all modern rhetoric came from a Radio Shack computer somewhere in Ohio, probably programmed by a twelve-year-old. It might be that my memory has exaggerated events somewhat, but there was unquestionably among us a poor regard for rhetoricians. Fortunately, Tom Waldrep couldn't let us go through life with such misconceptions.

He put together this book, and by God he was right: Rhetoricians are people, too! They dread writing as often as not, have false starts, turn things in late because they "like to work under pressure," abandon some projects altogether. They go at writing fifteen different ways from Sunday, rarely using "standard" methods of invention and organization. They write and teach writing by instinct as much as by anything else, but a foundation of theory is always there for them to draw from, just below the surface.

Maybe our class *was* a bit hasty in its judgment. In the year since I took 701, I've caught myself more than once going back to the textbooks for help in structuring my 101 and 102 classes. Several others in the class have admitted that they've done the same thing. Maybe it was just the way we were introduced to rhetorical theory, the way we were so overwhelmed by the mass of it, that led us to rebellion. Perhaps if we had been able to escape once in a while, to find rhetoricians who would talk to us about writing in a personal, practical context, and in ordinary language, perhaps then we might not have exploded and caused Harley Quackenbush to leave in such a huff.

I don't know. But I would advise you, especially those of you who find yourselves enrolled in courses such as The Theory and Teaching of Composition, to come back to this book now and then, to balance all of those theories of rhetoric with the actual practices of rhetoricians, real people. Besides giving you insight to theory and helping you cope with it, examining the writing methods of rhetoricians can come in handy: You never know when some professor might let you write an afterword to his book.